£6.99

332.153 TOU
3 wk

D1339922

The World Bank

A Critical Primer

ERIC TOUSSAINT

Translated by Elizabeth Anne, Vicki Briault,
Bertrand Declercq, Sushovan Dhar, Judith Harris,
Raghu Krishnan, Marie Lagatta, Christine Pagnoulle,
Véronique Renard, Gillian Sloane-Seale and Diren Valayden

Edited by Sylvain Dropsy

Pluto Press

LONDON • ANN ARBOR, MI

Between the Lines
TORONTO

David Philip Publishers
CAPE TOWN

in association with

CADTM, Committee for the
Abolition of Third World Debt
LIÈGE, BELGIUM

Originally published in French in 2006, as *Banque mondiale : Le Coup d'Etat permanent. L'Agenda caché du Consensus de Washington*, by CADTM-Syllepse-Cetim, Liège-Paris-Genève

First English language edition published 2008 by
Pluto Press, 345 Archway Road, London N6 5AA and 839 Greene Street, Ann Arbor, MI 48106. www.plutobooks.com

Published in Canada by Between the Lines, 720 Bathurst Street, Suite #404, Toronto, Ontario M5S 2R4. www.btlbooks.com

Published in southern Africa by David Philip Publishers, an imprint of New Africa Books (Pty) Ltd, 99 Garfield Road, Claremont 7700, Cape Town, South Africa
www.newafricabooks.co.za

British Library Cataloguing in Publication Data
A catalogue record for this book is available from the British Library

ISBN   978 0 7453 2714 3 (hardback)
ISBN   978 0 7453 2713 6 (Pluto paperback)
ISBN   978 1 897071 38 0 (Between the Lines paperback)
ISBN   978 0 86486 712 4 (David Philip Publishers paperback)

Library of Congress Cataloging in Publication Data applied for

Library and Archives Canada Cataloguing in Publication
Toussaint, Eric
    The World Bank, a never-ending coup d'état : the hidden agenda of the Washington consensus / Eric Toussaint.
Includes bibliographical references and index.
ISBN 978–1–897071–38–0
    1. World Bank. 2. Developing countries—Colonial influence.
3. Economic assistance—Developing countries—Evaluation.
4. Conditionality (International relations) I. Title.
HG3881.5.W57T68 2008   332.1'532   C2007-904371-2

This book is printed on paper suitable for recycling and made from fully managed and sustained forest sources. Logging, pulping and manufacturing processes are expected to conform to the environmental regulations of the country of origin.

10 9 8 7 6 5 4 3 2 1

Designed and produced for Pluto Press by
Chase Publishing Services Ltd, Fortescue, Sidmouth, EX10 9QG, England
Typeset from disk by Stanford DTP Services, Northampton, England
Printed and bound in India

Contents

Dedication

I would like to dedicate this book to Denise Comanne, at whose side I have been fighting for global justice for the self-emancipation of the oppressed for almost a quarter of a century. Happily, Denise miraculously side-stepped the appointment she had with death on 13 November 2005 and we have been able to fight on together.

It is also dedicated to all those who fight for human dignity.

And to those who attempt to cross the Straits of Gibraltar, the Rio Grande and all the dishonourable barriers that the governments of rich countries have put up to prevent people from crossing boundaries freely.

Acknowledgements

I am deeply grateful to Denise Comanne and Damien Millet without whom the present work could not have seen the light. They played an essential part in hunting out documents, drafting some of the passages, and reading through the text. Special thanks to Virginie de Romanet for her help in background research, checking texts and preparing the page layout. Nor do I forget the precious help I received from Sébastien Dibling with tables and research.

Elizabeth Anne, Vicki Briault, Bertrand Declercq, Sushovan Dhar, Judith Harris, Raghu Krishnan, Marie Lagatta, Christine Pagnoulle, Véronique Renard, Gillian Sloane-Seale and Diren Valayden translated my text into English. Without the unfailing support of Elizabeth Anne, Vicki Briault, Judith Harris and Christine Pagnoulle, we could not have completed the translation. I am aware of my debt to them.

I also wish to thank the following friends for their help and support, including their constructive criticism: Gilbert Achcar, Danielle Alverhne and Pierre Caron, Yigit Bener, Olivier Bonfond, Yannick Bovy, Freddy Delava, Suzanne Comanne, Julia Gérard, Denise Lagache, Daliah Luksenbourg, Alice Minette, Ajit Muricken, Guillermo Parodi, Griselda Pinero, Raul Quiroz, Hugo Ruiz Diaz, Juan Tortosa, and friends in the international network of the CADTM in Niger, Mali, Senegal, Congo-Brazzaville, the Democratic Republic of Congo, Ivory Coast, Tunisia, Syria, Morocco, India, Colombia, Venezuela, France, Switzerland and Belgium, as well of course as the whole CADTM team.

About this Book

This book is the result of an undertaking started in 1992. The writing itself was begun in March 2004 and took two years.

My main source consisted of documents produced by the World Bank, totalling over 15,000 pages. I also consulted numerous reports and studies published by other international institutions, principally by the International Monetary Fund (IMF), the United Nations Development Programme (UNDP), the United Nations Conference on Trade and Development (UNCTAD), the Organization for Economic Co-operation and Development (OECD) and the Bank for International Settlements (BIS). Also of great use were the publications and studies by some fifty authors whose analyses of the subject are listed in the Bibliography.

Since 1990 I have undertaken – mainly on behalf of CADTM – more than fifty missions and journeys in developing countries, mainly in Latin America, but also in Africa, Asia, and Central and Eastern Europe. The analysis developed in the pages of this book owes much to these missions and to the people I had occasion to meet.

Many direct contacts with the authorities of various developing countries also helped me develop this analysis. Outstanding among them were the invitations I received from the Ministry of the Economy of East Timor in March 2003 and from the Venezuelan parliament, the first in 1997 followed by others between 2003 and 2006, not to mention my regular contacts with Luis Ignacio Lula da Silva since 1990, including a meeting with him in June 2003 – eight months after his election as president of Brazil.[1] Since 1995, in my capacity as president of CADTM Belgium, I have also had several meetings and engaged in debate with three successive Belgian finance ministers: Philippe Maystadt (currently president of the European Investment Bank, EIB), Jean-Jacques Viseur and Didier Reynders. Since 1998, I have also met regularly with Belgian administrators of the World Bank and the IMF posted in Washington. Finally, I have taken part in public debates with top officials of the World Bank and the IMF in Prague, Geneva and Brussels.

Frequent contacts at grassroots level in developing countries and ongoing relations in the context of their social movements have been the compass that has constantly confirmed my course in the writing of this work.

Three chapters of this book are taken from my doctoral thesis in political science, which I defended in November 2004 in the Universities of Liège and Paris VIII.[2]

This book takes a chronological approach in analyzing the World Bank from its beginnings to 2006. Care has been taken to place World Bank policy in its political and geostrategic context. In addition, five studies of different countries are presented to illustrate World Bank policy: the Philippines (1946–90), Turkey (1980–90), Indonesia (1947–2005), South Korea (1945–98) and Mexico (1970–2005). This book aims to reveal the political, economic and strategic motives of the United States government with regard to the World Bank. The last part of this work touches on the justiciability of the World Bank. The book contains figures and tables, a World Bank data sheet and a glossary.

Given the magnitude of the subject under study, several problems will be examined in a further book entitled *Banque mondiale: l'horreur productiviste*. The following themes will be dealt with: the World Bank's support of the productivist model and its impact on the environment; the World Bank's view on poverty; the WB/IMF/WTO triumvirate; World Bank policy on women; and new studies of countries (DR Congo and Iraq).

As stated in the Acknowledgements, this book could not have been written without the help of others who are close to me. But the analyses developed here are entirely my own, personal responsibility. My dearest wish is that they should be taken, completed, amended and of course applied as widely as possible in the effort to free the oppressed people of the Earth, which is, after all, a lifetime struggle.

WHAT IS THE CADTM?

The Committee for the Cancellation of Third World Debt (the CADTM, *Comité pour l'annulation de la dette du Tiers Monde*) is an international network of individuals and local committees from across Europe and Latin America, Africa and Asia. It was founded in Belgium on 15 March 1990.

The network acts in close liaison with other movements and organizations fighting for the same ideals. Its main preoccupation, besides the debt issue, is the planning of activities and radical alternatives for the creation of a world respectful of people's fundamental rights, needs and liberties.

The CADTM has always been a pluralist association composed of both private individuals and legally constituted organizations. Its activities take place on the common ground occupied by the battles being waged by grassroots and cultural movements, trade unions, international solidarity committees and development NGOs. It is a member of the international council of the World Social Forum and is fully committed to its role within the international movement of citizens fighting for the 'other worlds possible'. This movement is gradually defining a new, alternative form of globalization, in contrast to that being pushed by those insisting on a globalized neoliberal capitalist model as the ultimate in human happiness, the natural state of society, the 'end of history', the inevitable destiny for all wherever they come from.

Consistent with its membership of the 'alterglobalization movement' refusing the neoliberal dogma, the CADTM's mission is to contribute to the emergence of a world based on the sovereignty of its peoples, on international solidarity, equality and social justice. Its aim is to 'improve the level of information and education on development issues, particularly in the North–South context; to take any initiative, organize any activity, publish any information, run any project helping to promote international solidarity between citizens of the world, in the North, South, East or West, facilitating the emergence of a fairer world more respectful of the peoples' sovereignty, of social justice, of equality between all human beings and between men and women' (extract from the CADTM statutes, as published in the *Moniteur belge*, Belgium's Official Journal, on 6 February 1992). The projects, tools and activities it develops share the dynamics generated by the coupling of action with research: publications (books, articles, analyses, reviews and so on), conferences and debates, seminars, training courses, international meetings and events, awareness-raising campaigns, concerts, etc.

The CADTM is thus both a grassroots organization for popular education and an action-oriented network. Its prime objective – and angle of attack – is the cancellation of the multilateral and bilateral debt of the countries of the Periphery (the Third World and ex-Soviet bloc), as well as the abandonment of the structural adjustment policies being imposed by the troika of the IMF, World Bank and WTO. The aim is to bring the infernal spiral of debt to an end and, ultimately, to establish socially equitable and ecologically sustainable models of development. The cancellation of the foreign debt payable by the countries of the Periphery is not, however, for the CADTM, an end in itself. It is far more a means, an insufficient but essential precondition, for achieving the genuinely sustainable and socially equitable development that is required, as much for the North as for the South of our planet.

<www.cadtm.org>

Eric Toussaint

Abbreviations

ADB	African Development Bank
BIS	Bank for International Settlements
DCs	Developing Countries
ECOSOC	The Economic and Social Council of the UN
EU	European Union
FAO	Food and Agriculture Organization
GDP	Gross Domestic Product
GNP	Gross National Product
HDI	Human Development Index
HIPCs	Heavily Indebted Poor Countries
IBRD	International Bank for Reconstruction and Development (World Bank Group)
ICSID	International Centre for Settlement of Investment Disputes (World Bank Group)
IDA	International Development Association (World Bank Group)
IFC	International Finance Corporation (World Bank Group)
IFIs	International Financial Institutions
ILO	International Labour Organization
IMF	International Monetary Fund
LDCs	Least Developed Countries
MDBs	Multilateral Development Banks
MIGA	Multilateral Investment Guarantee Agency (World Bank Group)
NGO	Non-governmental Organization
OAU	Organization of African Unity [replaced by African Union in 2002]
ODA	Official Development Assistance
OECD	Organization for Economic Cooperation and Development
OPEC	Organization of Petroleum Exporting Countries
PRGF	Poverty Reduction and Growth Facility
PRSP	Poverty Reduction Strategy Papers
SAP	Structural Adjustment Programme
SAPRI	Structural Adjustment Participatory Review Initiative

SUNFED	Special United Nations Fund for Economic Development
UNCTAD	United Nations Conference on Trade and Development
UNDP	United Nations Development Programme
UNO	United Nations Organization
USSR	Union of Soviet Socialist Republics
WB	World Bank
WCD	World Commission on Dams
WHO	World Health Organization
WTO	World Trade Organization

Terminology

Vocabulary is not neutral. The terms used to designate the different categories of countries convey the theoretical and political divergences in terms of analysis and strategy. Generally, these divergences are related to the social contents of the economic concepts: the economic categories are often presented as reflecting natural laws in which social relations and power struggles have a limited place. Thus, the conception of underdevelopment as being a simple time lag, sometimes ascribed to natural causes, largely dominates them.

1. Underdeveloped countries: this is the oldest term, but one that has gradually become obsolete as it implies a reference to the developed nations, and because very early on it appeared derogatory.
2. Developing countries: this expression is less derogatory than the first but it subscribes to the same problematic of time lag. Moreover, it presumes an improvement of the situation that is not always verified.
3. Least developed countries: a term used in the classifications of international authorities, but it combines all the preceding defects.
4. Third World: a term invented by Alfred Sauvy in 1952 (by analogy with the third state) and which was popular during the Cold War as a means of naming all the countries taking an independent stand whether with regard to the United States or to the USSR.[1] Two facts have rendered the use of the term more delicate, although the habit still persists: on the one hand, the disappearance of the USSR and the Soviet bloc, and on the other the growing heterogeneity of the former countries of the Third World.
5. Poor countries: a term that focuses on the economic poverty of the majority of the populations in the countries concerned and obscures the blatant inequalities that exist there. Moreover, a certain number of countries considered poor are actually very rich in natural resources, not to mention their cultural wealth. These countries should be called exploited countries.
6. Countries of the South: a convenient term to stigmatize the break with the countries in the northern hemisphere, often developed

and dominant, but having the double defect of ignoring the numerous exceptions to this geographic classification and letting people believe in a natural fatalism.

7. Peripheral countries: a term belonging to the Structuralist and Marxist problematics showing up the phenomena of domination at the heart of a global capitalism led by the most industrialized countries and their imperialist policies.

8. Emerging countries: a term designating the economies that have initiated an undeniable development process that distinguishes them from the body of the formerly more homogeneous Third World – China, India and Brazil being the principal examples. This term is often enough replaced by 'emerging markets', a substitution that clearly reflects the neoliberal vision of a development that can only be achieved through insertion in the international division of labour imposed by financial globalization.

9. Countries in transition: a euphemism for designating the countries of Eastern Europe, which, after the collapse of the USSR and the explosion of the Soviet bloc, followed a process of capitalist restoration.

Note: In this book, the following terms will be used as synonyms: Third World, countries of the South, South, Periphery, developing countries. The countries of the ex-Soviet bloc are placed in the Periphery. These terms are generally used in opposition to: Triad, (principal) industrialized capitalist countries, countries of the North, North, Centre, imperialist countries, which are also considered as synonyms.

Introduction

THE WORLD BANK'S PERMANENT COUP

The list of governments resulting from military coups that were supported by the World Bank is impressive. Among the best-known examples, we can mention the Shah's dictatorship in Iran after Prime Minister Mohammad Mossadegh was overthrown in 1953; the military dictatorship in Guatemala, which the United States set up after the democratically elected president Jacobo Arbenz was overthrown in 1954; Duvalier's in Haiti from 1957; General Park Chung Hee's in South Korea from 1961; the Brazilian generals' dictatorship from 1964, Mobutu's in the Congo and Suharto's in Indonesia from 1965; the Thai army leaders from 1966; Idi Amin Dada's in Uganda, General Hugo Banzer's in Bolivia in 1971, and Ferdinand Marcos' in the Philippines from 1972; Augusto Pinochet's in Chile; the Uruguayan generals' and Habyarimana's in Rwanda from 1973; the military junta in Argentina from 1976; Daniel Arap Moi's regime in Kenya from 1978; a dictatorship in Pakistan from 1978; Saddam Hussein's coup in 1979 and the Turkish military dictatorship from 1980.

Among other dictatorships that have been supported by the World Bank we should also mention the Somozas' in Nicaragua and Ceaucescu's in Romania. Some are still in power today: the dictatorial regime in China, Deby's dictatorship in Chad, Ben Ali's in Tunisia and Musharaf's in Pakistan, among many others. We should also remember the World Bank's support to dictatorships in Europe: General Franco's in Spain and General Salazar in Portugal.[1]

The World Bank has systematically supported despotic regimes, whether resulting from military coups or not, which carry out antisocial policies and perpetrate crimes against humanity. The Bank has displayed an utter lack of respect for the constitutional standards of some of its member countries. It has never shied away from supporting a military coup or downright criminals that would implement its policies against democratic governments, and this for a good reason: it considers that defending human rights is not part of its mission.

Its support to the apartheid regime in South Africa from 1951 to 1968 must not be forgotten. The World Bank explicitly refused to

1

implement the UN resolution that had been voted by the General Assembly in 1964, deciding that no UN agency was to further contribute any financial support to South Africa since that country had violated the UN Charter. This lasting support and the violation of international law it implies must not remain unpunished.

Finally, as the present book will show, in the 1950s and 1960s the World Bank consistently granted loans to colonial powers for them to carry out projects that increased the exploitation of their colonies' natural resources and populations to the benefit of the ruling classes in the metropolis. In this context the World Bank refused to implement a UN resolution voted in 1965 that urged it not to refuse any financial or technical support to Portugal as long as it did not give up its colonies.

The debts that Belgian, British and French colonies had contracted with the World Bank because of a decision made in the metropolis were later enforced on the newly independent countries.

The World Bank's support to dictatorial regimes is channelled through financial aid as well as technical and economic assistance. Thanks to such support these regimes could stay in power and perpetrate more crimes. The World Bank also contributed to these regimes not being isolated on an international level since such loans and technical assistance have always facilitated contacts with private banks and transnational corporations. The neoliberal model was gradually enforced on a global scale from Pinochet's dictatorship in Chile in 1973 and Ferdinand Marcos' in the Philippines in 1972. These two regimes were actively supported by the World Bank. When such regimes were eventually brought down the World Bank systematically forced the democratic regimes that took over to pay back the debts contracted by the former governments. In short, the WB's financial aiding and abetting of dictatorships turned into a burden for the populations. These now have to pay back for weapons dictators had bought the better to oppress them.

In the 1980s and 1990s a large number of dictatorships were brought down, some thanks to the struggle pursued by powerful democratic movements. The regimes that took over generally accepted the policies that the World Bank and IMF recommended or enforced and continued paying back what are in many cases odious debts. After being enforced via dictatorships the neoliberal model has been maintained thanks to the burden of the debt and of permanent structural adjustments. Indeed, since dictatorships were overthrown or collapsed, democratic governments have further implemented policies that break away from attempts at setting up a more autonomous development model. The new stage in globalization that started in the 1980s with the debt crisis has generally entailed an increased subordination of developing countries (the Periphery) to industrialized countries (the Centre).

THE HIDDEN AGENDA OF THE WASHINGTON CONSENSUS

Since the WB and the IMF started their activities a mechanism that is both easy to understand and difficult to set up has made it possible for the United States to control their policies. There have been some cases when a European government (the United Kingdom, France or Germany in particular) or Japan could make themselves heard, but they are few and far between. Frictions have occurred between the White House and the World Bank's and IMF's leaders, yet when we examine history since the end of the Second World War it appears that the US government has indeed enforced its views in those areas in which it is directly concerned.

The hidden agenda of the Washington Consensus aims both at maintaining the US global leadership and at freeing capitalism of the shackles it had to accept in the wake of the Second World War. These limitations resulted from powerful social mobilizations in countries both of the North and of the South, from nascent emancipation movements in the colonies, and from attempts at rejecting capitalism. The Washington Consensus also involves intensifying the productivist approach.

In recent decades, according to the Washington Consensus, the World Bank and the IMF have consolidated the ways in which they exercise pressure on many countries as they profited from the situation created by the debt crisis. The World Bank has developed branches (the International Finance Corporation (IFC), the Multilateral Investment Guarantee Agency (MIGA), the International Centre for Settlement of Investment Disputes (ICSID)) so as to weave a web tighter and tighter.

For instance, the World Bank will only grant a loan on condition that a country's water and sanitation services are privatized. As a consequence the public companies are sold to a private consortium, in which the IFC, a branch of the WB, happens to be a partner.

When the people who suffer under such privatization react against the sharp increase of prices and lower-quality services that result, while the government turns against the preying transnational corporation, the dispute is settled with the ICSID, which is both judge and party.

We thus reach a situation in which the World Bank Group controls all levels: (1) enforcement and financing of privatizations (World Bank); (2) investment in the private company (IFC); (3) guarantee for the company (MIGA); (4) dispute settlement (ICSID). This is what happened at El Alto (Bolivia) in 2004–05.

Cooperation between the World Bank and the IMF is also essential in order to exert maximal pressure on public authorities and to complete their control of the public sphere. To be able to further generalize the neoliberal model these two institutions have closely collaborated with the World Trade Organization (WTO) from its foundation in 1995. Such increasingly closer collaboration between the World Bank, the IMF and the WTO is part of the agenda of the Washington Consensus.

There is an essential difference between the declared agenda of the Washington Consensus and its hidden version. The official agenda aims at reducing poverty through growth, the free interaction of market forces, free trade, and a limited intervention by public authorities. The hidden agenda (the agenda that is actually carried out) aims at the submission of public and private sectors to the logic of maximum profits in a capitalist context. The implementation of such an agenda involves reproducing, not reducing poverty and increasing inequalities. It also involves a stagnation or even a degradation of living standards for a large majority of the world's population, combined with an ever greater concentration of wealth. It further involves a continuing degradation of the environment, which jeopardizes the very future of humankind.

One of the many paradoxes of the hidden agenda is that in the name of suppressing state dictatorship and liberating market forces, governments in their subservience to corporations, use the coercing action of multilateral public institutions (World Bank/IMF/WTO) to enforce their model to the populations.

BREAKING AWAY AS THE ONLY WAY OUT

This is why it is imperative to radically break away from the Washington Consensus and from the model enforced by the World Bank.

The Washington Consensus must not be understood as some power mechanism and project that would serve only the Washington government plus its three satellites. The European Commission, most European governments and the Japanese government subscribe to the Washington Consensus. They have translated it into their own languages, constitutional projects and political agendas.

Breaking away with the Washington Consensus, if it only means putting an end to the US leadership relayed by the World Bank, the FMI and the WTO, will not yield a real alternative since other world powers are ready to take over and aim at similar objectives. Imagine that the EU gets stronger than the US on a global scale: this would not improve the predicament in which the peoples on the surface of the earth find themselves, since it would merely mean replacing one capitalist bloc in the North (one of the poles in the Triad) with another. Imagine another possibility: the formation of a bloc made up of China, Brazil, India, South Africa and Russia that would become stronger than the countries of the Triad. If this bloc is motivated by the current logic of their present governments and by the economic system that underpins their functioning there would be no significant improvement either.

We have to replace the Washington Consensus with a consensus of peoples founded on a rejection of capitalism.

We must also radically question the notion of development that is tightly associated with a productivist model. Such a development model rules out the protection of cultures and their diversity; it exhausts natural resources and spoils the environment in ways that cannot be remedied. It sees the promotion of human rights as at best some long-term objective (in the long term we will all be dead); in many cases the promotion of human rights is rather perceived as an obstacle to growth; this model sees equality as an obstacle or even a stumbling block.

STEPPING OUT OF THE VICIOUS DEBT SPIRAL

Improving people's living conditions through public debt has proved a failure. The World Bank claims that in order to develop developing countries[2] must contract external debts and attract foreign investments. These loans are used to buy equipment and commodities from industrialized countries. Day after day, year after year for decades we have seen that this is not the case.

According to the dominant economic theory the development of the South has been delayed because of wanting domestic capital (not enough local savings). According to the same economic dogma, countries that wish to launch or accelerate their development have to call upon external capital flows through three kinds of policies: first, contracting loans; secondly, attracting foreign investment; thirdly, increasing exports to get the currency needed to buy foreign commodities allegedly necessary to their development. The poorer countries can also attract grants by their good behaviour as pupils of developed countries.

This theory is contradicted by facts: developing countries provide industrialized countries with capital, the US economy in particular. The World Bank even acknowledges this: *'Developing countries, in aggregate, were net lenders to developed countries.'*[3] In 2004–05, fairly low interest rates combining with decreasing hazard premiums and increasing prices for raw materials resulted in a sharp increase in the developing countries' currency reserves. By the end of 2005 they exceeded US$2,000 billion,[4] an unprecedented amount that is higher than the sum total of the developing countries' public external debt! If we add to this the money these countries' capitalists have deposited in banks located in industrialized countries, that is some US$1,500 billion, we can claim that developing countries are not debtors but creditors.

If they set up their own development bank and their own international monetary funds, they could easily do without the World Bank, the IMF and the private financial institutions of industrialized countries.

It isn't the case that developing countries have to contract debts to finance their development. Nowadays their loans are mainly used to make it possible for them to pay back more of their debts. In spite of extensive currency reserves governments and local ruling classes in the South do not increase investment or social expenditure, with one exception within the capitalist world: the Venezuelan government, which carries out a policy that aims to use oil revenues to help the most exploited classes and thus faces the frontal opposition of the local ruling classes and of the United States. How long can this last?

Never before has the situation been so favourable to developing countries from a financial perspective, yet nobody mentions a change in the rules of the game. This is because the current governments in China, Russia and the main developing countries (India, Brazil, Nigeria, Indonesia, Thailand, South Korea, Mexico, Algeria, South Africa) have no intention of changing the world situation to the benefit of their peoples.

However, on a political level, if they so wanted, the main developing countries could set up a powerful movement that would be able to introduce fundamental democratic reforms into the multilateral system. They could opt for a radical policy: call off the debt and implement a set of policies that break away from neoliberalism. The international context is favourable since the major world power is currently stuck in the Iraq war and the occupation of Afghanistan; it has to face strong resistance movements in Latin America, which lead either to humiliating failures (Venezuela, Cuba, Ecuador, Bolivia ...) or a dead-end (Colombia).

I am convinced that this will not happen: the radical scenario will not be implemented in the short term. The overwhelming majority of current leaders in developing countries wholeheartedly adhere to the neoliberal model. In most cases they collude with the interests of the local ruling classes, which can imagine no real distance, let alone break from the policies enforced by the industrial powers. Capitalists in the South snugly live off their annuities or at most try to expand their share of the market. This applies to capitalists in countries like Brazil, South Korea, China, Russia, South Africa or India who want their governments to get this or that concession from more industrialized countries in the context of bilateral or multilateral trade negotiations. Moreover, competition and conflicts among governments of developing countries, among capitalists of the South, are quite real and can easily become even sharper. The trade aggressiveness of capitalists in China, Russia or Brazil towards their competitors of the South leads to deeply anchored divisions. As a rule they agree (both among themselves and with the North) to enforce worse working conditions to workers in their countries, claiming that this is necessary for the sake of competitiveness.

But sooner or later peoples will throw off the burden of the debt. They will free themselves from the oppression they are subjected to by the ruling classes in the North and in the South. They will fight for a fair distribution of wealth and an end to the productivist model that destroys nature. Public authorities will then have to give absolute priority to meeting basic human needs.

To achieve this, an alternative approach is required: we have to step out of the vicious spiral of the debt without falling into policies based on charity that ultimately perpetuate a global system dominated by capital, by some powerful countries and transnational corporations. We have to set up an international system to redistribute revenues and wealth so as to compensate for the secular looting of which the colonized people were and still are the victims. Such compensation in the form of free grants does not give any right to industrialized countries to meddle in the policies implemented in recipient countries. In the South we have to invent mechanisms to decide on how funds are to be used and how the concerned populations and the concerned local public authorities can check what actually occurs. This certainly is food for thought and experiment.

On the other hand, the World Bank and the IMF have to be replaced by other global institutions based on democratic accountability. The new World Bank and the new International Monetary Funds, whatever their new names may be, must have radically different missions from those of the former institutions; they must make sure that international agreements on human (political, civic, social, economic and cultural) rights are actually carried through into action in the field of international credit and international monetary relations. These new global institutions must be part of a global institutional system controlled by a thoroughly reformed United Nations organization. It is an essential priority that as soon as possible developing countries join together in regional entities with a common Bank and a common Monetary Fund. During the South-East Asia and Korea crisis in 1997–98 an Asian Monetary Fund had been considered by the concerned countries. The project had failed because of Washington's intervention combined with the local governments' absence of political determination. In Latin America and the Caribbean a debate was launched by the Venezuelan government in 2005–06 on the possibility of building a Bank of the South. We'll have to see what comes out of it.

One thing must be clear: if what we want is the people's emancipation and human rights to be fully met, the new financial and monetary institutions, whether global or regional, must serve a social model that breaks away from capitalism and neoliberalism.

1
The Creation of the
Bretton Woods Institutions

The United States government began to plan for the creation of international financial institutions as early as 1941, not only to prevent a recurrence of economic crises such as the crash of 1929, but also to ensure world leadership in the post-war era. The World Bank and the International Monetary Fund saw the light of day at the Bretton Woods Conference of 1944 held in Bretton Woods, New Hampshire. Initially, the Roosevelt administration was in favour of creating strong institutions capable of imposing rules on the private financial sector, including Wall Street. But noticing the hostility of the banking world, Roosevelt backed down. Indeed, the distribution of votes within the World Bank and the International Monetary Fund clearly illustrates the will of certain major powers to exert domination over the rest of the world.

IN THE BEGINNING[1]

It was in 1941, the year the United States entered the Second World War, that discussions were initiated concerning the international institutions to be set up once this major conflict was over. In May 1942, the chief international economist at the US Treasury, Harry White, presented Franklin Roosevelt with a blueprint entitled *Plan for a United and Associated Nations Stabilization Fund and a Bank for Reconstruction and Development of the United Nations*. One of its objectives was to convince the allied nations currently at war with the Axis powers (Germany, Italy, Japan) that once peace was established, certain systems would need to be adopted to prevent the world economy entering a depression similar to that of the 1930s. Between 1941 and July 1944, when the Bretton Woods Conference assembled, several of the proposals contained in the initial plan were abandoned. But one of them came to fruition: the creation of the IMF (International Monetary Fund) and the IBRD (International Bank for Reconstruction and Development), better known as the World Bank.

To understand fully the roles attributed to these two institutions, we must go back to the late 1920s and the 1930s. The severe economic depression that gripped the United States during this period had a profound effect on world capitalism in general. One of the consequences was that in 1931 Germany ceased repaying its war debt to France, Belgium, Italy and Great Britain. In a domino effect, these countries stopped repayment of their external debt to the United States.[2] As for the latter, it drastically reduced capital exports in 1928 and even more in 1931.[3] At the same time, it cut down on imports. The result was that the flow of dollars from the United States to the rest of the world dried up, and countries with debts to the world's leading power did not have the dollars to pay it back. Nor did they have the dollars they needed to buy North American products. The machinery of world capitalism was grinding to a halt. Competitive devaluations followed as each country attempted to win market share at the expense of the others. The developed capitalist world was caught in a downward spiral.

In 1932, John Maynard Keynes made this ironic remark about the attitude of the United States:

The rest of the world owes them money. They will not take payment in goods; they will not take it in bonds; they have already all the gold there is. The puzzle which they have set to the rest of the world admits logically of only one solution, namely, that *some way must be found of doing without their exports*.[4]

One of the conclusions drawn by the United States government under Franklin Roosevelt (US President from 1933 to 1945) was that a great creditor nation must make currency available to debtor countries to be used for repayment of their debt. Another, bolder conclusion was that in certain cases, it was preferable to offer donations instead of loans if a state wanted its exporting industries to gain maximum and lasting profit. This question will be dealt with later in chapter 4 on the Marshall Plan for the reconstruction of Europe (1948–51).

Let us take a closer look at the 1930s before going on to discuss the creation of the Bretton Woods institutions during the Second World War.

CREATION OF THE EXPORT-IMPORT BANK OF WASHINGTON (1934)

The Export-Import Bank of Washington (the US public agency for export credit, later called Eximbank) was created in 1934 to protect and promote US exporters. It guaranteed US exports and at the same time granted long-term credit to foreign buyers for the purchase of US goods and services. Each dollar lent had to be spent on merchandise produced in the United States. The Export-Import Bank released funds only on receipt of proof of shipment of goods abroad. At the start, the total amount of loans granted by the bank was a modest one: US$60 million in the first five years. But the volume of loans increased rapidly from then on. In 1940, the bank's lending capacity was $200 million, and in 1945 it had reached $3,500 million. During its first years of operation, the Export-Import Bank targeted Latin America and the Caribbean, China and Finland, a reflection not only of the economic but also of the geostrategic interests at stake.

CREATION OF THE INTER-AMERICAN BANK (1940)

In 1940, another financial instrument was created: the Inter-American Bank. This was an inter-state bank founded on US initiative in the context of the Pan-American Union (the ancestor of the Organization of American States (OAS)). The original members included Bolivia, Brazil, the Dominican Republic, Ecuador, Mexico, Nicaragua, Paraguay and the United States. In some respects this bank was the forerunner of the World Bank, which came into being four years later.

The main architect on the US side was a fervent partisan of public intervention in the economy, an advocate of the New Deal: Emilio Collado, number two in the Department of State.[5] He played a prominent role in the discussions leading up to the Bretton Woods Conference, and in 1944 was appointed US first executive director of the World Bank. The Department of State was not the only player involved in the launch of the Inter-American Bank. The US Treasury was also represented in the persons of Henry Morgenthau and his assistant, Harry White.

Four basic reasons led the Roosevelt administration to approve the creation of the Inter-American Bank.

First, the government realized that it must not only lend money to foreign buyers of US products, but that it must also buy exports from those to whom it wished to sell its goods. Nazi Germany, with its dominance over part of Europe, was in the process of buying goods from, and investing in, Latin America.[6] The establishment of the Inter-American Bank would tighten the bonds between the United States and all its Southern neighbours.

Second, Washington considered that it could not count on the US private financial sector to lend capital to countries south of the Rio Grande when 14 Latin American countries were in partial or total default on payment of their external debt. In Washington's view, the big US banks were responsible for the 1929 crisis and its continuing effects. The creation of a public agency would enable the government to take serious action.

Third, to convince the governments of Latin America to actively engage in reinforced relations with the United States, they must be offered an instrument, which, officially at least, pursued objectives not directly answerable to the United States. A.A. Berle, deputy secretary of the Department of State, put it plainly:

In the past, movements of capital have been regarded as, frankly, imperialist. They usually led later to difficulties of one sort and another. The other country did not like to pay; the interests built up were frequently supposed to be tyrannous. We are still liquidating many of the nineteenth-century messes which were occasioned by the somewhat violent and not too enlightened moves of capital.[7]

Fourth, a bank had to be set up in which the borrowing countries played a part and had a voice. The reasoning was very simple: if borrowers were to repay their debts, they had better be part of the bank. The same principle was applied when planning the creation of the World Bank and the IMF.

As regards the distribution of votes within the Inter-American Bank, the criteria used were subsequently to be adopted by the World Bank and the IMF. The 'one country, one vote' principle was rejected in favour of a voting system based on the economic weight of a country (in this case, export volume).

The system implied an extra bonus for Latin American countries: the existence of a multilateral banking institution would protect them from strong-arm tactics on the part of creditors anxious to recover their funds. After all, it was not so very long ago that the United States and other powerful creditors had recourse either to military intervention or to direct control on customs and tax administration of indebted countries in order to recover what they claimed as their due.[8]

It should be noted that the firm attitude of a large number of Latin American countries (14 in all, including Brazil, Mexico, Colombia, Chile, Peru and Bolivia), which had decided to discontinue, either totally or partially, repayment of their external debt, scored a resounding victory. Three positive results ensued: their economic growth was higher than that in countries that continued to repay the debt; they won back a significant degree of autonomy vis-à-vis the rich countries; and, far from being excluded from sources of financing, they were wooed by various governments in the North eager to offer them public financing. An instructive lesson in the advantages of standing one's ground.

DISCUSSIONS WITH THE ROOSEVELT ADMINISTRATION

As of 1942, the Roosevelt administration pursued discussions concerning the economic and financial order to be established after the war. A number of ideas were regularly tabled on the subject of debt and capital movements: it was considered advisable to set up a number of public, multilateral institutions, which, to counteract the risky nature of private international investments, would provide public capital. These institutions should 'police international investment by private capital, so as to provide judicial and arbitral facilities for settlements of disputes between creditor and debtor, and to remove the danger of the use by creditor countries of their claims as a basis for illegitimate political or military or economic demands' (excerpt from a memorandum of the Council on Foreign Relations dated 1 April 1942).

AN AMBITIOUS PROJECT PROPOSED BY HARRY WHITE

As mentioned above, in 1941 Harry White at the Treasury was already preparing the groundwork for a plan to set up two major multilateral institutions. Franklin Roosevelt received a first draft in May 1942 based on the premise that before the war ended, it would be necessary to set up an Exchange Rate Stabilization Fund (the future International Monetary Fund) and an international bank to provide capital. White explained: 'Two separate, though linked agencies would be better than one, since one agency dealing with both tasks would have too much power and would run the risk of greater errors of judgment.'[9] The Fund and the Bank would bring together all nations, starting with the Allies. The relative weight of each member nation would be a function of its economic weight. Borrower countries would belong to the Bank, as this would motivate them to repay their loans. The two institutions would favour policies designed to ensure full employment.

The Fund would work to stabilize exchange rates, bring about a gradual discontinuance of exchange controls and the end of export subsidies. As for the Bank, it would provide capital for the reconstruction of the countries affected by the war and for the development of backward regions; it would help stabilize commodity prices. The Bank would lend money from its own capital and have its own currency: the *unitas*.

Harry White's ambitious project was drastically cut down to size in the years to come. Wall Street and the Republican Party were particularly hostile to several fundamental aspects of the White plan. They wanted nothing to do with two strong public institutions designed to regulate the flow of private capital, and which would in fact be in competition with them. Franklin Roosevelt decided to come to terms with them, with the result that in 1945, Congress eventually ratified, by a large majority, the Bretton Woods agreements of July 1944. The concessions made by Roosevelt were generous to the point of changing the nature of the original plan. Yet Wall Street effectively withheld its support of the Bank and the Fund until 1947.

Among the original proposals[10] withdrawn before the Bretton Woods conference were:

- The creation of a currency specific to the Bank. As we have seen, Harry White proposed calling it the *unitas*. John Maynard Keynes had meanwhile made a similar proposal, the *bancor*, which was no more successful.
- The Bank's use of its own capital when making loans. It was finally decided that the Bank would borrow the capital it needed to make loans from the private banking sector.
- The stabilization of commodity prices.

The two most influential countries in discussions with the US about the adoption of a final proposal were Great Britain and the USSR. Great Britain demanded privileged terms from Washington. For Churchill, any negotiation between Washington and London must be bilateral and secret.[11] Washington preferred to negotiate with all the Allies separately, on the divide-and-rule principle.

It seems that Franklin Roosevelt, seconded by Harry White and Henry Morgenthau (Secretary of the Treasury), genuinely wished to guarantee Soviet Russia's participation in the establishment of the Bank and the Fund. In January 1944 Morgenthau publicly disclosed that two Soviet delegates had arrived in Washington to discuss the creation of these two institutions.

THE GEOPOLITICAL AND GEOSTRATEGIC DIMENSION

Between 1 and 22 July 1944, the United Nations Monetary and Financial Conference, better known as the Bretton Woods[12] Conference, was attended by representatives from 44 countries.

The United States delegation was headed by Henry Morgenthau and Harry White, the British delegation by Lord John Maynard Keynes. These two delegations directed the work of the conference.

The Soviets were also in attendance. As a result of bargaining between Washington, Moscow and London, the USSR was to obtain third place in terms of voting rights, whereas it had wanted second place. Finally, Moscow did not ratify the final agreements and in 1947, at the UN General Assembly, denounced the Bretton Woods institutions as 'branches of Wall Street'. For the Soviet representative, the World Bank was 'subordinated to political purposes which make it the instrument of one great power'.[13]

The distribution of votes clearly reflected US and British dominance over the two institutions and painted a telling picture of the balance of power in the Allied camp (not counting the USSR) immediately after the war. In 1947, these two countries together had almost 50 per cent of the votes (34.23 per cent for the United States and 14.17 per cent for the United Kingdom on 30 August 1947).

Eleven most industrialized countries held more than 70 per cent of votes.[14] All the countries of the African continent together held no more than 2.34 per cent. Only three African countries had voting rights because practically all the others were still under colonial rule.[15] These three countries were: Egypt (0.70 per cent of votes); the Union of South Africa (1.34 per cent), governed by a white racist power that would introduce Apartheid a year later, and Ethiopia (0.30 per cent). In a word, black Africa under a black government (the Emperor Haile Selassie) held just one-third of 1 per cent of the votes.

South and East Asia held 11.66 per cent. Only three countries were members: Chiang Kai-shek's nationalist China (6.68 per cent), a US ally; the Philippines (0.43 per cent), a US colony until 1946; and India (4.55 per cent), which gained independence from the British crown in 1947.

Central and Eastern Europe held 3.90 per cent (Poland and Czechoslovakia each held 1.60 per cent and Tito's Yugoslavia 0.70 per cent).

The Near East and Middle East had 2.24 per cent (Turkey 0.73 per cent, Lebanon 0.32 per cent, Iran 0.52 per cent, Syria 0.34 per cent, Iraq 0.33 per cent).

The whole of Latin America and the Caribbean, a region considered to be firmly allied with the United States, held 8.38 per cent of the votes spread over 18 countries: Bolivia (0.34 per cent), Brazil (1.39 per cent), Chile (0.64 per cent), Colombia (0.64 per cent), Costa Rica (0.29 per cent), Cuba (0.64 per cent), Dominican Republic (0.29 per cent), Ecuador (0.30 per cent), El Salvador (0.28 per cent), Guatemala (0.29 per cent), Honduras (0.28 per cent), Mexico (0.96 per cent), Nicaragua (0.28 per cent), Panama (0.27 per cent), Paraguay (0.8 per cent), Peru (0.45 per cent), Uruguay (0.38 per cent), and Venezuela (0.38 per cent).

2
The First Years of the World Bank
(1946–62)

Contrary to common belief, the mission of the World Bank is not to reduce poverty in developing countries. The Bank's mission, as originally conceived by the victors of the Second World War, the United States and Great Britain in particular, was to help rebuild Europe and secondarily to promote the economic growth of the countries in the South, many of which were still under colonial rule. It was this second mission that went by the name of 'development', and which constantly increased in scope. The World Bank lent money first of all to the colonial powers (Great Britain, France and Belgium) to help them more effectively exploit their colonies. Then, when these colonies became independent, the Bank made them liable for the debt that had only been contracted by their former 'home countries' in order to better exploit their natural resources and population.

In the first 17 years of its existence, the projects supported by the World Bank focused on improvement of communication infrastructure and the production of power. The money lent by the Bank was to be spent essentially in industrialized countries. Projects approved by the Bank were designed to improve the South's export capacities to the North, thereby meeting the needs of Northern countries and enriching a handful of transnational companies in the relevant sectors. During this period, no projects were undertaken in the areas of education, health, drinking water supply and wastewater treatment.

From the start, the Bank's missions served to increase its ability to influence the decisions taken by the authorities of a country in a way that would benefit the shareholding powers and their companies.

World Bank policy evolved in response to the threat of spreading revolution and the Cold War. For the directors of the Bank, the political stakes were a central issue: their internal debates were heavily biased towards the interests of Washington or other industrialized world centres.

The World Bank effectively began operations in 1946. On 18 June that year, Eugene Meyer, editor of the *Washington Post* and a former banker, became its first president. He lasted six months.

The early days of the Bank were difficult. The hostile attitude of Wall Street was still acute even after Franklin Roosevelt's death in

April 1945. The banking world mistrusted an institution that, in their view, was still too influenced by the excessively interventionist, public policy of the New Deal. They would have preferred the United States to concentrate on developing the Export-Import Bank. They were overjoyed when Henry Morgenthau left the Treasury,[1] and were not particularly averse to Meyer's appointment as president of the Bank, but by no means welcomed those enthusiastic supporters of public control – Emilio Collado and Harry White – who were appointed executive directors of the World Bank and the IMF, respectively.

The witch-hunt

Operations at the World Bank and the IMF were largely influenced by the Cold War and the witch-hunt launched in the US. They were largely orchestrated by the Republican Senator of Wisconsin, Joseph McCarthy. Harry White, the 'father' of the World Bank and executive director of the IMF, was placed under investigation by the FBI (Federal Bureau of Investigation) as early as 1945, suspected of spying for the USSR.[2] In 1947, his case was put before the federal grand jury, who refused to prosecute. In 1948, he was questioned by the House Un-American Activities Committee (HUAC). Hounded by a spiteful and unrelenting campaign, he died of a heart attack on 16 August 1948, three days after appearing before the committee.[3] In November 1953, during Eisenhower's[4] presidency, the Attorney General brought posthumous charges against Harry White as a Soviet spy. He also accused President Truman of appointing Harry White executive director of the IMF in the knowledge that he was spying for Russia.

   The witch-hunt also had repercussions throughout the United Nations and its specialized agencies, since, at the end of his term of office, on 9 January 1953, President Truman adopted a decree ordering the UN Secretary General and the directors of specialized agencies to inform the United States of all applications made by US citizens for jobs at the UN. The United States would then carry out a full investigation to determine if the applicant was likely to engage in espionage or subversive activities (such as 'advocacy of revolution... to alter the constitutional form of government of the United States'[5]). During this period, the term 'un-American' was a common euphemism used to describe subversive behaviour. A subversive element could not be hired by the UN. Interference in the internal business of the UN went very far, as demonstrated by the tone and content of a letter sent by Secretary of State J.F. Dulles of the Eisenhower administration to the president of the World Bank, Eugene Black: 'Secretary Dulles has asked me [wrote his assistant secretary] to express to you the extreme importance he attaches to obtaining the full cooperation of all heads of the Specialized Agencies of the United Nations in the administration of Executive Order 10422. He believes it is manifest that without this full cooperation the objectives of the order cannot be achieved, and without such achievement, continued support of these Organizations by the United States cannot be assured.'[6]

However, in 1947 a number of changes were made in the Bank's higher echelons. A new trio favourable to Wall Street took the reins: John J. McCloy was made president of the World Bank in February 1947, seconded by Robert Garner, vice-president, while Eugene Black was brought in to replace Emilio Collado. Before their appointment, John J. McCloy had been a prominent business lawyer on Wall Street, Robert Garner vice-president of General Foods Corporation and Eugene Black vice-president of the Chase National Bank. Meanwhile, at the IMF Harry White had been fired. Wall Street was most happy about this. With the ousting of Emilio Collado and Harry White, the last proponents of public intervention and control of capital movements were gone. The financial world could 'get down to business'.

To lend money to its member countries, the World Bank had first to borrow from Wall Street by way of bonds.[7] Private banks required guarantees before lending to a public organization, especially since, at the beginning of 1946, 87 per cent of European bonds were in default on payment, as were 60 per cent of Latin American bonds and 56 per cent of Asian bonds.[8]

With the McCloy/Garner/Black triumvirate at the helm of the Bank, private bankers were willing to loosen the purse strings because they counted on recovering their outlay and making a profit too. They were not wrong.

During the first years of its operation, the Bank lent mainly to industrialized countries in Europe. It was only with the greatest caution that it began to grant loans to developing countries. Between 1946 and 1948, it granted loans for a total of just over $500 million to countries in Western Europe ($250 million to France, $207 million to the Netherlands, $40 million to Denmark and $12 million to Luxembourg), while only one loan was made to a developing country ($16 million to Chile).

The World Bank's lending policy to Europe was radically destabilized and curtailed by the introduction of the Marshall Plan in April 1948. The scope of the Plan far exceeded the Bank's capacities. For the Bank, one of the immediate consequences of the introduction of the Marshall Plan was the resignation a month later of its president, John J. McCloy, who went to Europe to take up the post of US High Commissioner for Germany. Eugene Black replaced him at the Bank; he occupied the post until 1962.

With the Chinese revolution of 1949, the United States lost a valuable ally in Asia, causing the leaders in Washington to incorporate the 'under-development' dimension into their strategy in order to prevent Communist 'contagion'. The terms of Point IV of President Truman's inaugural address in 1949 are very illuminating:

We must embark on a bold new program for making the benefits of our scientific advances and industrial progress available for the improvement and growth of underdeveloped areas. More than half the people of the world are living in conditions approaching misery. Their food is inadequate. They are victims of disease. Their economic life is primitive and stagnant. Their poverty is a handicap and a threat to them and to more prosperous areas. [...] I believe that we should make available to peace-loving peoples the benefits of our store of technical knowledge in order to help them realize their aspirations for a better life. [...] With the cooperation of business, private capital, agriculture, and labour in this country, this program can greatly increase the industrial activity in other nations and can raise substantially their standards of living. [...] Greater production is the key to prosperity and peace. And the key to greater production is a wider and more vigorous application of modern scientific and technical knowledge. [...] we hope to create the conditions that will lead eventually to personal freedom and happiness for all mankind.[9]

In the first page of the World Bank Annual Report, which appeared after President Truman's inaugural address, the Bank announced that it would henceforth work in the spirit of Point IV of Truman's speech:

As of the date of this report the full implications of the Point IV program, and the precise method of its implementation, are not yet entirely clear. From the standpoint of the Bank, however, the program is of vital interest. [...] The Bank's basic objectives in this field are essentially the same as those of the Point IV program.[10]

The words read like the minutes of a party meeting intent on executing an order from central committee. This being said, this fourth annual report, written under the dual impact of the Chinese revolution and Harry Truman's speech, was the first to point out that the political and social tensions caused by poverty and unequal distribution of wealth were an obstacle to development, as were poor distribution of land and its twin effects of inefficiency and oppression.

The report went on to say that diseases like malaria[11] must be eradicated, the rate of school attendance increased and public health services improved. In addition, said the report, the development of the South was also important for developed countries because their own expansion depended on the markets that these underdeveloped countries represented.

In subsequent reports, the social themes gradually disappeared; a more traditional view became prevalent.

As regards its lending policy, the World Bank did nothing to embrace the social dimension evoked in Point IV. It failed to support any project aimed at the redistribution of wealth and the granting of land to landless peasants. As regards improvement in health, education and provision of drinking water, it was only in the 1960s and 1970s that the Bank supported a small number of projects, even then, with the greatest circumspection.

SOME CHARACTERISTICS OF THE BANK'S LENDING POLICY

High costs for the borrower

The loans made by the World Bank to developing countries were very costly: a high interest rate (equal to that prevalent in the market or close to it) plus a management commission, and a relatively short period for repayment. This very quickly brought protests from the developing countries, who proposed that the UN should set up an alternative, less costly means of financing than that offered by the World Bank.

Today, the Bank lends money at close to the market rate in the case of developing countries with a per inhabitant annual income of more than $965. Like any conventional bank, it is careful to select profitable projects, making sure that it imposes drastic economic reforms. The money lent comes mainly from bonds issued on the financial markets ($13 billion in 2004). The solidity of the World Bank, guaranteed by the rich countries that are its biggest shareholders, allows it to procure these funds at a favourable rate. Repayment of loans is made over periods varying from 15 to 20 years, with a grace period of three to five years during which there is no repayment of capital. This lending business is very lucrative: the World Bank makes profits to the tune of several billion dollars per year at the expense of developing countries and their people.[12]

Not one loan for a school until 1962

The World Bank lends money for specific projects: a road, a port infrastructure, a dam, an agricultural project, etc.

In its first 17 years of operation, the Bank did not grant one single loan for a school, health unit, drainage system or drinking water conveyance!

Until 1962, all loans, without exception, were put into electrical power infrastructure, communications (roads, railways, etc.), dams, agricultural machinery, the promotion of export crops (tea, cocoa, rice, etc.), or, to a marginal extent, the modernization of processing industries.

Export-oriented investments

It is easy to see where the priorities lay: the idea was to increase the capacity of developing countries to export the raw materials, fuel and tropical agricultural products necessary to the well-being of the most industrialized countries.

An analysis of projects accepted or rejected by the World Bank clearly shows that, with a few exceptions, the Bank was unwilling to support industrial projects designed to satisfy the domestic demand of developing countries because this would result in reduced imports from the most industrialized countries. The exceptions to the rule concern a handful of strategically important countries possessing real bargaining power. India was one of these.

Money lent to the South found its way back North

The World Bank made its loans on condition that the money was spent by the developing countries on goods and services ordered from industrialized countries. During the first 17 years, more than 93 per cent of the money lent came back each year to the most industrialized countries in the form of purchases. Annual figures were provided by the World Bank until 1962. From the following year to the present, this kind of data has no longer been publicly available. The explanation is simple: up to 1962, the rich countries with the most influence in the Bank were happy enough to show that the money lent by the Bank came back to them immediately. They were proud to demonstrate that the Bank was an extremely profitable business for them. But as time went by, more and more recently independent countries joined the World Bank; it became embarrassing to show, in the Bank's Annual Report, that its activities in fact benefited the wealthiest countries most (see Tables 2.1, 2.2 and Figure 2.1).

Odious loans to colonial powers ...

Ten years after its creation, the World Bank counted only two members in Sub-Saharan Africa: Ethiopia and South Africa. In strict violation of the right of peoples to self-determination, the World Bank granted

Table 2.1 Geographic distribution of expenditure made with funds loaned by the World Bank, 1946–55

	1946–51	1952	1953	1954	1955
United States	73.1%	65.3%	63.5%	58.7%	47.1%
Europe	11.3%	25.3%	30.1%	38.1%	48.8%
Canada	6.6%	8.8%	4.3%	2.4%	2.9%
Sub-total industrialized countries	91.0%	99.4%	97.9%	99.2%	98.8%
Latin America	8.3%	0.5%	1.1%	0.4%	0.1%
Middle East	0.4%	0.0%	0.0%	–0.1%	0.0%
Africa	0.3%	0.2%	0.8%	0.3%	1.0%
Asia	0.0%	0.0%	0.2%	0.2%	0.1%

Source: World Bank, Annual Reports, 1946 to 1955

Table 2.2 Geographic distribution of expenditure made with funds loaned by the World Bank, 1946–62

	Until 1955	1956	1957	1958	1959	1960	1961	1962
Germany	4.1%	14.1%	18.6%	17.2%	16.3%	16.9%	13.5%	10.9%
Belgium	3.7%	2.9%	2.8%	2.9%	3.3%	2.1%	2.5%	1.6%
Canada	5.6%	7.0%	6.0%	1.1%	2.0%	2.3%	1.5%	1.1%
United States	63.4%	50.5%	44.3%	38.8%	29.7%	29.8%	29.6%	33.2%
France	2.7%	3.3%	3.5%	1.2%	5.2%	6.7%	12.0%	12.3%
Italy	0.9%	1.7%	3.0%	5.8%	6.3%	7.7%	6.6%	8.3%
Japan	0.%	0.2%	2.2%	8.3%	6.2%	3.9%	6.1%	5.0%
Netherlands	0.0%	0.0%	0.0%	0.0%	0.0%	0.0%	0.0%	2.5%
Sweden	0.7%	1.5%	2.7%	0.9%	2.1%	2.3%	3.1%	2.6%
Switzerland	2.1%	2.3%	1.9%	1.3%	2.7%	4.3%	4.5%	3.6%
United Kingdom	11.1%	13.2%	10.9%	18.8%	20.5%	16.5%	13.7%	13.7%
Sub-total industrialized countries	94.2%	96.7%	95.9%	96.3%	94.4%	92.5%	93.1%	94.7%
Other countries	5.8%	3.3%	4.1%	3.7%	5.6%	7.5%	6.9%	5.3%
Total	100.0%	100.0%	100.0%	100.0%	100.0%	100.0%	100.0%	100.0%

Source: World Bank, Annual Reports, 1946 to 1962

loans to Belgium, France and Great Britain to finance projects in their colonies.[13] As World Bank historians have recognized: 'These loans, which served to alleviate the dollar shortages of the European colonial powers, were largely directed to colonial interests, especially mining, either through direct investments or indirect assistance, as in the development of transport and mining.'[14] These loans enabled colonial powers to reinforce domination over the people they had

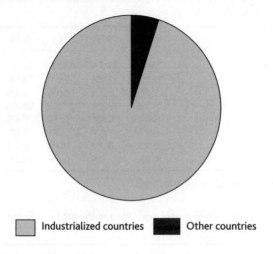

☐ Industrialized countries   ■ Other countries

Figure 2.1   Geographical distribution of the expenses made with loans from the World Bank, 1946–62

Source: World Bank, Annual Reports, 1946–62

colonized. They helped supply the colonial powers with minerals, agricultural products and fuel. In the Belgian Congo, the millions of dollars loaned to the colony for projects determined by Belgium were almost entirely spent by the colonial administration of the Congo on products exported by Belgium. The Belgian Congo received a total of $120 million in loans (in three phases), $105.4 million of which were spent in Belgium.[15]

... creating a heavy burden for young independent nations

When the above-mentioned colonies gained independence, the main shareholders came to an agreement to transfer the debt contracted by the colonial power to these new nations.

A blatant example can be seen in the case of Mauritania. On 17 March 1960, France stood surety for a loan of $66 million contracted by the Société Anonyme des Mines de Fer de Mauritanie (MIFERMA). Mauritania was living its last months as a colony, as independence was proclaimed on 28 November of the same year. This loan was to be repaid between 1966 and 1975. According to the Bank's Annual Report six years later, independent Mauritania had a debt to the Bank of $66 million.[16] The debt incurred at France's request while

Mauritania was its colony had been passed on to Mauritania a few years later. Transferring debts contracted by a colonial power to the new independent state was a current practice at the World Bank.

A similar case had already occurred in the past: it had been decided by the Treaty of Versailles. When Poland was reconstituted and made an independent state after the First World War, it was pronounced that the debts contracted by Germany to colonize the part of Poland under its domination would not be passed on to the new independent state. The Treaty of Versailles of 18 June 1919 stipulated thus: 'That portion of the debt which, in the opinion of the Reparation Commission, is attributable to the measures taken by the German and Prussian Governments for the German colonization of Poland shall be excluded from the apportionment to be made under Article 254.'[17] The Treaty stated that the creditors that had lent money to Germany for projects in Polish territory could only claim their due from this power, and not from Poland. Alexander-Nahum Sack, the theoretician of odious debt, states in his treatise of 1927: 'When the government contracts debts for the purpose of subjugating part of the people's territory or of colonizing it by nationals of the dominant nationality, etc., these debts are odious for the native population of this part of the territory of the debtor State.'[18]

This principle applies in every respect to the loans made by the Bank to Belgium, France and Great Britain for the development of their colonies. Consequently, the Bank acted in violation of international law by making the new independent states liable for debts incurred for the purpose of colonizing them. The Bank, with the connivance of its main colonial shareholders and the blessing of the United States, committed an act that should not go unpunished. These debts are null and void; the Bank should answer for them before the law. The states that have been victims of this violation should demand reparations and use the sums in question to repay the social debt due to their people.[19]

THE WORLD BANK'S MISSIONS

The World Bank is in the habit of sending specialists on missions to certain member countries. In its first twenty years, these specialists were in most cases sent from the United States.

In the beginning, the 'test' country most visited was undoubtedly Colombia. It was a key country from the point of view of strategic

US interests. One of Washington's priorities was to prevent Colombia falling into the Soviet camp or heeding the call of revolution.

In 1949, the Bank sent a well-manned mission to Colombia, including experts from the Bank, the IMF, the FAO (Food and Agriculture Organization of the United Nations) and the WHO (World Health Organization). Its task was to study the needs and determine a global development strategy for the country. The concrete projects supported by the Bank concerned the purchase from the United States of 70 bulldozers, 600 tractors and equipment for three hydroelectric stations! In 1950, it was learned that the Colombian government was studying the report delivered by the commission with a view to formulating a development programme on this basis. The next year – 1951 – a commission of independent Colombian experts finished drawing up such a development programme, which the government then put into action: budgetary and bank reforms; reduction and relaxing of import restrictions; relaxing of exchange controls; adoption of a liberal and accommodating attitude with regard to foreign capital.

Consultants designated jointly by the Bank and the Colombian government also drew up proposals concerning the railways, civil aviation, industrial investment and the issuing of public debt bonds. An economic adviser nominated by the Bank was taken on by the Colombian National Board of Economic Planning. This is what one of the top people at the IMF, Jacques Polack,[20] had to say about his participation in a mission to Colombia:

The oral instructions that I received as head of a Fund (IMF) mission to Colombia in 1955, formulated in a meeting between the vice-president of the Bank and the deputy managing director of the Fund, conveyed the same notion, expressed in the heartier language of these days: 'You twist their right arm and we'll twist their left arm.'[21]

As one can see, in general these missions served essentially to increase the capacity of the Bank (and other institutions, in particular the IMF) to influence the decisions taken by the authorities of a given country in a way that would benefit the shareholding powers and their companies.

WORLD BANK POLICY EVOLVED IN RESPONSE TO THE THREAT OF SPREADING REVOLUTION AND THE COLD WAR

In 1950 the US and its allies in the World Bank effectively expelled China when it became a Communist state and gave its seat to the anti-

Communist government of General Chiang Kai-shek, which had set up headquarters on the island of Taiwan.[22] To prevent the Communist contagion spreading to the rest of Asia, various strategies were used; certain countries were the focus of systematic intervention by the World Bank. Such was the case of India,[23] Pakistan, Thailand, the Philippines and Indonesia. Up to 1961, the Bank was not authorized to deal with South Korea, which was the exclusive domain of the United States.

Poland and Czechoslovakia, which were part of the Soviet bloc, left the Bank early on.[24] On its expulsion from the Soviet camp, Yugoslavia received financial support from the Bank.

In 1959 a tremendous revolutionary hurricane shook the Americas: in Cuba the struggle for revolution finally triumphed under the very nose of Uncle Sam.[25] Washington was obliged to grant concessions to the governments and people of Latin America to try to prevent revolution spreading like wildfire to other countries.

The Bank's historian, Richard Webb, ex-president of the Central Bank of Peru, recalled the effects of this phenomenon:

Between 1959 and 1960, Latin America received the full benefit of Fidel Castro's revolution. The first effects had already appeared with the decisions to establish an Inter-American Development Bank and to surrender – after a long resistance – to Latin American demands for a commodity price stabilization, a coffee agreement was signed in September 1959. The aid momentum increased in early 1960, following Cuba's sweeping expropriation, its trade pact with the USSR, and Eisenhower's trip to South America. 'Upon my return' he wrote 'I determined to begin ... historic measures designed to bring about social reforms for the benefit of all the people of Latin America.' [26]

President Eisenhower added:

Constantly before us was the question of what could be done about the revolutionary ferment in the world. [...] We needed new policies that would reach the seat of the trouble, the seething unrest of the people. [...] One suggestion was [...] to raise the pay of the teachers and start hundreds of vocational schools. [...] [We] had to disabuse ourselves of some of old ideas [...] to keep the Free World from going up in flames.[27]

Webb continued:

In April, secretary of State Christian A. Herter informed the Pan American Union of a sharp change in American foreign policy toward Latin America, including a decision to support land reform. Dillon presented a new aid program to Congress in August, which called for $600 million in funding for soft loans by the Inter-American Development Bank and stressed social expenditures to contend with income inequality and outdated institutions, two serious impediments to progress.

The bill was promptly enacted.

The perception of crisis in the region continued into 1961, and President Kennedy escalated the response: 'Next to Berlin it's the most critical area. [...] The whole place could blow up on us. [...] I don't know if Congress will give it to me. But now's the time, while they're all worried that Castro might take over the hemisphere.'[28] In March 1961 Kennedy demanded action to avert chaos in Bolivia. His staff decided to 'ignore proposals by both the IMF and State Department that Bolivia needed a good dose of an anti-inflationary austerity, and instead should offer immediate economic assistance. [...] Things were grim enough without calling for further sacrifice from those who had nothing to give.'[29] A week later Kennedy announced the Alliance for Progress with Latin America, a ten-year programme for cooperation and development, stressing social reform, with large-scale aid to countries that 'did their part'.[30]

The announcement of big reforms did not prevent the Bank and the United States from supporting corrupt and dictatorial regimes like that of Anastasio Somoza in Nicaragua, as demonstrated in the following example. On 12 April 1961, just five days before the United States was due to launch a military expedition against Cuba from Nicaraguan territory,[31] the directors of the Bank decided to grant a loan to Nicaragua although fully aware that the money would be used to reinforce the dictator's economic power. It was the price to pay for his support for the assault on Cuba. Below is an excerpt from the official minutes of the discussion between the Bank's directors on 12 April 1961:[32]

- Mr. [Aron] Broches. I am told that the Somoza Family is in everything and it would be difficult to find anything in Nicaragua which did not raise this problem.
- Mr. [Robert] Cavanaugh. I am concerned that we would appear to be fostering an arrangement under which people will be urged to sell land that the President wants...
- Mr. [Simon] Cargill. If the project itself is satisfactory I don't believe that the interest of the President is such a problem that the whole thing should be held up...

- Mr. Rucinski. I agree that it is too late to turn it down.
- Mr. Aldewereld. The problem of the land holding and Somoza ownership is an unfortunate one but it is one we have been aware of from the very start and I think it is too late to raise the question now.

A few months later, in June 1961, the same Bank directors were debating the question of a loan to Ecuador. The contents of this discussion are eloquent reminders of the global political stakes behind the Bank's action:[33]

- What is the political risk of the submerged Indians, representing half or two-thirds of the population, who are still completely out of the political and economic picture? ...
- Mr. [John] de Wilde. Ecuador has a good record. [...] [I]sn't [this] a strategic time for the agencies [...] such as the Bank to step into the picture [...] and [...] prevent a deterioration in the political situation?
- Mr. Knapp. [...] That is the sort of salvage job that the United States must perform.
- Mr. Broches. Where does Ecuador stand on the index of social injustices Mr Kennedy has been referring to?
- Mr. Knapp. Ecuador would appear to be the next country on the list to go 'Fidelistic'... [...] Mr [Orvis] Schmidt. While there is great disparity in the distribution of wealth in Ecuador, this is less so than in other countries in Latin America. [...] The Indians up on the mountains are still quiet although the Government has not really been doing very much on their behalf.
- Mr. Demuth. In looking at the Latin American feudal countries [...] to be realistic we must assume that revolutions are going to occur and only hope that the [new governments] will honour the obligations of former governments. [...]
- Mr. Aldewereld. Colonialism is certainly bad in Ecuador [...] even [...] worse than in the Far East. Something violent is going to happen. [...] I think that our projects do serve to relieve internal pressures. [...] I agree that we might consider more IDA money because of these political risks.
- Mr. Knapp. [...] But political situations do lead to defaults.

It could hardly have been put more clearly.

3
Difficult Beginnings between the UN and the World Bank

The World Bank and the IMF are specialized institutions of the UN, comparable in theory to the International Labour Organization (ILO) or the Food and Agriculture Organization of the United Nations (FAO). As such, they are supposed to cooperate closely with the various UN bodies and the other specialized institutions to achieve the objectives set out in the UN Charter and in the Universal Declaration of Human Rights.

From the outset, the World Bank and the IMF attempted to extricate themselves to a large extent from the obligations that bind member organizations of the United Nations system. In the case of the Bank, while its development aid mission should have led it to seek a rapprochement with the UN, its directors consistently managed to place the Bank outside the UN's sphere of authority. The Bank and the IMF were instrumental in heightening the Cold War and, later, in playing on the reactions of leaders in the most industrialized countries to the growing influence of developing countries calling for a new world economic order.

Having no Marshall Plan to promote their growth, the developing countries proposed that a new UN body, SUNFED (Special United Nations Fund for Economic Development), be created, based on a 'one country, one vote' system designed to facilitate loans to their industries. The industrialized countries were fiercely opposed to this move; they successfully imposed a counter-proposal, the International Development Association (IDA), a branch of the World Bank, thus effectively putting an end to SUNFED.

EARLY RELATIONS WITH THE UN

In March 1946, on the occasion of the first meeting of the governors of the World Bank and the IMF, the president of the Economic and Social Council of the United Nations (known by the acronym ECOSOC)[1] handed a letter to the directors of the World Bank asking it to set up liaison facilities with its organization. The Bank postponed discussion of this issue until the executive directors' meeting to be held in May 1946. In fact, the Bank dragged its feet so successfully that it was only in November 1947 that an agreement between the two parties was reached. According to Mason and Asher, the Bank's historians, the negotiations were not particularly cordial.[2] The first letter from ECOSOC having gone unanswered, a second letter was sent, to which the executive directors of the Bank replied that, in their view, a meeting on the subject would be premature. Meanwhile, the United Nations had already signed cooperation agreements with the International Labour Organization, UNESCO and the FAO.

In July 1946 a third attempt was made when the UN Secretary General proposed that the Bank and the IMF begin negotiations in September 1946. The directors of the IMF and the World Bank subsequently met and decided that such a meeting was still not timely. This is what Mason and Asher had to say about these stalling tactics: 'The Bank was very fearful that becoming a specialized agency of the UN would subject it to undesirable political control or influence and hurt its credit rating in Wall Street...'[3] The Bank finally adopted a draft text to be submitted for discussion with the United Nations. This text was more a declaration of independence than a declaration of cooperation. Then followed a day of discussions at the UN headquarters, during which the Bank's president, John J. McCloy, agreed to exercise a little more moderation.

The resulting agreement was accepted by ECOSOC's negotiating committee, but it raised a furore within ECOSOC itself and at the General Assembly. During ECOSOC's 1947 session, the Soviet Union delegate described the draft agreement as a flagrant violation of at least four articles of the UN Charter. Even more embarrassing for the Bank's directors, and obliquely, for the United States, was the attack led by the delegate from Norway (the native country of the current UN Secretary General, Trygve Lie). He declared that Norway could not tolerate such privileges being granted to the Bank and the IMF, because it would undermine UN authority. To which the United States delegate retorted that nothing would undermine UN authority more than the impossibility of its coming to an agreement with the Bank and the IMF. Finally, ECOSOC adopted (13 votes for, three against and two abstentions) the draft text which was ratified in September 1947 by the Bank's governing council (the governor representing Yugoslavia abstained). The agreement was approved by the UN General Assembly in November 1947.

This agreement ratified the Bank's status as a UN specialized agency, but, at the Bank's request, allowed it to operate as an 'independent international organization'. Following the same line, it authorized the Bank to use its own judgement as to what information could be usefully communicated to ECOSOC, which constituted a departure from Article 17, paragraph 3 and Article 64 of the United Nations Charter (Article 64 gives ECOSOC the right to obtain regular reports from specialized agencies). It was also a departure from Article 70, which allows for reciprocal representation at each deliberation. Yet in spite of this, the Bank and the IMF reserved the right to invite UN representatives only to the meeting of the governing council. In reviewing these events, the Bank's historians declare that this agreement was considered unsatisfactory by the United Nations secretariat, but it felt obliged to accept it. They go on to say that the Bank's president, 'McCloy, could not be classified as an admirer of the United Nations, and Garner (the Bank's vice president) was considered anti-UN'.[4]

THE CREATION OF THE IFC AND IDA[5]

From the beginning of World Bank operations, the governments of developing countries, starting with Latin America and followed by India, criticized the fact that their countries enjoyed no aid facilities similar to those of the Marshall Plan, which was restricted to Europe. Indeed, World Bank loans were granted at current market interest rates, while Marshall Plan aid was mainly given in the form of grants. A small proportion of Marshall Plan aid was in the form of interest-free loans or loans with interest rates lower than those of the market (see chapter 4).

In 1949, an Indian economist proposed creating a new international organization within the framework of the UN. He suggested it be called the 'United Nations Administration for Economic Development'. Some years later, the same idea took shape within ECOSOC, and SUNFED (Special United Nations Fund for Economic Development) was set up. From 1950 to 1960, several Third World countries, as well as the USSR and Yugoslavia, waged a systematic campaign within the UN to consolidate and reinforce SUNFED. For the US government and the governments of the other major industrial powers, the idea of a special fund controlled by the UN and separate from the World Bank was unacceptable.

Among the reasons behind the developing countries' demand for a specialized UN agency to finance their development was the question of voting rights. They wanted a UN specialized agency in order to ensure that the 'one country, one vote' rule was applied, as opposed to the census-type rule applied within the Bank. The same reason – but in reverse – was behind US and other major powers' opposition to the proposal: the small number of rich countries were afraid of becoming minority voters.

As recounted by the Bank historians Mason and Asher, and later by Catherine Gwin, in 1954 the United States made a first counter-proposal which the Bank put into practice in 1956 with the creation of the International Finance Corporation (IFC), whose role was to grant loans to private sector companies in developing countries.[6] This new initiative failed to quell dissatisfaction; the developing countries' campaign in favour of SUNFED gained strength. In 1958, this special United Nations fund was authorized to finance pre-investments in developing countries.

Unfortunately, the Third World camp quickly became divided. India, which had originally supported SUNFED, switched allegiance and declared itself favourable to the second US counter-proposal. This proposal involved the creation of an International Development Association (IDA), linked to the World Bank, as an alternative to SUNFED.[7] The pro-Washington Indian lobby was convinced that India would benefit from IDA since the major powers predominating in the Bretton Woods institutions would understand the necessity of giving India special treatment in view of its strategic position. And India was right: in the first year of IDA activity, it received 50 per cent of IDA loans.

By proposing the creation of IDA, the US government had a dual objective: on the one hand to prevent the United Nations continuing to reinforce SUNFED and thereby satisfying the needs of developing countries; on the other hand to find a way of using the currency reserves of developing countries that the US Treasury had been piling up since 1954 through the sale of its agricultural surpluses under Public Law 480.[8] Several authors agree that it was Senator Mike Monroney of Oklahoma who first floated the idea. He put a resolution before the Senate for the establishment of an IDA in cooperation with the World Bank and proposing that non-convertible currency reserves should be paid into this agency in order to grant long-term, low interest loans that would be paid back in local currency. Basically it meant that loans would be made to poor countries so that they could buy North-American agricultural surpluses.[9] Eugene Black, president of the World Bank, would later say: 'IDA was really an idea to offset the urge for SUNFED.'[10] It is worth quoting Mason and Asher here:

As an international organization affiliated with the World Bank, IDA is an elaborate fiction. Called an 'association' and possessed of Articles of Agreement, officers, governmental members galore, and all the trappings of other international agencies, it is as yet simply a fund administered by the World Bank.[11]

The United States provided 42 per cent of IDA's initial funding, thus ensuring US predominance within the agency.

At the same time that IDA was founded, the DAC (Development Assistance Committee of the OECD) was being set up in Paris. This was a structure designed to 'coordinate' bilateral development aid from the most highly industrialized countries. This spelt the final demise of SUNFED, the United States having imposed institutions where US control could be guaranteed.

IDA FINANCING

IDA does not borrow on the financial markets. The money it lends comes from donations made regularly by member countries (mainly the most wealthy industrial countries, plus the Organization of Petroleum Exporting Countries (OPEC)) since the 1970s, and from the repayments that it receives.

Every three or four years, the contributing countries haggle over the kitty. It is the stuff of great debates in the US Congress, which is where the payouts are decided. Bargaining proceeds smartly between Congress, the Washington government and the US presidency of the World Bank/IDA. Yet the amounts at stake are actually very modest. What is really important is to ensure that money loaned by IDA comes back to the donors in the form of purchases (linked aid).[12]

THE WORLD BANK'S REFUSAL TO COMPLY WITH UN DEMANDS CONCERNING PORTUGAL AND SOUTH AFRICA

From 1961, when most colonial countries had won independence and become UN members, the General Assembly on several occasions adopted resolutions condemning the apartheid regime in South Africa and Portugal's iron dominance over several African and Asian countries. In 1965, in view of the continued financial support of the Bank and the IMF for these regimes, the UN made a formal demand in the case of Portugal:

To all the specialized agencies of the United Nations, and in particular the International Bank for Reconstruction and Development and the International

Monetary Fund [...] to refrain from granting Portugal any financial, economic or technical assistance so long as the Portuguese Government fails to renounce its colonial policy, which constitutes a flagrant violation of the provisions of the Charter of The United Nations.[13]

It issued a similar demand concerning South Africa.

The Bank's directors met to take a position; a majority of the executive directors decided to continue making loans. To justify this decision, they invoked Article 4, section 10 of the Bank's statutes,[14] which forbids political involvement! All the most industrialized countries, backed by some Latin American states, voted to continue the loans. In 1966, the Bank approved a $10 million loan to Portugal and a $20 million loan to South Africa. Subsequently, under further pressure, the Bank stopped making new loans to these countries. However, a UN structure, the Decolonization Committee, continued for 15 years to denounce the fact that the Bank allowed South Africa and Portugal to apply for World Bank financing for projects in other countries. In addition, the Bank sought the favours of South Africa to obtain donations to IDA.[15]

4
The Post-1945 Context:
the Marshall Plan and US Bilateral Aid

The Marshall Plan replaced the World Bank's intervention since the US came to the conclusion that reconstruction gifts to Europe would be more efficient and cost-effective than loans. This bilateral policy aimed to buttress the capitalist Western bloc spearheaded by Washington against the Eastern bloc dominated by the USSR in the Cold War context.

The United States cancelled the debts of some of its allies. The most obvious instance of this kind was the way the German debt was largely cancelled by the 1953 London Agreement. In order to make sure that the economy of West Germany would thrive and become a key element of stability in the Atlantic bloc, the creditor allies led by the United States made major concessions to German authorities and corporations – concessions that went beyond debt relief. A comparison between the way West Germany was treated after the Second World War and the current attitude to developing countries is a telling story.

THE US GOVERNMENTS HAD LEARNT FROM
THE MISTAKES MADE IN THE 1920s AND 1930s

In the Treaty of Versailles at the end of the First World War, the victors demanded that Germany pay huge amounts as war debt and reparation.[1] Germany soon found it difficult to pay; social discontent grew as a consequence. The Wall Street crash occurred in 1929, leading to a global economic crisis. The US drastically reduced capital outflow, and Germany stopped paying its debt to France, Belgium and Britain; these countries in turn stopped paying their debts to the United States. The more industrialized world sank into recession and massive unemployment. International trade plummeted.

To prepare for a different outcome after the Second World War, Washington decided on policies that would be completely different from those implemented after the First World War and until the early 1930s. It set up the Bretton Woods institutions and the United Nations. This was the international institutions approach.

Let us now analyze the bilateral economic policies developed by the United States.

GIVE RATHER THAN LEND MONEY

The US government's major concern at the end of the Second World War was to maintain the full employment that had been achieved thanks to the tremendous war effort. It also wanted to guarantee that there would be a trade surplus in relations between the US and the rest of the world.[2] But the major industrialized countries that could import US commodities were literally penniless. For European countries to be able to buy US goods, they had to be provided with lots of dollars. But how? Through grants or through loans?

To put it simply, the US reasoning line went as follows: if we lend European countries on our side the money they need to rebuild their economies, how are they going to pay us back? They will no longer have the dollars we lent them since they used them to buy from us. So there are only three possibilities: first, they pay us back in kind; second, they pay us back in dollars; third, we give them the money so that they can recover.

In the first hypothesis, if they pay us back in kind, their goods will compete with ours on our home market, full employment will be jeopardized and profits will fall. This is not a good solution.

In the second hypothesis, they cannot use the dollars they received on loan to pay us back since they have used them to buy our goods. Consequently, if they are to pay us back, we have to lend them the same amount (which they owe us) again, with interest added. The risk of being caught in an infernal cycle of indebtedness (which puts a stop to or slows down the smooth running of business) is added to the risk attached to the first possibility. If Europeans try not to accumulate debts towards us they will try and sell their goods in our home market. They will thus get some of the dollars they need to pay us back. But this will not be enough to rid them of their debts; it will lower the rate of employment in the US.[3]

We are left with the third possibility: rather than lend money to Europeans (via the World Bank or not) it seems appropriate to give them the amount of dollars they need to build up their economies within a fairly short time. Europeans will use the donated dollars to buy goods and services from the US. This will guarantee an outlet for US exports, hence full employment. Once economic reconstruction is achieved Europeans will not be laden with debts and will be able to pay for what they buy from us.

The US authorities thus concluded that they had better proceed by grants, and therefore launched the Marshall Plan.

THE MARSHALL PLAN[4]

Between 1948 and 1951 the United States devoted more than \$13 billion (\$11 billion of which was freely given) to restore the economy of 17 European countries in the context of the Organization for European Economic Cooperation (OEEC, today OECD). The total of US aid amounted to approximately \$90 billion in current US dollars. The United States demanded a number of commitments in exchange for its aid: first, European countries had to coordinate reconstruction expenses within the OEEC – the US thus contributed to European cooperation, a prelude to the construction of Europe in order to reinforce the Western bloc against the Soviet bloc – then it

Table 4.1   Expenses involved in Marshall Plan economic assistance, 3 April 1948 to 30 June 1952 (in US\$ of the time)

Countries	Total	Grants	Loans
Total for all countries	\$13,335.8	\$11,820.7	\$1,505.1
Austria	677.8	677.8	–
Belgium–Luxembourg	559.3	491.3	68.0[a]
Denmark	273.0	239.7	33.3
France	2,713.6	2,488.0	225.6
Germany (FR)	1,390.6	1,173.7	216.9
Greece	706.7	706.7	–
Iceland	29.3	24.0	5.3
Ireland	147.5	19.3	128.2
Italy (including Trieste)	1,508.8	1,413.2	95.6
Netherlands (Indonesia)[b]	1,083.5	916.8	166.7
Norway	255.3	216.1	39.2
Portugal	51.2	15.1	36.1
Sweden	107.3	86.9	20.4
Turkey	225.1	140.1	85.0
United Kingdom	3,189.8	2,805.0	348.8
Regions[c]	407.0	407.0	–

Notes:
a. The loan included 65 million for Belgium and 3 million for Luxembourg.
b. Marshall Plan support to the Dutch East Indies (Indonesia) extended to the Netherlands after the former became independent on 30 December 1949.
c. Included the US contribution to the European Payments Union (EPU), a European social fund: 361.4 million.

demanded that the money received be used to buy goods produced by US industry.

To those grants within the Marshall Plan we must add the partial cancellation of France's debt to the US in 1946 ($2 billion was written off). Similarly, Belgium benefited from a reduction of its debt to the US as compensation for the uranium provided to make the first two atomic bombs, which were dropped on the Japanese cities of Hiroshima and Nagasaki and which resulted in the first nuclear holocaust. The uranium had been extracted in the mines of Shinkolobwé (near Likasi, then Jadotville) located in the province of Katanga in the Belgian Congo. First move: Belgium was granted debt cancellation thanks to its colony, whose natural resources it lavishly exploited. Second move: some 15 years later, Belgium transferred to the newly independent Congo the debts it had incurred in order to exploit those natural resources as well as its population (see chapter 2).

THE 1953 LONDON DEBT AGREEMENT, OR THE GERMAN DEBT

If West Germany could redeem its debt and rebuild its economy so soon after the Second World War, it was thanks to the political will of its creditors, i.e., the United States and its main Western allies (United Kingdom and France). In October 1950 these three countries drafted a project in which the German federal government acknowledged debts incurred before and during the war. They joined a declaration to the effect that:

the three countries agree that the plan include an appropriate satisfaction of demands towards Germany so that its implementation does not jeopardize the financial situation of the German economy through unwanted repercussions nor has an excessive effect on its potential currency reserves. The first three countries are convinced that the German federal government shares their view and that the restoration of German solvability includes an adequate solution for the German debt which takes Germany's economic problems into account and makes sure that negotiations are fair to all participants.[5]

Germany's pre-war debt amounted to DM22.6 billion, including interest. Its post-war debt was estimated at DM16.2 billion. In the agreement signed in London on 27 February 1953, these sums were reduced to DM7.5 billion and DM7 billion, respectively.[6] This amounts to a 62.6 per cent reduction.

The agreement offered the possibility to suspend payments and renegotiate conditions in the event of a substantial change limiting the availability of resources.[7]

To make sure that the West German economy was effectively doing well and represented a stable key element in the Atlantic bloc against the Eastern bloc, allied creditors granted the indebted German authorities and companies major concessions that far exceeded debt relief. The starting point was that Germany had to be able to pay everything back while maintaining a high level of growth and improving the living standards of its population. It had to pay back without getting poorer. To achieve this, the creditors accepted first that Germany pay its debt in its national currency; second, that Germany reduce imports (it could manufacture at home those goods that it formerly imported);[8] third, that it sell its manufactured goods abroad so as to achieve a positive trade balance. These various concessions were laid down in the declaration.[9]

Another significant aspect was that the debt service depended on how much the German economy could afford to pay, taking the country's reconstruction and the export revenues into account. The debt service/export revenue ratio was not to exceed 5 per cent. This meant that West Germany was not to use more than one-twentieth of its export revenues to pay its debt. In fact it never used more than 4.2 per cent (except once in 1959).

Another exceptional measure was that interest rates were substantially reduced (to between 0 and 5 per cent).

Finally, we have to consider the dollars the United States gave to West Germany: $1,173.7 million as part of the Marshall Plan from 3 April 1948 to 30 June 1952 (see Table 4.1 above) with at least $200 million added from 1954 to 1961, mainly via USAID.

Thanks to such exceptional conditions, Germany had redeemed its debt by 1960, in record time. It even beat the maturity dates.

SOME ELEMENTS TOWARDS A COMPARISON

It is enlightening to compare the way post-war West Germany was treated with the treatment of developing countries today. Although bruised by war, Germany was economically stronger than most developing countries. Yet it received in 1953 what is currently denied to developing countries.

Proportion of export revenues devoted to paying back the debt

Germany was allowed not to spend more than 5 per cent of its export revenues to pay back its debt.

In 2004, developing countries had to spend an average of 12.5 per cent of their export revenues to pay back their debts (8.7 per cent for Sub-Saharan African countries and 20 per cent for countries in Latin America and the Caribbean). The proportion was even higher than 20 per cent by the end of the 1990s.

Interest rate on external debt

As stipulated in the 1953 agreement on Germany's debt, the interest rate was between 0 and 5 per cent.

By contrast, the interest rates to be paid by developing countries were much higher. A large majority of agreements had rates that could be increased. From 1980 to 2000, the average interest rate for developing countries fluctuated between 4.8 and 9.1 per cent (between 5.7 and 11.4 per cent for Latin America and the Caribbean, respectively, and between 6.6 and 11.9 per cent for Brazil from 1980 to 2004).

Currency in which the external debt had to be paid

Germany was allowed to use its national currency.

No third world country can do the same barring exceptional cases for ludicrously small sums. All major indebted countries must use strong currencies (dollars, euros, yen, Swiss francs, pounds sterling).

Possibility of revising the agreement

The London Debt Agreement included the possibility to suspend payments and renegotiate conditions in the event that a substantial change should curtail available resources.

Loan agreements with developing countries do not include such a possibility.

Policy of import substitution

The London Debt Agreement stipulated that Germany could manufacture commodities it used to import.

By contrast, the WB and the IMF prohibit developing countries from manufacturing anything they can import.

Cash grants in strong currencies

Although it was largely responsible for the Second World War, Germany received significant grants in strong currencies as part of the Marshall Plan and beyond.

While the rich countries have promised developing countries assistance and cooperation, the latter merely receive a trickle by way of currency grants. Whereas they collectively pay back some $300 billion a year, they receive about $30 billion. The largest indebted countries in the Third World receive no cash aid whatsoever.

Undoubtedly, the refusal to grant indebted developing countries the same kind of concessions as granted to Germany indicates that creditors do not really want these countries to get rid of their debts. Creditors consider that it is in their better interest to maintain developing countries in a permanent state of indebtedness so as to draw maximum revenues in the form of debt reimbursement, but also to enforce policies that serve their interests and to make sure that the developing nations remain loyal partners within the international institutions.

What the United States had done via the Marshall Plan for industrialized countries that had been ravaged by war was repeated in the case of certain allied developing countries at strategic locations on the periphery of the Soviet Union and China. It gave them much higher amounts than those lent by the World Bank to the rest of the developing countries. This particularly applies to South Korea and Taiwan, which were to receive significant aid from the 1950s, an aid that largely contributed to their economic success story.

From 1953 to 1961, for example, South Korea received more from the United States than the Bank lent to all independent countries in the Third World (India, Pakistan, Mexico, Brazil and Nigeria included), namely, over $2,500 million vs $2,323 million. During the same period, Taiwan received about $800 million.[10] Because it was strategically located in relation to China and the USSR, a small farming country like South Korea benefited from US largesse. The Bank and the United States were tolerant towards economic policies in Korea and Taiwan that they banned in Brazil or Mexico. This will be developed in chapter 11 on Korea.

5

A Bank Under the Influence

The book commissioned by the World Bank to recount its first 50 years of existence shows that the concept of the Bank as a huge bureaucracy, gradually freed from the influence of the US, is far from reality. This mistaken conception is revealed in particular by the North American environmentalist Bruce Rich in his insightful book on the World Bank.[1] In real terms, the institution is firmly under the control of the US government, which negotiates, in concert with the governments of other major capitalist powers, the policies to be followed within the Bank and under its leadership. It has frequently failed to make the effort to reach a consensus with its principal partners (since the end of the 1950s, these are Japan, Germany, Great Britain and France) and imposes its views directly on the World Bank.

Relations have sometimes been tense between the US government and the Bank's president and/or its management in the wider sense. One must also consider the intervention (more or less active depending on the period) of Congress. On several occasions, the US executive has had to make a deal with Congress concerning the attitude to be taken with reference to the Bank and its activities.[2]

Although the World Bank is systematically subject to US influence, it nevertheless enjoys a certain measure of autonomy. It possesses a certain logic of its own, which sometimes comes into conflict with the immediate interests of the US government. The Bank's autonomy is very limited; the US government imposes its will on all issues that it considers important. Also, one must take into consideration the close links between the US business world (big capital) and the Bank.

THE INFLUENCE OF THE UNITED STATES ON THE BANK

Throughout the history of the International Bank for Reconstruction and Development (the World bank), the United States has been the largest shareholder and the most influential member country. U.S. support for, pressure on, and criticisms of the Bank have been central to its growth and the evolution of its policies, programs, and practices.[3]

These sentences introduce the chapter on relations between the US and the World Bank from 1945 to 1992, published in a book commissioned by the World Bank to recount its first 50 years of existence.[4]

Other excerpts from the same text, reproduced below, are so explicit as to need no comment:

And the top management of the Bank spends much more time meeting with, consulting, and responding to the United States than it does with any other member country. Although this intense interaction has changed little over the years, the way the United States mobilizes other member countries in support of its views has changed considerably. Initially, it was so predominant that its positions and the decision of the board were virtually indistinguishable.[5]

The United States has viewed all multilateral organizations, including the World Bank, as instruments of foreign policy to be used for specific U.S. aims and objectives.[6]

The United States is often impatient with the processes of consensus building on which multilateral cooperation rests.[7]

A preoccupation with containing communism, and the change in the relative U.S. power in the world explain much of the evolution in U.S. relations with the World Bank over the past fifty years.[8]

The debt crisis in the south and the collapse of communism in eastern Europe led to renewed U.S. interest in the Bank.[9]

REFERRING AGAIN TO THE ORIGIN OF THE WORLD BANK AND THE INFLUENCE OF THE UNITED STATES

In contrast to the IMF which is the result of intense negotiation between the United States and Britain, the Bank is largely an American creation. The role of the United States was acknowledged by John Maynard Keynes in his opening remarks at the Bretton Woods Conference.[10]

The result was a strong and enduring American imprint on all aspects of the Bank, including its structure, general policy direction, and the manner of granting loans.[11]

Among the issues that divided the participants at the Bretton Woods conference was the location of the Bank and IMF headquarters. The US Treasury wanted it to be established in Washington, within the reach of its influence, while several foreign delegations preferred New York, on the one hand to put it at a distance from the US government, and on the other hand to move it closer to the future headquarters of the United Nations. John Maynard Keynes explicitly asked that the Bank and the IMF be kept at a distance from the US Congress and, he added, from the influence of the embassies; New York must therefore be the choice of headquarters. In fact, Keynes initially tried to persuade the participants to choose London. Realizing it was a losing battle, he then tried to avoid Washington by proposing New York. The secretary of the US Treasury, Henry Morgenthau, replied that it was necessary to move the centre of the world from London and from Wall Street towards the US Treasury. Morgenthau's line of argument was clever with respect to other delegations since at the end of the Second World War, the British Empire, though shaky, was still dominant – hence the desire not to locate the headquarters of the new financial institution in London, close to the leading financial centre, the City of London. The second part of his argument was also clever in that Wall Street was synonymous with the domination of the business world that had produced the 1929 crash.

Basically, Morgenthau wanted, as he declared, to place the centre of the new financial institutions effectively in the control of the Treasury and maintain a distance in relation to Wall Street. Henry Morgenthau, Harry White and Emilio Collado later left or would be dismissed under the pressure of Wall Street (see chapter 2). In fact, the Bretton Woods institutions very quickly came under the double supervision of the Treasury and Wall Street (from 1947).

Out of the ten presidents of the World Bank from 1946 till today, seven, including the first, came directly from the business world.

Moreover, to avoid undue influence of the US government on the Board of Directors of the Bank, Keynes wanted its members (executive directors) to divide their activity between their country of origin and World Bank headquarters: he therefore proposed that they work on a part-time basis.[12] The Treasury's proposal prevailed: the Executive Directors were to be permanent residents in Washington and the headquarters of the two institutions just a five-minute walk from the White House.

During the vote in Congress on US participation in the World Bank and the IMF, an overwhelming majority emerged (345 against 18 in the House of Representatives; 61 against 16 in the Senate) – a very unusual state of affairs. This clearly proved that Congress was indeed satisfied with the choices made in the construction of these two institutions.

While the Bank was principally created to ensure reconstruction of the countries devastated by the Second World War, the US preferred to launch the Marshall Plan on its own initiative, because in this way it could totally control operations and also make donations to whomever it liked.

Although it in fact played a marginal role in reconstruction, nevertheless the Bank allocated certain loans to European countries, starting with the first in its history: $250 million to France in May 1947.[13] According to Catherine Gwin, the US government refused to grant any loan to France as long as the French Communist Party (PCF) was in the government. The State Department therefore took an explicit and formal step in this matter, and the PCF was pushed out of the governmental coalition; in the days that followed, the representative of the World Bank announced that the loan of $250 million was granted. This clearly shows the direct influence exercised by the US executive on the Bank and the political choices leading to this intervention. In the same study, the author indicated that, in 1947, the US intervened successfully in order to prevent the granting of a loan to Poland and Czechoslovakia on the grounds that the governments of these countries included communists.[14]

Since the start of operations, the policies of the World Bank were determined by the context of the Cold War and US interests in this regard.

THE PRESIDENT OF THE WORLD BANK HAS ALWAYS BEEN A US CITIZEN PROPOSED BY THE US GOVERNMENT

Since its origin and up to the present time, the president of the World Bank has been a US citizen proposed by its government. The members of the Board of Governors simply ratify the candidate presented by the US. This privilege does not figure in the statutes of the Bank. Although the statutes allow it, no governor has ventured up to now – or at any rate, publicly[15] – to propose a candidate of another country or even an American candidate other than the one selected by the government.[16]

THE US RIGHT OF VETO AT THE WORLD BANK

From its beginnings till today, the US is the only country to have a de facto right of veto at the World Bank. With the creation of the Bank, the US had 35.07 per cent of the voting rights;[17] since the last modification of voting rights, made in 2002, it enjoys 16.41 per cent. Since its origin in 1947 (the year the Bank went into operation), the majority required to modify the statutes was 80 per cent (held by at least 60 per cent of the member countries), which in fact gave the US a right of veto. The wave of newly independent countries in the South increased the number of member nations of the World Bank Group, gradually diluting the weight of the US vote. However, the US took care to preserve its right of veto: in 1966, it had only 25.50 per cent of voting rights but this percentage was still sufficient for the purpose.

When, in 1987, the situation was no longer tenable for the US, the definition of the qualified majority was modified in its favour. In fact, that year, Japan[18] negotiated a significant increase in its voting rights with the US, placing it as the second most important country ahead of Germany and Great Britain. In order to concede this increase to their Japanese allies, the US accepted a reduction of its voting rights provided that the required majority was raised to 85 per cent. In this manner it gave full satisfaction to Japan while maintaining its right of veto.

According to Catherine Gwin,

The United States is also the dominant member of the Bank's board – but only in part it is lead shareholder. Formally, most Bank decisions, including those affecting lending levels and loan allocations, require a simple majority vote of the board.

This means that the US could be made a minority. But, the author continues:

Decisions are, however, often worked out between the United States and Bank management before they ever get to the board, or among members of the board before they get to a vote. And most board decisions are taken by consensus. It is the weight of its voice, therefore, more than the exercise of its vote that gives the United States effective power on the board.[19]

THE INFLUENCE OF THE US ON THE BANK IN SPECIFIC CASES

I will present the cases of five countries in order to illustrate the influence of the US in the choices made by the Bank. To do this, I draw on the two books commissioned by the World Bank to narrate its own history,[20] as well as on the Annual Reports of the Bank, while comparing the information provided in other sources that are generally critical of the Bank. The choice has not been easy since there is a profusion of examples at our disposal. In fact, according to these two books, the instances in which the opinion of the US government did not prevail can be counted on the fingers of both hands.

Nicaragua and Guatemala

Central America is considered by the US government as part of its own exclusive sphere of influence. The policies adopted by the World Bank in terms of granting loans to the countries of the region are directly influenced by the political choices of the US government. The case of Nicaragua and Guatemala during the 1950s makes this clear.

Thus one of the largest developing country borrowers, in number of loans, was Nicaragua, a nation with one million inhabitants, controlled by the Somoza family.[21] 'Washington and the Somozas found their relationship highly convenient. The United States supported the Somozas and the Somozas supported the United States – in votes at the United Nations, in regional councils, and by offering Nicaragua as a base for training and launching the Cuban exile forces that met disaster at the Bay of Pigs in 1961. Between 1951 and 1956 Nicaragua received nine World Bank Loans, and one in 1960. An American military base was established in 1953 from which was launched the successful overthrow, by the U.S. Central Intelligence Agency (CIA), of Guatemalan President Jacobo Arbenz, who had legalized the Communist Party and threatened to expropriate the assets of the United Fruit Company. Guatemala itself, with three times the population of Nicaragua, and though it was one of the first countries to receive a survey mission (published in 1951), did not obtain a loan until 1955, after the overthrow of its "communist" regime'.[22]

After Somoza's fall in 1979, the US attempted, by different political, economic and military means, to destabilize and then overthrow the new Sandinista system. This led to a challenge by Nicaragua to the US in the International Court of Justice of The Hague, which delivered a verdict in 1986 condemning the United States for violation of obligations enforced by international law, in particular the ban on the use of force (Articles 2 and 4 of the UN Charter) and on violations of the sovereignty of another state.[23]

Concerning the attitude of the Bank with regard to the Sandinista regime during the 1980s and the influence that was brought to bear on it by the US government, I quote another excerpt from Gwin's study:

A more recent example in which the Bank's refusal to lend clearly coincided with U.S. policy is that of Nicaragua in the 1980s. The reason for the suspension of lending was the accumulation of arrears. However, in September 1984, the Nicaraguan government formally proposed a solution to its arrearages problem.[24]

Gwin details the concrete proposals formulated by Nicaragua and she explains that although these proposals were acceptable, the Bank made no effort to help the Sandinista regime. She points out that this was in contrast to the flexibility adopted by the Bank in respect to other regimes that were allies of the US.

Yugoslavia

In order to support Marshal Tito's regime vis-à-vis the Soviet Union, the US government incited the Bank to grant a loan to Yugoslavia at the end of the 1940s. As the following quotation shows, the US government preferred to assist Tito's Yugoslavia through the Bank rather than grant direct bilateral assistance for fear of being criticized in Congress by the numerous parliamentarians who opposed any support of a communist regime:[25]

The Bank lent to Yugoslavia soon after the break from the Soviet bloc in 1948. George Kennan[26] had recommended 'discreet and unostentatious support' by the West, fearing Russian reaction, and aware that Congress would be unwilling to assist a Communist country. The 'international Bank' was an appropriate vehicle for such a role, and a mission travelled to Belgrade the following year.[27]

The president of the Bank, Eugene R. Black, went in person to negotiate directly with Marshal Tito.

Chile

After the election of Salvador Allende in 1969 and the government's setting up of the Popular Unity, the Bank, under US pressure, suspended its loans to Chile from 1970 to 1973. The Chilean case shows that there can be a contradiction between the judgement of the Bank and the position of the US government, the latter finally getting the Bank to modify its position. Although the Bank's management considered that Chile fulfilled the conditions to receive loans, the US government made sure that no loan was granted to the Salvador Allende government. Gwin summarizes this emblematic case as follows:

The United States pressured the Bank not to lend to the Allende government after nationalization of Chile's copper mines. Despite the pressure, the Bank sent a mission to Santiago (having determined that Chile was in compliance with Bank rules requiring that for lending to resume after nationalization, procedure for compensation had to be under way). Robert McNamara subsequently met with Allende to indicate that the Bank was prepared to make new loans contingent upon government commitments to reform the economy. But the Bank and the Allende regime could not come to terms on the conditions for a loan. Throughout the period of the Allende regime, Chile received no new loans. Shortly after Allende's assassination in 1973 during a coup that brought General Pinochet's military junta to power, the Bank resumed lending, providing a fifteen-year credit for copper mine development. [...] The suspension of lending in 1970–73 was cited in the 1982 U.S. Treasury report as a significant example of the successful exercise of U.S. influence on the Bank and although the Bank reached an agreement in principle on new lending in June 1973, the loan proposals were not formally considered by the board until after the September coup that brought General Pinochet to power.[28]

As a complement to this information there is a document preserved in the archives of the World Bank, in which the Chilean government, on the occasion of a meeting of the Bank in September 1972, protested against the suspension of loans and pointed out that precisely defined projects had already been submitted to the Bank.[29] Under pressure from the US, the Bank took no action as long as Allende was in power. Several internal working documents of the Bank critically refer back to the Bank's policies towards Chile under Allende and under Pinochet (see following chapter).

Some twelve years later, when the atrocities committed by the Pinochet regime were provoking widespread protests in the US, and even within Congress, the US government asked the Bank to delay a discussion on granting loans to Chile in order to avoid opposition in Congress. This request was rejected by the president of the Bank, Barber Conable, in a letter addressed to James Baker, Secretary of the Treasury, on 29 October 1986. One can deduce that the request of the US government was simply paying lip service to public opinion, designed to depict the government as being sensitive to expressed democratic concerns, while remaining fully aware that, in a well-rehearsed distribution of roles, the president of the Bank would keep to the political course recommended by the government. It was a question of pleasing everyone.

Vietnam

From the 1960s until the end of the Vietnam War in 1975, the US successfully encouraged the Bank, through its affiliate IDA, to grant loans regularly to the South Vietnam regime – an ally of the

US. After the end of the war and the defeat of the US, the World Bank sent two successive fact-finding missions, which concluded that the Vietnamese authorities, although not pursuing a totally satisfactory economic policy, fulfilled the conditions required to receive concessional loans. Shahid Husain, director of the Bank's mission, specified that the economic performance of Vietnam was not inferior to that of Bangladesh or Pakistan, which received aid from the Bank. In spite of this, the Bank management, under pressure from the US, suspended loans to Vietnam and its president, Robert McNamara, affirmed in *Newsweek* (20 August 1979) that the suspension was based on the negative report of the mission. This affirmation is factually false, as pointed out by Gwin: 'The mission's contention, in contrast to what McNamara said publicly in *Newsweek*, was that on substantive grounds there was no basis for stopping all lending to Vietnam.'[30]

Conclusion concerning the country case studies

The World Bank management justifies allocation or non-allocation of loans on purely economic grounds. But we have seen that, in reality, the policies of granting loans is first and foremost determined by the intervention of the US government in the Bank's business, on the basis of mainly political objectives.

This is not to say that economic objectives have no importance, but they are subordinated or supplementary to political and strategic choices. Catherine Gwin, who defends the generally positive result of US influence on the World Bank, from the US standpoint, adopts a rigorous approach in which she does not conceal the contradictory aspects of the policies of both the US and the Bank management. In this regard, the following remark is particularly interesting:

Although one need not dispute the Bank's economic policy assessments of Allende's Chile, Vietnam, and Nicaragua under the Sandinistas, it is worth noting that equally harsh assessments could have been made, but were not, of Somoza's Nicaragua, Marcos's Philippines, and Mobutu's Zaire, regimes that were all important cold war allies of the United States.[31]

THE INFLUENCE OF THE US CONCERNING SECTORAL LOANS

From the 1970s, the US systematically used its influence in an attempt to convince the Bank not to grant loans that would facilitate the production of goods that would compete with US products. Thus the US regularly opposed the production of palm oil,[32] citrus fruits and sugar. In 1987, it got the Bank to drastically reduce loans granted to the steel-manufacturing industry in India and Pakistan. In 1985, the US successfully opposed an investment project by the International Finance Corporation (IFC/World Bank Group) in the Brazilian steel industry and later a loan from the Bank to support the restructuring of the steel manufacturing sector of Mexico. It also threatened to use its power of veto to block a loan for the Chinese steel industry in the 1980s. The US also blocked a loan from the IFC to a mining company for the extraction of iron ore in Brazil. It took similar action regarding an investment by the IFC in the Chilean copper industry.

In addition, the US actively influenced the Bank in its policy on the oil sector. The US was in favour of loans for oil drilling but not refining. No comment is necessary.

CASES OF CONVERGENCE BETWEEN THE US AND ANOTHER POWER (GREAT BRITAIN, FOR EXAMPLE)

On several occasions, US interests coincided with those of other powers; the attitude adopted by the Bank is then the result of close consultation between the United States, the other concerned power(s) and the Bank. Two examples may be cited: the attitude of the Bank concerning the Aswan Dam construction project under the regime of Gamal Abdel Nasser in Egypt, and in Iraq since the occupation of that territory by troops from the US, Great Britain and their allies in March 2003.

The Aswan Dam project in Egypt

The project for the construction of the Aswan Dam on the Nile preceded the accession of Colonel Nasser to power in 1952 but took its final form during that year. In January 1953, the Egyptian finance minister wrote to Eugene Black, president of the World Bank, proposing the co-financing of this gigantic project. Although the execution of this infrastructure corresponded to the priorities of the Bank, its management was reluctant to be involved because Great Britain, at that time the second power in terms of voting rights within the Bank's Board of Governors, considered the progressive military regime to be a threat to its strategic interests. In effect, the Egyptian military in power challenged the occupation of the Suez Canal by British troops. Black personally visited Egypt and discussed the project; the Bank sent engineers, and so forth. The project involved a dam whose capacity of 130 billion cubic metres would be four times greater than those of the largest artificial dams yet built. The vast scope of this project offered huge prospects to international construction firms.

The negotiations between Egypt and Great Britain for the departure of British troops resulted in an agreement, which reduced the reluctance of Great Britain and the pressure it was placing on the Bank management not to grant loans. The North American and British governments gave the Bank management their go-ahead for negotiations, but imposed restrictions by dividing the execution of the project into two phases: the financing of the first phase was guaranteed while the financing of the second would depend on the political position of the Egyptian authorities. Of course, this was not explicitly expressed in the agreements but that was how the Egyptian government interpreted it. The Egyptians wanted to start the work in July 1957, which meant that the contract had to be signed in July 1956. Consequently, they asked the Bank to confirm the granting of loans as quickly as possible.

In December 1955, a meeting of the executive directors of the Bank gave Eugene Black the green light to pursue negotiations with the Egyptians on the basis of the conditions laid down by the United States and British governments. The Egyptians gave the Bank's conditions a cold reception. Meanwhile, the British authorities learned that the Egyptians had signed a commercial agreement with the Soviet Union with a view to a cotton-for-arms exchange.[33] The historians Mason and Asher commented on the appearance of the Soviet Union on the scene as follows: 'These manoeuvres had simply heightened the desire of the Western powers to associate themselves with the dam.'[34] Black, before going to Cairo to finalize the agreement with the Egyptians, contacted the US government, who confirmed the go-ahead. On his way to Cairo, Black also met the British Prime Minister in London. After ten days of negotiations in Cairo, one fundamental point of disagreement remained: the Egyptians would not accept the conditions fixed by the US and Great Britain. On his return to Washington, Black proposed pursuing negotiations because he was eager to reach an agreement. On the other hand, in Washington and especially in London, hesitation was growing as the Egyptian regime took on an Arab nationalist orientation. The opposition of the British increased further when King Hussein of Jordan on 1 March 1956 sacked the entire British command of the Arab Legion. Black now found himself more and more isolated, but the governments let him pursue negotiations, implying that they could succeed, while it appears to the Bank historians that the decision to refuse had already been taken.

At the beginning of July 1956, thanks to tenacious negotiating, Black got Gamal Abdel Nasser, the Egyptian Prime Minister, to declare his acceptance of the conditions fixed by the Western powers. Nevertheless, when the Egyptian ambassador officially announced Egypt's agreement on 19 July 1956, he was told that in the present circumstances the US government had decided not to participate in financing the Aswan Dam. On 20 July, the British Parliament was advised that the British government had withdrawn from the project. Mason and Asher specify that the State Department informed the Bank of its decision to withdraw from the project only one hour before the official communication was made to the Egyptian ambassador. They add that in this communication, the US used the pretext of a negative judgement by the Bank, justified by economic reasons. While the printed version of this text was already being circulated in the chancelleries, the Bank's president persuaded the US government to withdraw this argument from the text released to the press.

To come back to the fundamental political consequences, I once again refer to the judgement made by Mason and Asher:

The dramatic sequel is well known. On July 26, 1956, Premier Nasser announced that the government was taking control of the property and operations of the Suez Canal Company. On October 29, after a series of border incidents, Israeli troops invaded Egypt, and on December 2, British and French military action against Egypt began – ostensibly for the purpose of protecting the Canal Zone but, in the opinion of many observers, actually for the purpose of overturning Premier Nasser.[35]

The Aswan Dam affair shows how the US government can work with another government to exert influence on the decisions of the World Bank when their interests coincide. It also reveals that the US can take refuge behind a so-called refusal of the Bank to oppose a project, thus making the Bank seem responsible for its failure.

In a limited number of cases, the US government has allowed other powers to use their means of influence on the Bank. This has happened when the strategic interests of the United States were not directly concerned. For example, France was able to exert influence on the Bank to persuade it to adopt a policy in accordance with 'French' interests in Ivory Coast.

The occupation and reconstruction of Iraq

The military intervention of March 2003 against Iraq, followed by the occupation of its territory, was carried out without the agreement of the UN and against the opinion of several major powers including France, Germany, Russia and China. The US, at the head of the coalition that launched the attack against Iraq, had the active support of three other members of the G7 (Great Britain, Japan and Italy) and of medium-size powers such as Spain and Australia. As early as April 2003, the US took the initiative of negotiating with the G7 and within the framework of the Paris Club a substantial reduction of the debts contracted by the Saddam Hussein regime. The idea was to reduce the burden of this debt so that the 'new' Iraq, allied to the United States, would be in a position to contract new loans and to repay them. In addition to this approach, which I have analyzed elsewhere,[36] the US government put pressure on the World Bank and the IMF to lend to the new Iraqi authorities, which were directly under their control through the civil administrator of Iraq, the American Paul Bremer. In several declarations from the end of March to the end of May 2003, it can clearly be seen that the president of the World Bank and the director of the IMF were very reluctant. The necessary conditions for granting loans were not met. What were the problems?

1. The legitimacy of the authorities at the head of Iraq was not recognized, particularly because they exercised no real sovereignty in view of the role played by Paul Bremer and the occupation authorities.

2. In principle, the World Bank and the IMF respect the following rule: they do not grant new loans to a country that has defaulted on payment of its sovereign debt. The pressure exerted by the US on the Bank and the IMF on the one hand, and the powers opposing the war on the other, gradually removed the obstacles inasmuch as the UN Security Council, at its meeting on 22 May 2003, entrusted the US and its allies with the management of Iraqi oil and lifted the embargo against Iraq. The Security Council did not recognize the war but recognized the *fait accompli* of the occupation. The US and its allies got the World Bank and the IMF to agree to actively participate in the donor conference for the reconstruction of Iraq held in Madrid on 23 October 2003. The case of Iraq demonstrates that the US can constitute an alliance to determine the orientation of the Bank and the IMF despite the

reluctance of their principal directors, James Wolfensohn and Horst Kölher.[37] In October 2004, the United States managed to get the member nations of the Paris Club (to which it also belongs) to agree to make a three-phase cancellation[38] of 80 per cent of their $38.9 billion claim against Iraq.[39]

DIVERGENCES BETWEEN THE WORLD BANK MANAGEMENT AND THE UNITED STATES

In the early 1970s, divergences appeared between the US executive and the Bank management. This was because Robert McNamara, president of the Bank since 1968, was directly aligned with the Democratic Party: he entered politics thanks to President John F. Kennedy, who made him his adviser in 1961; his career continued under the next Democratic president, Lyndon B. Johnson (as Defense Secretary), and whose administration appointed him president of the Bank in 1968. In 1969, the position changed when Republican president Richard Nixon took office while McNamara's term was still running. Several skirmishes between the Nixon administration and the management of the Bank occurred during 1971. For example, the executive ordered the executive director representing the United States to vote against a loan that the Bank had decided to grant to Guyana. In 1972, the option was to renew McNamara's term (of five years) or to replace him. The Republicans were favourable in principle to the appointment of one of their own but, in the end, the executive reluctantly renewed McNamara's mandate.

During his second term, tensions increased considerably. The government foiled an initiative to which McNamara was strongly committed: he had negotiated with the OPEC member nations for the creation of a new development financing fund fuelled by petrodollars. The government, which wanted to break the OPEC monopoly, aborted this initiative. During this tense period, Secretary of State Henry Kissinger led the offensive against McNamara. As an alternative to the creation of a special fund fuelled by OPEC, Kissinger proposed increasing the funds made available for the International Financial Corporation and the World Bank.[40]

Relations between McNamara and the executive improved substantially again with the arrival of the new Democratic President, Jimmy Carter, in the white House. Robert McNamara was even invited to participate in the meetings of the National Security Council to discuss an increase in financial resources for the IDA.

The end of Robert McNamara's term was somewhat eventful owing to the election of a new Republican president, Ronald Reagan, in January 1981. Reagan and the Republicans campaigned in favour of a radical change in US foreign policy with immediate consequences for the World Bank. Reagan proposed a drastic reduction in multilateral aid, and therefore the US contribution to the IDA, in favour of bilateral aid, notably by a major increase in military assistance.

The bill presented in January 1981 by David Stockman, director of the Office of Management and Budget, eloquently reflects the spirit of the Reagan camp. Its adoption would have meant the end of US contributions to the IDA and to the UN, and an increase in expenditure for military assistance. In 1986, Stockman summed up in the following manner the contents of the bill that he had presented jointly with parliamentarian Phil Gramm to Congress in January 1981:

The Gramm–Stockman budget plan had called for deep cuts in foreign economic aid on the basis of pure ideological principle. Both Gramm and I believed that the organs of international aid and so-called Third World development... were infested with socialist error. The international aid bureaucracy was turning Third World countries into quagmires of self-imposed inefficiency and burying them beneath mountainous external debts they would never be able to pay.[41]

THE INFLUENCE OF THE US AS SEEN BY THE EXECUTIVE

A report from the US Treasury in 1982 praised the pre-eminence of the US in the multilateral financial institutions:

The United States was instrumental in shaping the structure and mission of the World Bank along Western, market-oriented lines... We were also responsible... for the emergence of a corporate entity with a weighted voting run by a board of directors, headed by a high-caliber American-dominated management, and well-qualified professional staff. As a charter member and major share-holder in the World Bank, the United States secured the sole right to a permanent seat on the Bank's Board of Directors. [...] Other significant actors – management, major donors, and major recipients – have recognized the United States as a major voice in the [multilateral development] banks. They know from past experience that we are capable and willing to pursue important policy objectives in the banks by exercising the financial and political leverage at our disposal.[42]

According to Walden Bello, another passage in this Treasury document specifies that:

in a study of fourteen of 'the most significant issues' that sparked debate at the Bank – ranging from blocking observer status for the Palestine Liberation Organization (PLO) to halting Bank aid to the Vietnam and Afghanistan – the United States was able to impose its view as Bank policy in twelve cases.[43]

A passage in another Treasury report dated the same year is also devoted to the World Bank and to the other development banks:

On the whole, the policies and programs of the World Bank Group have been consistent with U.S. interests. This is particularly true in terms of general country allocation questions and sensitive policy issues. The international character of the World Bank, its corporate structure, the strength of the management team, and the Bank's weighted voting structure have ensured broad consistency between its policies and practices and the long term economic and political objectives of the United States.[44]

Elsewhere in the same report, one reads:

By promoting economic and social development in the Third World, fostering market-oriented economic policies, and preserving a reputation for impartiality and competence, the MDBs encourage developing countries to participate more fully in an international system based on liberalized trade and capital flows... This means expanding opportunities for U.S. exports, investment, and finance.[45]

In a letter from President Reagan to Robert Michel, Republican leader of the House of Representatives, asking him to support the increase in World Bank capital in 1988, one finds a very useful list of middle-income countries that are strategic allies of the US and supported by the Bank. Here is an excerpt from that letter:

The Bank commits the vast majority of its funds in support of specific investment projects in the middle income developing nations. These are mostly nations (such as the Philippines, Egypt, Pakistan, Turkey, Morocco, Tunisia, Argentina, Indonesia and Brazil) that are strategically and economically important to the United States.[46]

THE FINANCIAL ADVANTAGES ENJOYED BY THE US THANKS TO THE EXISTENCE OF THE WORLD BANK AND ITS INFLUENCE ON THE BANK

Catherine Gwin has made an estimate of what the Bank and its activities brought to the US between 1947 and 1992.[47] First, one must distinguish two contributions: first, income received by US citizens possessing bonds issued by the Bank (according to her, this represents

$20.2 billion for this period); second, the operating expenditures of the Bank on US territory (this represents $11 billion for the same period). Next, she writes, one must above all take into account the lever effect of US investment in the World Bank and the IDA. Since the creation of the World Bank, the US would have made only a minimum outlay of $1.85 billion while the World Bank granted loans for a total amount of $218.21 billion (this is more than a hundredfold increase). These loans have generated large orders for US firms. She provides no estimate regarding the amount of the orders (flow-back, in Bank jargon). In the case of the IDA, the United States has made a larger outlay than for the World Bank: $18 billion to finance IDA loans to the tune of $71 billion.

THE INFLUENCE OF US BUSINESS CIRCLES AND BIG CAPITAL ON THE WORLD BANK

The fact that the World Bank, since its creation, obtains the bulk of its financial resources by issuing bonds keeps it in a permanent and privileged relationship with the big private US financial bodies. These are some of the biggest holders of Bank bonds and they exert a considerable influence.

The link between US business circles, big capital and the World Bank is also immediately perceptible when one looks more closely at the careers of the ten American citizens who have succeeded each other at the head of the Bank up to the present day.

Eugene Meyer, the first president, who lasted only eight months, was the publisher of the *Washington Post* and a former banker. The second, John J. McCloy, was a leading business lawyer on Wall Street and was subsequently appointed Commissioner-in-Chief of the Allies in Germany and, later, chairman of the Chase Manhattan Bank. The third, Eugene R. Black, was vice-president of Chase National Bank and later became Special Adviser to President Lyndon B. Johnson. The fourth, George D. Woods, also a banker, was president of the First Boston Corporation. Robert S. McNamara had been CEO of the Ford Motor Company, then Secretary for Defense under Kennedy and Johnson. His successor, Alden W. Clausen, was president of the Bank of America (one of the principal US banks deeply involved in the Third World debt crisis), and to which he returned on leaving the World Bank. In 1986, Barber Conable, a former Republican member of Congress, succeeded him. Lewis T. Preston, formerly chairman of the executive committee of the J.P. Morgan bank, arrived in 1991.

James D. Wolfensohn, president from 1995, was a banker on Wall Street with Salomon Brothers. At the end of his presidency in May 2005, Wolfensohn joined the management of Citibank-Citigroup, the leading banking group worldwide. Paul Wolfowitz was Deputy Secretary for Defense until he took office as the tenth president of the World Bank in May 2005.

In summary, and in general, a close link has been established between US political power, business circles (or if one prefers, the hard core of the US capitalist class) and the presidency of the Bank.

Table 5.1   The ten presidents of the World Bank

Name	Term	Past Career
Meyer	June 1946–December 1946	Merchant banker on Wall Street, publisher of the Washington Post
McCloy	March 1947–June 1949	Director of the Chase National Bank (later to become Chase Manhattan)
Black	July 1949–December 1962	Vice-president of Chase Manhattan Bank
Woods	January 1963–March 1968	President of First Boston Corporation
McNamara	April 1968–June 1981	CEO of Ford, then US Secretary of Defense
Clausen	July 1981–June 1986	President of Bank of America
Conable	July 1986–August 1991	Member of Congress and the Congress Banking Commission
Preston	September 1991–May 1995	President of JP Morgan & Co.
Wolfensohn	June 1995–May 2005	H Schroder Bank, then Salomon Brothers Bank, later, president of James Wolfensohn Inc.
Wolfowitz	June 2005	US Deputy Secretary for Defense

6
World Bank and IMF Support of Dictatorships

After the Second World War, in a growing number of Third World countries, policies diverged from those of the former colonial powers. This trend encountered firm opposition from the governments of the major industrialized capitalist countries whose influence held sway with the World Bank and the IMF. WB projects have a strong political content: to curtail the development of movements challenging the domination/rule of major capitalist powers. The prohibition against taking 'political' and 'non-economic' considerations into account in Bank operations, one of the most important provisions of its charter, is systematically circumvented. The political bias of the Bretton Woods institutions is shown by their financial support to dictatorships in Chile, Brazil, Nicaragua, Congo-Kinshasa and Romania.

ANTI-COLONIAL AND ANTI-IMPERIALIST MOVEMENTS IN THE THIRD WORLD

After 1955, the spirit of the Bandung Conference (Indonesia)[1] spread a mighty wind across much of the planet. It followed in the wake of the French defeat in Vietnam (1954) and preceded Nasser's nationalization of the Suez Canal. Then came the Cuban (1959) and Algerian (1954–62) revolutions and the renewed Vietnamese liberation struggle. In more and more Third World countries, policies implemented were a decisive rejection of the former colonial powers. This often meant import substitution and the development of policies turned towards the internal market. This approach met with firm opposition from the governments of the major industrialized capitalist countries, who held sway at the World Bank and the IMF. A wave of bourgeois nationalist regimes carrying out populist policies (including Nasser in Egypt, Nehru in India, Peron in Argentina, Goulart in Brazil, Sukarno in Indonesia and Nkrumah in Ghana) and outright socialist regimes (Cuba, People's Republic of China) appeared on the scene.

In this context, World Bank projects have an underlying political purpose: to thwart the development of movements challenging domination by major capitalist powers.

THE WORLD BANK'S POWER OF
INTERVENTION IN NATIONAL ECONOMIES

As early as the 1950s, the World Bank established a network of influence that was to serve it greatly in later years. In the Third World, it sought to create demand for its services. The influence it enjoys nowadays is to a large extent the outcome of the network of agencies it built up in states that became its clients and, by so doing, its debtors. The Bank exercises a real policy of influence to support its network of loans.

From the 1950s onwards, one of the primary goals of Bank policy was 'institution building'. This most often meant setting up para-governmental agencies based in the client countries.[2] Such agencies were expressly founded as relatively financially independent entities with respect to their own governments and outside the control of local political institutions, including national parliaments. They became natural relays for the WB and owed it a great deal, including their very existence; and in some cases, their funding.

Establishing such agencies was one of the WB's primary strategies to get a foothold in the political economies of Third World countries. These agencies, operating according to their own rules (often developed on the basis of Bank suggestions) staffed with Bank-backed technocrats, were used to create a stable and trustworthy source for the Bank's needs: 'viable' loan proposals. They also provided the WB parallel power bases through which it succeeded in transforming national economies, and entire societies, without going through the bother of democratic control and open debates.

In 1956, the WB founded the Economic Development Institute with significant backing from the Ford and Rockefeller Foundations. The EDI offered six-month training courses to official delegates from member countries. 'Between 1957 and 1971, more than 1300 officials had passed through EDI, a number of them already having risen to the position of prime minister or minister of planning or finance in their respective countries.'[3]

This policy had disturbing implications. The New York-based International Legal Center (ILC) study of WB policy in Colombia from 1949 to 1972 concluded that the independent agencies founded by the Bank had a profound impact on the political structure and social development of the entire region, undermining the political party system and minimizing the role of the legislative and judicial branches.

From the 1960s on, the WB has certainly found singular and novel means of continual involvement in the internal affairs of borrower countries. And yet, the WB vigorously denies that such involvement is political. It insists on the contrary that its policies are unrelated to power structures and that political and economic matters are separate spheres.

HOW POLITICAL AND GEOPOLITICAL CONSIDERATIONS INFLUENCE WORLD BANK LENDING POLICY

Article 4, section 10 of the World Bank charter stipulates:

The WB and its officers shall not interfere in the political affairs of any member; nor shall they be influenced in their decisions by the political character of the member or members concerned. Only economic considerations shall be relevant to their decisions, and these considerations shall be weighed impartially in order to achieve the purposes (set by the WB) stated in Article I.

Nevertheless, the World Bank has found many systematic means of getting round the prohibition on taking 'political' and 'non-economic' considerations into account in its operations, one of the primary stipulations of its charter. From its very beginnings, as mentioned in the preceding chapter, the Bank refused loans to post-liberation France as long as there were communists in the government. The day after they left the government in May 1947, the loan France had requested, blocked until then, was granted.

The Bank has repeatedly contravened Article 4 of its own statutes. In truth, it has made many choices based on political considerations. The quality of governments' economic policies is not the determining element in its choices. The WB has often lent money to the authorities in countries despite the dismal quality of their economic policies and a great deal of corruption: Indonesia and Zaire are two cases in point. Specifically, its choices relative to countries that play a major political role in the eyes of its major shareholders are regularly linked to these shareholders' interests and outlooks, starting with the United States.

From 1947 to the collapse of the Soviet bloc,[4] WB and IMF decisions were determined in large part by the following criteria:

- Avoid shoring up self-reliant models;
- Provide funding to large-scale projects (WB) or policies (IMF) enabling the major industrialized countries to increase exports;

- Refuse to help regimes seen as a threat by the United States government or other important shareholders;
- Attempt to modify the policies of certain governments in the so-called socialist countries so as to weaken the cohesion of the Soviet bloc. This is why support was granted to Yugoslavia, which had dropped out of the Moscow-dominated bloc from 1948, or to Romania from the 1970s at the time when Ceaucescu was attempting to distance himself from Comecon and the Warsaw Pact;
- Support strategic allies of the Western capitalist bloc and in particular of the US (i.e., Indonesia from 1965 to the present day, Mobutu's Zaire, the Philippines under Marcos, Brazil under the dictators after the 1964 coup, dictator Somoza's Nicaragua, apartheid South Africa);
- Attempt to avoid or limit as far as possible, closer links between Third World countries and the Soviet bloc or China: for example, by distancing the USSR from India and Sukarno-era Indonesia.

To carry out this policy, the WB and the IMF have generalized a tactic: greater flexibility towards right-wing governments (less demanding in terms of austerity measures) facing a strong left opposition than to left-wing governments facing strong opposition from the right. Concretely, that means the international financial institutions (IFIs) are more demanding and make life more difficult for left-wing governments to weaken them and ease the right's path to power. By the same logic, they have made fewer demands on right-wing governments facing a left-wing opposition to avoid weakening them and preventing the left from coming to power. Monetarist orthodoxy has variable geometrics: the variations depend on many political and geopolitical factors.

Some concrete cases – Chile, Brazil, Nicaragua, Zaire and Romania – provide cases in point: these were countries selected by both the WB and the IMF since such choices are determined, overall, by the same considerations and subject to the same influences.

The IMF and WB did not hesitate to support dictatorships when they (and other major capitalist powers) found it opportune. The author of the *Human Development Report* published by UNDP (1994 edition) says so in black and white:

But rhetoric is running far ahead of reality, as a comparison of the per capita ODA received by democratic and authoritarian regimes shows. Indeed, for the United States in the 1980s, the relationship between aid and human rights has been perverse. Multilateral donors also seem not to have been bothered by such considerations. They seem to prefer martial law regimes, quietly assuming that such regimes will promote political stability and improve economic management. After Bangladesh and the Philippines lifted martial law, their shares in the total loans given by the WB declined.[5]

IFI POLITICAL BIAS:
EXAMPLES OF FINANCIAL SUPPORT TO DICTATORSHIPS

Support to General Augusto Pinochet's dictatorship in Chile

Under Allende's democratically elected government (1970–73), Chile received no World Bank loans. Under the Pinochet government, after the 1973 military coup, the country suddenly became credible. And yet, no WB or IMF leader could fail to be aware of the deeply authoritarian and dictatorial nature of the Pinochet regime. The link between lending policies and the geopolitical context is blatant in this case.

One of Robert McNamara's principal assistants, Mahbub ul Haq, drafted in a memorandum in 1976 a very critical note entitled 'The Bank's mistakes in Chile'[6] with a view to modifying the orientation of the WB. It reads: 'We failed to support the basic objectives of the Allende regime, either in our reports or publicly.' McNamara decided

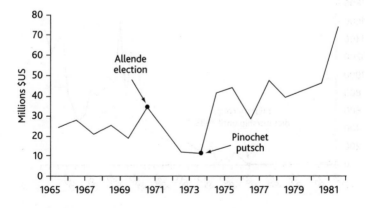

Figure 6.1   Multilateral disbursements to Chile, 1965–82

Source: World Bank, CD-ROM, *Global Development Finance*, 2001

to ignore it.[7] Mahbub ul Haq tried, unsuccessfully, to persuade the Bank management to suspend loans to Pinochet until such time as it should be 'reasonably satisfied that Pinochet's government is not merely restoring the unstable elitist economic society'. He adds that Pinochet's policies have 'worsened the country's distribution of income'.[8]

Support for the Brazilian military junta after the overthrow of President Joao Goulart

President Joao Goulart's democratic government was overthrown by the military in April 1964. WB and IMF loans, suspended for three years, resumed very soon afterwards.[9]

A brief timeline: in 1958, Brazilian President Kubitschek was about to undertake negotiations with the IMF to gain access to a loan of $300 million from the United States. In the end, Kubitschek refused the IMF-imposed conditions and did without the US loan. This earned him wide popularity in Brazil.

His successor, Goulart, announced that he would implement a radical land reform programme and proceed to nationalize petroleum refineries: he was overthrown by the military. The United States recognized the new military regime one day after the coup. Not long afterwards, the WB and IMF resumed their suspended lending policy. As for the military, it rescinded the economic measures the United States and the IMF had criticized. Note that the IFIs were of the view

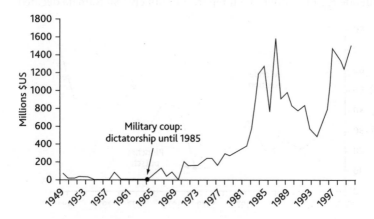

Figure 6.2   World Bank disbursements to Brazil, 1949–97

Source: World Bank, CD-ROM, *Global Development Finance*, 2001

that the military regime was taking sound economic measures.[10] Yet, the GDP fell 7 per cent in 1965 and thousands of firms declared bankruptcy. The regime organized harsh repression, outlawed strikes, caused a dramatic drop in real wages, eliminated direct ballot voting, disbanded trade unions and made systematic use of torture.

After his first trip in May 1968, McNamara visited Brazil regularly and made a point of meeting the military rulers. The World Bank's public reports systematically praised the policies of the dictatorship in reducing inequalities.[11] However, inside the Bank, the discussions took a bitter turn. When Bernard Chadenet, vice-president of projects at the WB, declared that the Bank's image would suffer through its support of the repressive government of Brazil, McNamara recognized that there was a tremendous amount of repression, but noted that it 'is not necessarily a great deal different from what it had been under previous governments, and it did not seem to be a lot worse than in some other member countries of the WB. Is Brazil worse than Thailand?'[12] Some days later, McNamara added that 'No viable alternative to the Government by generals seemed open.'[13]

The WB was well aware that inequalities would not diminish and that its loans in the agricultural sector would reinforce the big landowners. Nevertheless, it decided to maintain the loans because it absolutely wanted to get the government under its influence. Now, at this juncture, the Bank ran into a patent failure: the military regime proved extremely wary of the Bank's desire to strengthen its presence. Finally, at the end of the 1970s, they took advantage of a profusion of loans from international private bankers granted at a lower rate of interest than that of the WB.

After supporting Anastasio Somoza's dictatorship, the WB called off its loans when the Sandinista, Daniel Ortega, was elected president of Nicaragua

The Somoza clan had held power since the 1930s thanks to United States military intervention. On 19 July 1979, a powerful popular movement overthrew the dictatorship and dictator Anastasio Somoza was forced to flee. The Somoza family had a stranglehold on a huge proportion of the country's wealth and encouraged the implantation of large foreign firms, especially from the US. The people hated them. The World Bank had showered loans on Somoza's dictatorship. After the dictatorship fell, an alliance government brought together the traditional democratic opposition (led by top businessmen) and the Sandinista revolutionaries. The latter made no secret of their

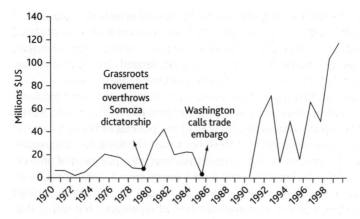

Figure 6.3   World Bank disbursements to Nicaragua, 1970–99

Source: World Bank, CD-ROM, *Global Development Finance*, 2001

sympathy for Cuba or their desire to undertake certain economic reforms (land reform, nationalization of certain foreign firms, confiscation of Somoza clan landholdings, a literacy programme and so on). Washington had supported Anastasio Somoza to the bitter end but feared that the new government might spread communism in Central America.

The Carter administration, in office when the dictatorship was overthrown, did not immediately take an aggressive stance. But things changed overnight when Ronald Reagan moved in to the White House. In 1981, he announced his commitment to bring down the Sandinistas. He provided financial and military backing to a rebellion by former members of the National Guard ('Contrarevolu-cionarios' or 'Contras'). The US Air Force mined several Nicaraguan ports. Faced with such hostility, the Sandinista majority government opted for more radical policies. During the 1984 elections, the first democratic elections in half a century, the Sandinista Daniel Ortega was elected president with 67 per cent of the ballot. The following year, the United States called a trade embargo against Nicaragua, isolating the country in relation to foreign investors. The World Bank had halted its loans from the time of the Sandinista presidential election victory. The Sandinistas actively urged the WB to resume its loans.[14] They were even ready to accept a draconian structural adjustment plan. The WB decided not to follow up on this and did not resume the loans until the Sandinista electoral defeat in February

1990, when Violeta Barrios de Chamorro, the US-backed conservative candidate, won the vote.

Support to the Mobutu dictatorship

As early as 1962, a report by the United Nations Secretary-General revealed that Sese Seko Mobutu had looted several million dollars, earmarked to finance his country's troops. In 1982, a senior IMF official, Erwin Blumenthal, a German banker and an ex-governor of the Bundesbank, wrote a damning report on Mobutu's administration of Zaire. Blumenthal warned the foreign lenders not to expect repayment as long as Mobutu remained in power. Between 1965 and 1981, the Zairean government borrowed approximately $5 billion abroad, and between 1976 and 1981, its foreign debt was subject to four Paris Club rescheduling measures amounting to $2.25 billion in all.

Mobutu's gross economic mismanagement and systematic misappropriation of a portion of the loans did not result in the IMF and World Bank halting aid to his dictatorial regime. It is striking to observe that after the Blumenthal report was submitted, WB payouts actually increased[15] (as did IMF payouts, but they are not shown here). It is clear that sound economic management criteria are not the deciding factor in WB and IMF decisions. Mobutu's regime was a strategic ally of the United States and other influential powers in the Bretton Woods institutions (including France and Belgium) during

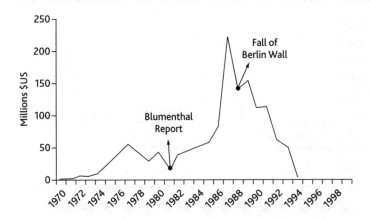

Figure 6.4   World Bank disbursements to Congo-Kinshasa (Zaire under Mobutu)

Source: World Bank, CD-ROM, *Global Development Finance*, 2001

the Cold War. After 1989–91, with the fall of the Berlin Wall followed soon after by the implosion of the Soviet Union, Mobutu's regime was no longer worthy of interest. Moreover, in many African countries, including Zaire, national conferences were making democratic demands. World Bank loans started to dry up, and ceased completely in the mid-1990s.

World Bank support to the Ceaucescu dictatorship in Romania

In 1947, Romania was brought into the Soviet bloc. In 1972, Romania was the first Soviet satellite country to join the World Bank.

Since 1965, Ceaucescu had been secretary-general of the ruling Communist Party. In 1968, he criticized the USSR's invasion of Czechoslovakia. Romanian troops did not take part in the Warsaw Pact operation. This distancing from Moscow clearly made up Washington's mind to contemplate closer ties with the Romanian regime, through the WB.

As early is 1973, the WB undertook negotiations with Bucharest to determine a loan policy; very soon this reached a very appreciable level. In 1980, Romania became the eighth most important WB borrower. Bank historian Aart van de Laar tells a significant anecdote from 1973. Early that year, he attended a meeting of the WB directors, with the beginning of loan grants to Romania on the agenda. Certain directors were sceptical of the lack of thorough studies on Romania, but Robert McNamara declared he had great trust in the financial morality of socialist countries in terms of debt reimbursement. The

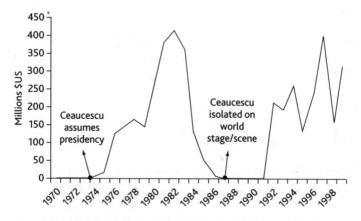

Figure 6.5   World Bank disbursements to Romania, 1970–99

Source: World Bank, CD-ROM, *Global Development Finance*, 2001

story goes that one of the Bank vice-presidents attending piped up to ask whether Allende's Chile had perhaps not yet become socialist enough.[16] This met with McNamara's stony silence.

WB choices did not depend on reliable economic criteria. First, while the Bank has regularly refused loans to countries that had failed to repay old sovereign debts, it began lending to Romania although the latter had not settled disputes over outstanding debts. Secondly, most of Romania's economic exchanges took place within Comecon in non-convertible currency. How could the country reimburse debts in hard currency? Thirdly, from the outset Romania refused to hand over the economic data the Bank required. Political considerations were obviously the reason for the WB developing close relations with Romania. The lack of internal democracy and systematic police repression were no greater a stumbling block for the Bank in this case than in others.

Romania became one of the World Bank's biggest clients and the latter financed large-scale projects (including opencast coal mines and thermal electric generators) whose negative impact in environmental terms was patently obvious. To operate the opencast coal mines, the Romanian authorities displaced former farming communities. In another field, the Bank supported the population planning policy whose aim was a higher birth rate.

In 1982, when the debt crisis came to the fore internationally, the Romanian regime decided to impose shock therapy on its people. Romania slashed its imports to the bone to come up with the surplus in hard currency to pay off its foreign debt as soon as possible. 'Romania was, in a sense, a "model" debtor, at least from the creditors' point of view.'[17]

CONCLUSION

Contrary to section 10 of Article 4 of the World Bank charter, the Bank and the IMF have systematically lent to states in order to influence their policies. The examples given in this study show that the political and strategic interests of the major capitalist powers are determining factors. Regimes with the backing of major capitalist powers have received financial aid even though their economic policies did not meet official IFI criteria or they failed to respect human rights. Furthermore, regimes seen as hostile to the major powers were deprived of IFI loans on the pretext that they were failing to respect the economic criteria set by these institutions. These policies of the Bretton Woods institutions, far from being abandoned at the end of the Cold War, continue to the present day. Examples are loans to Yeltsin's and Putin's Russia, to Suharto's Indonesia until his fall in 1998, to Chad under Idriss Déby, to the People's Republic of China, to Iraq under foreign occupation, to mention but a few.

7
The World Bank and the Philippines (1946–90)

The 1946 US decision to grant the Philippines its independence inaugurated a period of prosperity in the country. For a number of geostrategic reasons, in the wake of the Second World War the Americans were willing to let the Philippine government pursue policies that they ruled out elsewhere. The Philippine government was allowed to implement independent policies that fostered the country's economic development. However, American tolerance was short-lived. From 1962 onwards, and with the backing of the IMF and the World Bank, the Conservatives (who had won a majority of seats in the Philippine Congress in the 1959 elections) imposed radically different policies. These new policies sparked massive capital flight, crippling debts, devaluation, and a drop in wages for the population. It was in this context of crisis that Ferdinand Marcos declared martial law in 1972. The dictator earned the admiration of the Bank for pursuing policies very much in line with Washington's expectations. Massive corruption increased popular discontent and brought about the downfall of Ferdinand Marcos and his replacement by Corazon Aquino in 1986. Aquino was the leader of the democratic opposition but was also closely connected to the plantation owners. She carried out intransigently neoliberal economic policies bearing the unmistakable imprint of the World Bank. To be sure, this was a great disappointment to the people.

The Philippines remained a Spanish colony until 1898, when Spain was defeated in a war declared by the United States. The US then occupied the country itself; this occupation was interrupted by the Japanese occupation during the Second World War. In 1946, the US granted the Philippines independence in exchange for its acceptance of a number of conditions: a fixed exchange rate between the Philippine peso and the American dollar to protect US companies against the effects of devaluation, free trade agreements and so forth. At the beginning, the arrangement worked relatively well since the US was bringing in a large amount of dollars to the Philippines, primarily through its strong military presence in the country.

However, in 1949 the flow of dollars slowed down dramatically. The Philippine government established strict exchange controls to avoid a heavy drain on the currency. Private companies were forbidden to borrow money from foreign investors. The US government and the IMF tolerated this measure in order to stay on good terms with their Philippine ally. The introduction of controls over currency exchange, capital flows and imports sparked an economic boom in the country, driven in particular by the growth of industry. This period of economic growth ended twelve years later, in 1962, when the control measures were abandoned under pressure from the United States, the IMF and the WB.[1]

During the 1950s, the manufacturing sector grew annually from 10 to 12 per cent, the annual inflation rate was kept below 2 per cent, foreign exchange reserves were strong and the external debt was extremely low. However, this was not to everyone's liking; American and other foreign companies complained about having to reinvest all their profits in the country's economy. Capitalist export firms were forced to deposit their hard currency export earnings in the Central Bank, which returned them in pesos at an unfavourable rate. This was a source of enormous revenue for the state. In 1954, bolstered by its success, the Philippine government demanded that the US alter the rules of the game laid down in 1946 at the time of independence. Washington submitted to this demand, which strengthened the position of the Philippine authorities.

Of course, one has to be careful not to idealize the achievements of the Philippines in this period. It remained a profoundly unequal capitalist society; industrialization did not go much beyond assembly and light manufacturing. Nevertheless, the situation of the 1950s was certainly promising in comparison with all that has transpired since 1962. Indeed, it was these promising developments that triggered the united offensive led by the US, the IMF and the WB – together with the most conservative sectors of the Philippine ruling classes – aimed at putting an end to the experience.

In 1962, the Conservatives, who had won a majority in the Philippine Congress after the elections of 1959, eliminated controls on capital movements. The IMF and the US government showed their approval by immediately granting a loan of $300 million. The elimination of controls led to massive capital flight towards foreign countries; the resulting deficit was financed by one set of external loans after another. The external debt increased sevenfold between 1962 and 1969 – from $275 million to $1.88 billion!

Transnational corporations and Philippine exporters of agricultural products and raw materials rejoiced as their profits jumped. On the other hand, the manufacturing sector oriented towards the domestic market rapidly declined. In 1970, the peso had to be sharply devalued. The incomes and earnings of small producers slumped.

It was in this context of a crisis of the policies supported by the United States, the IMF, the WB and the Conservatives, that Ferdinand Marcos set up a dictatorship in 1972. His objective was to consolidate neoliberal policies through force.

One year later, on the other side of the Pacific, Augusto Pinochet took power in Chile with exactly the same objectives, the same overlords and the same backing!

THE ROLE OF THE WORLD BANK

The first loans granted by the World Bank to the Philippines date back to 1958. But the loans remained extremely low until McNamara became World Bank president in 1968. McNamara argued that the Philippines – where there were American military bases, as in Indonesia and Turkey – was of such strategic importance that it was absolutely necessary to strengthen its ties to the World Bank. Lending money was a way to get greater leverage. World Bank historians do not mince words:

McNamara and his staff were annoyed at the way the Philippines legislature was stalemating policy reforms. Thus the Philippines was an instance in which martial law triggered the takeoff of Banking lending. Marcos dismissed the legislature and started ruling by presidential decree in August 1972. McNamara and the Bank staff welcomed the move.[2]

One of the first measures taken by the Marcos dictatorship was the removal of the ceiling on public indebtedness, initially established by the Philippine Parliament in 1970. The regulation had established a debt margin of $1 billion with an annual ceiling of $250 million. Marcos put an end to this limitation, to the great satisfaction of the World Bank.[3] McNamara announced that the Bank was ready to at least double the amounts granted.[4] At the time it was too late to increase the loans granted for 1973, much to McNamara's displeasure. That is why the Bank did the job in double-quick time and increased by 5.5 times the total amount for 1974 ($165 million instead of $30 million).[5]

The WB and the IMF publicly supported the dictatorship to such an extent that they held their 1976 annual general meeting in Manila. That year, Bernard Bell, vice-president of the Bank for East Asia and Pacific Region, declared: 'The risk in lending to the Philippines was lower than for Malaysia or Korea.'[6] It is also worth noting that the Bank established one of the three centres of research on the green revolution in the Philippines, in partnership with the Ford and Rockefeller Foundations.

However, Marcos did not quite carry out the economic policy the Bank had hoped for. The Bank was disappointed since it was on very good terms with the dictator and the team of academics he had gathered around himself – some of whom later became officials of the Bank, such as Gerardo Sicat, secretary for planning and then president of the Philippines National Bank, the main bank of the country.

The World Bank did not criticize in the slightest the regime's repressive measures. However, it was concerned about the slowness with which structural reforms were being implemented. It wanted the dictatorship to replace what remained of the import-substitution industrialization model with the export-oriented industrialization model that it championed. In order to exert greater influence on the Filipino government, the Bank decided to grant two huge structural adjustment loans in 1981 and 1983, aimed at export promotion. The Bank was perfectly aware of the fact that most of these funds ended up in the bank accounts of Marcos and his generals; nevertheless, it considered it worthwhile to pay off members of the ruling clique in exchange for an acceleration of the neoliberal counter-reform.

At this juncture, in 1981, a banking crisis broke out in the Philippines following a huge case of corruption involving local capitalists and sections of the state bureaucracy. The crisis spread gradually to the whole financial system, threatening the two largest public banks with bankruptcy. The crisis spread from 1981 to 1983–84 and was exacerbated by the external debt crisis that broke out internationally in 1982. Foreign private banks stopped granting credits to the Philippines. This was a clear failure for the World Bank and its good friends, Ferdinand Marcos, Gerardo Sicat and Prime Minister Cesar Virata.

Popular discontent rose sharply. A number of key sectors of the ruling classes clashed with the Marcos regime. The crisis deepened following the murder of one of the members of the landed oligarchy opposed to Marcos: Senator Benigno Aquino, previously exiled to the

United States, was gunned down at Manila airport upon his return to the country in August 1983.

In spite of the growing opposition to Marcos, the Bank opted to stand behind the dictator. Departing from its plans, it massively boosted its loans to the Philippines: $600 million in 1983, or more than double the previous year's loans of $251 million. The Bank historians write that it was a matter of loyalty towards a good friend.[7]

Popular mobilizations became more radical until the opposition within the ruling classes and the army removed Marcos. They did so with the assistance of the Americans – represented in Manila by Paul Wolfowitz[8] – who supported the Marcos regime until the end and then forced him into exile.[9] Corazon Aquino – leader of the opposition among middle-class and landed sectors and widow of Benigno Aquino – took over the reins in 1986.

The World Bank then hesitated over which course to follow. Its president for East Asia and Pacific region, Attila Karaosmanoglu (see chapter 8 on Turkey), wrote a rather unenthusiastic internal note on the new democratic regime: 'We expect that the decision making process will be more difficult than in the past, because of a more collegial nature of the new team, the enhanced role of the legislative branch and the populist tendencies of the new government.'[10] Finally the Bank, the IMF and the US sought to make the best of the situation by backing President Corazon Aquino since she had made a commitment to keep her country on the right side and even to deepen the neoliberal reforms. The World Bank lent $300 million in 1987 and $200 million in 1988: it was all about greasing the wheels of the privatization of state-owned firms. Between 1989 and 1992, the World Bank lent the Philippines $1.3 billion to finance structural adjustment. The US threatened to block these loans in the event that the Philippines carried out its plan to close American military bases on its territory.

As for the land reform demanded by the powerful popular movement that led to the overthrow of Marcos and became even stronger in 1987, Corazon Aquino sided with the landed oligarchy she came from. Between 1986 and 1990, the state only acquired 122 hectares![11]

All told, the government of Corazon Aquino went even further than Marcos as far as the implementation of neoliberal policy prescriptions was concerned. This was cause for great satisfaction at the World Bank.

8
The World Bank's Support of the Dictatorship in Turkey

The World Bank's strategy in Turkey clearly recalls its policy towards Ferdinand Marcos' dictatorship in the Philippines from 1972 and Augusto Pinochet's in Chile from 1973, and the economic model they promoted. Geopolitical reasons are once again a determining factor: a hinge between Europe and Asia, Turkey is an essential pawn on the Middle East chessboard. Consequently it is necessary to subordinate this country to Washington's interests by giving full support to an authoritarian regime. The WB works in this direction when, in perfect agreement with the military leaders, it develops neoliberal economic policies that open the door wide to investments by transnational corporations and suppresses both trade unions and far-left parties. Such policies consolidate the role of Turkey as a spearhead for the United States in a historic new context.

In the 1950s the World Bank got off to a bad start in Turkey. Its signing officer, Pieter Lieftinck, from the Netherlands, was expelled by the Ankara authorities on the grounds of excessive interventionism.

Under Robert McNamara, Turkey's geostrategic importance led the Bank to increase its efforts to improve matters. A few months after becoming Bank president, in July 1968, Robert McNamara visited Turkey. He knew the country well since it had been a military ally of the United States. As Defense Secretary until 1967 he was in close contact with Ankara. Anxious not to repeat what had happened with Pieter Lieftinck, the Bank took great care not to appear too openly intrusive in the 1970s.[1] By the end of the decade it had gradually increased its pressure on the Turkish government, particularly in 1978 when the left-wing nationalist, Bülent Ecevit, became Prime Minister. In particular, the Bank tried to force an increase in the price of electricity.

The September 1980 military coup, which resulted in a dictatorship that lasted until May 1983, was very convenient for the World Bank, since the military leaders agreed to maintain the neoliberal plan it had drawn up with Süleyman Demirel[2] and Turgut Özal.

Turgut Özal[3] had been appointed state undersecretary for economic coordination by the then Prime Minister Süleyman Demirel. The two were to launch the neoliberal economic programme in January 1980. But its implementation was made difficult by trade union actions, the sense of insecurity resulting from confrontations between right-wing and left-wing students, manoeuvres in the Muslim Party, which drove a hard bargain for its parliamentary support of Demirel's minority government, and the army's thirst for power, intent on destabilizing the government with the help of the US. However, the military regime, which dissolved parliament and put Demirel in jail in September 1980, appointed Özal as plenipotentiary minister for economic affairs. He was then able to implement neoliberal policies for two years, until the financial crash that resulted in his eviction.

The World Bank enthusiastically supported the policies developed by the military leaders and Özal since they led the way to 'increasing export incentives, improving external debt management, eliminating the budget deficit […], reducing the level of public investment'.[4]

The historians of the World Bank wrote: 'the Turkish program became a prototype for the institution's structural adjustment loan series'.[5] Several factors made such developments easier:

- The close connections between Turkish political leaders and Turkish senior officers in the World Bank. In addition to already cited names we can mention Attila Karaosmanoglu[6] and Munir Benjenk,[7] men of the Bank *par excellence*.[8]
- In 1977 a highly indebted Turkey experienced a crisis, and, unlike other indebted countries, it was granted significant aid by Western powers (United States, Germany), the WB and the IMF so that it did not go under.[9]

Turkey's neoliberal turnabout was not easy since the constitution that had been drafted in the early 1960s stipulated that the country develop an industrialization policy aiming at import substitution, and implement both protectionism and public investment to this end.

The military coup in September 1980 therefore had the Bank's wholehearted sympathy. It is likely that Robert McNamara knew about preparations for the coup for he entertained close relations with the Carter administration.

The example of Turkey is another illustration of how thoroughly the World Bank's policies are determined by geostrategic interests, particularly those of the United States.

Historians of the Bank even acknowledge this openly: 'Personally as a global statesman, McNamara was not blind to Turkey's geopolitical salience.'[10] Faced with the danger of the 1979 Iranian revolution, which was hostile to the United States' policy, Turkey's stability had to be ensured by supporting an authoritarian regime.[11] The military coup in Turkey was prepared with the help of the United States.

In neighbouring Iraq, Saddam Hussein's 1979 coup against a pro-Soviet regime was part of the same convergence of strategic interests. Later Saddam would serve the interests of the United States and of Western Europe when he launched the war against Iran in 1980.

This is not something the historians of the World Bank ever mention. However, their comments on Turkey are clear enough:

The Bank seemed to take special pains to attribute benign motives to the Turkish military and avoid exhibiting displeasure at its interventions. The institution's formal comments to the effect that the military takeover in 1980 would not displace the Bank's lending intentions were extremely polite.[12]

When the military leaders handed power back to civilians, Turgut Özal and his Motherland party led the government.

In subsequent years Turkey received five structural adjustment loans (until 1985). In 1988 the World Bank wrote: 'Among the Bank's clients, Turkey represents one of the most spectacular success stories.'[13]

Such a self-congratulatory observation deserves comment. If we look at one of the Bank's major objectives, namely, reducing inflation, there is little success to be celebrated: the annual inflation rate in Turkey before structural adjustment was between 40 and 50 per cent at the end of the 1970s; under the military dictatorship that implemented adjustment, inflation reached 46 per cent in 1980–83, 44 per cent in 1984–88 and 60 per cent in 1989. In the following decades it reached an average of 70 per cent, with peaks as high as 140 per cent.

In short, the objective of reducing inflation was definitely not achieved. The same applies to the public internal debt, which exploded, and to the external debt, which increased even further.

But if we consider the Bank's hidden agenda, it can indeed be said that it achieved a remarkable victory in the 1980s:

• Turkey remained one of the Western powers' staunch allies;
• It completely relinquished the industrialization model by import substitution with a high level of protectionism and a high level of public investment;

- It developed a model focusing on exports by increasing its competitiveness, forcing down real wages and devaluing its currency in significant proportions;
- The trade union movement and both the reformist and the revolutionary left were repressed thanks to the dictatorship.

From the end of 1979 to 1994 the relative value of the US dollar to the Turkish lira multiplied by 900; this process started with a 30 per cent devaluation in 1980. In the 1970s real wages had significantly increased as a result of the trade unions' influence and the political position of the far left among young people and workers. The 1980 military coup made it possible to ban trade unions and strikes, reduce wages and increase profits.

Turkey thus became a veritable haven for corporate investments. Turgut Özal was rewarded and elected President from 1989 to 1993.

The World Bank steadily supported the military regime and the subsequent regime through loans of close to $1 billion year.

In 1991, in exchange for its services to the United States and its allies in the first Gulf War, Turkey benefited from reparations paid by a defeated Iraq.

We can thus claim that the World Bank's strategy in Turkey clearly recalls its policy towards Ferdinand Marcos' dictatorship in the Philippines from 1972, Augusto Pinochet's in Chile from 1973, and the economic model they promoted.

In 1999–2001 Turkey went through a financial crisis as severe as that of Argentina. Geostrategic interests again prevailed in the decisions taken: the IMF abandoned Argentina in December 2001 when it refused a new loan to President de la Rua, while it simultaneously pursued its policy of loans to Turkey in order to prevent social disruption that would destabilize an essential pawn on the Middle East chessboard.

Now, as everywhere else, the aid provided by the IMF and the WB only increases the debt of recipient countries and Turkish citizens have a right to refuse further reimbursement to the Bretton Woods institutions. The debt that was contracted to the IMF and the WB is odious by any standards.

9
The World Bank in Indonesia – A Textbook Case of Intervention

The World Bank's policy on Indonesia is a textbook case in many ways. Everything is there: interference in a country's internal affairs, support for a dictatorial regime guilty of crimes against humanity, backing for a regime responsible for aggression against a neighbouring country (the annexation of East Timor in 1975) and the development of mega-projects, which simultaneously imply massive transfers of population, the plundering of natural resources for the profit of transnational corporations and aggression against indigenous populations.

In 1997, Indonesia was hit hard by the South-East Asian crisis. The prescribed remedies of the World Bank and the IMF worsened the economic situation and brought about social disasters. The 2004 tsunami drama changed nothing for the Bank. The creditors maintained their pressure for repayment of Indonesian debts and imposed an additional dose of neoliberal adjustment.

In 1947, the World Bank granted a $195 million loan to the Netherlands – the second loan in the Bank's history. Two weeks before the loan was approved, the Netherlands launched its offensive against the Indonesian nationalists who were demanding independence. In the next two years, as many as 145,000 Dutch occupying troops were sent into the country: it was a large-scale operation that could hardly go unnoticed. Within the United Nations and in the US, criticism was voiced concerning Dutch policy in Indonesia and the World Bank's involvement. The Bank replied that the loan had been granted to the Dutch government for spending within the Netherlands. The critics objected in their turn that since money is fungible by nature, it was easy for the Dutch government to use the Bank loan to support its military effort in Indonesia.[1]

The US put pressure on the Netherlands, giving it $400 million under the Marshall Plan so that it could grant independence to Indonesia. The US objective was to open a new field of trade and investment for its own companies. On 27 December 1949, the transfer of sovereignty was signed. Indonesia became a republic and the nationalist Sukarno was elected President. He set about maintaining a balance between the various factions in the country, while amassing personal power. In 1955, following the first elections, Sukarno decided to collaborate with the Communist Party (PKI) in order to establish his legitimacy. The PKI won 16 per cent of the votes and Sukarno's party, the PNI, 25 per cent.

In external affairs, Sukarno made skilful use of the two opposing blocs in the Cold War; there too, he managed to maintain an equilibrium until 1963, when the US, exasperated by the USSR's assistance to Indonesia, explicitly asked him to choose his camp. The IMF played the role of intermediary by proposing financial assistance strictly conditioned by terms of close cooperation. In March 1963, negotiations for loans got under way with the US, the IMF and the member states of the OECD, but everything went haywire in September 1963 when the British proclaimed the Federation of Malaysia without any outside consultation. Sukarno saw it as a destabilizing manoeuvre and retaliated by nationalizing the British companies, which led to the cancellation of the agreements with the IMF. Despite everything, the UN endorsed the creation of Malaysia; Sukarno, unable to prevail, walked out of the UN in 1965.

At the height of the Cold War, Sukarno nationalized all foreign private companies (except the oil companies). Indonesia left the IMF and the World Bank in August 1965 and decided to manage its affairs without them. On 30 September 1965, General Mohamed Suharto staged a military coup, supported by Washington. As chief of the armed forces, he launched a massive repression against the leftist parties, making the PKI his prime target: between 500,000 and one million civilians were assassinated simply for being members of or even sympathizers of the PKI. In March 1966, Suharto finally forced Sukarno to make an official transfer of power. Six days later, the US government announced that it was opening a line of credit for Indonesia amounting to $8.2 million so that it could buy American rice.[2] On 13 April 1966, Indonesia joined the World Bank.[3] In 1966, US President Lyndon B. Johnson went to visit US troops in Vietnam and insisted, in one of his speeches, on the Indonesian model.[4] This model, 'the New Order' of the Suharto era, regularly used terror and assassination, and in effect aligned its policy on that of the United States.

THE WORLD BANK AND SUHARTO'S DICTATORSHIP

When Robert McNamara became president of the World Bank in April 1968, he observed that Indonesia (with Mao's China) was the only highly populated country with which the Bank did not have an important relationship. It was necessary to make up for lost time and his first trip abroad as WB president was to Indonesia in June 1968. He felt quite at home there: the dictator Suharto had already surrounded himself with economists trained in the US, courtesy of the Ford Foundation.[5]

Relations between them were idyllic: 'He (McNamara) and President Suharto admired each other.'[6] 'While they were engaged in daily policy discussion, the Bank and the government acted like a couple of old cronies.'[7] 'Indonesia was the presidentially designated jewel in the Bank's operational crown.'[8]

Moreover, the historians of the Bank admit that: 'President Suharto (he had assumed the office in 1967) was a general, and his government, in good part, was a government of generals, many of whom were corrupt.' [9]

Indonesia officially rejoined the ranks of the IMF in February 1967; the rewards were not long in coming: the Western countries immediately granted aid of $174 million in order to absorb the effects of the Indonesian crisis. Thereafter, in the early 1970s, the good relations between Indonesia, the US and the financial institutions took the form of a substantial debt reduction.

Indeed, at the end of 1966, $534 million should have been repaid as debt servicing (interest, principal and arrears), a sum that represented 69 per cent of the estimated earnings from exports. Without a rescheduling, debt servicing would have destroyed the effect of financial assistance. The Western creditor countries accepted a long-term moratorium[10] until 1971 on repayment of the principal and interests on the debt contracted before 1966. However, the effects of the moratorium were only temporary; in 1971, repayments were supposed to start again. Consequently, the creditors signed the most favourable agreement ever granted at that time to a Third World country:[11] the pre-1966 debt (contracted under Sukarno) must be repaid in 30 annual instalments over a period extending between 1970 and 1999. The creditors agreed that Indonesian repayments would not exceed 6 per cent of the earnings from exports.[12] This operation had the effect of cancelling 50 per cent of the debt.[13]

This reduction of debt was coupled with a reprehensible complacency regarding corruption. As soon as the World Bank returned to Indonesia to support the military dictatorship, its representatives became aware of the extent of the corruption. But Robert McNamara and the enormous Bank staff who settled in permanently in Djakarta[14] decided not to make it a cause for divorce. Thus they were clearly accomplices.

Bernard Bell, who headed the Bank resident staff in Indonesia, recalls the question of the enormous misappropriation of funds caused by high-level government corruption. On 11 February 1972 he described this corruption to Robert McNamara, as 'unacceptable to small but potentially vigorous elements of the public'. And that was only the beginning. Indeed, the *Global Corruption Report 2004* by Transparency International estimated embezzlement by Suharto and his entourage at $15 to $35 billion. The World Bank itself nurtured the corruption since one of its own reports mentioned that 20 to 30 per cent of the budgets related to development funds were misappropriated.[15] The Bank continued its loans while knowing perfectly well that they were likely to be diverted.

THE PERTAMINA AFFAIR

During the 1970s, oil incomes exploded, and so did the diversion of funds by corrupt generals for their own benefit. In 1975, a major crisis came to a head between the US and Indonesia. Ironically, the invasion and annexation of East Timor by Indonesia that year had nothing to do with this.

The Indonesian generals had developed the public oil company Pertamina so successfully that in February 1975 it had become the largest Asian company (Japan not included). The Pertamina conglomerate not only extracted and refined hydrocarbons, but also possessed a chain of hotels and numerous oil tankers. Pertamina improved the country's harbour infrastructure, and built roads and hospitals. This public company was active in the field of insurance with offices in Hong Kong, Los Angeles, Singapore and Tokyo. It played a key part in a strategy of industrialization by import substitution. This was less and less to the liking of the US, and naturally, to the World Bank. To put it bluntly, Pertamina was an obstacle to the development of the large US oil companies. Consequently, the US found it advisable to weaken and even dismantle Pertamina. Under pressure, Suharto bowed to its demands during the summer of 1975. Robert McNamara wrote to him: 'I applaud the comprehensive and systematic way in which you have moved to re-establish appropriate priorities.'[16] As a consolation prize, McNamara added that he would see to it that the World Bank increased its loans.

It was only during his last visit to Indonesia on 15 May 1979 that McNamara privately spoke his mind:

It was also necessary to maintain the emphasis on reducing corruption. Outside Indonesia, this was much talked about and the world had the impression, rightly or wrongly, that it was greater than in any but perhaps one other country... It was like a cancer eating away at society.[17]

However, at the end of 1980, the World Bank was still supporting Suharto's Indonesia to such an extent that it granted a loan without respecting (imposing) the usual conditions. A similar situation can be seen nine years later when the Bank, anxious to maintain good relations with China, failed to distance itself from China after the 1989 spring.[18]

THE BANK'S SILENCE REGARDING THE ANNEXATION OF EAST TIMOR

Thirty years after Indonesia's invasion of Timor, certain US archives were made public. Undoubtedly they establish what had long been suspected: in December 1975, Indonesia invaded East Timor with the connivance of the American, British and Australian governments, with the result that the country would undergo 24 years of bloody occupation and systematic violation of human rights. According to these documents, as early as March 1975, the State Department, then headed by Henry Kissinger, aware of Indonesia's preparations for invasion, estimated that the US 'has considerable interests in Indonesia and none in Timor'. When he learned about the special operations leading up to the invasion, Kissinger asked his colleagues: 'Can I trust you to keep quiet about this?' His fear was that Congress would decree an embargo on arms deliveries to Indonesia, Washington's ally in the Cold War.[19] One can well understand that during this time, the World Bank neither made any allusion to, nor criticized the invasion and the annexation of East Timor! Submission to the interests of the US and its allies, the UK and Australia, and complicity regarding the dictatorship were constant components of the Bank's behaviour.

THE WORLD BANK'S SUPPORT FOR
THE TRANSMIGRATION PROGRAMME[20]

The World Bank actively collaborated in the sinister transmigration project, certain facets of which constitute crimes against humanity. This project concerned the displacement – in certain cases, forced

– of millions of people from the islands of Java and Sumatra to other islands of the archipelago and the dispossession of the indigenous people of these islands.

The World Bank, especially during the 15 years of the programme's heyday (1974–89), was its principal source of external financing. The Bank's historians recognize this responsibility of the Bank: 'During the middle and later 1970's, the Bank, as well, supported and assisted the government's controversial program of official and subsidized transmigration of families from Java to the outer islands.'[21] This contribution was not only restricted to financial and technical support. The Bank also supported the project politically.

Between 1950 and 1974, the government displaced 664,000 people within the framework of the transmigration programme. However, from 1974 on, with the World Bank's support, 3.5 million people were displaced and assisted, and approximately 3.5 million people migrated on their own initiative. The World Bank directly contributed to displacements and relocations. Owing to its loans it was possible, on the one hand, to almost totally cover the 'official' migrations of 2.3 million people, and on the other hand to 'catalyze' the relocation of some 2 million people transmigrating spontaneously.

Although the World Bank qualified this transmigration as 'the biggest programme in the world for voluntary relocation', it soon appeared that the programme was also used to rid Java of undesirable inhabitants. Thus, in the principal Javanese cities, 'nonconformists', elderly people, sick people (including those with leprosy), beggars and vagrants were forced either to disappear into the countryside (where their chances of survival were slim) or to transmigrate. In the latter case, they were herded into army trucks during the night and brought to 'transit camps' where they were given training for their relocation.[22] Marriage was an obligatory criterion for selection: the authorities organized forced marriages of single people before their departure. One should note that the World Bank played a large role in recruitment operations for homeless people and political prisoners in order to send them to the remotest and least desirable transmigration sites.

The transmigration projects most heavily supported by the World Bank were those involving private domestic or foreign firms likely to promote foreign trade and attract more ambitious transnational investments (particularly projects for industrial plantations).

Unrestricted foreign exploitation of the resources of the outer islands was pursued for the benefit of the central government and firms operating in the country, but to the detriment of the local populations who saw a great portion of their habitat and their means of subsistence destroyed forever. The lands of the outer islands were regarded as 'empty' because the inhabitants who lived there for millennia did not have ownership certificates. These lands were then declared to be 'at the state's service' and were forcefully confiscated, most often without compensation. In fact, the World Bank supported the government in its acts of expropriating land belonging to indigenous people, although it never acknowledged it officially.

The people of the transmigration programme received land that was not reserved for forest concessions and was generally far from productive. For the government officials appointed to locate the sites to be cleared, it did not matter whether they were cultivable or not. Their job was to fill up a chart with information relating to site access, the number of hectares to be cleared and the number of families that could possibly be located there.

The forest – a vital resource for the native dwellers – gradually disappeared following the operations of forestry companies and commercial plantations, on the one hand, and government teams entrusted with clearing the areas intended for agriculture and the installation of migrants, on the other. In addition, mining companies (as in the case of the American mining company Freeport McMoran[23]) destroyed complete mountainsides and daily poured tons of industrial waste into the rivers, polluting them beyond recovery. These rivers being the only source of water for indegenes, major health disasters occurred. Oil extraction along the coasts also caused great damage to the marine fauna and flora, another source of food for the indigenous populations.

The real culprits in this matter were those who devised, carried out and financed the project. Primarily they were the Indonesian authorities and the international institutions (the WB first and foremost), as well as certain Western governments (the US, the UK, Germany and Israel, for example) and the national and foreign companies involved in the project's materialization. Among the devastating effects of the project were the development and proliferation of intensive operations for the exploitation of natural resources and a rapid increase in the surface areas intended for commercial plantations as a result of programmes financed by international loans. These loans were always conditioned by the opening up of markets at all levels – the removal of tariff barriers, attraction of foreign capital, priority on monocultures for export, liberalization and privatization of the goods and services distribution sectors, etc.

At the end of 1980, vociferous criticism increased, as much inside as outside the archipelago, accusing the World Bank of having taken part in a project of geopolitical domination typified by social and ecological blunders and infringing human rights in the course of its procedures.[24] The WB indeed played a major part in this project with harmful and irreversible consequences: control of the indigenous populations of the outer islands and violation of their right to land ownership; the exorbitant cost of displacement ($7,000 per family according to Bank estimates[25]) in relation to the results achieved, because according to a 1986 World Bank study, 50 per cent of the displaced families lived below the poverty level and 20 per cent below subsistence level; there were persistent problems of density in Java, massive deforestation of the outer islands, etc.

The World Bank, accused on all sides, decided to cease financing the installation of new transmigration sites and the costs of transmigration travel. Nevertheless, it concentrated its loans on the reinforcement of already existing villages[26] and on maintenance of the commercial plantations, thus only partially renouncing its participation in the programme.

The Bank obviously denied all the allegations brought by observers. In 1994, it decided to carry out an internal evaluation study[27] of the projects it financed, in order to determine its eventual responsibilities. In this report, the Bank accepted a very small share of responsibility, stating that the project in Sumatra 'had negative and probably irreversible effects' on the Kubu, a nomadic people whose survival relied on fallow cultivation, hunting and gathering in the forest. The audit admits that 'although the existence of Kubu in the zones of the project was known since the project was planned, few initiatives were carried out to avoid problems'.

The loans of the World Bank for the transmigration programme correspond in all respects to the constitution of an odious debt: they were contracted by a despotic regime, which used them for repression and not for the well-being of the population. Consequently, this debt is null and void: it must be cancelled. But it should not stop there. The transmigration project supported by the Bank implied the forced displacement of certain populations. The Bank cannot simply claim that it was not aware of this. It was also an accomplice to the violation of the rights of the indigenous people who lived in the zones colonized by the transmigration project. These very serious acts should not go unpunished.

THE CRISIS OF 1997–98 AND ITS CONSEQUENCES

From the 1980s, and especially during the first half of the 1990s, the World Bank and the IMF got the Indonesian government to agree to free circulation of capital. This had the effect of placing Indonesia (like the Philippines, Thailand, Malaysia and South Korea) at the mercy of international speculation.

In the IMF's annual report for the year 1997, one can read the compliments it pays to the Indonesian authorities: 'the administrators congratulated the authorities for Indonesia's economic results during the previous years, particularly the appreciable reduction of poverty and the improvement of many social indicators'.[28] Further on, the administrators of the IMF compliment the Indonesian authorities for 'the importance attached to maintaining free circulation of capital',[29] while earlier in the document they themselves point out the risks: 'powerful entries of capital posed important challenges for the authorities'. They continue their analysis by praising the authorities, implying that they are capable of controlling the situation: 'the flexibility with which the authorities adapted the proportioning of economic measures according to the evolution of the situation was one of the ingredients of their success and will remain an essential tool for taking up these challenges'.

In 1997, a massive economic and financial crisis broke out in South-East Asia. After its appearance in Thailand in February 1997, it spread to Malaysia, Indonesia and the Philippines by July 1997. These four countries, described previously by the IMF, the World Bank and the private banks as role models by reason of their opening up to the world market, their low rate of inflation and high growth rate, were now unable to resist the onslaughts of speculators. Between 2 July 1997 and 8 January 1998, the Indonesian rupee was depreciated by 229 per cent in relation to the US dollar.

After having been praised to the skies by the WB and the IMF, the Indonesian authorities were now strongly criticized for leaving too much power in the hands of the state; a state which, in addition, would have been wrong in accepting that the private financial and industrial institutions were overly involved in debt and speculation.

South-East Asia's crisis of 1997 dealt a hard blow to Indonesia. In the space of less than a year, foreign capital was withdrawn from the country. Mass unemployment set in. At the end of 1998, according to government statistics, 50 per cent of the population lived below the poverty line, estimated in Indonesia at $0.55 per day for cities and $0.40 for the countryside.

The IMF imposed its 'shock' measures to resolve the crisis of 1997. They worsened the situation, particularly by causing the bankruptcy of a large section of the banking sector and of many entrepreneurs. The IMF and the WB pressed the government to transform the private debt of the banks into a public debt. The Indonesian public debt, which accounted for 23 per cent of the gross national product (GNP) before the crisis (1997) literally exploded as a consequence of the policies imposed by the IMF and the Bank. In 2000, the public debt amounted to 93 per cent of GNP.

On the other hand, real wages plunged: whereas there had been an increase of 46 per cent between 1990 and 1996, they lost 25.1 per cent of their value in 1998.

The population directly suffered the effects of these measures and started protesting vigorously. On 5 May 1998, within the framework of the agreements signed with the IMF, Suharto eliminated the subsidies on basic commodities so that the price of kerosene, electricity and petrol increased by 70 per cent. This intensified the huge popular mobilization that had begun several months before. Fifteen days later, deserted by Washington and denounced by the people, Suharto was forced to step down, bringing an end to a dictatorial regime of 32 years.

Today, the largest portion of the state budget is devoted to repayment of the debt. In 1999 and 2000, 50 per cent and 40 per cent, respectively, were devoted to debt servicing. In 2004, the figure was close to 28 per cent. According to the projections of the Indonesian finance minister, repayment of the external public debt would increase in 2006 and reach a peak in 2008, remaining at a high level thereafter.[30]

After the December 2004 tsunami, resulting in the death of 150,000 people in the Indonesian province of Aceh, the World Bank and the governments of the creditor countries had promised to show generosity. The reality is quite different: financial aid, at first turned into a mega media event, has been provided in a chaotic and transitory way. While this show was being made to offer financial resources for reconstruction, the creditors in the Paris Club (who in addition direct the World Bank and the IMF), decided to deduct late-payment interest from the portion of debt servicing that was not made in 2005.[31] The moratorium granted by the Paris Club is thus only a show of generosity, since the states that accept it will make their populations pay, right down to the last cent. The Indonesian government, under pressure from its creditors, imposed a steep increase (+ 29 per cent) on the price of fuel on 1 March 2005, which occasioned deep popular discontent. The tax revenue resulting from this rise was intended mainly for replenishing the budget deficit and repaying the debt.[32]

As for human development, many indicators are particularly worrying:

Table 9.1   Indicators of human development

Share of population living with less than $2 per day	52.4 %
Life expectancy at birth	66.6 years
Rate of mortality among children (< 5 years of age)	45 per 1,000
Share of childbirth assisted by qualified personnel	64%
Share of population suffering from malnutrition	6%
Share of population without access to a water supply installation	22%
Net rate of school attendance at the primary level	92%
Literacy rate of adults (> 15 years of age)	87.9 %

Source: UNDP, *World Report on Human Development 2004*

BY WAY OF CONCLUSION

The 1965 military *coup d'état* deprived the Indonesian people of the possibility of determining their own future. Yet with the Bandung Conference in 1955, Indonesia had begun to affirm itself on the international scene. It was the threat of seeing one of the most populous countries on earth playing a key role in establishing a new world order that led the United States and the Bretton Woods institutions to provide active support for the Suharto dictatorship.

These institutions based their choice on political and geostrategic factors. Their financial support enabled Suharto to carry out policies that went counter to human rights. Suharto served the interests of the major Western powers in the region and enabled transnational corporations based in the industrialized countries to draw liberally on Indonesia's natural resources. The World Bank and the IMF were active accomplices in these policies. The local ruling class supported Suharto and did not seek to invest in the development of the country.

It preferred to abet the plundering of Indonesia's natural resources by transnational corporations.

Starting from the crisis in 1997, IMF-imposed measures aggravated the economic situation and brought about a sharp increase in the internal and external public debt. The historical balance sheet of the IMF's and WB's role in Indonesia is an unqualified disaster. In consequence, the claims they hold against this country must be cancelled in full. Moreover, the WB and the IMF must be brought to account for their complicity in the Suharto regime and for projects such as transmigration, which in many respects constitute a crime against humanity.

The bilateral debts are in the hands of countries that directly backed the Suharto dictatorship, so they too must be cancelled. The same applies to debts owed to foreign private companies that played a part in the corruption of the Indonesian regime, the pillaging of the country's natural resources and the exploitation of its workers.

A review of Indonesia's debt shows a totally negative result in the matter of human development. Between 1970 and 2003, Indonesia received $139 billion in the form of loans intended for the authorities and it has refunded $164 billion. Yet Indonesia's external public debt has increased twenty-fold.[33] Between 1970 and 2003, total debt repayment represents 46 times the amount of the initial debt stock. Since 1985, Indonesia has refunded annually more than it has received in the form of loans. This is irrefutable proof that the debt system is a fatal mechanism for extracting the country's wealth.

10
The World Bank's
Theories of Development

The World Bank claims that, in order to progress, the developing countries[1] should rely on external borrowing and attract foreign investments. The main aim of thus running up debt is to buy basic equipment and consumer goods from the highly industrialized countries. The facts show that day after day, for decades now, the idea has been failing to bring about progress. The models that have influenced the Bank's vision can only result in making the developing countries heavily dependent on an influx of external capital, particularly in the form of loans, which create the illusion of a certain level of self-sustained development. The lenders of public money (the governments of the industrialized countries and especially the World Bank) see loans as a powerful means of control over indebted countries. Thus the Bank's actions should not be seen as a succession of errors or bad management. On the contrary, they are a deliberate part of a coherent, carefully thought-out, theoretical plan, taught with great application in most universities. It is distilled in hundreds of books on development economics. The World Bank has produced its own ideology of development. When facts undermine the theory, the Bank does not question the theory. Rather, it seeks to twist the facts in order to protect the dogma.

In the early years of its existence, the World Bank was not much given to reflecting upon the type of political economy that might best be applied to the developing countries. There were several reasons for this: first, it was not among the Bank's priorities at the time – in 1957, the majority of the loans made by the Bank (52.7 per cent) still went to the industrialized countries;[2] secondly, the theoretical framework of the Bank's economists and directors was of a neoclassical bent – now neoclassical theory did not assign any particular place to the developing countries;[3] finally, it was not until 1960 that the Bank came up with a specific instrument for granting low-interest loans to the developing countries, with the creation of the International Development Association (IDA – see chapter 3).

However, the fact that the Bank had no idea of its own did not prevent it from criticizing others. Indeed, in 1949, it criticized a report by a United Nations' commission on employment and economics, which argued for public investment in heavy industry in the developing countries. The Bank declared that the governments of the developing countries had enough to do in establishing a good infrastructure, and should leave the responsibility for heavy industry to local and foreign private initiative.[4]

According to World Bank historians Mason and Asher, the Bank's position stemmed from the belief that public and private sectors should play different roles. The public should ensure the planned development of an adequate infrastructure: railways, roads, power stations, ports and communications in general. The private sector should deal with agriculture, industry, trade, and personal and financial services, being held to be more effective than the public sector in these areas.[5] What this really meant was that anything that might prove profitable should be handed over to the private sector. On the other hand, providing the infrastructure should fall on the public sector, since the costs needed to be met by society, to help out the private sector. In other words, the World Bank recommended privatization of profits combined with the socialization of the cost of anything that was not directly profitable.

Growth and development planning (in both industrialized and developing economies) is given remarkable importance in World Bank documents and the literature of the time dealing with development issues from the 1950s until the 1970s. Until the end of the 1970s, planning was considered important for several reasons: first, planning emerged during the prolonged depression of the 1930s as a response to the chaos resulting from laissez-faire policies; secondly, the reconstruction of Europe and Japan had to be organized; thirdly, this was still part of the 30 years of continuous economic growth that followed the Second World War and had to be managed and planned for; fourthly, the success, real or supposed, of Soviet planning undoubtedly exercised a great fascination, even for the sworn enemies of the so-called 'communist bloc'. The idea of planning was completely rejected from the early 1980s, when neoliberal ideologies and policies came back with a vengeance.

Another major preoccupation in the early days that was rejected after the 1980s was the decision by several Latin American countries to resort to import substitution and the possibility that other newly independent countries might follow their example.

Let us briefly review some of the economists whose work had a direct influence on and in the Bank.

An ethnocentric and conservative vision of the world

The World Bank's vision is marked by several conservative prejudices. In the reports and speeches of the first 15 years of its existence, there are regular references to backward and underdeveloped countries. The Bank sees the reasons for underdevelopment from an ethnocentric point of view. In the World Bank's eighth Annual Report, we read that:

> There are many and complex reasons why these areas have not been more developed. Many cultures, for instance, have placed a low value on material advance and, indeed, some have regarded it as incompatible with more desirable objectives of society and the individual...[6]

One of the causes of backwardness identified in the report is the lack of desire or absence of will to make material progress and to modernize society. Hindus' deep respect for cows becomes shorthand for the inherent backwardness of India. As for Africa, World Bank president Eugene Black declared in 1961: 'Even today the bulk of Africa's more than 200 millions are only beginning to enter world society...'[7] The reactionary nature of World Bank vision has by no means been attenuated by the passing years. In the *Global Development Report* of 1987, the Bank wrote:

> In his *Principles of Political Economy* (1848), John Stuart Mill mentioned the advantages of 'foreign trade'. Over a century later, his observations are as pertinent as they were in 1848. Here is what Mill had to say about the indirect advantages of trade: 'A people may be in the quiescent, indolent, uncultivated state, with all their tastes either fully satisfied or entirely undeveloped, and they may fail to put forth the whole of their productive energies for want of any sufficient object of desire. The opening of a foreign trade, by making them acquainted with new objects, or tempting them by the easier acquisition of things which they had not previously thought attainable, sometimes works a sort of industrial revolution in a country whose resources were previously undeveloped for want of energy and ambition in the people: inducing those who were satisfied with scanty comforts and little work to work harder for the gratification of their new tastes, and even to save and accumulate capital, for the still more complete satisfaction of those tastes at a future time.'[8]

The massive return of the neoconservatives in the administration that President G.W. Bush set up in 2001 has exacerbated its deeply materialistic and reactionary tendencies. The appointment of Paul Wolfowitz, one of the leading neocons, to the presidency of the Bank in 2005, has further entrenched this orientation.

THE HOS MODEL (HECKSCHER–OHLIN–SAMUELSON)

Ricardo's theory of comparative advantages gained force in the 1930s through the studies of Swedish economists, Heckscher and Ohlin, later joined by Samuelson. It is the synthesis produced by the latter that is known as the HOS model. The HOS model raises the issue of factors of production – these factors are work, land and capital – and claims that each country has an interest in specializing in the production and export of goods that make greatest use of that country's most abundant production factor – which will also be the cheapest. Free trade would then make it possible to balance out what the factors earn among all the countries taking part in free trade agreements. The abundant factor, which would be exported, would grow scarcer and thus more costly; the rare factor, which would be imported, would increase and its price would fall. This system of specialization would bring about optimal distribution of factors in a now homogeneous market. This model would enable all economies to aim for maximal integration in the global market with positive outcomes for all the trading partners. Various studies carried out later, especially those by Paul Krugman,[9] to test the HOS model have shown it to be inaccurate.

THE FIVE STAGES OF ECONOMIC GROWTH ACCORDING TO WALT W. ROSTOW

In 1960, Walt W. Rostow[10] postulated five stages of development in a book entitled *The Stages of Economic Growth: a Non-Communist Manifesto*.[11] He claimed that all countries fell into one of the five categories and that they could only follow this route.

The first stage is traditional society characterized by the predominance of agricultural activity. Technical progress is nil, there is practically no growth in productivity and minds are not ready for change.

Next, in the stage before take-off, exchanges and techniques begin to emerge, people's mentalities become less fatalistic and savings rates increase. In fact, this is how European societies evolved from the fifteenth to the early eighteenth century.

The third stage is take-off, a crucial stage corresponding to a qualitative leap, with a significant increase in savings and investment rates and a move towards cumulative growth.[12]

The fourth stage is the 'march towards maturity', where technical progress takes over in all fields of activity and production is diversified.

Finally, the fifth stage coincides with the era of mass consumerism.[13]

Rostow claimed that at the take-off stage, an influx of external capital (in the form of foreign investments or credit) was indispensable.

Rostow's model is marred by over-simplification. He presents the stage of development reached by the USA after the Second World War both as the goal to aim for and the model to reproduce. Similarly, he considers that the British take-off model, with the agricultural revolution followed by the industrial revolution, should be reproduced elsewhere. He thus completely ignores the historical reality of other countries. There is no reason why each country should go through the five stages he describes.

INSUFFICIENT SAVINGS AND THE NEED TO RESORT TO EXTERNAL FUNDING

In neoclassical terms, savings should precede investment and are insufficient in the developing countries. This means that the shortage of savings is seen as a fundamental factor explaining why development is blocked. An influx of external funding is required. Paul Samuelson, in *Economics*,[14] took the history of US indebtedness in the nineteenth and twentieth centuries as a basis for determining four different stages leading to prosperity: young borrowing nation in debt (from the War of Independence in 1776 to the Civil War of 1865); mature indebted nation (from 1873 to 1914); new lending nation (from the First to Second World Wars); and mature lending nation (1960s). Samuelson and his emulators slapped the model of US economic development from the late eighteenth century until the Second World War on to one hundred or so countries that made up the Third World after 1945, as though it were possible for all those countries to quite simply imitate the experience of the United States.[15]

As for the need to resort to foreign capital (in the form of loans and foreign investments), an associate of Rostow's, Paul Rosenstein-Rodan, found the following formula:

Foreign capital will be a pure addition to domestic capital formation, i.e. it will all be invested; the investment will be productive or 'businesslike' and result in increased production. The main function of foreign capital inflow is to increase the rate of domestic capital formation up to a level which could then be maintained without any further aid.[16]

This statement contradicts the facts. It is not true that foreign capital enhances the formation of national capital and is all invested. A large part of foreign capital rapidly leaves the country where it was temporarily directed, as capital flight and repatriation of profits.

Paul Rosenstein-Rodan, who was the assistant director of the Economics Department of the World Bank between 1946 and 1952, made another monumental error in predicting the dates when various countries would reach self-sustained growth. He reckoned that Colombia would reach that stage by 1965, Yugoslavia by 1966, Argentina and Mexico between 1965 and 1975, India in the early 1970s, Pakistan three or four years after India, and the Philippines after 1975. What nonsense that has proved to be!

Note that this notion of self-sustained growth is commonly used by the World Bank. The definition given by Dragoslav Avramoviæ, then director of the Economics Department, in 1964, was as follows: 'Self-sustained growth is defined to mean a rate of income increase of, say, 5 per cent p.a. financed out of domestically generated funds and out of foreign capital which flows into the country...'[17]

Development planning as envisaged by the World Bank and US academia amounts to pseudo-scientific deception based on mathematical equations. It is supposed to give legitimacy and credibility to the intention to make the developing countries dependent on obtaining external capital. There follows an example, advanced in all seriousness by Max Millikan and Walt W. Rostow in 1957:

If the initial rate of domestic investment in a country is 5 per cent of national income, if foreign capital is supplied at a constant rate equal to one-third the initial level of domestic investment, if 25 per cent of all additions to income are saved and reinvested, if the capital–output ratio is 3 and if interest and dividend service on foreign loans and private investment are paid at the rate of 6 per cent per year, the country will be able to discontinue net foreign borrowing after fourteen years and sustain a 3 per cent rate of growth out of its own resources.[18]

More nonsense!

CHENERY AND STROUT'S DOUBLE DEFICIT MODEL

In the mid-1960s, the economist Hollis Chenery, later to become chief economist and vice-president of the World Bank,[19] and his colleague Alan Strout drew up a new model called the 'double deficit model'.[20] Chenery and Strout laid emphasis on two constraints: first, insufficient internal savings, and then insufficient foreign currency. Charles Oman and Ganeshan Wignarja summarized the Chenery–Strout model as follows:

Essentially, the double deficit model hypothesises that while in the very first stages of industrial growth insufficient savings can constitute the main constraint on the rate of formation of domestic capital, once industrialization is up and running, the main constraint may no longer be domestic savings per se, but rather the availability of currency required to import equipment, intermediary goods and perhaps even the raw materials used as industrial input. The currency deficit can thus exceed the savings deficit as the main constraint on development.[21]

To resolve this double deficit, Chenery and Strout propose a simple solution: borrow foreign currency and/or procure it by increasing exports.

The Chenery–Strout model is highly mathematical. It was the 'in thing' at the time. For its supporters, it had the advantage of conferring an air of scientific credibility upon a policy whose main aims were, firstly, to incite the developing countries to resort to massive external borrowing and foreign investments, and secondly, to subject their development to a dependency on exports. At the time, the model came under criticism from several quarters. Suffice it to quote that of Keith Griffin and Jean Luc Enos, who claimed that resorting to external inflow would further limit local savings:

Yet as long as the cost of aid (e.g. the rate of interest on foreign loans) is less than the incremental output–capital ratio, it will 'pay' a country to borrow as much as possible and substitute foreign for domestic savings. In other words, given a target rate of growth in the developing country, foreign aid will permit higher consumption, and domestic savings will simply be a residual, that is, the difference between desired investment and the amount of foreign aid available. Thus the foundations of models of the Chenery–Strout type are weak, since one would expect, on theoretical grounds, to find an inverse association between foreign aid and domestic savings.[22]

THE WISH TO INCITE THE DEVELOPING COUNTRIES TO RESORT TO EXTERNAL AID SEEN AS A MEANS OF INFLUENCING THEM

Bilateral aid and World Bank policies are directly related to the political objectives pursued by the USA in its foreign affairs.

Hollis Chenery maintained that 'The main objective of foreign assistance, as of many other tools of foreign policy, is to produce the kind of political and economic environment in the world in which the United States can best pursue its own social goals.'[23]

In a book entitled *The Emerging Nations: their Growth and United States Policy*, Max Millikan[24] and Donald Blackmer, both colleagues of Walt W. Rostow's, clearly described in 1961 certain objectives of US foreign policy:

It is in the interest of the United States to see emerging from the transition process nations with certain characteristics. First, they must be able to maintain their independence, especially of powers hostile or potentially hostile to the United States [...] Fourth, they must accept the principle of an open society whose members are encouraged to exchange ideas, goods, values, and experiences with the rest of the world; this implies as well that their governments must be willing to cooperate in the measures of international economic, political and social control necessary to the functioning of an interdependent world community.[25]

Under the leadership of the USA, of course.

Later in the book, it is explicitly shown how aid is used as a lever to orient the policies of the beneficiary countries:

For capital assistance to have the maximum leverage in persuading the under-developed countries to follow a course consistent with American and free-world interests the amounts offered must be large enough and the terms flexible enough to persuade the recipient that the game is worth the effort. This means that we must invest substantially larger resources in our economic development programs than we have done in our past.[26]

As we shall see further on, the volume of loans to developing countries increased at a growing pace throughout the 1960s and 1970s, as the consequence of a deliberate policy on the part of the USA, the governments of other industrialized countries and the Bretton Woods institutions, whose aim was to influence the policies of countries in the South.

PRIORITY ON EXPORTS

In one of their main contributions, Chenery and Strout claimed that resorting to import substitution was an acceptable method of reducing the deficit in foreign currency.[27] They later abandoned this position, when maintaining import-substitution policies as practised by certain developing countries became one of the main criticisms levelled by the Bank, the IMF, the OECD and the governments of the major industrialized countries.

This is how other studies by economists directly associated with the World Bank turned to measuring the effective rates of protection of economies and the resulting bias in terms of utilization of productive resources and of profitability of investments. They favoured redirecting strategies towards exports, abandoning protectionist tariffs, and, more generally, a price-fixing policy more closely related to market mechanisms. Bela Balassa, Jagdish Bhagwati and Anne Krueger[28] systematized this approach, and their analyses were to leave their mark on the international institutions and become the theoretical justification for opening up trade during the 1980s and 1990s. Anne Krueger[29] wrote:

A regime promoting exports can free a country's economy from the Keynesian yoke of under-employment since, unlike a regime of import substitution, the effective demand for its products on international markets may be virtually infinite, and thus it can always get closer to full employment, unless there is a world recession. A small export-oriented economy will be able to sell whatever quantity of goods it may produce. In other words, the country's only constraint will be its capacity to supply the goods.[30]

More eyewash.

THE TRICKLE-DOWN EFFECT

The trickle-down effect is a trivial metaphor that has guided the actions of the World Bank from the outset. The idea is simple: the positive effects of growth trickle down, starting from the top, where they benefit the wealthy, until eventually at the bottom a little also reaches the poor. This means that it is in the interests of the poor that growth should be as strong as possible, if they are to be able to lap up the drops. Indeed, if growth is weak, the rich will keep a larger part than when growth is strong.

What are the effects of this on the World Bank's conduct? Growth should be encouraged at all costs so that there is something left for the poor at the end of the cycle. Any policy that holds back growth for the sake of (even partial) redistribution of wealth or for the sake of protecting the environment reduces the trickle-down effect and harms the poor. In practice, the actions of the Bank's directors are conducted in line with this metaphor, whatever the more sophisticated discourse of certain experts. Moreover the Bank's historians devote about 20 pages to discussions of the trickle-down[31] theory and acknowledge that 'This belief justified persistent efforts to persuade borrowers of the advantages of discipline, sacrifice, and trust in the market, and therefore of the need to hold the line against political temptation.'[32] They maintain that the belief gradually fell into disrepute from 1970, following cutting remarks from an impressive number of researchers concerning the situation in both the United States and the developing countries.[33] Nevertheless, the historians note that in practice this did not have much effect,[34] particularly since from 1982, the trickle-down theory made a triumphant comeback at the World Bank.[35] Obviously, the trickle-down issue is inseparable from that of inequality, which will be discussed in the next section.

THE QUESTION OF INEQUALITY IN THE DISTRIBUTION OF INCOME

From 1973, the World Bank began to examine the question of inequality in the distribution of income in the developing countries as a factor affecting the chances of development. The economics team under the direction of Hollis Chenery gave the matter considerable thought. The major World Bank book on the subject, published in 1974, was coordinated by Chenery himself and entitled *Redistribution with Growth*.[36] Chenery was aware that the type of growth induced by the Bank's loans policy would generate increased inequality. The World Bank's main worry was clearly expressed by McNamara on several occasions: if we do not reduce inequality and poverty, there will be repeated outbursts of social unrest which will harm the interests of the free world, under the leadership of the United States.

Chenery did not share Simon Kuznets' point of view,[37] that after a necessary phase of increased inequality during the economic take-off, things would subsequently improve. The World Bank was firmly convinced of the need for increased inequality. This is borne out by the words of the president of the Bank, Eugene Black, in April 1961: 'Inequalities in income are a necessary by-product of economic growth (which) makes it possible for people to escape a life of poverty.'[38] Yet empirical studies carried out by the World Bank in Chenery's day disproved Kuznets' claims.

However, after Chenery's departure in 1982 and his replacement by Anne Krueger, the World Bank completely abandoned its relative concern about increasing or maintaining inequality to the extent that it decided not to publish relevant data in the *World Development Report*. Krueger did not hesitate to adopt Kuznets' argument, making the rise of inequality a condition for take-off of growth, on the grounds that the savings of the rich were likely to feed into investments.

Not until François Bourguignon became chief economist in 2003 did the Bank show any real renewal of interest in this question.[39] In 2006, the World Bank's *World Development Report* subtitled *Equity and Development* again refers to inequality as a hindrance to development.[40] At best, this approach is considered to be good marketing by James Wolfensohn (president of the World Bank from 1996 to 2005) and his successor, Paul Wolfowitz.

11
South Korea: the Miracle Unmasked

What is often presented as South Korea's success story is actually the result of policies that in no way conform to the World Bank's recommendations. Instead of a virtuous accumulation favoured by free trade, South Korea's economic development was made possible by 'a ruthless primitive accumulation that used the most coercive methods in order to forcefully impose a "virtue" of sorts' (J.-P. Peemans). Korea achieved the results we have become familiar with under the yoke of a repressive dictatorship that enjoyed US protection in order to counter so-called socialist regimes. It enforced a productivist model of development that was deeply detrimental to the environment. The Korean way is neither commendable nor reproducible, but it deserves to be examined in some detail.

The World Bank claims that South Korea is an undeniable success story. In the Bank's version, the country's authorities have used external loans efficiently, have attracted foreign investments and used them to set up a successful development model based on export substitution. The industrialization model through export substitution represents the World Bank's (and others') alternative to the industrialization model through import substitution (which implies producing the imported commodities within the country itself). Instead of producing what it imported, Korea has channelled its export activities towards meeting the demands of the world market while successfully developing industries that yield high added value. It has replaced the export of unprocessed or minimally processed commodities with the export of commodities that have required advanced technology. The World Bank claims that the state has intervened in a modest measure to support private initiatives and ensure the free play of market forces.

Yet in actual fact the Korean way to industrialization and sustained growth largely runs counter to the Bank's official version.

I must start by saying that I cannot see Korea as a model to be imitated, and that my position rests on ethical, economic and social reasons. Korea achieved the recorded results under a harshly repressive dictatorship protected by the United States to counter so-called socialist regimes. Korea developed a productivist model that completely disregards environmental considerations. The Korean way is neither commendable nor reproducible. But it should be examined carefully.

The Korean success is the result of several factors: a high degree of intervention from the state (which has steered the process with an iron hand), substantial US technical and financial support (in the form of grants), a radical land reform carried out from the start, a 25-year period during which the industrialization model based on import substitution was gradually converted into export substitution (the latter being impossible without the former), state control of the banking sector, the enforcement of authoritarian planning, strict control of currency exchange and capital flows, state-enforced prices for a wide range of products, and not least, the protection afforded by the US, allowing Korea to implement policies that it condemned elsewhere. The Korean government has also made great progress in education, thus ensuring a ready supply of highly skilled manpower to private enterprise.

Paradoxically, the scarcity of natural resources has been an asset in the country's development in that it has not attracted the greed of transnational corporations or the US. The US saw Korea as a military strategic zone to counter the communist bloc, not as a strategic source of supplies (as is the case for Venezuela, Mexico or countries in the Persian Gulf). Had Korea been endowed with large oil fields or other raw materials, the country would have been treated as a supply zone and would not have been allowed the same margin of flexibility to develop its powerful industrial network. The US is not prepared to deliberately promote the emergence of powerful competitors possessing large natural reserves as well as diversified industrial activities.

THE POLITICAL AND GEOSTRATEGIC CONTEXT

In an agreement signed in 1905, the United States and Japan defined their respective areas of influence in East Asia. The US would control the Philippines, which it had conquered in 1902. Taiwan (which was annexed as early as 1895) and Korea fell into the Japanese zone. In 1910 Japan annexed Korea and turned it into a food-producing convenience, and later into a kind of all-purpose appendix to Japanese industry. When Japan's imperialism was defeated at the end of the

Second World War it left Korea with modern transport and electricity networks, a significant industrial infrastructure ranging from textiles and armaments to chemicals and mechanical construction, and a fully developed banking system. Yet Korean industry was not a consistent whole since it was created to meet Japan's needs. Industrialization was more advanced in the north of the country, the part that would become North Korea, while the south was more geared to farming. The middle class had hardly developed since Japan's domination granted it very limited room. Compared with Argentina at the same period Korea was definitely backward in terms of industrial development.

As a result of the February 1945 Yalta agreement between the US, the UK and the USSR, particularly the section about the Soviet Union's involvement in the war against Japan, Korea was to be occupied by the Soviet army and the US army. The Soviet army arrived first, in August 1945, and Soviet soldiers were welcomed as liberators with the support of an anti-Japanese liberation movement that had organized into a network of people's committees and was to be the basis of the state apparatus. The state soon set up a number of national, democratic and anti-capitalist reforms. Among the measures that met with powerful popular support was a radical land reform. The later evolution of the North Korean regime and its bureaucratic and authoritarian degeneration should not blind us to its early economic success.

In the south things turned out differently. While US soldiers had not yet reached Korean shores, Washington agreed with Japan, without any consultation with Moscow, that the Japanese would capitulate to US troops just south of the 38th parallel.[1] This led to the de facto partition of Korea, which had not been foreseen in the Yalta agreements. US troops arrived only on 8 September 1945, two days after a national assembly of anti-Japanese people's committees had officially proclaimed the People's Republic of Korea in Seoul, which lies south of the 38th parallel.

These new authorities had not waited for the US army's arrival before they disarmed the Japanese troops, liberated political prisoners and arrested collaborators. Yet when the nationalists tried to meet the US staff to propose a form of collaboration, their demand was rejected. On 9 September the US Military Government in Korea (USAMGIK) was set up. It would be the main authority in this part of the country until 1948. In February 1946 the US headquarters set up a Korean civilian government under the supervision of the USAMGIK. This civilian government was presided by Syngman Rhee, a right-wing politician who had returned to Korea in October 1945 after spending 39 out of the 41 previous years in the US. Washington wanted the Korean Democratic Party (KDP) in power, an anti-communist party that had been legally constituted under Japanese occupation in order to represent the interests of the Korean upper class. The KDP soon underwent a hasty facelift under the new name of Liberal Party. Next to Syngman Rhee we thus find former collaborators of the Japanese occupying forces; the new state apparatus retains a number of former colonial officers, particularly among repressive forces. A Korean CIA was set up and significantly called the KCIA (Korean Central Intelligence Agency).

The government that the US had set up was most unpopular. In 1946 and 1948 protest took the form of popular uprisings that were harshly repressed. The General Council of Korean Trade Unions (GCKTU), led by activists from the Communist Party, included hundreds of thousands of members and led the protest marches. It was the prime target of repressive actions and was eventually suppressed in 1948. Repression was still powerful after 1948, the UN commission on Korea indicated in August 1949 that within the eight months before 30 April 1949, some 89,710 people had been detained. Thousands, if not tens of thousands of people, were killed. Several historical leaders of the struggle against Japan, though not related to the communists, were assassinated by the Syngman Rhee regime.

When the country's division was made official in 1948 with the creation of the Republic of Korea south of the 38th parallel, a large majority of the country's political elite was against it. When the Korean War started in June 1950, the rapid advance of North Korean troops in the south was only marginally related to military reasons. It was also a logical consequence of the lack of popular support for the Syngman Rhee government. According to the US army's official history of the Korean War, the South Korean army 'disintegrated'.[2] There were mass desertions.

The war lasted for three years and brought the world to the brink of a third world war. The US army was massively involved with the support of its Western allies, 300,000 Western soldiers fought on the side of the South Korean army with a UN mandate.[3] They fought against the North Korean army and a strong Chinese support (estimates vary between 500,000 and 850,000 men). The war resulted in three million dead among the Korean population. During the war the Syngman Rhee government exerted a fierce repression against the South Korean left wing. Some sources mention execution or assassination of as many as 100,000 anti-government activists.[4] The armistice on 27 July 1953 brought the two armies virtually to their starting point, on either side of the 38th parallel.

THE KOREAN BOURGEOISIE BECOMES A STATE WARD

Left as it was with an obsolete industry and a financial system formerly controlled by the Japanese,[5] the Syngman Rhee government would use it, with the blessing of the USAMGIK, to reward and comfort the upper class's loyalty, since after all they were the basis of its political power. The new industrialists made thriving business, not thanks to their own investments, for they hardly had any equity, but thanks to tax incomes and US subsidies that the dictatorship generously handed out. Moreover, a strictly protectionist policy protected them from foreign competition. Later, the Park Chung Hee dictatorship (1961–79) would create industrial and financial conglomerates called *chaebols*.

Finding 1: The Korean bourgeoisie developed in the shadow of the state, which was its guardian and protector.

US EXTERNAL FINANCIAL AID

The World Bank passes over the fact that Korea did not rely on loans for 17 years after the end of the Second World War and that later it only contracted limited loans until 1967. From 1945 to 1961 it neither borrowed money nor received any foreign investments. According to the criteria of the World Bank and neoclassical economics, such a situation is a complete anomaly.

On the other hand, it received over $3,100 million in grants from the United States over the same period.[6] No other external aid was received. But the amount is more than significant. It represents twice what the Benelux countries received from the Marshall Plan, one-third more than France received, 10 per cent more than Britain. The grants Korea received from 1945 to 1961 amount to more than the World Bank's total loans to newly independent developing countries (colonies not included).

From 1962 onwards, Korea would borrow, though only moderately. From 1962 to 1966, US grants still amounted to 70 per cent of inflowing capital, while loans accounted for 28 per cent and foreign investments for 2 per cent. Only from 1967 did capital inflow mainly consist of loans from foreign (mainly Japanese) banks. And foreign investments only became significant in the late 1980s once Korea had successfully carried out its industrialization.

Finding 2: Korea's initial industrialization was in no way dependent on external loans or foreign investments.

LAND REFORM AND THE STATE'S COERCION OF PEASANTS

At the end of the Second World War, southern Korea was still an essentially agrarian country. Until the early 1950s, over 75 per cent of its population lived in the countryside.

US military authorities then proceeded to implement a drastic land reform to counter the communist influence.[7] The large estates that had been taken from the Japanese[8] without any compensation and from Korean landowners with compensation were broken up and most peasants became owners of small pieces of land[9] (estates could not exceed 8 acres for one family[10]). The state's intervention was active and coercive. The rent that peasants used to pay to their landlords was replaced by taxes to be paid to the state. The state took over the farming surplus that formerly went to estate owners. The state made it compulsory for farmers to reach given production quotas for certain products. This quota was to be delivered to state entities at a price determined by the authorities. The set price was very low, often less than production cost.[11] It has been estimated that 'until 1961, the price at which rice was bought did not cover farmers' production costs and remained well below market price until 1970. Until 1975, public trading offices controlled at least 50 per cent of the amount of rice and 90 per cent of the amount of barley placed on the market.'[12]

To sum up, Korean farmers were freed from the grip of estate owners and could farm their own land, but they had to work for the state.

Finding 3: When it imposed a radical land reform largely based on the expropriation without any compensation of Japanese estates, the state interfered in a despotic way. The land reform was meant to undermine any communist appeal. Peasants were subjected to a strong constraint from the state.

FARMING SURPLUSES USED TO SERVE CITIES AND INDUSTRIALIZATION

Since it set the prices at which products were bought (from farmers) and sold (to consumers), the state was supplying food (and essentially rice) at subsidized (and therefore low) prices to those social sectors that were regarded as strategic, such as the vast state bureaucracy.

Moreover, if a bowl of rice could be afforded by the urban population, and particularly by the industrial proletariat, wages could be kept at a very low level.

In addition, taxes paid by farmers were used by the state to invest in infrastructures for communications, electricity and industry.

As J.-P. Peemans observed, writing about the demands made on farmers, 'It was in no way a virtuous accumulation resting on the virtues of the market, but a brutal form of primitive accumulation resting on the most coercive methods to create "virtue" by force.'[13]

Finding 4: The state did not allow market forces to determine prices: it fixed them (up) on its own authority.

Finding 5: The state enforced heavy taxes on peasants. Neoliberals regularly inveigh against the state's taxing mania: South Korea is an excellent illustration.

USING EXTERNAL FINANCIAL AID

Korean state finances relied on two main sources of supply: taxes (principally from farmers) and US external aid. It must be specified that until 1961, about 40 per cent of US aid consisted of US farming surpluses (amounting to 40 per cent of the aid granted). This obviously did not contribute to the state's finances. The remaining part, which was paid in US dollars, was used to pay for imports from the United States. Part of these imports consisted of capital goods used to industrialize the country. Seventy-one per cent of investments by the state were financed thanks to US aid until 1961.[14] Military aid which amounted to more than $1,500 million, should also be taken into account.[15] A large part of it went into the building of roads, bridges and other infrastructural projects that were used for industrial production. Finally, we have to add what the US expeditionary corps in Vietnam ordered – in the early 1970s they amounted to 20 per cent of South Korean exports.

Finding 6: South Korea benefited from massive US external aid. Only very few other countries have received the same kind of preferential treatment: Taiwan and Israel are two of them.

INDUSTRIALIZATION BY IMPORT SUBSTITUTION

The industrial development in the 1950s was mainly organized around the production of goods that would replace imports so as to meet the needs of the domestic market, particularly in the food and textile industries. These amounted to 55 per cent of the industrial production in 1955. Production focused on the processing of cotton, sugar and rice flour. Manufacturing industry only accounted for 10 per cent of the GDP in 1955.

Finding 7: In the 1950s Korea developed an industrialization policy that aimed at replacing imports; this was to be reinforced in the 1960s.

ECONOMIC POLICY UNDER PARK CHUNG HEE'S MILITARY DICTATORSHIP (1961–79)[16]

Syngman Rhee's corrupt dictatorship was overthrown by the urban uprising students initiated in April 1960. A powerful movement of political centralization quickly developed among urban masses that mobilized under the banner 'a peaceful unification for the whole of Korea' put forward by the students' movement since the late 1960s.

Mobilizations were stopped by General Park Chung Hee's coup, which set up a military dictatorship, further reinforcing the state's intervention in the economy. The new government nationalized the whole financial system, from the largest bank to the smallest insurance company, to turn it into its instrument in the economy.

From 1962, the structure of external financing would gradually change but grants were still the main supply source until 1966. The United States urged Korea to resume economic relations with Japan. Japan signed a ten-year agreement (1965–75) that included economic aid to the amount of $500 million, $300 million of which was in the form of grants.

Korea contracted its first loan with the WB in 1962 and signed its first agreement with the IMF in 1965 (under US pressure). The Korean dictatorship's willingness to cooperate with the WB was determined by a political rather than an economic agenda.

A posteriori Mahn-Je Kim, who had been deputy prime minister, finance minister and minister for economic planning under dictator Chun Doo Hwan in the 1980s[17] and then became CEO of a steel company (POSCO), declared his satisfaction at the government's excellent relations with the World Bank and gave a favourable assessment of the dictatorship. He wrote that the Bank helped dictator Park to gather support on the domestic as well as on the international level:

Such recognition from the Bank – the world's most authoritative international development organization – positively influenced Korea's international relations, but was even more important domestically. It provided a powerful and persuasive justification to the Korean public for the existence of a dictatorial government devoted to economic development.[18]

The World Bank's complicity with the dictatorship cannot be more bluntly stated.

General Park Chung Hee tried to win greater autonomy from Washington in his economic policies. Calling on World Bank's loans from 1962 onwards, then mainly on loans by private foreign banks since 1967 was part of this determination to gradually diminish Korea's dependence on financing by the US government. This also suited Washington since the US administration had started to take measures to limit the outflow of US dollars in 1963.

Finding 8: The WB supported Park Chung Hee's dictatorship. The dictator used this support to consolidate his position both in the country and on the international scene.

General Park Chung Hee implemented an accelerated industrialization policy underpinned by the strictest planning. The first five-year plan was launched in 1962. Korea took a firm protectionist stand with regard to its agricultural production (a ban on rice imports) and industrial output. In the mid-1960s, Korea already had a number of light industries supplying the domestic market and winning market share abroad. These industries were basically making products – using a massive cheap labour force – by processing or assembling goods imported from abroad. The dictatorship sought to radically change this situation by consolidating the country's industrialization. It decided to reinforce the industrialization model based on import substitution. Korea would attempt to produce the products it had until now imported. To achieve this objective, starting from the end of the 1960s Korea concentrated on developing a heavy steel and capital goods industry (machine tools, assembly lines, turbines, etc.) as well as a petrochemical industry. Park's government further sought to produce for export.

The state favoured the development of *chaebols*, vast conglomerates bringing together a number of private companies selected by Park to spearhead the new industry.

These *chaebols* are now known the world over: Samsung, Hyundai, Lucky Goldstar, Daewoo,[19] Kia, and so on. Year after year they have benefited from substantial and virtually free financial help from the state. The government's or the banks' borrowings (at market price) mainly from US banks before Japan took pride of place in the 1970s provided the *chaebols* with a virtually inexhaustible source of fresh capital at very low interest rates, when not at a loss for the loaning party. Direct subsidies from the state were added to this. In actual fact it took over the management of the country's economy through a board for economic planning. And steered all development choices within the *chaebols* with a steely determination.

Five-year plans followed one another. During the first plan (1962–66) priority was given to the development of energy, fertilizers and cement. The second one (1967–71) highlighted synthetic fibres, the petrochemical industry and electric appliances. The third (1972–76) focused on the steel industry, transport facilities, household appliances and shipbuilding.

Finding 9: The state planned the country's economic development with an iron hand. In a sense, it was the state that created the Korean capitalist class.

THE WORLD BANK'S RELUCTANT SUPPORT

At first the Bank considered Korea's intention to develop a heavy industry as premature[20] and tried to dissuade the authorities. But faced with Seoul's insistence and, anxious to safeguard its influence in the country, the Bank changed tack and supported the import-substitution industrialization policy. It should be mentioned that this was when Robert McNamara became World Bank president (1968) and that his chief economist Hollis Chenery was not opposed to developing countries using the import substitution model.[21]

The Korean argument went as follows: (1) we need to have a heavy industry (steel, petrochemicals) and to manufacture capital goods so that we can supply our light industries ourselves, reduce imports and improve our balance of payments; (2) on the world market, competitor nations can quickly win market share from us by producing the same goods at a lower cost by using lower-paid labour than ours. We must therefore acquire a heavy industry in order to diversify our exports towards higher value-added products that contain more components produced by ourselves. The other nations will have a hard time competing with us in this area; (3) in addition to the development of heavy industry, we are going to step up the pace in technology and make increasing investments in higher education and research; (4) at the start, our heavy industry will not be competitive compared to foreign competitors who can access our domestic market, so we must protect our young industries and close our borders to foreign competition; (5) the state must use public money to finance and control all this.

In the mid-1970s, when Korea was on the way to developing a powerful heavy industry sector, the World Bank once again voiced its doubts about the chosen strategy. It felt that Korea was over-ambitious and suggested that the country scale down its efforts in this sector.[22] The Korean authorities chose not to follow these recommendations.

The most dramatic illustration of this policy was the programme for the development of heavy industries in 1977–79. For two years, 80 per cent of all state investments were devoted to this end. Its financing was supported by a huge increase of the economy's indebtedness, of the state as well as of the banks and private companies, but also by the immobilization of all pension funds and the enforced use of private savings.[23]

Mahn-Je Kim describes in diplomatic terms, and with a hint of irony, the attitude of the World Bank economists:

The flexibility of the World Bank economists should be emphasized. They were typical neoclassical markets economists, and they contributed greatly to the indoctrination of Korean officials with the ideals of the market economic system. The Bank's economists in general were not dogmatic and knew how to harmonize textbook principles with real-world constraints.[24]

Mahn-Je Kim is referring to the period leading up to the early 1980s.

Finding 10: South Korea did not adhere to the World Bank's recommendations.

SOCIAL CHANGES BETWEEN 1960 AND 1980

During Park Chung Hee's dictatorship the structure of South Korean society was deeply modified. The urban population increased from 28 per cent in 1960 to 55 per cent in 1980. In the capital, Seoul, the population doubled between 1964 and 1970, from 3 to 6 million. In 1980, it was close to 9 million. The structure of the active population changed radically, too. In 1960, 63 per cent worked on the land, 11 per cent in industry and mining and 26 per cent in services. Twenty years later, the proportions had changed as follows: 34 per cent in agriculture, 23 per cent in industry and mining, and 43 per cent in services. In 1963, there were 600,000 industrial workers; in 1973, 1.4 million; and in 1980, over 3 million, half of whom were trained workers. They were subjected to extreme exploitation: in 1980 the wage costs of a Korean worker amounted to one-tenth of those of a German worker, 50 per cent of a Mexican worker and 60 per cent of a Brazilian worker. One of the components in the Korean miracle was the exploitation of industrial manpower. A Korean worker's working week in 1980 was the longest in the world. There were no legal minimum wages. After the General Council of Korean Trade Unions was crushed between 1946 and 1948, workers had no right to a genuine trade union any more. In 1946 the Syngman Rhee government created the Federation of Korean Trade Unions with the support of the US and of the US trade union council AFL-CIO. The FKTU was the only legal trade union confederation in South Korea until the 1990s. It was a mere relay for the dictatorship and the bosses. The working class was shackled, at least until the 1980s.

Next to plant workers other social categories became significant. In 1980 there were 100,000 engineers and 130,000 technicians. The number of students in higher education also rose dramatically to reach about one million students in 1980.

Finding 11: Between 1960 and 1980 the social structure was deeply modified and came closer to that found in industrialized countries.

Finding 12: The dictatorship prevented the working class from developing independent trade unions and used harsh repressive measures. One of the components in the Korean miracle was the exploitation of workers.

Washington a party to the May 1980 massacres

The armed forces of the Korean Republic were placed under joint US–Korean command, itself under the control of the commander-in-chief of the US forces in South Korea. The only exceptions were a garrison in the capital and a section of paratroopers under direct presidential authority. The greater part of the Korean Republic's armed forces could not be mobilized without the permission of the US forces' commander-in-chief. At the time of the Kwangju uprising in May 1980, the troops from the garrison in the capital had been mobilized to keep order in Seoul and paratroop units sent to Kwangju. If there had been further uprisings – on a similar or greater scale than the Kwangju uprising – the government could not have responded since it had no more reserve forces under its direct command.

It was for this reason that the United States, following a request from the South Korean government, quickly made available some of the troops under the joint command. On 19 May, the 31st division was dispatched to Kwangju. And for the final thrust, four regiments – totalling 7,800 men – were detached from the joint command and sent to Kwangju. In addition, the American aircraft carrier *Coral Sea*, at the time heading for the Middle East, was ordered to change course and advance full speed for the Korean peninsula.

When the students of Kwangju sent a desperate message to Democrat President Jimmy Carter[25] asking him to intervene on behalf of their rights, the United States ignored the appeal on the pretext that 'it had not come through the official channels'. What, we may ask, are the 'official channels' in the case of a city under siege? The *Washington Post* of 1 June 1980 reported the words of a prominent American official: 'It is not a matter of human rights. It is a matter concerning the national interest of the United States in creating and maintaining stability in north-east Asia.'

It should be noted that the Japanese government also sided with Chun Doo Hwan against the Korean people.

FROM THE PARK CHUNG HEE TO
THE CHUN DOO HWAN DICTATORSHIP

Throughout Park's dictatorship, in spite of repressive measures, large protest movements developed at regular intervals, often ignited by students. We can mention the 1965 protest marches against the signing of the treaty between Japan and Korea, and those in 1972 against martial law and a new Constitution that made it possible for the dictator to stay in power till he died.

In October 1979, fiercely repressed student demonstrations in the city of Pusan led to a government crisis that resulted in the assassination of Park Chung Hee on 26 October. Park was shot by his closest collaborator Kim Jae Kyu, who was then at the head of the KCIA. On 16 October, a large student march in Pusan had led to violent confrontations with the police. Park's government immediately proclaimed a state of emergency in that city and sent in an infantry division. However, demonstrations spread to other towns such as Masan, another industrial city with several export companies. Many workers were involved in street protest. Park proceeded to proclaim a state of emergency in Masan. Over the four days of confrontation 4,207 people were arrested. Student demonstrations reached the capital city, Seoul.[26] The KCIA chief considered that if he got rid of Park, the situation could be saved.

On the day after the death of General Park the army was divided: part of it evoked the possibility of liberalizing the regime. Demonstrations were still organized. In early December 1979 most political prisoners (some of whom had to serve long sentences) were released. On 12 December, Major-General Chun Doo Hwan took everybody by surprise and successfully carried out a coup within the army. He had his main opponent General Ching arrested and took complete control of the armed forces. The demonstrations continued. On 14 April 1980, Chun Doo Hwan was appointed at the head of the KCIA while retaining his functions within the army. Demonstrations proceeded apace.

Undisguised military dictatorship was back on 18 May 1980. Fierce repression resulted in all opposition leaders being arrested, which led to violent urban uprisings culminating in the Kwangju insurrection.

Immediately after martial law had been proclaimed anew on 18 May 1980, several thousand students from the Chonam University in Kwangju took to the streets. Paratroopers were sent out and killed demonstrators (including young girls) with their bayonets. On the following day over 50,000 people assembled to face the army. In the ensuing confrontations over 260 of them were killed. After four days of street fighting some 200,000 inhabitants out of 750,000 were in the streets and determined to be heard. They eventually took control of the city. Radio stations were set on fire by demonstrators who were incensed by the radio silence on the struggle resulting from censorship imposed by the martial law. The insurgents took over weapons left behind by retreating soldiers and organized committees to manage the town administration. On 23 May, the province of Cholla in the south of the country was entirely controlled by students and the insurgent population. Kwangju students took over buses and lorries, and, fully armed as they now were, travelled from town to town and thus extended the movement through the country. When new paratroopers marched on Kwangju, the insurgents formed a crisis committee in order to negotiate with the authorities in charge of martial law. They demanded that the authorities apologize to the people of Kwangju for the atrocities for which they had been responsible, pay compensation for the wounded and the dead, promise no reprisals, and undertake that military leaders would not move their troops before an agreement was reached.

Yet, in spite of the negotiations, about 17,000 soldiers marched on the town in the early hours of 27 May and set up a military occupation. Several hundred students and inhabitants were killed.[27] Repression was carried out with the blessing of Washington and the US army.[28] In the following months repression was introduced across the country. According to an official report dated 9 February 1981, over 57,000 people were arrested during the 'Social Purification Campaign' that had been launched in summer 1980. Some 39,000 of them were sent to military camps for 'physical and psychological re-education'.[29] In February 1981 dictator Chun Doo Hwan was received at the White House by the new US President Ronald Reagan.[30]

Finding 13: A powerful social movement spearheaded by the students challenged the dictatorship. After the assassination of Park in October 1979 and a brief democratic interlude, a brutal new dictatorship was established thanks to the bloody repression of May 1980 supported by Washington and Tokyo.

THE ECONOMIC POLICY OF DICTATOR CHUN DOO HWAN (1980–87)

After the assassination of dictator Park Chung Hee in 1979 and his replacement by General Chun Doo Hwan, the country's economic orientation remained basically unchanged. Korea, which during the 1970s was heavily in debt to foreign banks, mainly Japanese, was harder hit than the other developing countries by the brutal hike in interest rates because it had mainly borrowed at variable rates. In 1983, South Korea was fourth on the list of most heavily indebted countries in absolute figures ($43 billion), behind Brazil ($98 billion), Mexico ($93 billion) and Argentina ($45 billion). But once again, its geostrategic position meant that it received a different treatment from that of the other developing countries. Japan came to the rescue by paying Korea $3 billion (by way of war reparations), which Korea used to keep up debt repayment to Japanese bankers. In this way Korea avoided having to appeal to the IMF and comply with its strict conditions.[31] In exchange, the Japanese government was able to avoid bankruptcy for some of its banks and obtain more flexible investment facilities from South Korea.

Finding 14: Contrary to the World Bank's version of the story, the massive external debt incurred with private banks came close to costing South Korea very dear. If it had not occupied a key geostrategic position in the eyes of the US and Japan, it might have suffered the fate of countries like Argentina, Brazil and Mexico, all of which had been forced to submit to IMF conditions. As we shall see later, Korea was able to pursue a partially independent course of development until the 1980s.

Korea was also affected by the second oil crisis in 1979 (soaring oil prices caused by the Iranian revolution and the overthrow of the Shah), but managed to absorb its impact. Authoritarian control of the economy was maintained, with the government ordering the various industries to produce certain specific products in preference to others. It decided to reorganize the transport vehicle industry and put two *chaebols* in charge of manufacturing automobiles.

The Bank objected to this development and recommended that Korea discontinue the production of finished vehicles and focus on the production of spare parts for export. It explained that Korean-made cars would not find buyers.

The Korean authorities stood their ground. And in the mid-1980s, Hyundai (wholly controlled by private Korean capital backed by the public authorities) succeeded in exporting its cars to the US and winning substantial market share.

At this period, the World Bank had stopped making concessions for the industrialization model via import substitution. In 1981, under the Reagan administration, the last economists in favour of state intervention had been replaced by hardcore neoliberals headed by chief economist Anne Krueger. A few years previously, she had written a book on Korea to demonstrate the superiority of export substitution over import substitution.[32] Seoul's determination to produce cars for export was an aggressive example of export substitution, and in theory it should have received the World Bank's full support. However, this was not to be, because Seoul's decision was seen as a threat to the US automobile industry. The flexibility of World Bank economists is quickly stretched to the limits when US interests are at stake.

Finding 15: The Chun Doo Hwan regime once again refused to follow the recommendations of the World Bank, and its decision paid off. The Bank nevertheless continued to support the dictatorship because its ultimate aim was to maintain influence over it. At the same time, the United States began to view the appetite of South Korean companies with distrust.

THE LAST YEARS OF THE CHUN DOO HWAN REGIME (1980–87)

During 1979–80, workers in many companies were seeking to form their own trade unions. The idea was to create new 'independent' unions that would openly challenge the collaboration policy of FKTU management while being legally obliged to comply with it. Following the crackdown by Chun Doo Hwan, a hundred or so local sections of the FKTU were disbanded, 191 officials were dismissed and some of them were sent to camps.

The driving force behind the move to create independent unions were the young people, workers and student protesters who had chosen to take to the factories to pursue the political struggle begun in the universities.

The student movement gathered strength in 1983–84 and went through a process of radicalization and intense politicization. From January to May 1986, 166,000 students took part in demonstrations.[33] The scale of the movement in the universities[34] is reflected in the number of students among political prisoners: 800 out of 1,300.

The factory workers resumed the struggle in 1985. For the first time, a major strike broke out in a *chaebol* – in this case Daewoo Motors. It had a successful outcome and a new, independent trade union was created.

On 12 February 1986, the NKDP (New Korean Democratic Party) launched a petition to change the constitution (the objective being to introduce presidential election by direct suffrage instead of by an electoral college). In the months following, a series of rallies took place, attended by tens of thousands of people in major cities around the country. Students participated independently in the democratic movement with radical slogans such as 'Down with the military dictatorship', 'No to the presence of 40,000 US soldiers in the country' and 'Yes to a popular constitution'.

On 29 November 1986, the regime deployed 50,000 policemen in Seoul to prevent an NKDP rally. The government hoped to forcibly quell the opposition but this policy misfired as a tide of democratic fervour swept through every level of society. Endless negotiations ensued between the regime and the opposition on electoral procedures. The government's position was weakened by the political fallout of the murder of a student in a police station. It was in this context that a demonstration was organized by all the opposition forces, including the new coalition resulting from a split in the NKDP. The day before the demonstration, due to take place on 10 June 1987, the police arrested 3,000 people, placed 140 opposition leaders under house arrest and sent in an advance guard of thousands of policemen. These precautions were to no avail, and on 10 June and in the days after, protest spread throughout the country, with clashes of such violence that the regime had to back off. It was a victory for direct presidential elections.[35] Washington finally coerced the regime to loosen its grip.

In the factories, the movement went far beyond electoral concerns. The South Korean labour force was quick to move into the breach created by the mass demonstrations of June 1987, which had been largely spearheaded by students.

In the summer of 1987 South Korea dictatorship was weakened by an unprecedented number of strikes. Between 17 July and 25 August, 1,064 labour disputes[36] were recorded whereas the annual average over the previous ten years was a mere 200.[37] All sectors of the economy were affected, including the *chaebols* (24,000 workers in the Hyundai naval shipyards, 15,000 coalminers, etc.). The strikers used forceful measures: occupation of company premises, including directors' offices, blocking of railway lines and occupation of railway stations, rejection of lockout tactics. These disputes resulted in substantial pay increases and the recognition of independent, democratic trade unions.

In 1988, there were already 2,799 democratic unions. In 1989, the number rose to over 7,000. January 1988 saw the creation of the Korean Trade Union Congress, which a few years later would become the Korean Confederation of Trade Unions (KCTU). Yet up until 2000 the creation of a trade union confederation was an unlawful act.

On the political scene, elections by universal suffrage were organized in 1988 – a first for Korea. But the opposition was divided and three candidates were put forward, the 'three Kims': Kim Youngsam, Kim Daejung and Kim Jongpil. General Roh Taewoo, the candidate supported by the incumbent and who was by his side at the *putsch* of 1979 and the Kwangju massacre of May 1980, was elected.

Finding 16: Assailed on all sides by protest movements and faced with the growing strength of a young, combative workforce, the dictatorship loosened its grip and organized the first free elections. Washington had finally brought pressure to bear. Thanks to a divided opposition, the regime's candidate managed to win the elections, but movements within the factories were intensifying.

THE DECISIVE 1990s

From the 1980s to the mid-1990s, Korea went from strength to strength in terms of its position in world industry: from the manufacture of bulldozers and IT equipment to shipbuilding (in the 1980s it ranked no. 2 shipbuilder worldwide after Japan). Korea was shaping up to be a serious competitor for US and European transnationals in several fields.

During the same period, China drew closer to Washington, having for some time curtailed its support for movements in various countries that threatened the stability of US allies. China joined the World Bank in 1980. Meanwhile in Russia, Gorbachev signed geostrategic agreements with Washington in the late 1980s, the Berlin Wall came down in 1989 and the USSR imploded in 1991. The Cold War was at an end.

The international politico-military situation left over from the Second World War, the victory of the Chinese revolution of 1949 and the Korean War of 1950–53 had fundamentally changed. Washington considered it would be better in future to avoid supporting declared dictatorships battling with powerful opposition movements and social unrest. In the face of opposition forces prepared to fight to the end, it would be wise to ease the pressure (as in June 1987) and safeguard what was essential – in other words, maintain favourable relations with the regime that was replacing the dictatorship. In addition, it was thought that a democratic government could more efficiently apply a neoliberal agenda, since it reduced the possibility of conflict with a democratic opposition and a social movement opposed to neoliberalism.

In 1992, following the merger of the party in power and two opposition parties, Kim Youngsam, a former moderate opposition leader, was elected with the backing of Roh Taewoo. Kim Youngsam was the first civilian president for 32 years, but nevertheless depended on the support of the military and sided openly with Washington.[38] His agenda was clearly a neoliberal one.

Korea continued to occupy a strategic military position, but the United States government, which had 37,000 soldiers posted in the country, decided it was time to curb Korea's economic appetite. Washington applied pressure, using various measures such as tariff protection against Korean products. It requested that Korea comply with the recommendations of the World Bank and the IMF, and was partially successful, as can be seen from the report of the mission sent to Korea by the IMF in November 1996 and from the minutes published after a debate between IMF directors. Here are some extracts:

(1) **On the removal of trade barriers or other forms of import restrictions:** 'Since 1994, the authorities have gradually removed obstacles to importation and reduced customs duties in accordance with the Uruguay Round[39] agreement. Granting of import licences is now automatic except for a small number of products that are a health or security risk.'[40]

(2) **On privatization:** 'Over the last ten years, the authorities have partially applied two privatization programmes. The programme implemented in December 1993 was designed to see the privatization, between 1994 and 1998, of 58 of the 133 State-owned companies. At mid-1996, 16 companies had been privatized.'[41]

(3) **On the liberalization of capital movements:** 'The administrators of the IMF are also pleased to see the recent liberalization of capital movements. Although some administrators have advocated a gradual process in this matter, others consider that rapid, full liberalization in this area offers numerous advantages at Korea's present stage of economic development.'[42]

Finding 17: From 1985 on, Washington gradually modified its policy relative to dictator allies in a new climate reflecting the end of the Cold War. This turning point was seen in its relations with Brazil in the second half of the 1980s, the Philippines in 1986, South Korea in 1987, and in the next decade with South Africa in 1994, progressively with Chile and with Indonesia in 1998. From the US viewpoint, the bottom line was positive: essential interests had been safeguarded. What, one wonders, would have happened if Washington had persisted in supporting its dictator allies in the face of mass opposition and protest? The turning point was not a global

one, however. Washington continued to support dictatorships in
Arab countries, starting with Saudi Arabia.

THE ASIAN CRISIS OF 1997 AND ITS CONSEQUENCES

Between 1990 and 1996, South Korean workers obtained a 67 per cent
increase in real wages[43] – an impressive achievement. The neoliberal
agenda met with resistance from workers in Korea as elsewhere. On
26 December 1996, the first general strike since 1948 was declared.
The workers came out in protest against a reform in the labour code
that would make layoffs easier. After 24 days on strike, they got
their way: the labour code reform was deferred. The KCTU emerged
stronger from this strike.

However, the major advances won by the workers faced a new
challenge with the Asian crisis of 1997, and the employer class was
quick to take its revenge.

In addition, what the United States and the other industrial
powers had obtained by negotiation up to 1996 was heightened by
the crisis of 1997, brought on by a speculative wave of attacks on
South-East Asian and Korean currencies. This wave was facilitated by
the capital movement liberalization measures mentioned above. After
the South-East Asian countries (Thailand was the first to be affected
in July 1997), the crisis hit South Korea in November 1997. Between
November 1997 and 8 January 1998, the Korean unit of currency,
the won, depreciated by 96 per cent against the American dollar. In
December 1997, the government in Seoul bowed to the conditions
forced on it by the IMF (while Malaysia refused to do so).[44]

A veritable restructuring operation was put in place: many
financial establishments were closed, massive redundancies ensued,
the central bank was made independent from government, interest
rates shot up (plunging local industries and workers into recession),
major investment projects were abandoned, certain *chaebols* were
dismantled, certain companies were sold to transnational corporations
in highly industrialized countries. The modification of the labour
code – deferred following the general strike of January 1996 – was
adopted, allowing employers to make massive cuts in the labour force.
The neoliberal cure imposed on Korea had radical results. The country
sank into deep recession: the GDP fell by 7 per cent in 1998.

The loans granted by the IMF, the World Bank and private banks
all carried a risk premium. These institutions were therefore able
to collect hefty revenues when repayments were due. The tens of

billions of dollars loaned to Korea were immediately channelled into repayment to the banks. All parties to the 'rescue scheme' were refunded thanks to export revenues and drastic cuts in public spending. An increasing slice of tax revenues was used to pay back the external debt. Korea's public debt grew spectacularly after the state took over the debt of private companies. Representing 12 per cent of GDP before the crisis, it almost doubled to 22.2 per cent by the end of 1999.

The increased public debt served as a pretext for making additional drastic cuts in social spending and further promoting the privatization scheme and the opening up to foreign capital.

The enforcement of these measures also aimed at disempowering Korean workers and weakening the labour unions, which had grown stronger over the previous years. The real wage of a Korean worker fell by 4.9 per cent in 1998 as a result of the crisis.

Reinforced measures to open up trade had a brutal effect on the small farmers of South Korea, who stepped up resistance movements throughout the country and regularly sent delegations abroad to attend WTO summits: Cancun in September 2003, Hong Kong in December 2005.

In the opinion of the World Bank, Korea is now a developed country. But many battles remain to be waged.

Among the recent mass actions led by the 800,000 member-strong KCTU was a general strike in March 2006 for the repeal of a law reinforcing the precariousness of part-time labour.[45]

12
The Debt Trap

In the 1970s, the debt of developing countries rose at a tremendous rate because the financial conditions of the loans seemed to be extremely favourable. Developing countries were actively encouraged to take on loans by the World Bank, private banks and the governments of highly industrialized countries. Then there was a radical change at the end of 1979, when the US Treasury imposed a sudden rise in interest rates as neoliberal policies kicked in. This jump in interest rates, combined with the drop in the commodities market, completely changed things. During the 1980s the creditors were making huge profits. Since the 1997 South-East Asia and Korean financial crises, the net financial transfer on debt in favour of the creditors (including the World Bank) has been growing at a considerable rate, while, at the same time, the debt has continued to soar to peaks never seen before.

Figures 12.1 and 12.2, along with Table 12.1, show the structure of the external debt of developing countries (DCs) first from the point of view of the creditors, then from that of the debtors. Data is as provided by the World Bank for 2004, rounded off here; the data refers to 1970–2004, a long period that saw both the 1982 crisis and those that came after it.

The second column in Table 12.1 shows the change in the *total* external debt stock of all the DCs for which the World Bank provides data[1] (long-term and short-term debts owed and guaranteed by the governments of the DCs and also the debt owed by private companies of the DCs). Column 4, with the title 'External public debt', shows the change in the total stock only of that part of the external debt that *is owed and/or guaranteed by the government* of the DC. Column 6, entitled 'Debt owed to the World Bank', shows that part of the external debt of DCs that is owed to the World Bank (IBDR and IDA). Columns 3, 5 and 7 show the net financial transfer on these three types of debt stock.

What is the net transfer on debt? It is the difference between what a country receives in the form of loans and what it pays back (capital and interest). If the figure is negative, that means the country has paid back more than it received.

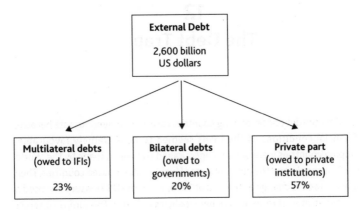

Figure 12.1   External debt of developing countries from the creditors' point of view

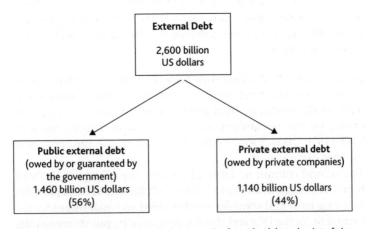

Figure 12.2   External debt of developing countries from the debtors' point of view

INTERPRETATION OF TABLE 12.1

From 1970 to 1982, the DCs greatly increased their loans. The total external debt (public and private) in current dollars was multiplied by ten (going from $70 billion to $716 billion). The external public debt was also multiplied by ten (from $45 billion to $442 billion). The public external debt owed to the World Bank was multiplied by 7.5. During this period, the net transfer on debt was consistently

Table 12.1   Debts of developing countries, 1970–2004

	ALL DEVELOPING COUNTRIES (DCs) (in US$ billions)					
	Total External Debt		External Public Debt		Debt owed to the World Bank	
	Total Debt Stock	Net Debt Transfer	Total Debt Stock	Net Debt Transfer	Total Debt Stock	Net Debt Transfer
1970	70	4	45	4	6	0.3
1971	81	7	53	5	7	0.5
1972	95	10	61	6	9	0.7
1973	113	10	74	8	10	0.9
1994	141	20	92	12	11	1.3
1975	171	27	113	20	13	1.9
1976	209	29	139	20	17	2.0
1977	283	51	177	24	20	2.0
1978	358	39	231	28	23	1.8
1979	427	44	278	31	27	2.6
1980	541	51	339	29	32	3.0
1981	629	41	383	26	38	4.1
1982	716	21	442	30	45	4.6
1983	782	–14	517	17	53	4.9
1984	826	–21	571	9	54	5.0
1985	929	–27	672	–5	71	4.4
1986	1,020	–25	782	–5	91	3.7
1987	1,166	–13	920	–2	116	2.7
1988	1,172	–24	932	–10	116	0.6
1989	1,238	–22	982	–16	120	0.4
1990	1,337	–8	1,039	–14	137	2.4
1991	1,414	–3	1,080	–14	147	–08
1992	1,480	31	1,099	–6	149	–2.8
1993	1,632	45	1,193	9	158	–08
1994	1,792	0	1,290	–16	174	–2.6
1995	1,972	61	1,346	–16	184	–2.1
1996	2,045	27	1,332	–24	180	–0.9
1997	2,110	4	1,309	–24	179	1.9
1998	2,323	–54	1,395	–7	192	1.6
1999	2,347	–98	1,405	–30	198	0.9
2000	2,283	–127	1,363	–52	199	–0.4
2001	2,261	–114	1,326	–65	202	–0.5
2002	2,336	–87	1,375	–67	212	–7.3
2003	2,554	–41	1,450	–81	223	–7.0
2004	2,597	–19	1,459	–26	222	–6.1

Source: World Bank, *Global Development Finance*, 2005

positive, which means that the DCs borrowed more than they paid back. They were encouraged to take out more loans since the real interest rates were extremely low. Furthermore, the export revenue with which they were reimbursing the debt was increasing, since the price of raw materials was high. Consequently, the DCs on the whole did not have repayment problems.[2]

The table does not immediately reflect the downturn, which started at the end of 1979 with the sudden increase in interest rates imposed on the world unilaterally by the United States government. The real interest rates exploded at the beginning of the 1980s: 8.6 per cent in 1981 and 8.7 per cent in 1982, compared with –1.3 per cent (the real interest rate was actually negative) in 1975, 1.1 per cent in 1976 and 0.3 per cent in 1977.[3]

This increase in interest rates, which meant an increase in the sums to be repaid, was compounded by a drop in the commodities market (although initially crude oil was not included in this downturn).

When this drop finally brought down the price of crude oil, the main debtors, who were oil-producing nations such as Mexico, were no longer able to pay. This situation started in 1982.[4]

Going back to the table, it can be seen that at this point, the DCs moved into a debt payment crisis and there was a negative net financial flow on the total public and private debt between 1983 and 1991 (nine consecutive years of negative net transfer).

During this time, while the DCs were paying back more than they were borrowing, their total external debt did not go down at all. Between 1983 and 1991 it went up by $632 billion, that is to say, increased by 81 per cent.

Why? Because the DCs were in difficulty owing to their drop in revenue and the high interest rate, they took on further loans mainly in order to be able to make the payments due, or in other words, to be able to service the debt. In such conditions the new loans were even more expensive (high interest rates and high risk premiums[5]).

It should also be noticed that the net transfer on the external public debt moved into negative values with a time lag of two years. Why is it that in 1983 and 1984 the net transfer on the public external debt was still positive? Because the governments at that point started to borrow considerable amounts (from the IMF and the World Bank) in order to begin to accumulate debts that had initially been taken out by the private sector but which the governments had agreed to take over. These enormous loans, for which the nation pay-back began a few years later, explain the subsequent negative flow from 1985 onwards.

This was especially true for Argentina, where $12 billion of private debt was transferred to the state by the military junta.[6]

Between 1982 and 1984, the public external debt increased by $129 billion (from $442 billion to $571 billion (see column 4) while the private external debt went down by $19 billion (from $274 billion to $255 billion).[7]

Taking the period 1982–88, the public debt increased by more than 100 per cent (from $442 billion to $932 billion – see column 4) while the private external debt went down (from $274 billion to $240 billion). The capitalists in the DCs escaped their debt by getting the Treasury of their country to pay it for them, that is to say, the salaried workers, smallholders and the poor, who pay proportionally far more tax than the capitalists. Furthermore, it will be seen in a later chapter that a very high proportion of these loans go straight back to the creditor countries through capital flight. That is to say, the capitalists of the DCs sent a large part of the loans that had been taken out by the country straight back to the North!

Looking at column 5, for the period 1985–2004, it can be seen that after 1985, the net transfer on debt was consistently negative except in 1993. Over 20 years, the negative transfer weighed heavily on public finance, reaching a total of $471 billion, i.e., the governments of the DCs transferred to their creditors an amount equivalent to five Marshall Plans. At the bottom of column 5, it can be seen that between 2000 and 2004, the negative transfer increased. Over this period, this negative transfer totalled $291 billion, i.e., the equivalent of three Marshall Plans were provided by the DCs in just five years.

After 20 years of negative transfer, economic reasoning would make it logical to suppose that the authorities of a country had paid off their debt. Obviously, if they reimbursed more than they borrowed, it would be assumed that the principal sum was going down or could even reach zero.

However, Table 12.1 shows that in fact the exact opposite happened: that the external public debt of the DCs more than doubled over the period 1985 to 2004, i.e., from $672 billion in 1985 it had gone up to $1,459 billion by 2004.[8]

Thus we see that what this table shows us is:

- The management of the external debt of the DCs has resulted in a powerful mechanism of capital flow from the debtor countries to the various creditors (public and private).

- Despite enormous and continuous repayment, the total debt has not gone down.

During the 1960s and 1970s, developing countries were encouraged to take out more and more loans, until the trap finally closed on them. As we saw above, the turning point was 1979, with the sudden jump in the interest rate and the start of the drop in the commodities market (which did not affect crude oil at the beginning, but then did so in 1981).

The theoretical virtuous circle of taking out external loans to promote development and well-being and which would result in self-perpetuating growth[9] did not work. It turned into a vicious circle of permanent debt with enormous capital flow to the creditors.

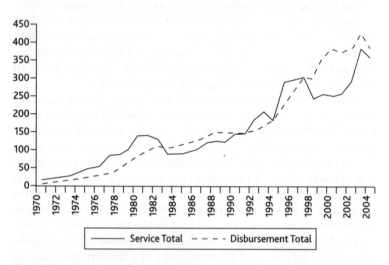

Figure 12.3 Comparison of the amount taken out in new loans yearly and the amount reimbursed each year (total external debt) (US$ billions)

Source: World Bank, *Global Development Finance*, 2005.

Note: In 1983 and 1991, the developing countries repaid more than they borrowed, as was also the case between 1998 and 2004.

If we go back to Table 12.1 and look at column 3, for the period between 1983 and 2004, it can be seen that the net transfers were negative up to 1991, and then became positive between 1992 and 1997. From 1998 onwards they were very strongly negative, reaching minus $127 billion for the year 2000. How can this be explained? During the 1980s, the flow was negative up to 1989, both for the private companies within the DCs and for the governments of these countries. As we saw above: (1) the private sector freed itself of its debts by transferring part of its debt to the public sector and was repaying only a part of what remained, and (2) the public sector continued increasing its debt to cover the debts it had taken over from the private sector, and was paying most of the reimbursements. Around 1990, the private sector, having been released from much of its debt, took out new loans, which became massive debts between 1992 and 1997 (the external debt of the private sector rose from $381 billion to $801 billion, an increase of more than 110 per cent). The loans taken out by the private sector were temporarily higher than the repayments made. The low point in 1994 corresponds to the Mexican crisis, which was accompanied by massive capital flight.

The situation changed again from 1998, when the South-East Asian crisis (Thailand, Malaysia, the Philippines and Indonesia) and the South Korean crisis occurred, followed by crises in Russia and Brazil in 1999, and in Argentina and Turkey in 2001. Repayments from the private and public sectors were enormous and the negative net flow attained its maximum in 2000–01.

In 2003 and 2004, the net flow remained negative, but lessened since the private sector and public authorities of the DCs took on new loans under conditions that were temporarily favourable because of:

- relatively low interest rates,
- considerably reduced risk premiums, and
- an increasing export revenue owing to an upward trend in the commodities market (oil, gas, etc.).

Instead of taking advantage of this situation to pay off existing loans, and with encouragement from the creditors, most medium income DCs took on new loans. Those which, like Thailand, Brazil and Argentina, chose advance reimbursement of the IMF,[10] or those which, like Russia or Brazil, reimbursed the Paris Club, simply replaced their debts to public creditors by new debts to private creditors (who were offering temporarily favourable conditions). These countries considerably increased their internal public debt.

The last two columns of Table 12.1 concern the DCs' debt to the World Bank. It can be seen that this debt has increased steadily, as has that to all the creditors. It is the final column, which gives the total net transfer, that changes. The total net transfer remains positive with regard to the World Bank up to 1990 whereas it becomes negative from 1983 as far as the total debt is concerned (column 3) and from 1985 for the public external debt (column 5). This is mainly due to the fact that during the 1980s, the WB provided the DCs with loans so that they would be able to reimburse the private banks of the North who were liable to go bankrupt if they did not have this inflow. Of course it is the IMF that plays the major role at this level, but in close coordination with 'The Bank'.

The net transfer with respect to the World Bank became negative from 1991 to 1996, then positive from 1997 to 1999 before becoming negative again, with the greatest negative net flow ever in 2002, 2003, and 2004. The negative transfer over the period 2000–04 totals a staggering $21.3 billion. This is to be compared to the total amount provided in loans each year by the World Bank, which is less than $20 billion a year.

What is even more serious is that this enormous negative net transfer does not in the slightest lead to the DCs freeing themselves from debt, but actually causes an increase in the debt owed to the World Bank.

This outcome shows the total cynicism inherent in the system, which results in artificially increased debt loads that in no way correspond to the money injected into the economies of these countries.

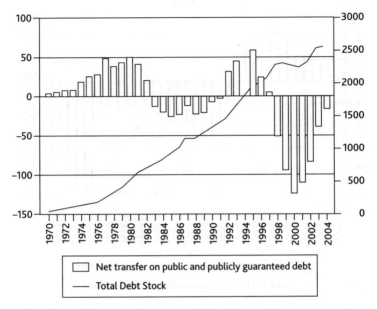

Left-hand scale: Net transfer on the total external debt (public + private) of all the DCs together (US$ billions)
Right-hand scale: Change in the total external debt (public + private) of the DCs (US$ billions)

Figure 12.4   Change in total debt stock compared with the total net transfer on the debt

Source: World Bank, *Global Development Finance*, 2005.

Figure 12.4 illustrates the content of columns 2 and 3 of Table 12.1. It can be seen that the net transfer is positive from 1970 to 1982, the year when the debt crisis occurred. It became negative between 1983 and 1991. Then from 1992 to 1997 it was positive again except in 1994, the year of the Mexican crisis. From 1998 (the South-East Asian and Korean crises) and up to 2004, the net transfer was negative. Over the period 1970–2004, the debt stock spiralled upwards from $70 billion in 1970 to $2,597 billion in 2004.

Figures 12.5 to 12.10, which follow, illustrate the public external debt of the major regions of the world.

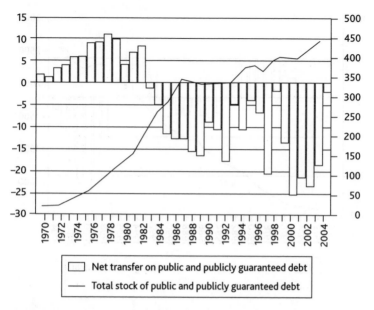

Left-hand scale: Net transfer on the total external public debt of Latin America and the Caribbean (in US$ billions)
Right-hand scale: Change in the total external public debt of Latin America and the Caribbean (in US$ billions)

Figure 12.5   Change in total debt stock compared with the total net transfer on the public external debts in Latin America and the Caribbean

Source: World Bank, *Global Development Finance*, 2005.

The net transfer on the public debt became negative in 1983 and remained negative up to 2004.

Population of Latin America and the Caribbean in 2004: 540 million.

List of countries:[11] (Antigua-and-Barbuda), Argentina, Barbados, Belize, Bolivia, Brazil, Chile, Colombia, Costa Rica, (Cuba), Dominica, Dominican Republic, Ecuador, El Salvador, Grenada, Guatemala, Guyana, Haiti, Honduras, Jamaica, Mexico, Nicaragua, Panama, Paraguay, Peru, St Kitts and Nevis, St Lucia, St Vincent and the Grenadines, (Suriname), Trinidad and Tobago, Uruguay, Venezuela.

Total external public debt in 1970: $16 billion.

Total external public debt in 2004: $442 billion.

This area, Latin America and the Caribbean, is emblematic of the way the debt crises are managed in order to protect the interests of the creditors.

A quick overview (Figures 12.6 to 12.10) of the change in the public debt and the net flow on the debt in the other five major developing regions shows that the debt crisis of 1982, which started in Latin America, gradually spread to all the other regions. Apart from obvious differences, what stands out is that the net transfer became negative everywhere at the end of the 1990s. This illustrates the fact that nowhere in the world has the crisis been resolved. It also shows that at the beginning of the twenty-first century, the debt is even more of an obstacle to be overcome than it was in the 1980s.

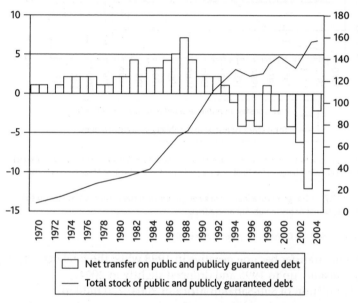

☐ Net transfer on public and publicly guaranteed debt

— Total stock of public and publicly guaranteed debt

Left-hand scale: Net transfer on the total external public debt in South Asia ($US billions)
Right-hand scale: Change in the total external public debt in South Asia ($US billions)

Figure 12.6   Change in total debt stock compared with the total net transfer on the public external debts in South Asia

Source: World Bank, *Global Development Finance*, 2005.

The net transfer became negative in 1994 while the total debt stock has continued rising.

Population of South Asia in 2004: 1.450 billion.

List of countries:[12] (Afghanistan), Bangladesh, Bhutan, India, the Maldives, Nepal, Pakistan, Sri Lanka.

Total external public debt in 1970: $12 billion.

Total external public debt in 2004: $156 billion.

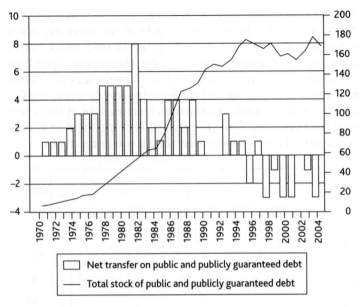

Left-hand scale: Net transfer on the total external public debt in Sub-Saharan Africa (US$ billions)
Right-hand scale: Change in the total external public debt in Sub Saharan Africa ($US billions)

Figure 12.7   Change in total debt stock compared with the total net transfer on the public external debts in Sub-Saharan Africa

Source: World Bank, *Global Development Finance*, 2005.

The net transfer became negative in 1998 while the total debt stock rose steadily up to 1995 and dropped slightly in 2004.

Population of Sub-Saharan Africa in 2004: 720 million.

List of countries:[13] Angola, Benin, Botswana, Burkina Faso, Burundi, Cameroon, Cape Verde Islands, Central African Republic, Chad, Comoros, Congo-Brazzaville, Democratic Republic of Congo, Ivory Coast, Eritrea, Ethiopia, Gabon, Gambia, Ghana, Guinea, Guinea-Bissau, Kenya, Lesotho, Liberia, Madagascar, Malawi, Mali, Mauritius, Mauritania, Mozambique, (Namibia), Niger, Nigeria, Rwanda, São Tome and Principe, Senegal, Seychelles, Sierra Leone, Somalia, South Africa, Sudan, Swaziland, Tanzania, Togo, Uganda, Zambia, Zimbabwe.

Total external public debt in 1970: $6 billion.

Total external public debt in 2004: $165 billion.

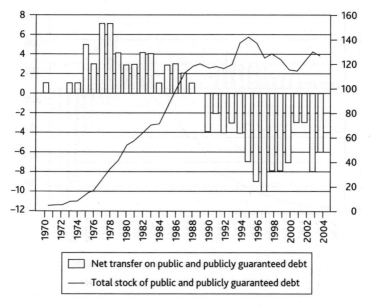

Left-hand scale: Net transfer on the total external public debt in North Africa and the Middle East (in $US billions)
Right-hand scale: Change in the total external public debt in North Africa and the Middle East (in $US billions)

Figure 12.8   Change in total debt stock compared with the total net transfer on the public external debts in North Africa and the Middle East

Source: World Bank, *Global Development Finance*, 2005.

The net transfer became negative from 1990 onwards. In spite of these considerable reimbursements, the debt has not been noticeably reduced.

Population of North Africa and the Middle East in 2004: 290 million.

List of countries:[14] Algeria, Djibouti, Egypt, Iran, (Iraq), Jordan, Lebanon, (Libya), Morocco, Oman, (Saudi Arabia), Syria, Tunisia, Yemen.

Total external public debt in 1970: $4 billion.

Total external public debt in 2004: $126 billion.

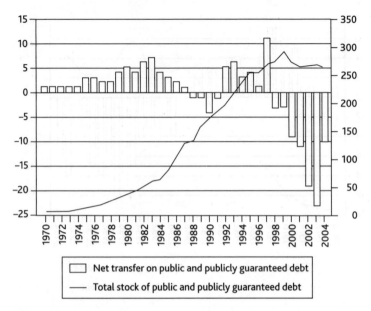

Left-hand scale: Net transfer on the total external public debt in East Asia and the Pacific (US$ billions)
Right-hand scale: Change in the total external public debt in East Asia and the Pacific (US$ billions)

Figure 12.9   Change in total debt stock compared with the total net transfer on the public external debts in East Asia and the Pacific

Source: World Bank, *Global Development Finance*, 2005.

The net transfer was negative between 1988 and 1991, and from 1999 became negative again but even more strongly. In 1999, the public debt shot up after the private debts became public and the IMF provided 'emergency' loans. In spite of such a negative net transfer, the debt has not gone down.

Population of the DCs in East Asia and the Pacific in 2004: 1.870 billion.

List of countries:[15] Burma-Myanmar, Cambodia, China, (East Timor), Fiji, Indonesia, (Kiribati), Laos, Malaysia, Mongolia, (North Korea and South Korea[16]), Papua New Guinea, Philippines, Solomon Islands, Samoa, Thailand, Tonga, Vanuatu, Vietnam.

Total external public debt in 1970: $5 billion.

Total external public debt in 2004: $262 billion.

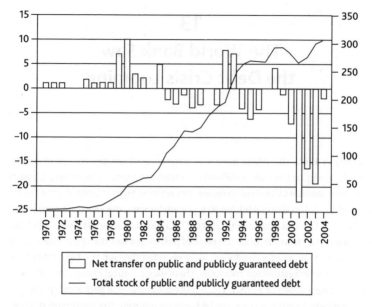

Left-hand scale: Net transfer on the total external public debt in Eastern Europe and Central Asia ($US billions)
Right-hand scale: Change in the total external public debt in Eastern Europe and Central Asia ($US billions)

Figure 12.10   Change in total debt stock compared with the total net transfer on the public external debts in Eastern Europe and Central Asia

Source: World Bank, *Global Development Finance*, 2005.

The net transfer became negative in 1985 and remained negative through to 2004 apart from the years 1992–93 and 1998. In spite of the extremely large negative transfers between 2000 and 2003, the external public debt continued to rise.

Population of Eastern Europe and Central Asia in 2004: 470 million.

List of countries: Albania, Armenia, Azerbaijan, Belarus, Bosnia-Herzegovina, Bulgaria, Croatia, Czech Republic, Estonia, Georgia, Hungary, Kazakhstan, Kyrgyzstan, Latvia, Lithuania, Macedonia, Moldavia, Poland, Romania, Russia, Serbia Montenegro, Slovakia, Slovenia, Tajikistan, Turkey, Turkmenistan, Ukraine, Uzbekistan.

Total external public debt in 1970: $3 billion.

Total external public debt in 2004: $310 billion.

13
The World Bank Saw
the Debt Crisis Looming

Already in 1960, the World Bank was beginning to see the danger of a debt crisis looming, as the main indebted countries were struggling to keep up with the rising amounts they had to repay. The warning signs increased until the oil crisis of 1973. The World Bank leaders, private bankers, the Pearson Commission and the US General Accounting Office (GAO) published reports warning of the risk of a crisis. However, once the price of petroleum had started to rise in 1973 and huge amounts of petrodollars were recycled through the big commercial banks of the industrialized countries, there was a radical change of tone. The WB no longer spoke of a crisis. Yet indebtedness was still gathering speed. The WB competed with the commercial banks in granting the maximum number of loans as fast as possible. Until the debt crisis broke in 1982, the Bank held a double discourse. One, intended for the public and the indebted countries, claimed that there was nothing to worry about and that if there were problems, they would be short-lived; this is what appeared in official documents available to the public. The other discourse took place behind closed doors at internal meetings. One internal memorandum comments that if banks see risks rising, they will cut down on loans and 'We may see a larger number of countries in extremely difficult situations' (29 October 1979).[1]

After 1960, there were plenty of warning signs.

In 1960, Dragoslav Avramoviæ and Ravi Gulhati, two eminent World Bank economists,[2] published a report that clearly highlighted the danger of seeing the developing countries reach an unsustainable level of indebtedness owing to the gloomy prospects of earning much in export revenues:

In several major debtor countries, most of which already have high debt service ratios, service payments are predicted to rise in the next few years. [...] In some cases uncertain export prospects and heavy debt service schedules constitute a serious obstacle to substantial amounts of further borrowing.[3]

This was just the beginning of a long series of warnings that appeared in different successive WB documents until 1973.

On page 8 of the World Bank's 1963–64 Annual Report we read:

The heavy debt burden that weighs on an increasing number of its member countries has been a continuing concern of the World Bank group... the Executive Directors have decided that the Bank itself may vary some terms of its lending to lighten the service burden in cases where this is appropriate to the debt position of the country.[4]

The 20th Annual Report, published in 1965, carries a large section on the debt. It emphasizes that exports of agricultural produce are increasing faster than the demand from the industrialized countries, triggering a fall in prices:[5]

agricultural export commodities growth has tended to be more rapid than the growth of demand in the industrialized countries. Consequently, the developing countries suffered from a sustained decline in the prices of their agricultural exports during 1957–1962.

For example, while coffee exports increased by 25 per cent of volume between 1957 and 1962, the export revenues they brought in *fell* by 25 per cent.[6] Cocoa and sugar prices also fell. The report showed that exports from the developing countries were essentially raw materials for which Northern demand was slow and erratic. The prices of raw materials were falling.[7] The report also indicated that financial flows towards the developing countries were insufficient, whether in terms of donations and loans or of foreign investments, because of the large amounts paid out in debt repayments and repatriation of profits on foreign investments.

The report mentioned that the debt had increased at an annual rate of 15 per cent between 1955 and 1962 and had then accelerated to a rate of 17 per cent between 1962 and 1964. Just over 50 per cent of the debt was concentrated in eleven countries. All were big clients of the Bank (India, Brazil, Argentina, Mexico, Egypt, Pakistan, Turkey, Yugoslavia, Israel, Chile and Colombia).

The growth rate of the external public debt of the developing countries was very high. Between 1955 and 1963, the debt increased by 300 per cent, from $9 billion to $28 billion. In just one year from 1963 to 1964, the debt increased by 22 per cent to reach $33 billion. The total amount of debt service increased fourfold over that whole period (1955–64).

In 1955, debt servicing came to 4 per cent of export revenues. By 1964, it had tripled to 12 per cent. In the case of certain countries, it was almost 25 per cent!

The report placed the accent on the need to properly define the conditions under which the World Bank and other creditors granted loans. What was the underlying reasoning?

The harsher the conditions, the higher the repayments. The higher the repayments, the higher the volume of aid would have to be. Consequently, the relative harshness or flexibility of conditions was as important as the volume of aid. Two key factors determined the harshness or flexibility: first, the percentage that was donated; secondly, the actual terms and conditions of loans (the duration and interest rate).

The report noted that the share of donations had fallen (mainly those of the USA). Interest rates had dropped slightly and the conditions of loans had toughened up. In other words, harshness had been increased on one side and reduced a bit on the other. Note that the USSR lent money at a considerably lower interest rate than that fixed by the 'West'.[8] Great Britain announced that in future it would grant interest-free loans to the poorest countries. Canada said much the same. The report pleaded for greater flexibility in the conditions carried by loans. None of the 19 annual reports that had preceded this one contained this kind of analysis. How can the particular tone and the original contents of this report be explained?

In fact, the report was written under pressure of events. Numerous Third World countries had joined the Non-aligned Movement. They had a majority within the UN General Assembly and in 1964 they had managed to have the United Nations Conference on Trade and Development founded. UNCTAD is the only UN institution run by representatives of the developing countries.[9] These countries were strongly critical of the attitude of the industrialized countries. The World Bank itself counted 102 member states at the time, most of which were Third World countries. The Bank's leaders were obliged to take account of the recriminations of the South in their analysis.

The 21st Annual Report published in 1966 also discussed loan conditions, pleading for greater flexibility and pointing out that under the present logic, the debt was bound to increase permanently:

While the increasingly heavy debt burden of developing countries points to the need for funds on easier terms... the average terms of total bilateral assistance may become less, rather than more, concessionary... A higher level of aid on inappropriate terms, however, could make the external debt problem even more difficult. If aid is not made available on average terms which are more concessionary, the gross volume of assistance will have to be steeply and continuously increased in order to maintain any given level of real resources transfer.[10]

To summarize, the World Bank had clearly detected the persistent danger of a debt crisis breaking out owing to the countries' inability to sustain rising debt payments. The solutions proposed by the Bank in the extracts quoted above consisted of increasing the volume of loans and proposing more favourable conditions: lower interest rates, and longer periods for repayment. In fact, the Bank did not see the problem in terms of financial flows. It merely saw that for the indebted countries to be able to repay their debt, they would need to borrow more money on easier terms. Plainly, this was the start of the vicious circle where new debts serve to repay old ones, both in theory and in practice.

In the same reports, the Bank expressed confidence in an increase of private capital flows (loans and investments) towards the developing countries. The increase of private loans was considered as an important objective. Such an increase would reduce expectations linked to public finance, according to the reports.

The 20th Annual Report published in 1965 reads:

The World Bank group and other international organizations [...] are making strenuous efforts to encourage and enlarge the flow of private capital into the less developed countries. There is no doubt that this flow can be expected to increase [...] thereby accelerating the pace of development and relieving the pressure on public funds.[11]

In the next report in 1966, the need to free up international movement of capital is highlighted: 'It is to be hoped that conditions can be established in world [private] capital markets which will permit a freer movement of capital internationally.'[12]

Then, remarkably, after a long discussion of the difficulties of repaying the debt, the Bank declares that there should be no reduction in loans: 'None of this, however, should be taken to mean that developing countries cannot afford, and hence should avoid, any increase in debt service obligations.'[13]

The designation of the Pearson Commission in 1968 by Robert McNamara, the new president of the World Bank, is one of the ways in which the US leaders tried to deal with the growing indebtedness and demands of the South. *Partners in Development*, the report published by the Pearson Commission in 1969, predicted that the burden of debt would increase to reach crisis proportions in the following decade. The percentage of new gross loans used to service existing debt reached 87 per cent in Latin America in 1965–67.

In 1969, Nelson Rockefeller, brother of the president of the Chase Manhattan Bank, explained in a report to the US President about the problems Latin America had to face:

Heavy borrowing by some Western hemisphere countries to support development has reached the point where annual repayments of interest and amortization absorb a large share of foreign exchange earnings... Many of the countries are, in effect, having to make new loans to get the foreign exchange to pay interest and amortization on old loans, and at higher interest rates.[14]

In 1969, the General Accounting Office (GAO) handed the government an equally alarming report:

Many poor nations have already incurred debts past the possibility of repayment... The US continues to make more loans to underdeveloped countries than any other country or organization and also has the greatest loss ratio. The trend toward making loans repayable in dollars does not ensure that the funds will be repaid.[15]

Some time later, in 1970, in a report to the US President, the president of the Bank of America, Rudolph Peterson, sounded the alarm:

The debt burden of many developing countries is now an urgent problem. It was foreseen, but not faced, a decade ago. It stems from a combination of causes [but] whatever the causes, future export earnings of some countries are so heavily mortgaged as to endanger continuing imports, investment, and development.[16]

In short, from the late 1960s, diverse influential and interrelated sources in the USA considered that a debt crisis could break in the ensuing years.

DESPITE BEING AWARE OF THE DANGER ...

For his part, Robert McNamara also considered the rate at which Third World indebtedness was growing to be a problem. He declared that by the end of 1972, the debt would come to $75 billion and the annual service of the debt would exceed $7 billion. The amount paid in debt servicing had increased by 18 per cent in 1970 and 20 per cent in 1971. The average rate of increase of the debt since the 1960s represented almost double the growth rate of the export revenues with which the indebted countries had to service the debt. McNamara added that the situation could not go on indefinitely.[17]

... FROM 1973 ON, THE WORLD BANK SET OUT TO INCREASE DEBT IN COMPETITION FROM THE COMMERCIAL BANKS

Yet the World Bank presided over by McNamara kept up the pressure on the countries of the Periphery to get them even more into debt.

The rise in prices of petroleum products and other raw materials in 1973 led countries to rush blindly into even greater debt. The publications of the World Bank, the IMF and bankers, showed less and less pessimism concerning the repayment difficulties that the developing countries were faced with.

Take for example the IMF's Annual Report for 1975, which contained the following dispassionate message:

The investment of the surpluses of oil-exporting countries in national and international financial markets together with the expansion of international financing (through both bilateral arrangements and multilateral facilities) has resulted in a satisfactory channeling of funds into the current account deficits of the oil-importing countries.[18]

It is interesting to note that this diagnosis is at loggerheads with the one that would appear when the debt crisis had arisen. No sooner had the crisis broken in 1982 than the IMF blamed it on the two oil crises of 1973 and 1979. Yet this 1975 quotation implies that, for the IMF, the recycling of petrodollars combined with public lending had largely solved the problems of oil-importing countries.

WHY DID THE WORLD BANK ENCOURAGE DEBT IN THE 1970s?

The World Bank absolutely wanted to increase its influence over the maximum number of countries that clearly positioned themselves in the capitalist camp or at least kept a distance from the USSR (like Yugoslavia) or were trying to do so (like Romania).[19] To maintain or increase its influence, it needed to strengthen its leverage by constantly upscaling the amounts it lent. Now, commercial banks also wanted to increase their lending and were ready to offer more competitive rates than the World Bank.[20] This sent the Bank off in search of projects that might require loans. Between 1978 and 1981, the amounts lent by the Bank rose by 100 per cent.

Robert McNamara made a great show of confidence in the 1970s. In 1977 he declared in his annual presidential address that 'the major lending banks and major borrowing countries are operating on assumptions which are broadly consistent with one another', and concluded that 'we are even more confident today than we were a year ago that the debt problem is indeed manageable'.[21]

Some big commercial banks also showed great serenity.[22] In 1980, Citibank declared:

Since World War II, defaults by LDC's, when they have occurred, have not normally involved major losses to the lending banks. Defaults are typically followed by an arrangement between the government of the debtor country and its foreign creditors to reschedule the debt... Since interest rates or spreads are typically increased when a loan is rescheduled, the loan's present discounted value may well be higher than that of the original credit.[23]

This statement is to be taken with the greatest caution as to the motivations of its author. In fact, by 1980, Citibank, one of the most active banks in the 1970s in terms of Third World lending, was beginning to sense that the wind was changing. At the time these lines were written, it was already preparing to withdraw, and was granting almost no more new loans.

The text was meant for smaller banks, especially local banks in the USA, of the Savings and Loans type, that companies like Citibank were trying to reassure so that they would continue to grant loans. In Citibank's view, the money that Savings and Loans continued to send to the countries of the South would enable them to repay the big banks. In other words, for the indebted countries to carry on repaying the big banks, there had to be other lenders. They could be private (small or middle-sized banks, less well informed than the bigger ones or misinformed by them) or public (the World Bank, the IMF, public export credit agencies, governments...). There had to be lenders of last resort for the big banks to be sure of getting fully repaid. In this respect, it might be said that in falling over themselves to be reassuring in the run-up to the crisis, institutions like the WB and the IMF connived with the big banks that were on the lookout for lenders of last resort. The smaller banks that continued to lend capital to the developing countries were forced into bankruptcy after the 1982 crisis and were bailed out by the US Treasury, that is, by US taxpayers.

THE WATERSHED, 1979–81

The second oil crisis of 1979 (after the Iranian revolution) coincided with a fall in prices of other raw materials.

At the end of 1979, two factors forced up the cost of the debt: a very sharp rise in interest rates and the appreciation of the dollar. Attempts from the South to revive negotiations for a New World Order failed and, in Cancun in 1981, the dialogue between the North and the South fell through. Moreover, the United States did not apply the budget austerity it imposed on the countries of the South. Instead it reduced taxes, increased military spending and spent more on consumer goods.

The general about-turn towards what the World Bank called *structural adjustment* was announced in a speech made by Robert McNamara at the UNCTAD conference in Manila in May 1979.

THE DOUBLE DISCOURSE OF THE WORLD BANK

Until the debt crisis broke in 1982, the World Bank promoted a double discourse. One, intended for the public and the indebted countries, claimed that there was nothing to worry about and that if there were problems they would be short-lived; this is what appeared in official documents available to the public. The other discourse took place behind closed doors at internal meetings.

In October 1978, one of the vice-presidents of the World Bank, Peter Cargill, in charge of finance, addressed a memorandum to the president, Robert McNamara, entitled 'Riskiness in IBRD's loans portfolio'. In it, Cargill urged McNamara and the whole of the World Bank to pay a lot more attention to the solvency of indebted countries.[24] Cargill claimed that the number of indebted countries in arrears regarding payments to the World Bank and/or that were seeking to renegotiate their multilateral debt had risen from three to 18 between 1974 and 1978! McNamara himself made known his worries internally on several occasions, particularly in a memorandum in September 1979. One internal memorandum reads that if banks see risks rising, they will cut down on loans and 'We may see a larger number of countries in extremely difficult situations' (29 October 1979).[25]

The *World Development Report* published by the World Bank in 1980 gives an optimistic view of the future, predicting that interest rates would stabilize at the very low level of 1 per cent. This was completely unrealistic, as was proved by real events. It is edifying to learn through the World Bank historians that in the first, unpublished, version of the report, there was a second hypothesis based on a real interest rate of 3 per cent. That projection showed that the situation would eventually be unsustainable for the indebted countries. McNamara managed to get that gloomy scenario left out of the final version![26]

The World Bank's *World Development Report* of 1981 mentions that it seemed very likely that borrowers and lenders would adapt to the changing conditions without starting a general crisis of confidence.[27] McNamara's presidential mandate at the World Bank ended in June 1981, a year before the crisis broke and became common knowledge. The US President, Ronald Reagan, replaced him with Alden William Clausen, president of the Bank of America, one of the major private creditors to the developing countries. Rather like putting a fox in the chicken-run...

14
The Mexican Debt Crisis
and the World Bank

Robert McNamara and Mexican President Luis Echeverria (1970–76) were thick as thieves. Echeverria had cracked down on the radical left. From 1973, Mexico's foreign currency revenue soared thanks to the tripling of oil prices. This increase in currency revenue should have prevented Mexico from borrowing. However, the volume of World Bank loans to Mexico rose sharply: these quadrupled from 1973 to 1981 (from $118 million in 1973 to $460 million in 1981). Mexico also borrowed from private banks with the World Bank's backing. The volume of loans from private banks to Mexico increased six times between 1973 and 1981. US banks led the field, followed in decreasing order by banks from the UK, Japan, Germany, France, Canada and Switzerland. The amounts loaned by private banks were ten times those borrowed from the World Bank. When the crisis broke in 1982, there were no fewer than 550 banks to which the Mexican government owed money! Lending money to Mexico was the Bank's way of keeping its hold on Mexican authorities. From 1974 to 1976, the predicament of Mexican public finances seriously worsened. Yet the Bank insisted that Mexico should contract more debts while the alarm signals were flashing.

On 3 February 1978, the World Bank boldly projected a rosy future for Mexico:

The Mexican government almost certainly will experience a large increase in the resources at its disposal by the early 1980s. Our most recent projections show that ... the balance of payments will show a surplus on current account by 1982 ... large increases in export revenues, mainly from petroleum and products, should make both the foreign debt problem and the management of public finance much easier to manage by the 1980s. The debt service ratio of 32.6 per cent (of export revenue) in 76, will increase progressively to 53.1 per cent in 78, and thereafter will decline to 49.4 per cent in 1980 and about 30 per cent in 1982.[1]

The exact opposite was to occur. Every word of this prediction was contradicted by facts!

In October 1979, when Paul Volcker, then chairman of the US Federal Reserve, decided on a steep hike in interest rates that would inevitably lead to the debt crisis (which was to start in Mexico), the World Bank had reassuring words. On 19 November 1979 we read:

Both the increase in Mexico's external public debt and especially the increase in the debt service ratio, which in 1979 may become as high as 2/3 of its exports [...], suggest a very critical situation. *In fact, the truth is exactly the opposite* [author's emphasis].[2]

This is quite simply astounding.

The World Bank's message consists of repeating that even when everything suggests that there is cause for alarm, actually all is well, the situation is excellent, and you should just contract further debts. What would we think of a crossing-keeper who would tell pedestrians they should cross the railway lines when a red light clearly indicates that a train is arriving? What would a court say if such behaviour had resulted in loss of life?

Private banks of the North loaned exponentially higher amounts to developing countries, starting with Mexico.

One of the Bank's economists in charge of monitoring the situation sent a most alarming report on 14 August 1981.[3] He explained that he disagreed with the optimistic view held by the Mexican government and its representative Carlos Salinas de Gortari, minister of planning and budget.[4] He later had serious problems with his hierarchy, and even decided to lodge a lawsuit against the WB (which he won).[5] In 1981 the Bank granted Mexico $1.1 billion (scheduled over several years): it was by far the largest loan granted by the WB since 1946. In the early months of 1982, the World Bank still claimed that the increase in the Mexican GDP would average 8.1 per cent a year between 1983 and 1985. On 19 March 1982, i.e., six months before the crisis, the president of the World Bank, Alden W. Clausen, sent the following letter to the Mexican President José Lopez Portillo:[6]

Our meeting in Mexico City with your top aides reinforced my confidence in the economic leaders of your country. You, Mr. President, can be rightfully proud of the achievements of the last five years. Few countries can claim to have achieved such high growth rates, or have created so many jobs... I wish to congratulate you on the many successes already achieved. As I stated during our meeting, *the recent setback for the Mexican economy is bound to be transient*, and we will be happy to be of assistance during the consolidation process [author's emphasis].[7]

Less than a year earlier, Clausen still chaired the Bank of America, which was busy providing loan after loan to Mexico.

On 20 August 1982 Mexico, which had paid back considerable amounts over the first seven months of the year, stated that it could not pay any more. It decreed a six-month moratorium (August 1982 to January 1983). It had only $180 million in reserve and was expected to pay $300 million on 23 August. Already in early August Mexico had told the IMF that its currency reserve was down to $180 million. At the end of August the IMF convened with the Federal Reserve, the US Treasury, the Bank for International Settlements (BIS) and the Bank of England. The director of the IMF, Jacques de Larosière, told the Mexican authorities that the IMF and the BIS were willing to grant currency loans in December 1982 on the twofold condition that the money be used to refund private banks and that Mexico implement drastic structural adjustment measures. Mexico accepted. It sharply devalued its national currency, considerably increased domestic interest rates and saved Mexican private banks from bankruptcy by nationalizing them and taking over their debts. In exchange, it seized the $6 billion cash the banks had on hand. President José Lopez Portillo presented this measure to the Mexican people as though it were a nationalist move. He of course refrained from divulging that the $6 billion would be used to pay back foreign bankers.

Who was really responsible for the Mexican debt crisis? Did Mexico start it?

Generally speaking, the reasons are obvious: a rise in interest rates decided in Washington, plummeting oil revenues and a huge debt are the structural causes. The first two are external factors and Mexico was helpless against them. The third one results from choices made by the Mexican leaders, whom the WB and private bankers encouraged to take on enormous loans.

Beyond these structural causes, which are fundamental, an analysis of how one thing led to another shows that private banks of the North started the crisis in that they significantly reduced the loans granted to Mexico in 1982. Aware that almost all the available currency in the Mexican Treasury had been used to pay back the debt, they considered it was time to reduce their loans. In this way they brought one of the world's largest indebted countries to its knees. Seeing that Mexico was facing the combined effects of a rise in interest rates – from which they profited – and a fall in its oil revenues, they chose to act fast and move out. An aggravating circumstance was that foreign bankers had aided and abetted Mexican ruling circles (CEOs and leaders of the party-state called the Institutional Revolutionary Party) who were frantically transferring their capital abroad in order to invest it safely. It is estimated that in 1981–82, no less than $29 billion left Mexico as capital flight.[8] After precipitating the crisis private bankers benefited from it further – and left it for others to mend matters. The evidence can be seen in the following tables.

Table 14.1 traces the growth of loans granted by private foreign banks without any guarantee by the state. We note that after a huge increase from 1978 to 1981, loans fell drastically in 1982. Repayments, however, did not decrease. On the contrary, they increased by close to 40 per cent in 1982. In 1983 bank loans had completely stopped. Yet repayments were still well under way. The evolution of debt net transfer, which had been positive until 1981, became seriously negative from 1982. All in all, between 1978 and 1987, negative net transfer accounted for more than $10 billion in profits for the bankers.

Table 14.2 shows the growth of loans from foreign private banks that were guaranteed by the Mexican state. We note the increase in loans from 1978 to 1981. In 1982 loans decreased by 20 per cent while repayments increased. Bank loans decreased sharply until 1986. By contrast, repayments by the Mexican state continued at a very high level. Net transfer on the public debt to foreign banks contracted with a state guarantee, which had been positive from 1978 to 1982, became very seriously negative from 1983. All in all, the net negative transfer between 1978 and 1987 accounts for over $10 billion in profits for the banks.

If we add up negative transfers in the two tables we reach a sum of over $20 billion. Private banks in the North had extracted substantial benefits from the Mexican people.

Table 14.3 shows the growth of World Bank loans to Mexico. We note a sharp increase from 1978 to 1981. The WB was then frantically competing with private banks. In 1982 and 1983 we note a moderate decrease. Loans increased again from 1984 on. The Bank behaved as a last resort lender. Loans were conditional on the Mexican state repaying private banks, a majority of which were North American. Net transfer remained positive because Mexico used WB loans to repay private banks.

Table 14.4 shows the growth of IMF loans to Mexico. There were none between 1978 and 1981. Yet in those years Mexico repaid old loans. From 1982, the IMF loaned massive amounts on two conditions: 1) the money had to be used to repay private banks; 2) Mexico had

Table 14.1 Foreign banks' loans to Mexico without any state guarantee and repayments to the banks, 1978–87 (US$ million)

	1978	1979	1980	1981	1982	1983	1984	1985	1986	1987
	Foreign banks' loans without any state guarantee and repayments to the banks									
Loans from the banks	931	1,576	2,450	3,690	590	0	2,144	1,115	1,700	247
Repayments	860	1,390	1,450	2,090	2,890	1,546	4,630	3,882	3,490	2,453
Net transfer	71	175	1,000	1,600	−2,300	−1,546	−2,486	−2,767	−1,790	−2,206

Source: World Bank, *Global Development Finance*, 2005

Table 14.2 Foreign banks' loans to Mexico with state guarantee and repayments to the banks, 1978–87 (US$ million)

	1978	1979	1980	1981	1982	1983	1984	1985	1986	1987	Total
	Foreign banks' loans with state guarantee and repayments to the banks										
Loans from the banks	7,235	9,465	7,625	10,063	8,085	5,284	3,134	1,878	198	4,486	57,453
Repayments	5,349	8,582	6,706	7,226	7,260	7,571	7,654	6,922	5,345	5,170	67,785
Net transfer	1,886	883	919	2,837	825	−2,287	−4,520	−5,044	−5,147	−684	−10,332

Source: World Bank, *Global Development Finance*, 2005

Table 14.3 World Bank loans to Mexico and repayments, 1978–87 (US$ million)

	1978	1979	1980	1981	1982	1983	1984	1985	1986	1987	Total
WB loans	167	326	422	460	408	360	682	840	1,016	983	5,664
Repayments	184	220	255	283	328	399	485	597	819	1,072	4,642
Net transfer	–17	106	167	177	80	–39	197	243	197	–89	1,022

Source: World Bank, *Global Development Finance*, 2005

Table 14.4 IMF loans to Mexico and repayments, 1978–87 (US$ million)

	1978	1979	1980	1981	1982	1983	1984	1985	1986	1987	Total
IMF loans	0	0	0	0	222	1,072	1,234	300	870	786	4,484
Repayments	261	178	138	70	0	26	115	202	413	650	2,053
Net transfer	–261	–178	–138	–70	222	1,046	1,119	98	457	136	2,431

Source: World Bank, *Global Development Finance*, 2005

Table 14.5 Loans from countries of the North to Mexico and repayments, 1978–87 (US$ million)

	1978	1979	1980	1981	1982	1983	1984	1985	1986	1987	Total
Loans from countries	156	229	439	578	673	539	540	446	848	700	5,148
Repayments	171	388	223	286	372	481	583	573	488	377	3,942
Net transfer	–15	–159	216	292	301	58	–43	–127	360	323	1,206

Source: World Bank, *Global Development Finance*, 2005

Table 14.6 Growth of Mexican external debt, 1978–87 (US$ million)

	1978	1979	1980	1981	1982	1983	1984	1985	1986	1987	Total
Total debt stock	35,712	42,774	57,378	78,215	86,081	92,974	94,830	96,867	100,891	109,471	5,148
Repayment	7,423	11,595	10,962	14,340	15,684	14,825	16,960	15,293	12,944	12,087	132,113
Net total transfer	1,512	3,623	8,757	11,483	–1,799	–15,804	–12,144	–10,932	–6,648	–4,227	–26,179

Source: World Bank, *Global Development Finance*, 2005

to implement a structural adjustment policy (reduction of social expenditure and expenditure for infrastructure, privatization, rise in interest rates, increase in indirect taxation, etc.). Net transfer remained positive because Mexico used IMF loans to repay private banks.

Table 14.5 shows the growth of loans granted by the most industrialized countries. Like private banks and the World Bank, countries of the North sharply increased their loans to Mexico from 1978 to 1981. Then they did more or less what the WB and the IMF were doing. While private banks reduced their loans, they followed the IMF and the WB in loaning to Mexico in order to make sure that it could repay private banks and implement its structural adjustment programme.

Table 14.6 shows the growth of Mexico's total external debt. This multiplied three times between 1978 and 1987. During this period the amounts that were paid back were 3.5 times the amount owed in 1978. Total negative net transfer accounts for over $26 billion.

Since 1982, the Mexican people have been bled dry to assuage their various creditors. Indeed, the IMF and the World Bank have exacted the last cent back from what they loaned to the country so that it could pay private banks. Mexico has been forcefully subjected to the logic of structural adjustment. The shock of 1982 first led to a steep recession, massive layoffs and a dramatic drop in purchasing power. Next structural measures resulted in hundreds of publicly owned companies being privatized. The concentration of wealth and a large part of the national assets in the hands of a few Mexican and foreign industrial and financial corporations is staggering.[9]

In a historical perspective it is evident that the road to over-indebtedness in the 1960s and 1970s, the explosion of the debt crisis in 1982 and the way it was managed in the following years marked a radical break with the progressive policies implemented from the start of the Mexican revolution in 1910 to the 1940s with Lazaro Cardenas as President. From the revolution to the 1940s, living standards notably improved, Mexico made great strides in economic terms and adopted an independent foreign policy. From 1914 to 1946 Mexico did not pay back any debt and eventually won a resounding victory over its creditors when the latter agreed to give up 90 per cent of the amount owed in 1914 without claiming any interest either. Since the 1982 crisis, Mexico has lost control of its destiny. Historically, this has been the US's objective since the nineteenth century.

In 1970, Mexico's public external debt amounted to $3.1 billion. Thirty-three years later, in 2003, it had multiplied by 25, reaching $77.4 billion (public and private external debts together amounted to $140 billion). Meanwhile, the Mexican government paid back $368 billion (120 times the amount owed in 1970). Net negative transfer from 1970 to 2003 amounts to $109 billion. From 1983 to 2003, i.e., over a period of 21 years, net transfer on the public external debt was positive only in 1990 and 1995.

We trust the day is approaching when the Mexican people will be able to win back the freedom to decide their own future.

15

The World Bank and the IMF: the Creditors' Bailiffs

In July 1981, Alden W. Clausen, then president of the Bank of America, was made president of the World Bank. The Bank of America is one of the biggest US banks at risk in case of non-payment of debt by the developing countries. By placing Clausen at the head of the World Bank, President Reagan was sending a strong signal to US banks (and other commercial banks around the world) that their interests would be duly considered.

US banks were the most at risk compared to European and Japanese banks because they lent proportionately more. The 1982 crisis particularly affected Latin America, the US banks' preferred hunting ground. The amounts they lent, compared to their capital, were enormous and imprudent. All the US banks taken as a whole had lent the equivalent of 152 per cent of their own capital. Of those, the top 15 had lent the equivalent of 160 per cent of their capital. The nine biggest, including the Bank of America, had committed the equivalent of 229 per cent of their capital.

In August 1982, when Mexico announced that it was unable to pay up, the big movers and shakers of world finance got together to bail out the commercial banks. The quartet that orchestrated the strategy was composed of Jacques de Larosière, managing director of the IMF, Paul Volcker, president of the US Federal Reserve, Gordon Richardson, director of the Bank of England, and Fritz Lentwiler, president of the Bank for International Settlements (BIS). The president of the World Bank was not invited to the preliminary meetings.

The strategy adopted may be summarized as follows:

- The crisis should be treated as though it was caused by a short-term liquidity problem that could be resolved by the IMF and the major central banks;
- Priority would be given to the debts of the three most indebted countries: Brazil, Mexico and Argentina;
- Private debt should be converted into public debt for the indebted countries;

- Creditors should act collectively while the indebted countries would be dealt with individually, making it impossible for them to present a united front ('divide and rule');
- Indebted countries must at all cost continue to repay the interest on the debt;
- No cancellation or reduction of the interest rate should be granted by the creditors – the payments could only be rescheduled;
- New loans would only be granted by commercial banks on condition that the indebted countries concerned promise to implement austerity policies in agreement with the IMF.

This was the strategy that was largely maintained throughout the 1980s, but it had to be modified to take into account the amplitude of the crisis and the reactions of the commercial banks. The latter, instead of following the last point of the strategy mentioned above, practically stopped all lending and made do with gathering repayments, which sent their profits soaring! The profits that the Citibank took from Brazil in 1983 and 1984 alone represented 20 per cent of its total profits.

Karin Lissakers (who was later to become the executive director for the USA at the IMF) claimed that the dividends distributed by the big US banks in 1984 were to double what they had been in 1980.[1] In fact, the IMF and the public money-spinners mentioned above, later joined by the World Bank, adopted a tough strategy with regard to the indebted countries in order to protect the commercial banks. They could hardly have done more to promote the interests of big private international finance, or in other words, big international capital. They had become bailiffs at the service of commercial banks. As Lissakers herself points out: 'The IMF was in a sense the creditor community's enforcer.'

Jacques Polak, who was director of research at the IMF, then executive director of the IMF for the Netherlands, writes of the strategy outlined above:

In the second half of the 1980s, however, commercial banks began to exploit this approach. No longer afraid of becoming the victims of a generalized debt crisis, the banks began to realize they could insist on favorable terms for themselves by blocking a country's access to Fund credit (and to other credit linked to a Fund arrangement). The Fund was thus pushed increasingly into being used by the commercial banks in the collection of their debts.[2]

What has been said about the IMF goes for the World Bank, too, which behaved in exactly the same way.

The US banks did very well for themselves. So did European banks, by obtaining enormous tax breaks for stocking huge funds as provision against possible losses on their loans. Furthermore, European and Japanese banks had the advantage of the depreciation of the dollar, which reduced the weight in their portfolios of their loans in dollars to indebted countries.

The governments of the indebted countries arranged for their country's Treasury (and thus its citizens) to take on the burden of the external debt run up by their country's private companies. The case of Argentina was typical: subsidiaries of transnational corporations indebted towards their parent company managed to get their debts paid off by the Argentine Treasury![3]

In doing this, governments of the developing countries submit to the combined pressure of local capitalists, the transnationals implanted in their countries, and the big public moneylenders of the North, themselves under the thumb of the big commercial banks of the North.

It was the very same big public moneylenders, particularly the IMF and the World Bank, who gradually replaced commercial banks as creditors to the countries in the greatest distress. Here again, the risks and the costs were transferred from the private sector to the public sector. Table 15.1 shows how commercial banks dissociated themselves from indebted countries encountering repayment difficulties. Their credits to these countries fell from $278 billion in 1982 to $200 billion in 1992, i.e., a reduction of 28 per cent. Over the same period, the official creditors (IMF, World Bank, states) took over,

Table 15.1   Real debt of developing countries with debt-servicing difficulties, 1982–92 (US$ billion)

Year	To commercial banks	To official creditors	Share of official creditors in total
1982	278	115	29.3
1984	286	143	33.3
1986	278	187	40.2
1988	254	232	47.7
1990	222	251	53.1
1992	200	252	55.7

Source: Michael Dooley (1994), 'A Retrospective on the Debt Crisis', paper prepared for the Fiftieth Anniversary of Essays in International Finance, Princeton University, table 2.[4]

with their credits going from \$115 billion to \$252 billion between 1982 and 1992, or an increase of 120 per cent).

On the recommendation of or at the injunction of the IMF and the World Bank, the indebted countries use loans that they obtain from public creditors (IMF, World Bank, states) to repay the commercial banks, which have no intention of lending them any more money. Not until they have been fully repaid.

However, not only do the loans made by public creditors increase the debt stock that will have to be repaid in any case, but they are far too modest to repay the colossal debts owed to the banks, particularly as the interest rates are extremely high. Concerning the exorbitant interest rates paid by the developing countries, the UNDP has this to say in the *Human Development Report 1992*:

During the 1980s, when interest rates were at 4 per cent in the industrialized countries, the developing countries were bearing an effective interest rate of 17 per cent. On the outstanding debt of over a thousand billion dollars, that represents a cost increase of 120 billion dollars on top of the net transfers on debt which are negative and came to 50 billion dollars in 1989.[5]

The question of negative net transfer on debt mentioned in this UNDP report is fundamental, and deserves closer scrutiny.

THE DEBATE INSIDE THE WORLD BANK ON CALCULATING THE NET TRANSFER ON DEBT

In 1984, the debate over this issue caused a rumpus in the World Bank. For that very year, a team of Bank economists, led by Sidney Chernick and Basil Kavalsky, produced a report that questioned the Bank's presentation of external debt flows.[6] Hitherto, the Bank had only considered net flows on debt, which it defined as the difference between the capital lent and the capital repaid, without counting the interest. This team of economists took a different stance, by declaring that interest payments should be included in the calculation so that the debt problem could be presented more realistically.

Table 15.2 illustrates the crux of the debate. It shows how the amount of total external debt increased between 1979 and 1987. Using the World Bank's traditional approach, i.e., without including interest payments, the transfer appears positive throughout the period considered. Such a presentation of the transfers leads one to wonder how anyone could realize that a debt crisis broke out in 1982 and has been carrying on until now.

On the other hand, using the approach advanced by the Bank's team of economists, the result is totally different. It can be seen clearly that the transfer was positive until 1982 and became negative as of 1983. It is perfectly justifiable to calculate the net transfer on debt by deducting the amounts repaid in terms of both capital and interest, from the amounts lent. Moreover, the fact that the crisis was caused by a rise in interest rates can only be seen and understood when the interest payments are taken into account.

The report received a cold reception when it reached the management level of the Bank. Ernest Stern, one of the Bank's senior members and vice-president for Operations, sent a fax saying: 'I am not prepared to circulate a paper which is analytically based on the net transfer concept.'[7] In his view, there was no question of presenting the payment of interest as a burden since it was simply the remuneration for capital lent. And that was that.

After a meeting of the New York Federal Reserve to which the Bank had been invited, Ernest Stern wrote a memorandum to the Bank's managing committee in which he said: 'the issue of net transfers was raised and was greeted with a veritable firestorm of negative comments, from several governors and other participants. The World Bank was also attacked by several speakers for having endorsed this concept.'[8] The subject was taboo.

Such an outcry clearly shows that it was a particularly sensitive and important issue. It is impossible to grasp the full significance of debt repayment without including the payment of interest as well as the repayment of the capital. Table 15.3 uses the same procedure as the previous one applied to Latin America and the Caribbean. The Bank's erroneous traditional presentation only reveals a slight problem of negative transfer on debt, and one limited to 1983. On the other hand, taking the interest paid into account reveals the true situation, that transfers were overwhelmingly negative from 1983.

Calculations have shown that between 1982 and 1985, transfers from Latin America to creditors represented 5.3 per cent of the continent's gross domestic product (GDP). The burden is enormous when you consider, by way of comparison, that the reparations imposed on Germany by the Treaty of Versailles came to 2.5 per cent of the German GDP between 1925 and 1932.[9]

For the Bank's managing committee, the internal debate over net transfers had a direct bearing upon its interests as a creditor. The Bank (and also the IMF) wanted to maintain its status as a privileged creditor since this enabled it to claim a right to prior repayment over

Table 15.2 Total external debt incurred by developing countries, 1979–87 (US$ million)

All developing countries	1979	1980	1981	1982	1983	1984	1985	1986	1987
Total external debt	427,421	540,923	628,610	715,788	781,947	826,434	929,186	1,020,494	1,166,248
Net transfer without interest payments (i.e. net flow)	67,298	94,821	96,739	83,194	45,366	42,397	38,208	36,327	48,037
Net transfer with interest payments	44,247	51,359	40,708	20,341	−14,282	−27,744	−27,614	−24,846	−12,895

Source: World Bank, *Global Development Finance*, 2005

Table 15.3 Total external debt incurred by Latin America and the Caribbean, 1975–87 (US$ million)

Latin America and the Caribbean	1979	1980	1981	1982	1983	1984	1985	1986	1987
Total external debt	197,472	242,835	295,301	333,142	361,668	376,004	387,807	406,001	442,010
Net transfer without interest payments	35,901	45,710	54,261	37,893	−317	6,211	4,537	2,276	8,515
Net transfer with interest payments	23,221	21,359	21,413	299	−34,971	−29,040	−30,204	−27,774	−19,814

Source: World Bank, *Global Development Finance*, 2005

other creditors – private or bilateral. Ernest Stern explained, in an internal note made in preparing a speech that the president of the Bank was to give at the World Economic Forum in Davos in January 1984, that the Bank should refrain from asking commercial banks to maintain positive net transfers (including interest paid) as this could have a backlash for the Bank. For naturally, such a requirement could also be applied to the Bank. The issue should therefore be fudged by referring only to net loans, or net flows on debt, thus excluding interest payments from the calculation. There follows an extract from this internal note:

If we hold the commercial bank responsible for maintaining net transfers... then we are saying that... the World Bank itself at some future point can be held responsible for not maintaining positive net transfers. We are arguing in other fora that one thing that distinguishes the World Bank from other banks, and justifies our separate treatment in rescheduling, is that we maintain net disbursements – not net transfers. If we accept the net transfer argument in a public speech by the President, our basis for rejecting attempts to draw us into rescheduling when our net transfer payments are no longer positive will be much weaker.[10]

Two important points emerge from the end of this extract. First, that the World Bank's leader already foresaw that the net transfer between the Bank and its clients should also become negative; and second, that he was worried that as a result, the Bank would no longer be able to refuse the rescheduling of debts owed to it.

The next table shows transfer on debts owed to the Bank. Using the method preferred by Ernest Stern, transfer appears to remain positive. By applying the alternative approach, the transfer becomes negative as from 1987.[11]

There is one more reason why the Bank refused to discuss negative transfers. In the 1980s, middle-income countries like Mexico, Brazil, Argentina, Venezuela and Yugoslavia, were the main countries affected by the debt crisis. They were also the World Bank's main clients. These countries funded it through interest payments (added to the repayment of borrowed capital). Indeed, the World Bank owed its positive results to the interest paid by the middle-income countries that made use of its services. The rich countries did not finance the World Bank (the IBRD) since the latter borrowed on the financial markets. The World Bank used its IDA branch to lend to poor countries. In other words, it was the indebted middle-income countries who enabled the Bank to lend to the poor countries at low

Table 15.4 Debt owed to the World Bank by developing countries, 1979–87 (US$ million)

All developing countries	1979	1980	1981	1982	1983	1984	1985	1986	1987
Debt owed to the World Bank (IBRD)	24,356	28,570	33,706	33,426	46,612	63,411	83,372	79,871	80,981
Net transfer without interest payments	3,972	4,229	5,144	5,556	5,100	5,667	5,027	3,743	3,329
Net transfer with interest payments	2,239	2,217	2,728	2,700	1,838	837	–767	–2,801	–2,738

Source: World Bank, *Global Development Finance*, 2005

interest rates without making a loss. The Bank had to conceal this fact since the middle-income countries, were they aware of it, could then have demanded the right to examine the Bank's policies towards the poorest countries. But defining that policy is the prerogative of the rich countries that control the Bank.

INTELLECTUAL TERRORISM WITHIN THE WORLD BANK

The World Bank historians claim that a system of spying was officially set up under the presidency of Alden W. Clausen with a view to detecting people who deviated from the Bank's managing committee's politico-economic line. The Bank historians say:

Between early 1983 and 1986, the Bank's Personnel Department informed the institution's senior managers that the Economics Department had adopted an 'intelligence' system to detect staff divergences from establishment positions, that it was categorizing staff by schools of economic thought and openly favouring 'loyalists', and that it was hiring staff on fixed-term contracts to render them more pliable. ERS (Economic Research Staff), the personnel people said, increasingly was seen as a unit selling ideology instead of objective research.[12]

Intellectual terrorism and neoliberal obscurantism were such that, during Anne Krueger's term as vice-president and chief economist, out of 37 researchers at management level of the research department, 29 left between 1983 and 1986.[13] Even more seriously for the institution's functioning, for two years more than ten posts remained vacant because no-one in the other services wanted to take the place of those who had left.

The World Bank historians report a crisis that arose between the World Bank's leadership, especially Anne Krueger, and the editor of a new World Bank review, *WB Economic Review*, Mark Leiserson. In 1986, Leiserson, backed by the entire editorial committee, had decided to publish an article by Jeffrey Sachs written in 1985. Anne Krueger prevented publication of the article. The editor resigned in protest after having tried in vain to persuade the Bank leaders to respect the editorial committee. This was not an isolated phenomenon as a few months later, the editor of another World Bank review, *WB Research Observer*, also resigned for similar reasons.

When you consider that Sachs had just finished setting up a very tough structural adjustment plan for Bolivia, and was thus in the neoliberal camp of the World Bank and the IMF, you can appreciate the degree of intellectual terrorism and obscurantism wielded by Krueger, the Bank's chief economist, on those in the Bank who cautiously tried to give people from outside the institution a chance to make themselves heard. Krueger did not like Sachs' proposal that the World Bank and the IMF should ask commercial banks to agree to cancel the debts of extremely indebted countries. In short, Sachs was proposing that the private sector should make an effort, and Krueger found that quite unacceptable! Bank historians acknowledge that even the Bank's most important publication, *World Debt Tables*, came in for censorship.[14]

Anne Krueger left office in 1987. In 2000, she became no. 2 in the IMF, and occupied that post until August 2006. However, it is important not to see things in personal terms. Krueger acts as the representative of the US administration. She is no unfortunate accident in the history of the IMF and the World Bank.

RADICAL CHANGES IN WORLD BANK DISCOURSE ON DEVELOPING COUNTRIES AND THEIR LEADERS

Until the debt crisis broke out, the World Bank could not praise the leaders of the countries enough, in a desire to encourage them to take on debts and follow the policies the WB recommended. Some time after the start of the crisis, there was a radical change of tone. The Bank criticized the governments of the developing countries and blamed them for the crisis. On no account was it going to examine its own responsibilities.

The change is clearly apparent in the following two quotations. In 1982, just before the outbreak of the crisis, the Bank wrote in the *World Development Report*:

the developing countries, despite the rise in their current account deficits from $40 billion in 1979 to $115 billion in 1981, have been much more successful than the industrialized countries in adjusting to the new situation.[15]

Four years later, it claimed the opposite (*World Development Report 1986*):

at the root of the poor performance and debt problems of developing countries lies their failure to adjust to the external developments that have taken place since the early 1970s, coupled with the magnitude of the external shocks.[16]

In 1984, one of the Bank's economists, Carlos Diaz-Alejandro, produced a qualified analysis of the developing countries' attitudes in the crisis, with emphasis on the fact that they had been subject to powerful external forces. Ernest Stern retorted:

The countries which borrowed $10–15 billion a year are playing in the big league. They thought they had the capacity – they often said so. They did so with their eyes open. They were very proud of what they were doing at the time – and much of what they did was sound. But they miscalculated. That can happen, and the cost of miscalculation can be high. But, if they want to be partners in an open and interlinked international economic system, it is time that they equip themselves to do so properly, and you should not put the burden of failure on the shoulders of everyone but themselves – it is not so. I believe it is a view they, in fact, share.[17]

There were several aims behind the Bank's attitude here. First, it sought to avoid criticism for the policy of indebtedness that it had been recommending for decades before the crisis and especially in the 1970s. Second, it wished to convince its partners that they should apply radical austerity policies within the framework of structural adjustment without demanding an effort of solidarity on the part of the governments of the rich countries.

Stanley Fisher, who replaced Anne Krueger as the Bank's chief economist in 1987, wrote in an internal memorandum in 1990:

I very much fear giving them [the less developed countries] any encouragement to believe the international community will do much to help them, and thus tend to emphasize that they have to handle their own problems...[18]

As the Bank historians point out:

Anyone interested in the intellectual history of the debt crisis would be struck by the degree to which the intellectual debate was dominated by voices from the US, in contrast to the virtual absence of voices from the countries bearing the brunt of the crisis.[19]

Later they add that the studies published by the World Bank reflect the political interests of its principal shareholders, especially the USA and major commercial banks.

COMPLICITY BETWEEN BANKERS OF THE NORTH AND THE RULING CLASSES OF THE SOUTH

Several studies show the link between the growing indebtedness of the Latin American countries in the 1970s and 1980s and capital flight from the South to the North. A very large portion of the money lent by Northern bankers returned to their coffers in the form of deposits. The Bank historians say of this:

The ratio of capital flight to the increase in external debt in the period 1978–82 is estimated to have ranged from 50 to 100 percent for Argentina, Mexico, and Venezuela. In the case of Brazil it was of the order of 10 percent.[20]

Other studies, one of which is presented in Table 15.5, produce results that corroborate this.

Table 15.5   Capital flight from selected Latin American countries, 1973–87 (US$ million and percentages)

Country	Capital flight (1973–87)	Stock assets abroad in (1987)	Assets abroad as % of the External debt (1987)
Argentina	29,469	43,674	76.9
Brazil	1,556	20,634	18.3
Colombia	1,913	2,994	19.5
Mexico	60,970	79,102	73.3
Peru	2,599	4,148	23.0
Venezuela	38,815	48,027	131.5

Source: IFRI, Ramses 93, Paris, 1992, p. 235
Based on M. Pastor, 'Capital flight from Latin America', World Development, January 1990

The World Bank historians draw an extremely pertinent conclusion from all this:

Capital flight increasingly placed private assets in overseas havens, in the very banks that held national debt. The elite of Latin American countries were unlikely to countenance any scheme entailing default that would place their private assets at risk.[21]

Indeed, the affluent elite of the developing countries had clearly no interest in their country suspending payments on its external debt.

To end this section, how to resist the pleasure of reproducing the delicate exchange of internal notes between Stanley Fisher of the World Bank and Jacob Frenkel, his colleague at the IMF? The IMF had published in a study an optimistic prognosis of the end of capital flight and its return to its country of origin. Fisher writes to his IMF colleague:

Bank staff are concerned with the Fund's projections of substantial return capital flight in the financial gap analysis for some countries. We are unaware of the economic analysis on which such projections are based, and believe that it would generally be a self-denying prophesy to argue that a financing gap will be closed by return capital flight, which depends above all on confidence in overall macroeconomic and financial stability.[22]

Jacob Frenkel replies:

the issue you raise concerning projections of return capital flight in financial gap analysis is one which, as you are aware, *embraces considerations other than purely analytical ones*[23] [my emphasis].

In other words, the IMF makes optimistic projections for political reasons.

STRUCTURAL ADJUSTMENT IN EVERY DIRECTION

In a book published in 1974, the American economist Cheryl Payer, a critic of the IMF and the World Bank, lists the measures that the IMF imposes on developing countries that call on its services:

- abolition or liberalization of control of currency exchange and imports;
- devaluation of the currency;
- restrictive monetary policies to control inflation, as follows:
  a) raised interest rates and, in some cases, an increase in exchange reserves;
  b) control of the public deficit: spending cuts; increases in taxes and tariffs for public services and companies; abolition of subsidies on consumer products;
  c) limits on salary rises in the civil service;
  d) dismantling of price controls;
- greater hospitality for foreign investments.

In order to define these measures, Payer had analyzed IMF policy as applied in the 1960s in the Philippines, Indonesia, Brazil, Chile, India, Yugoslavia and Ghana.

From 1981–82 on, when the debt crisis broke, a considerable number of countries called upon the services of the IMF (often under pressure from their main creditors, whether public or private), to try to solve the problem of their balance of payments. The IMF then had greater powers at its disposal to generalize the economic measures listed above. The whole set of measures was to become increasingly known by the expression 'structural adjustment policy'.

One of the bitter ironies of history, as was mentioned earlier, was when the price of petrol shot up in 1973 and the IMF declared that no structural adjustment was necessary. Yet the oil crisis had considerably modified the international situation. Oil-exporting countries saw a huge increase in their foreign currency revenues, while there was a huge demand for foreign currency on the part of the non-oil-producing developing countries.

In a book edited by John Williamson and published in 1990, an IMF functionary reports:

The worry at this time (that is, the oil crisis of 1973) was that countries might try to adjust too fast for such an attempt if it were carried out collectively could lead to a regrettable deepening of the global recession.[24]

When the debt crisis broke out as a consequence of the combined effects of the rise in interest rates decreed by the US Federal Reserve and the fall in prices of raw materials, the IMF and the World Bank completely modified their version of what had happened. They blamed the debt crisis largely on the oil crisis. Suddenly, the adjustment they had deemed unnecessary in the mid-1970s became unavoidable.

The World Bank pioneered the launch of the first structural adjustment loans in 1980. It was on the initiative of Robert McNamara that the Bank initiated these new loans. McNamara used the following prediction to justify the policy: after the second oil crisis in 1979, the price of oil would continue to rise throughout the 1980s. (In fact he was wrong, the opposite happened.) This meant that the developing countries should carry out structural adjustment.[25]

The adjustment measures presented by McNamara were those outlined above. Between 1980 and 1983, the Bank granted 14 structural adjustment loans to nine countries.[26]

Throughout the 1980s, there were regular clashes between the Bank and the IMF who could not seem to manage to coordinate their actions. This led to a concordat between the two institutions in 1989.[27] The following year, in 1990, the concept of the Washington Consensus was born, codifying the policies to be adhered to within the structural adjustment framework.[28] To the measures listed by Cheryl Payer and cited above were added a dimension of mass privatization and a policy of cost recovery in sectors like education, health, water distribution, etc. Note that the Washington Consensus concerns not only the IMF and the World Bank, but also the US executive represented by the Treasury. The novelty of the Washington Consensus was not so much in the economic measures to be applied (most of which were already in effect) as in the public proclamation of an agreement between the Bretton Woods institutions and the executive.

As well as this, the World Bank produces an enormous number of studies and reports that aim to provide a theoretical foundation and codification for structural adjustment policy. Among these, one report is of particular interest: *Accelerated Development in Africa South of the Sahara*, edited by the economist Elliot Berg. It emanated from an order from Robert McNamara. This report was to underpin the World Bank's policy line for a long period. Emphasis was placed on the lack of adequate support given to private initiative and over-reliance on the public sector.

The report advocated increased aid for cash crops along with even more reduction of subsistence crops. Berg and his team felt that on no account should countries aim for nutritional self-sufficiency, for, they wrote, 'most African countries have a distinct comparative advantage in the area of cash crops'. Far better to export tropical products and import other foodstuffs, since 'a policy of self-sufficiency based on sacrificing cash crops would prove costly in terms of lost revenue'.[29] The report criticized foreign aid for having reinforced the public sector! It blamed African leaders for most of the misfortunes of Africa while exonerating the international financial institutions and the countries of the North!

The Berg Report might be seen as the World Bank's answer to the Organization of African Unity's (OAU) Lagos Plan adopted in 1980. The Bank's leadership was astonished by the negative reactions the Berg Report received, particularly as the African officials at the Bank had approved the report without a murmur. The Bank's management committee was taken off-guard and had to ask two external experts to sound out the African leaders on what they thought of the Bank. The results of the survey confirmed their worst fears: the Bank's image was frankly terrible.

The World Bank's historians sharply denounced the Bank's theoretical output during the 1980s and the way the Bank and the IMF shared the roles in this field:

The Bank emerged as the headquarters, the fountainhead – some half-jokingly said the Vatican – of neo-orthodox development economics. It was the most authoritative articulation of the longer-term side of the so-called Washington consensus (the IMF dominated the short run) concerning appropriate relations between states and markets, including international and interacting national economic policies.[30]

TIMID ATTEMPTS AT RESISTANCE ON THE PART OF THE DEVELOPING COUNTRIES

The divide-and-rule strategy drawn up in Washington when the crisis broke out was in full spate. Latin American governments did not have the political will to create a united front to deal with the crisis and the creditors.

In January 1984 there was to be a secret meeting in Cuzco, Peru, between the finance ministers of Argentina, Brazil, Colombia, Mexico and Peru. The plan was to try to agree on a common strategy. The meeting was called off at the last minute owing to the sudden resignation of the Peruvian minister, Carlos Rodriguez Pastor, who was to have hosted it. The decision to cancel the meeting came so late in the day that one of the ministers invited actually arrived at the meeting venue, not having been informed in time.[31]

Richard Webb, one of the World Bank historians, had been governor of the Central Bank of Peru. He reported that in June 1984, Peru was confronted with a dilemma: whether to continue servicing its external debt and cancel imports needed for growth, or to go ahead with the imports needed to maintain growth and only partially suspend debt repayments. The government had just failed to meet the budget austerity goals demanded by the IMF. As governor of the central bank, Webb suggested that Peru should declare unilaterally a partial moratorium, which caused panic in the government. Webb was accused by the prime minister of the time of 'stabbing the country in the back'. Dismissal proceedings were started against him, and he was accused of having destroyed Peru's financial credibility abroad.[32]

When Alan García, then President of Peru, announced in 1985 that henceforth his country would devote no more than 10 per cent of export revenues to repaying the debt, the World Bank made an internal study of the issue and concluded that should García carry out this plan, Peru would be able to manage very well, provided it spent the money saved on bolstering up its economy. Obviously, the results of this study were never published.[33]

The Argentine economists Alfredo Eric Calcagno and Alfredo Fernando Calcagno summarized the experiment that Peru carried out from August 1985:

In August 1985, the government of president Alan García made known its decision to no longer pay more than the equivalent of 10 per cent of its export revenues, giving priority to multilateral financial organizations. Thus the net transfers which had been negative to the tune of –488 million dollars in 1984 and –595 million in 1985 became positive at 112 million dollars in 1986, 89 million in 1987 and 90 million in 1988. Peru was subjected neither to reprisals nor to trade restrictions; in 1986 and 1987 it increased its imports by an extraordinary amount (by 44 per cent and 18 per cent respectively) in spite of a fall in exports of 15 per cent in 1986 (these showed a slight recovery in 1987). Concerning external finance, non-payment of the major part of the debt largely compensated for the breaking off of loans from private financiers and the reduction in official and multilateral loans. In 1986 and 1987, the gross domestic product increased by 8.9 per cent and 6.5 per cent respectively, sustained by the fact that more domestic demands were met by national productive capacity and by an increase in imports made affordable by the reduction in outpayments on the debt. However there was a shortage of big investments over this period and the dynamizing effects had fizzled out by 1988, when the GDP fell by 7.5 per cent and inflation rose sharply. So in fact Peru's crisis over the subsequent years was linked to problems of internal economic policy rather than external trade sanctions or adverse effects of cutting down on debt repayments. On the contrary, the reduced amounts disbursed for external payments opened up an opportunity that the government failed to make the best use of.[34]

During the 1980s, other Latin American countries totally or partially suspended payments of their external debts for several months[35] but despite the large campaign led by the Cuban government in 1985, no common strategy was adopted. The campaign led by Fidel Castro on the theme 'The debt cannot be paid' enjoyed a sympathetic reception among social organizations and left-wing parties of the continent but a cooler one from its governments.

Nevertheless, Cuba's 1985 initiative found an echo beyond the borders of Latin America – in Sub-Saharan Africa, for example. The young President of Burkina Faso, Thomas Sankara, made the following address to the African heads of state present at the 25th conference of the Organization of African Unity (OAU) on 29 July 1987 in Addis Ababa:[36]

In debt we see neocolonialism in another guise, with the colonialists recast as 'technical assistants'. In fact, we should say technical assassins. And they are the ones who offered us funding, and financial backers. [...] Those financial backers were recommended to us, we were advised to turn to them. We were shown enticing files and financial packages. We got ourselves into debt for the fifty, sixty years ahead and even more. In other words, we were persuaded to compromise our people for upwards of fifty years.

The debt in its present form is a carefully organized reconquest of Africa, forcing its growth and development to obey norms which are completely foreign to it. So that each of us will become a financial slave, which means a slave, of those who had the opportunity, the cunning, the dishonesty to place funds at our disposal which we would have to repay. [...] Who, among us here present, does not wish to see the debt quite simply cancelled? Those who do not wish it can leave, take a plane and go straight to the World Bank and pay up. I would not like Burkina Faso's proposal to be seen as coming from young, immature politicians without experience. Neither would I like people to think that only revolutionaries speak in these terms. I would like them to acknowledge that we are motivated merely by obligation and objectivity. I can give examples of both revolutionaries and non-revolutionaries, among those who have said we should not pay the debt. I will cite, for example, Fidel Castro. He has already said that we should not pay. He is a lot older than me, even if he is a revolutionary.

Three months later, the impetuous Thomas Sankara was assassinated. Since then, his country has become a docile pupil of the World Bank, the IMF and the Paris Club under the leadership of Blaise Compaoré.

Jean-Philippe Peemans puts in a nutshell the relationship of complicity between the World Bank, the IMF and the governments of the developing countries that show themselves to be good pupils:

For the South, the role of international institutions like the IMF and the World Bank has been essential in this area, as the governments that do as they are told are guaranteed permanent access to multilateral credit. This guarantees them permanent access to global flows, however much their national economy may contract due to adjustment. These external flows enable capital holders to invest their assets abroad with no trouble, while the debt grows in proportion to their withdrawal of capital.[37]

SHOULD THE DEBT BE CANCELLED?

In October 1985, James Baker, the new secretary of the US Treasury, announced a plan aiming to solve the problems of the 15 highly indebted middle-income countries.[38] The plan was proclaimed with much media coverage during the annual meeting of the IMF and the World Bank in Seoul.[39] Debt cancellation had yet to be mentioned.

Inside the World Bank, in a small inner circle, the debate had begun over whether or not it was necessary to cancel part of the debt of certain countries, especially Argentina, but no-one would commit publicly to such a measure. In the draft copy of the *World Development Report 1988* there appeared a sentence on the need for partial cancellation of the concessional debt. It did not appear in the final version.[40] Among the arguments against cancellation was one that still comes up over and over again two decades later. It is that once a country has benefited from cancellation, it will find it hard to regain access to credit. This argument is and always has been totally fallacious – in fact, the opposite happens. Generally, as soon as a country has benefited from debt reduction, the commercial banks offer to lend it money as its subsequent capacity to repay has been improved.

In 1992 Stanley Fisher explained that, throughout a large part of the 1980s, the US, British (Margaret Thatcher) and German (Helmut Kohl) governments prevented any discussion about debt cancellation.[41]

The turning point when debt reduction (i.e., partial cancellation) was at last envisaged came in 1988, at the G7 in Toronto, in recognition of the failure of all previous policies. The poorest countries were promised cancellation[42] once the USA had changed its mind on the subject. For the first time, in 1990 in Houston, the G7 extended the possibility of partial cancellation to highly indebted middle-income countries like Mexico, Argentina, Brazil and the Philippines. This change of heart was initiated by Washington in March 1989 under the George Bush Senior administration while Nicholas Brady was secretary of the Treasury. Once again, the US government sets the tone. The IMF, the World Bank and the G7 just go along with it.

The Brady Plan consisted of restructuring part of the debt of a series of middle-income countries through the issue of new debt paper called 'Brady bonds'. When the indebted countries issued their Brady bonds, bankers of the North accepted a reduction of their credit. In exchange, they were guaranteed generous returns. To issue Brady bonds, the countries concerned first had to buy US Treasury bonds as a guarantee. Thus the indebted countries found themselves financing the policy of indebtedness of the world's most powerful country.[43]

At first, the Brady Plan seemed to work. The successful outcome for Mexico and its President Salinas de Gortari was trumpeted, to the extent that in 1994 the very neoliberal British weekly, *The Economist*, proclaimed Carlos Salinas de Gortari to be one of the great men of the twentieth century. In December that year, Mexico was struck down by the Tequila crisis and went into its deepest recession in 60 years! A few years later, Carlos Salinas de Gortari and his brother Raul were prosecuted and charged with fraud and massive embezzlement by the Mexican judiciary. Raul Salinas de Gortari served his prison sentence while Carlos Salinas chose exile in Ireland where he works for the Dow Jones Corporation, which among other things owns the *Wall Street Journal*. The Mexican judicial authorities managed to get their counterparts in Switzerland to order Swiss banks to cede back to Mexico the money embezzled by the Salinas brothers and deposited in their coffers.

In the second half of the 1990s, it was clear that the 1982 debt crisis had not been resolved. Measures to reduce the debt had failed. Structural adjustment policies had made countries vulnerable to financial speculation. This led to a succession of financial crises for the major indebted countries. Mexico was the first to be affected at the end of 1994, then the countries of South-East Asia and Korea in 1997–98, Russia in 1998, Brazil in 1999, and in 2000–01 Argentina and Turkey. As for the poorest countries, the partial cancellation of debt conceded to a few good pupils at the G7 summit in Toronto in 1988, and to a few more in London in 1991, Naples in 1994, Lyon in 1996 and Cologne in 1999, has not provided any lasting solution.

16
Presidents Barber Conable
and Lewis Preston (1986–95)

The Republican Congressman Barber Conable succeeded the banker Allan W. Clausen for a term that started in July 1986 and ended in August 1991. James Baker, Secretary of the Treasury, and Ronald Reagan chose him because of his thorough knowledge of all the mysteries of the US Congress. Indeed, the executive had its hands full with its parliamentary majority since several Republican representatives questioned the weight of the World Bank in US foreign policy (see chapter 5). Barber Conable had 20 years' experience in Congress and had chaired the committee on finance. Baker and Reagan wanted Conable to appease the recalcitrant Republicans and persuade them to let the White House steer the World Bank. The issue was complex and Conable soon found himself in a precarious situation. While he wished to expand the Bank's activities, the White House made some concessions to the recalcitrant elements, limited the resources granted to the Bank and demanded that Conable reduce its expenditures. When he did this a number of senior executives and all of the staff turned against him. In 1987 the internal reorganization of the Bank was a veritable game of musical chairs. Several top managers resigned.[1]

Conable also met other obstacles. Several of the Bank's large-scale model projects were challenged by the people concerned and by environmental associations. The three projects that prompted the most determined protests were the Polonoroeste programme in Brazilian Amazonia,[2] the various dams on the Narmada river in India, the transmigration project and the Kedung Ombo dam in Indonesia.[3] The largest demonstration occurred in India where some 50,000 people from all parts of the country marched in the city of Harsud (Madhya Pradesh) in September 1989. A fourth WB programme also raised strong opposition from human rights organizations, namely the Ruzizi II hydroelectric project that concerned Zaire (as the Democratic Republic of Congo was then called) and Rwanda and involved the displacement of some 2,500 farmers without any significant compensation.[4] Conable promised that the Bank would in the future take the environmental impact into account and would see to it that affected people receive decent compensation.[5] This was truly a titanic task since in India alone the WB financed 32 projects involving the displacement of some 600,000 people from 1978 to 1990.[6]

In 1988, the World Bank–IMF annual assembly in West Berlin was greeted by 80,000 demonstrators who denounced their anti-social policies. This was the first mass demonstration against the Bretton Woods institutions.

The uprisings triggered by the policy of structural adjustment and the consequent deterioration in the 'adjusted' peoples' standards of living in the countries concerned led the WB to broach the issue of poverty after ten years of silence. The *World Development Report 1990* is entirely devoted to it.

It was also with Barber Conable as president that the Bank started to systematically refer to 'good governance'. In 1990 he told a number of African governors of the Bank:

Let me be frank: political uncertainty and arbitrary rule in so many sub-Saharan African countries are major obstacles to their development.... In saying this, I'm not talking politics. Rather, I'm speaking as a defender of increased openness and responsibility, of respect for human rights and the rule of law. Governability is linked to economic development. Donor countries are increasingly indicating that they will cease to back inefficient systems which do not meet the population's basic needs.[7]

This change in the Bank's policy reflects the change in Washington's policy towards the end of the 1980s. It is analyzed above in chapter 11 on Korea. The Bank's discourse on respect for the law and human rights was never evidenced in the conditionalities it imposed on countries under structural adjustment. Indeed, its discourse did not prevent it from supporting, for example, Suharto's dictatorship in Indonesia until 1998.

LEWIS PRESTON'S TERM OF OFFICE (1991–95)

With the appointment of Lewis Preston as president of the World Bank in 1991, President George Bush again placed a first-rate banker at the helm of the institution. Preston had up to then been CEO of

J.P. Morgan & Co. He had had a remarkable career at the head of this leading New York bank, allowing him to take full advantage of the debt crisis that broke in 1982.

Preston's mandate began in June 1991 with the huge political and financial scandal of the Bank of Credit and Commerce International's bankruptcy, which came close to directly implicating the World Bank. Specializing as it did in money laundering, the BCCI was closed by order of the British authorities in July 1991. Its closure is said to have induced the loss of some $20 billion for two million small savers. The BCCI was convicted of the following crimes: involvement in money laundering, bribery, support of terrorism, arms trafficking, the sale of nuclear technologies, the commission and facilitation of tax evasion, smuggling, illegal immigration and illicit purchases in the banking and property sectors. The BCCI was present in 78 countries with over 400 branches, and was closely related to the CIA.[8] Bruce Rich writes that the World Bank had occasionally used the BCCI for the disbursement of loans in African countries. He also establishes that several of the Bank's senior officers had close relationships with the BCCI's senior officers.[9]

Preston gave his first major speech on the occasion of a huge media circus staged by the World Bank and the IMF in Bangkok for their joint annual meeting in October 1991 (this was the first meeting held in a Third World country since Seoul in 1985). Fifteen thousand bankers and political leaders from all over the world met there for three days. The cost for the Thai authorities amounted to dozens of millions of dollars. Preston gave an enthusiastic speech supporting globalization and asserting that the Bank was close to poor people, attentive to environmental issues and committed to improving the lot of women. Here is a short excerpt:

Poverty reduction, to which I personally am fully committed, remains the World Bank Group's overarching objective [...] The World Bank Group takes into account the interest of the poor so that growth is equitable; environmental aspects so that development is sustainable... and the role of women who are vital to the development effort.[10] The future is bright, since the world is now one after the fall of the Berlin Wall.[11]

The challenge posed by the Bank was to include all East European countries in the globalized world. A few hundred yards away from where the meeting was being held, 20,000 people demonstrated against the new dictatorship that had been established in Thailand eight months earlier,[12] and demanded a return to democracy.

In December 1991 Lawrence H. Summers, the World Bank's chief economist, wrote a confidential memorandum on the 1992 *World Development Report* (which was being drafted). The report was entirely devoted to the environment in view of the Earth Summit due to be held in May 1992. Summers argued for exporting polluting industries to countries of the South, which are largely under-polluted, as a rational means of creating industrial development while alleviating the pressures of pollution in the North.

Here are two excerpts from Summers' memorandum: 'Shouldn't the World Bank be encouraging more migration of the dirty industries to the lesser developed countries?'; 'The economic logic behind dumping a load of toxic waste in the lowest wage countries is impeccable and we should face up to it.'[13] A favourable wind took this document to the environmental organization Greenpeace, which immediately made it public. The British neoliberal weekly *The Economist* published it at the end of December 1991,[14] just when Preston was beginning his first tour in Africa. He was set upon by journalists asking whether he approved of his chief economist when he wrote: 'I've always thought that under-populated countries in Africa are vastly under-polluted.'[15]

In February 1992 Willi Wapenhans, the Bank's vice-president, handed Preston a confidential assessment report on all projects financed by the Bank (almost 1,300 projects in progress in 113 countries). Its conclusions were alarming: 37.5 per cent of projects proved unsatisfactory when completed (as against 15 per cent in 1981), and only 22 per cent of the financial commitments conform to the Bank's instructions.

In May 1992, a few days before the beginning of the Earth Summit, the Bank's management received the results of the independent survey on the Narmada River dam in India. Preston had entrusted US representative Bradford Morse with coordinating the survey. The report considers that the dams and its canals would result in 240,000 displaced persons, not 100,000 as originally foreseen. Such conclusions caused panic in the Bank management. The report had to be kept secret until the Earth Summit was over. This goal was achieved.

The WB did very well out of the Earth Summit in Rio de Janeiro. It was attended by 118 heads of state and covered by some 9,000 journalists. At the end of it the Bank was entrusted with the management of the GEF (Global Environment Facility), i.e., the global funds for the environment through which the majority of amounts of monetary sums related to the implementation of Agenda 21 adopted at the end of the global meeting were to pass.

The World Bank would also support the transition of countries from the former Eastern bloc to a capitalist economy. This resulted in a large-scale sell-off of public companies that were privatized and given over to a new class of mostly *mafiosi* capitalists. Joseph Stiglitz, the Bank's chief economist from 1997 to 2000, shows very clearly that WB policy in Russia was far removed from the good governance it otherwise advocated. About the time when Preston was president of the Bank he writes:

It is not surprising that many of the market reformers showed a remarkable affinity to the old ways of doing business: in Russia, President Yeltsin,[16] with enormously greater powers than his counterparts in any Western democracy, was encouraged to circumvent the democratically elected Duma (parliament) and to enact market reforms by decree.[17]

Public companies were sold for peanuts: '... pressured by the United States, the World Bank and the IMF to privatize rapidly, [the Russian government] had turned over its state assets for a pittance'.[18] Privatization was a large-scale looting of the country for the benefit of oligarchs who invested part of their pilferage in the West in order to launder it and remove it from the reach of the law:

Privatization accompanied by the opening of the capital markets, led not to wealth creation but to asset stripping. It was perfectly logical. An oligarch, who has just been able to use political influence to garner assets worth billions, after paying only a pittance, would naturally want to get his money out of the country.[19]

During Preston's mandate the World Bank and the IMF celebrated in great style their fiftieth anniversary in Madrid. On this occasion a large coalition of social movements (among them the main trade unions in Spain, UGT and Worker's Commissions), Third World movements and NGOs came together under the name *The other voices of the earth* and organized a four-day conference with many debates and a demonstration by some 20,000 people who chanted, '50 years is enough'.

The end of Lewis Preston's term was marked by the Tequila crisis that hit Mexico from December 1994. Mexico was the first in a series of financial crises that would strike other emerging countries during the term of the next president, James Wolfensohn.

17

James Wolfensohn Switches on the Charm (1995–2005)

In 1995, Bill Clinton, the President of the United States, nominated James Wolfensohn, a New York banker, as the World Bank's ninth president.

Wolfensohn, born an Australian citizen, began his banking career in Sydney in 1959. From 1968 to 1977 he was one of the directors of the highly controversial London and New York banking group J. Henry Schroder.[1] According to Patrick Bond,[2] James Wolfensohn was the treasurer of the 'American Friends of Bilderberg', an anti-communist pressure group.[3] He left the Henry Schroder Bank to become an executive partner in Salomon Brothers, the investment bank. In 1980–81, Robert McNamara was looking for a successor, and Wolfensohn, who was thought to be on the list, became a US citizen so as to better qualify for the post.[4] However, President Reagan nominated Alden W. Clausen as the president of the World Bank, and Wolfensohn founded his own investment bank, James D. Wolfensohn Inc., which was a very active player in the flurry of mergers and acquisitions of the 1980s and through the first half of the 1990s, before being bought by Banker's Trust.

Wolfensohn became president of the Bank at a time when it had become urgent to restore its public image. Structural adjustment policies were getting very bad press and a series of financial crises were starting to hit the developing countries. It was necessary to quickly draw attention away by bringing back the terms 'poverty reduction', 'good governance' and loans for projects that respected the environment. There was an onslaught of PR, and Wolfensohn became an expert in dealing with the press. His charm and eloquence made a good impression.

ALLURING WAYS[5]

The HIPC initiative

The Highly Indebted Poor Countries (HIPC) initiative was launched in 1996, its aim being to offset the increasing demands for cancellation of debts to developing countries. With great press coverage, the Bank announced 'its' solution. There was immediately much criticism of the basic concept of the HIPC initiative and its ability to actually reach the goals or fulfil the aims it announced. At the end of Wolfensohn's mandate, its failure was patently obvious. Instead of the 42 countries that were supposed to benefit from up to 80 per cent cancellation of their debt as announced in 1996, or even 90 per cent as was said in June 1999 at the G8 in Cologne, in fact only 18 countries would see some reduction in their debt. While it was supposed to finally sort out the problem of the debt for these 42 countries, this initiative has turned into a fiasco: their debt went down from $218 billion to $205 billion, i.e., a reduction of only 6 per cent between 1996 and 2003.

From SAPs to PRSPs

Wolfensohn introduced the Poverty Reduction Strategy Programmes (PRSPs) to replace the much-discredited Structural Adjustment Programmes (SAPs) that had been the Bank's and IMF's main approach to development since the 1980s. In fact, only the name changed – the macroeconomic framework of privatization and liberalization remained the same. The World Bank and the IMF actually imposed more stringent conditions on their loans, because now they were working hand in hand with the WTO, which came into existence in 1995.[6] At the same time, the much-vaunted 'participation' of civil society – which was presented by the World Bank as a profound policy change – was very difficult to find or observe in reality.

The SAPRI initiative

The very first 'constructive engagement' exercise to which Wolfensohn committed the Bank was a three-way assessment of SAPs between the Bank, civil society and governments called SAPRI (Structural Adjustment Participatory Review), which was launched in 1997.

SAPRI was designed as a tripartite field-based exercise, with a Bank team appointed by Wolfensohn to develop a transparent and participatory global methodology for gathering and documenting evidence of the impacts of World Bank–IMF SAPs at local and national levels in seven countries. Walden Bello and Shalmali Guttal (2005) are devastating in their criticism:

Despite agreement on the common rules of the exercise and the review methodology, the World Bank team played an obstructionist role throughout the SAPRI process. For example, at public fora, instead of trying to listen to and learn from the evidence presented by civil society representatives about the impacts of SAPs, Bank staff almost always argued points and in the end, claimed that the fora presentations (which were part of the agreed-upon qualitative input) constituted 'anecdotal evidence'.

As the Bank's ability to control country processes decreased, so also did its ability to control the output of the Review. Even before the final and concluding national fora were reached, field investigations already indicated major problems in all aspects of adjustment programmes.

Reluctant to go public with these findings, the Bank team backed off from an earlier (written) agreement to present all SAPRI findings in a large public forum in Washington DC, with Wolfensohn present. Instead, the Bank team insisted on a closed technical meeting and a small session in Washington DC scheduled when Wolfensohn was not in town. Most important, the Bank now insisted that it and civil society each write separate reports. The Bank report used the Bank's own commissioned research as the basis for its conclusions and barely referred to the five-year SAPRI process. In August 2001, the Bank pulled out of SAPRI and buried the entire exercise, and except to say that it had learned a lot from SAPRI, the Bank did not commit itself to reshaping its lending policies based on the SAPRI findings.

On 15 April 2002, the full SAPRI report (under the name SAPRIN, to include findings from the two countries where civil society conducted investigations without Bank involvement) was released to the public and received immense media coverage.

Wolfensohn expressed regrets that he and his staff had not been in touch with SAPRI and promised to read the report and discuss it seriously in the near future. To date, however, neither the Bank, nor Wolfensohn have shown any commitment to review and make changes to their adjustment lending. On the contrary, structural adjustment policies continue to be the mainstay of Bank-Fund lending through PRSPs and the Poverty Reduction and Growth Facility (PRGF).[7]

Corruption

The World Bank's stated aim of promoting 'good governance' was very much contradicted by the revelations that came to the fore due to the Asian crisis. The Bank's relationship with the corrupt Suharto dictatorship in Indonesia continued well into the Wolfensohn era. According to Jeffrey Winters, a specialist on Indonesia, the Bank accepted erroneous statistics and tolerated the fact that 30 per cent of every dollar in aid it dispensed to the regime was siphoned off by corrupt individuals.

In Sub-Saharan Africa,

The Bank took more hits as news of corruption and malpractice came to light in Bank supported infrastructure projects. Prominent among these were the Lesotho Highlands Water Project (LHWP) and the Bujagali Falls dam in Uganda. In 2001, the Lesotho High Court started investigating charges of bribery against several major international dam-building companies and public officials in connection with the LHWP. Instead of supporting a nationally accountable legal process, the Bank quietly conducted its own internal investigation of three of the companies charged with paying bribes and concluded that there was insufficient evidence to punish them for corruption. In 2002, the Lesotho High Court eventually succeeded in convicting four companies for paying bribes, among them Acres International, a long term ally and pet contractor of the World Bank and who the Bank had cleared in its internal investigation. It took the Bank well over a year to eventually announce that it would disbar Acres International from World Bank contracts for a period of three years.[8]

THE WORLD COMMISSION ON DAMS (WCD)

Established in 1997, the World Commission on Dams was to conduct a comprehensive and independent global review of the effectiveness for development of large dams and to propose internationally acceptable standards for such projects. Over a period of two-and-a-half years, the WCD commissioned a massive volume of research and received nearly a thousand submissions from around the world relating to environmental, social, economic, technical and institutional factors on the performance of large dams.

Although the WCD worked independently from the World Bank, the Bank played a more active role in the development of the WCD Report than any other institution and was consulted at every stage of the WCD's work programme. Wolfensohn applauded the WCD process as a model for future multi-stakeholder dialogues. However, the inadmissible happened: the Bank rejected the WCD's findings because they went too far. The final report, 'Dams and Development: A New Framework for Decision-Making', was presented by Nelson Mandela in London in November 2000. Wolfensohn justified his refusal to follow the report's guidelines by saying that the Bank had to consult its shareholders and the relevant government agencies in the major dam-building countries. In a statement published on 27 March 2001, the Bank said:

Consistent with the clarification provided by the WCD Chair, the World Bank will not 'comprehensively adopt the 26 WCD guidelines', but will use them as a reference point when considering investments in dams.

It even added,

This was an unprecedented and highly productive dialogue between all parties. The World Bank believes that such dialogues are very important for the many controversial development issues, and will continue to engage in them in the future.[9]

The Bank's tactics are clear. Faced with criticism and opposition, the Bank itself announces the setting up of a participatory mechanism, commissions and actively participates in studies and reports, declaring its intention to take into account the results, and then, when the reports are published, uses evasive rhetoric about the future, while assuring the public that it will continue to engage in such 'highly productive dialogue' in the future.

The Extractive Industries Commission

The experience of the WCD was replayed in the Extractive Industries Review (EIR). Challenged in a public meeting by Friends of the Earth, Wolfensohn responded – to the surprise of his staff – that the Bank would undertake a global review to examine whether Bank involvement in extractive industries was consistent with its stated aim of poverty reduction.

Having learnt its lesson from the WCD process, the Bank kept a much tighter rein on the EIR, which was less independent and less participative than the WCD. However, the EIR Report, published in Lisbon on 11 December 2003, turned out to be a surprisingly strong document in spite of the Bank's interference. It firmly recommended that the Bank and its private sector arm, the International Finance Corporation (IFC), phase out their involvement in oil, mining and natural gas. The report demanded that the Bank shift its financing to renewable energy. The Report caused an outcry among private financiers (such as Citibank, ABN Amro, WestLB and Barclays) for whom Bank involvement in the oil, mining and gas industries is essential for as long as they are not able to totally finance such projects themselves.

In the 17 June 2004 edition of *The Financial Times*, Emil Salim, who presided over the EIR, published an opinion article in which he stated,

Having overseen the review, I came to the conclusion that the World Bank must radically alter its approach to supporting extractive projects – and even stop supporting some altogether. The reason for this conclusion was clear. The Bank is a publicly supported institution whose mandate is poverty reduction. Not only have the oil, gas and mining industries not helped the poorest people in developing countries, they have often made them worse off.

As with the WCD Report, the World Bank decided once again, in August 2004, to ignore most of the EIR Report's important recommendations. For example, it actually continued to defend the construction of the Chad–Cameroon pipeline.[10] The Bank continued to justify its direct involvement in extractive industries on the principle that this puts it in a position to ensure the industries' compliance with social and environmental standards!

JAMES WOLFENSOHN STRUGGLES WITH CIVIL SOCIETY

When Wolfensohn arrived at the World Bank in 1995, the '50 Years is Enough'[11] campaign was in full steam in the US and was gathering momentum throughout the world. Then came the Jubilee 2000 Coalition, which was especially strong in countries that are mainly Christian, in both the North and the South. The Jubilee 2000 campaign, which started in 1997 and ended in 2000, collected more than 20 million signatures on a petition asking the Bank to go further than the HIPC initiative and to 'cancel the backlog of unpayable debts of the most impoverished nations'. It also organized several large demonstrations, including the human chain of 80,000 people in Birmingham, UK during the G8 summit in May 1998, and the 35,000 demonstrators during the G8 in Cologne in June 1999.

The growing opposition between civil society and Wolfensohn came to the boil during the tumultuous World Bank–IMF annual meeting held in Prague in September 2000, which had to be cut short owing to massive demonstrations. Confronted with a list of thoroughly documented charges at the famous Prague Castle debate, Wolfensohn lost his cool, exclaiming, 'I and my colleagues feel good about going to work every day.' It was an answer that was matched only by IMF managing director Horst Koehler's equally famous line at the same debate: 'I also have a heart, but I have to use my head in making decisions.'

The World Bank has instigated a highly proactive approach towards NGOs and some local authorities, setting up a strategy of integration/ recuperation, which it calls 'soft loans'. These soft loans are destined to provide micro-credits (especially for NGOs concerned with women), to be used for local education and health initiatives and to best manage financial input from migrants. The Bank has created a specific structure for loans and donations to help NGOs. This strategy of the Bank to woo civil society and regain some legitimacy in the eyes of the public is producing results.

Wolfensohn played the open-to-dialogue card in order to defuse criticism of the Bank and to win over some of the contestation movements. The three initiatives in three different domains – SAPRI, the World Commission on Dams and the Extractive Industries Commission – were all aimed at bringing the Bank's critics around the table, and implied that the Bank was willing to change its way of working and to take their demands into account. In fact, this proved not to be the case. The Bank did not play by the rules since it rejected the results of these commissions. It was above all a lesson for those who were still hanging on to their illusions that negotiation could lead to a change in the Bank's policies and workings.

INTERNAL CRISES AND THE CRISIS OF LEGITIMACY

During Wolfensohn's mandate, in 1999–2000, the Bank's leadership went through an internal crisis resulting in the departure of two key members of staff, namely Joseph Stiglitz, the chief economist and vice-president of the Bank, who resigned at the end of 1999, under pressure from the secretary of the US Treasury, Lawrence Summers, and in June 2000 Ravi Kanbur, the director of the World Bank's annual *World Development Report*. Stiglitz and Kanbur were inside reformers whose departure was a clear message that there is no place for reform from within the Bank itself.

The World Bank is also strongly contested in the US Congress, as can be seen from the report of the Meltzer Commission, which was published in February 2000 (see next chapter).

THE END OF WOLFENSOHN'S SECOND MANDATE

The arrival of the conservative administration at the White House in 2001 complicated Wolfensohn's mandate. He spent his last four years as president acquiescing in the increasingly aggressive programme of G.W. Bush's administration. From time to time he dug his heels in, but invariably ended up doing what Bush and his team required him to do. He himself said in an interview shortly before the end of his mandate, 'I've had the impression from the administration that they are perfectly pleased with what has happened here in recent years.'[12]

In Afghanistan, as well as pledging $570 million and fronting the US effort to raise billions of dollars for reconstruction, Wolfensohn expressed interest in the Bank's participation in financing a fuel pipeline to channel massive gas reserves through Afghanistan from landlocked Turkmenistan to India or Pakistan, a project greatly desired by US energy corporations backed by US vice-president Richard Cheney.

In Iraq, Wolfensohn, under incentive from Washington, committed $3 billion to $5 billion for reconstruction and agreed to manage the Iraq Trust Fund to channel money to development projects undertaken by the occupying regime, especially those aimed at 'capacity building' in the private sector, a priority aim of the Bush administration.

Despite all his efforts, James Wolfensohn could not stop the erosion of his authority and prestige. No longer appreciated at the White House because of his sympathies with Bill Clinton and John Kerry – the Democrat candidate in 2004 – Wolfensohn was also increasingly mistrusted by those who had believed in his reformist rhetoric. It was perfectly obvious very early on that were George W. Bush to be elected for a second term, there was no chance of Wolfensohn's mandate being renewed in 2005. Indeed, in March 2005 Bush appointed one of his close collaborators as the president of the World Bank, namely Paul Wolfowitz, the deputy defense secretary.

As for James Wolfensohn, in 2005–06 he was charged with a mission in relation with the Bank in the Gaza Strip, but as a full-time job he joined the board of the largest international bank group, Citibank.

18
Debates in Washington at the Start of the Twenty-first Century

THE MELTZER COMMISSION ON THE IFI AT THE US CONGRESS IN 2000

The succession of crises that swept over the so-called emerging countries in the 1990s and the ensuing disastrous IMF and World Bank interventions provoked a worldwide debate concerning the future and the role of these Bretton Woods institutions. A number of establishment intellectuals played a part in these discussions, for instance, Allan Meltzer, Paul Krugman, Joseph Stiglitz and Jeffrey Sachs. At the same time, Congress in Washington has never been keen to provide additional financial means to the IMF to overcome such crises. All it ended up in doing was setting up an *ad hoc* bipartisan[1] commission. This commission, entitled the 'International Financial Institutions Advisory Commission' delivered its report at the start of 2000. The report focused on seven multilateral institutions: the IMF, the World Bank, the Inter-American Development Bank, the Asian Development Bank, the African Development Bank, the WTO and the Bank of International Settlements. This study is only concerned with the report's conclusions concerning the IMF and the World Bank.

The Meltzer Commission comprised eleven experts (six Republicans and five Democrats), parliamentarians, academics and bankers. Among them were Allan H. Meltzer (its president), Edwin Feulner (president of the extremely reactionary Heritage Foundation and former president of the Mont Pelerin Society) on the Republican side and Jeffrey Sachs, Fred Bergsten and Jerome Levinson on the Democrats'. A large part of the commission's work, including documentation of its internal disagreements, is available on the Internet.[2]

All the commission's meetings and hearings were held in public and since its work casts an interesting light on the terms of debate in Washington, it is worth scrutinizing in some detail.

A short resolution was adopted unanimously by the commission while the entire report was approved by eight votes to three. The three votes against were Democrats (Fred Bergsten, Jerome Levinson and Esteban Edward Torres). Two Democrats (including Jeffrey Sachs) voted with the Republicans.

The resolution adopted unanimously reads as follows:

(1). The IMF, the World Bank and the Regional Development banks should write off in their entirety all claims against Heavily Indebted Poor Countries (HIPCs) that implement an effective economic and social development strategy in conjunction with the World Bank and the regional development institutions, and (2). The IMF should restrict its lending to the provision of short term liquidity. The current practice of extending long-term loans for poverty reduction or other objectives should end.

The report is over a hundred pages long. Essentially, its recommendation is not that these multilateral institutions be abolished or somehow combined, but, instead, that they should be profoundly reformed. The report contains some extremely critical points concerning the political management of the IMF and the World Bank; it also severely lambastes the WTO. It proposes that the World Bank should completely stop its loans to those countries that already have access to financial markets and restrict itself to giving aid only to those countries that do not.

In a similar vein, the report states that the IMF must no longer grant short-term loans and ought to give up its mission of combating poverty, a mission that should only be the preserve of the World Bank and regional banks. It goes on to say that the Bank should henceforth be renamed the World Development Agency. The report also denounces the governments of the rich countries, the IMF and the World Bank for short-circuiting decision-making bodies and legislative authorities. In a similar vein, it criticizes the WTO for abusing its powers, commenting that the WTO does not have the automatic right to impose its rules on member states. Instead, WTO decisions must be endorsed by the parliaments of each member state.

Below are some of the more outstanding comments of the report. They start in a congratulatory fashion, praising the role of the US in the world, and go on to confirm the commission's neoliberal credentials.

These institutions, and the U.S. commitment to maintain peace and stability, have had remarkable results. In more than fifty postwar years, more people in more countries have experienced greater improvements in living standards than at any previous time.

Our former adversaries are now part of the expanding global market system.

The United States has been the leader in maintaining peace and stability, promoting democracy and the rule of law, reducing trade barriers, and establishing a transnational financial system.

The Commission believes that to encourage development, countries should open markets to trade, and encourage private ownership, the rule of law, political democracy and individual freedom.

What these Republican and Democrat establishment figures have to say here will cause few eyebrows to be raised. But it is the rest of the report that is more surprising. The commission criticizes the actions of the IMF and the G7 governments and takes issue with the shock policies imposed by the IMF and World Bank.

THE PRINCIPAL CRITIQUES IN THE MELTZER REPORT

Critique of the IMF intervention in the Mexican debt crisis

In August 1982 the Mexican government announced that it could not service its external debts. The IMF organized and supervised the administration of a plan to reschedule the private commercial debts that the Mexican government had incurred over the previous decade. IMF lending did not channel net new funding to Mexico. Rather it lent the money to enable Mexico to service the debt. *Mexico's debt increased*, but it avoided default. The IMF made its loans conditional on the implementation of a package of long-term economic reforms. *Many of the conditions required sacrifices by the local population, loss of jobs and deep reductions in living standards.* Other developing countries, particularly in Latin America, found that net private capital inflows declined or became negative.

Critique of the SAP imposed by the IMF

Transformation of the IMF into a source of long-term conditional loans *has made poorer nations increasingly dependent on the IMF* and has given the IMF a degree of influence over member countries' policymaking that is unprecedented for a multilateral institution. Some agreements between the IMF and its members specify scores of required policies as conditions for continued funding. *These programs have not ensured economic progress. They have undermined national sovereignty and often hindered the development of responsible, democratic institutions that correct their own mistakes and respond to changes in external conditions.*

The Meltzer Report criticizes the IFI intervention during the 1994 Mexican debt crisis

After the IMF, the U.S. Treasury, and the foreign creditors had been repaid, however, *the Mexican taxpayer was left with the bill*. The cost of the banking system bailout is currently estimated at roughly 20 percent of Mexico's annual GDP. Real income per capita in 1997, despite ups and downs, was no higher in 1997 than twenty years earlier. *Real wages of the lowest paid workers, those receiving the minimum wage, have fallen 50 per cent since 1985. Mexico's total (public and private) external debt, expressed in 1996 U.S. dollars, has grown fivefold over the period since 1973, or fourfold when expressed on a per capita basis.* Real wages are lower and the burden of financing the debt is much higher for each Mexican worker.

Critics also claimed that, by preventing or reducing the losses borne by international lenders, the IMF's 1995 Mexican program sent the wrong message to international lenders and borrowers. By preventing or reducing losses by international lenders, the IMF had implicitly signaled that, if local banks and other firm institutions incurred large foreign liabilities and governments guaranteed private debts, the IMF would provide the foreign exchange needed to honor the guarantees. Economists give the name 'moral hazard' to the incentive inherent in such guarantees.

Cutting government expenditure, raising taxes and interest rates and closing banks aggravated the crises.

The Meltzer Commission also criticizes the IMF in the pay of the G7

The G7 governments, particularly the United States, use the IMF as a vehicle to achieve their political ends. This practice subverts democratic processes of creditor countries by avoiding parliamentary authority over foreign aid or foreign policy and by relaxing budget discipline.

The IMF in the pay of the rich

Numerous studies of the effects of IMF lending have failed to find any significant link between IMF involvement and increases in wealth or income. *IMF-assisted bailouts of creditors in recent crises have had especially harmful and harsh effects on developing countries.* People who have worked hard to struggle out of poverty have seen their achievements destroyed, their wealth and savings lost, and their small businesses bankrupted. Workers lost their jobs, often without any safety net to cushion the loss. Domestic and foreign owners of real assets suffered large losses, while foreign creditor banks were protected. These banks received compensation for bearing risk, in the form of high interest rates, but did not have to bear the full (and at times any of the) losses associated with high-risk lending. The assistance that helped foreign bankers also protected politically influential domestic debtors, encouraged large borrowing and extraordinary ratios of debt to equity.

The commission disapproves of the IMF's policies in Latin America

The Commission does not approve of the IMF's policies in Latin America in the 1980s and in Mexico in 1995, or in many other cases. IMF loans to these countries protected U.S. and other foreign banks, financial institutions, and some investors at great cost to the citizens of the indebted countries. The loans delayed resolution of the 1980s crises by permitting lenders and borrowers to report the debt as fully serviced. [...] *The Commission believes that lenders who make risky loans or purchase risky securities should accept the true losses when risks become unpleasant realities.*

The commission criticizes the interlinked World and regional banks

There is a wide gap between the Banks' rhetoric and promises and their performance and achievements. The World Bank is illustrative. In keeping with a mission to alleviate poverty in the developing world, *the Bank claims to focus its lending on countries denied access to the capital markets. Not so*; 70 per cent of World Bank non-aid resources flow to 11 countries that enjoy easy access to the capital markets.

The total resource flow to public-sector activities in countries without capital market access, but with stabilizing policies and institutions, was $2.5 billion for the seven years 1993–1999. This is less than 2 per cent of World Bank Group financing, excluding aid.

The future of the World Bank group according to Meltzer

The World Bank's role as lender would be significantly reduced. The commission adds that above all the Bank will have to make donations. Moreover, the commission thinks the World Bank no longer has a *raison d'être*.

The International Finance Corporation should become an integral part of the redefined World Development Agency. Its capital base would be returned to shareholders as existing portfolios are redeemed.

MIGA *should be eliminated*. Many countries have their own political insurance agencies. In addition, private-sector insurers have entered the market.

The IMF's role redefined according to Meltzer

The mission of the new IMF. The Commission recommends that the IMF be restructured as a smaller institution with three unique responsibilities:

a)   to act as a quasi-lender of last resort to solvent emerging economies by providing short-term liquidity assistance to countries in need;

b)   to collect and publish financial and economic data from member countries, and disseminate those data in a timely and uniform manner;

c)   to provide advice (but not impose conditions) relating to economic policy as part of regular 'Article IV' consultations with member countries.

The IMF's Poverty and Growth Facility should be closed.

The IMF would not be authorized to negotiate policy reforms.

IMF loans should have a short maturity (e.g., a maximum of 120 days, with only one allowable rollover.)

THE DEMOCRATS' MINORITY REPORT

The three democrats who voted against the report (Fred Bergsten, Jerome Levinson and Esteban Torres) considered that this was far too harsh on the IFI and the WTO, regarding it as likely to impinge too greatly on their respective powers and remits, and Levinson even went as far as to write a 20-page defence of them. In this alternative vision to that of the rest of the commission, Levinson emphasized the Democrats' involvement with the trades union movement – the AFL-CIO. However, he did condemn the World Bank's and the IMF's hostility to workers' rights. Indeed, both the World Bank and the IMF have made sure that workers and workers alone have paid the price of financial crises. Levinson should be very well aware of this, having been in Brazil at the time of the military coup, itself backed by the US, the World Bank and the IMF.[3]

He summarizes correctly how the holders of capital and governments provoke and use crises, which have then led to systematic attacks on the working class. The following extract from the Meltzer Commission's report is revealing in this respect.

The syndicated bank lending of the decade of the 70s, the tesobono and East Asian financing fiascos, all have common characteristics: in each instance, banks and investors, awash with liquidity, seek a higher financial return than they can obtain in their home bases; without 'due diligence', they invest (tesobonos), or loan (East Asia, 1970s, syndicated bank loans) to governments or banks and corporations in the developing countries; much of the resources are not used for productive investments; a combination of external and internal shocks leads to an international crisis, which is perceived to put at risk the international financial system.

The IMF and the World Bank are charged with overseeing the workout; the financial institutions, who were equally responsible for the crisis by their imprudent lending or investing, are bailed out and rewarded: they are enabled to buy into local banks and financial institutions at bargain basement prices (Mexico and East Asia); the debtor countries are counseled to export their way out of the crisis, which, in practice, means flooding the U.S. market with goods and services because that is the only market that is effectively open to them; and, in order to make their goods more internationally competitive, the IMF and World Bank require governments in the debtor countries to adopt labor market flexibility measures – making it easier for companies to fire workers without significant severance payments, weakening the capacity of unions to negotiate on behalf of their members, all for the purpose of driving down labor costs and benefits. Workers in both the industrialized and developing countries, particularly in the unionized part of the labor market, bear a disproportionate part of the burden of adjustment ....

Levinson also quotes Joseph Stiglitz (former chief economist at the World Bank) who argues in the same vein:

Even when labor market problems are not the core of the problem facing the country, all too often workers are asked to bear the brunt of the costs of adjustment. In East Asia, it was reckless lending by international banks and other financial institutions combined with reckless borrowing by domestic financial institutions – combined with fickle investor expectations – which may have precipitated the crisis; but the costs in terms of soaring unemployment and plummeting wages were borne by workers.

Levinson is scathing towards the World Bank's hypocrisy. When this learned institution is asked to promote workers' rights, he notes, it apologizes, saying that it is forbidden by Section 10 Article 4 of its constitution to take any political factors into account. Yet when it comes to setting conditionalities, he goes on to argue, it is quick enough to impose the maximum amount of labour flexibility, thus making it easier to sack people, weaken the negotiating power of trades unions and reduce the incomes of urban workers.

It must be stressed, however, that Levinson is fully in favour of pro-market economic liberalism and privatization. He regards such measures as necessary, but believes that for them to work, they have to be accompanied by a trade union counter-balance. Levinson's vision is close to that advocated by Tony Blair in Great Britain or Gerhard Schroeder in Germany.

THE MELTZER COMMISSION IN CONTEXT

In a study published in 1998, Anne Krueger, who was chief economist at the World Bank from 1981 to 1987, underlined the differences between the 1970s and the end of the 1990s. Her article is useful for understanding certain terms of the debate. She indicates that at the start of the 1970s, the United States forced the World Bank and the IMF to switch from bilateral to multilateral aid.[4] According to Krueger, from then on, private capital flows, encouraged by the spread of liberalization, proved dominant and reduced the room for manoeuvre for the Bank and IMF. Moreover, the Cold War had finished. She notes:

Up until the end of the Cold War, political support for IMF and World Bank aid programs came from two groups: those from the right who were concerned about security issues and those from the left who supported development objectives from a humanitarian point of view. With the end of the Cold War, political support from the right slipped away and the Bank's efforts to extend its activities into new areas can be seen as its seeking out a wider base of political support.[5]

According to her, the World Bank tends to do too much:

Many of the criticisms levelled at the Bank's lack of organization can be traced back to its tendency to over-reach itself in all the countries it is concerned with. In becoming involved in environmental issues, cooperating with NGO's, attempting to combat corruption and so on, the bank can be considered to have exceeded its basic competencies. In doing so, it has gone beyond its remit.

As far as the future of the Bank is concerned, Krueger believes it has three options:

1) to withdraw gradually from economically middling nations and limit itself to 'helping' exceptionally poor countries whilst maintaining its overall development role; 2) To pursue its activities in all its client countries but to concentrate solely on 'soft issues' of development such as environmental preservation, women's rights and the encouragement of NGO's; 3) Shut up shop.[6]

While Krueger is not convinced by the latter option and is open to persuasion on the first two, she notes that something must be decided sooner or later. She is also clear as to the Bank's operational factors: the change to a 'one country, one vote' system must be resisted. Krueger maintains that, though a merger between the World Bank and the IMF cannot be ruled out, this would be unwelcome as it would mean drafting a new constitution along this 'one country, one vote' line, something she believes must be avoided.[7] The whole affair must remain in the control of the major powers.

THE CONTEXT OF THE MELTZER COMMISSION

In order to understand the Meltzer Commission's proposals, one must, of course, put them in their international context: namely, the successive financial crises of the peripheral countries and the superseding catastrophic intervention of the IMF and the World Bank. But this would only be scratching the surface, since the real determining factor was the US national context. It must be borne in mind that, at the time of the commission, the Republican majority was conducting a fierce campaign against Bill Clinton's Democrat administration. This element of internal politics is crucial in understanding why and how the commission attacked the executive so ruthlessly and exploited the IMF in order to intervene in world affairs, all without Congressional agreement.[8] Furthermore, a number of the commission's political goals were linked to the need to split the Democrat appointees at the heart of the commission, in order to win enough of them over to the opinion of Meltzer and his colleagues. It was also a matter of hitting the Clinton administration and its electoral and political base at one of their most sensitive points.

THE MELTZER COMMISSION'S POSITION
TOWARDS WASHINGTON'S POLICY

There are areas of agreement between the commission and Washington. Since the start of his presidency in 2001, G.W. Bush's political strategy has been to move in the direction of the Meltzer Commission recommendations. For example:

1. There is fundamental agreement between them over the pursuit of a neoliberal agenda: 'The Commission believes that in order to encourage development all countries must open up their markets, promote private property, respect for the law, political democracy and individual freedom.' These points are considered essential.

2. Both see the necessity of retaining existing international financial institutions: 'These institutions together with American involvement in the world have had remarkable results in terms of keeping the peace and maintaining stability.'

3. There is of course agreement over keeping and strengthening US dominance over these institutions.

4. There is agreement over cancelling all or nearly all the debt of the HIPCs and other poor countries, as long as these nations follow the neoliberal agenda and conform to the interests of the United States. The thinking behind this is quite simple: these countries are of no use to the US if their debts stop them from buying US goods and services. So, in order to prevent this, it would be better to write off or to substantially reduce these debts.

5. It is in the US interest to pressurize the World Bank into giving aid to poor countries, and to do so itself, since it is certain that these countries will spend the money on goods primarily from the most industrialized nations. Poor nations immediately spend what they are given on goods from the North because they themselves do not produce enough of what they need. This has been the impact of liberalization and competition over the last 25 years on local producers and firms in developing countries.

6. Corruption in recipient countries must be rooted out in order to ensure that the maximum amount of aid money ends up being spent on products from the North.

7. The politics of aid also has the advantage of keeping recipient countries in a state of dependence on donor countries.

8. The amounts of money involved in aid and donations are trifling to countries like the United States. It is far less, for instance, than the $400 billion spent on the 'War against Terror' in Iraq and Afghanistan between September 2001 and April 2006.

HOW THE MELTZER COMMISSION VIEWS THE POLITICS OF AID

The commission concludes that loans should be largely replaced by recourse to donations. The example given by the commission, though, clearly shows that the aim of this strategy is that the donor country becomes involved in the decision-making processes of HIPCs and thus short-circuit their national politics:

Example: A country with $1,000 per capita income qualifying for 70% grant resources decides that vaccination of its children against measles is a desired goal. If the development agency confirms the need, the government would solicit competitive bids from private-sector suppliers, nongovernmental organizations such as charitable institutions, and public sector entities such as the Ministry of Health. Suppose the lowest qualifying bid is $5 per child vaccinated, the development agency would agree to pay $3.50 (70%) for each vaccination directly to the supplier. The government would be responsible for the remaining $1.50 (30%) fee. Payments would only be made upon certification by an agent independent of all participants – the government, the development agency and the supplier of vaccinations. Under a system of user fees, grants are paid after audited delivery of service. No results, no funds expended. Payments would be based upon number of children vaccinated, kilowatts of electricity delivered, cubic meters of water treated, students passing literacy tests, miles of functioning roads. [...] Execution is substantially free of political risk. The supplier of the service, not the government, receives the payment.

And, later in the text:

From vaccinations to roads, from literacy to water supply, services would be performed by outside private-sector providers (including NGOs and charitable organizations) or public-sector entities, and awarded on competitive bid. Quantity and quality of performance would be verified by independent auditors. Payments would be made directly to providers. Costs would be divided between recipient countries and the development agency. The subsidy would vary between 10% and 90%, depending upon capital-market access and per capita income.

Even if the arguments contained in the Meltzer Report are useful in describing the overall effects of the IMF's and the World Bank's actions, the solutions it extols would be as disastrous as they are unconvincing. To use donations and aid as a new way of entrenching the commodification of essential services, such as health, water services and education, as the report does, is a policy that has to be rejected. It is unacceptable for donor countries to use aid as a way of imposing their demands and wishes on recipient nations.

A very different approach is needed. Some way must be found of breaking the wretched cycle of debt while avoiding a politics of charity – something that would only perpetuate the current global system dominated by capitalism, the major powers and transnational corporations. This alternative would create an international order that could redistribute wealth so as to compensate for the wholesale plunder that people of the Periphery have endured in the past and still endure today. Such reparations in the guise of aid should, under no circumstances, give the more industrialized countries leverage over the internal political affairs of the nations they are compensating. This new strategy would be aimed at creating decision-making bodies that would control the destination of aid but leave how it is utilized in the hands of the populations and public authorities concerned. This would necessarily open up a huge space of reflection and experimentation.

Furthermore, in opposition to the Meltzer Commission, which wants to retain the IMF and the World Bank with slight reforms, it is a contention of this book that these bodies must be abolished and replaced with different global institutions that would operate democratically. The 'New World Bank' and the 'New Monetary Fund', to give them their new titles, would have radically different remits from their predecessors – they would, for instance, guarantee the fulfilment of international treaty obligations in terms of political, civil, social, economic and cultural rights as well as in the domains of international monetary and credit relations. These new institutions must play a role in a global institutional system headed by a radically reformed United Nations. It is an absolute priority that developing countries mobilize themselves as soon as possible into regional entities, equipped with banks and monetary funds in common. The establishment of an Asian Monetary Fund for the countries affected had been suggested in the wake of the near economic meltdown there in 1997–98, yet all such talk was quashed under pressure from the US and the IMF. However, with a little help from the Venezuelans, debate has started in Latin America and the Caribbean about the possibility of setting up a 'Bank of the South'. Obviously, if one is striving for emancipation and the full respect of human rights, these new, more regional, financial institutions must be subservient to a social movement totally opposed to capitalism and neoliberalism.

19
The World Bank's Accounts

Since the World Bank came into existence in 1946, each year without exception, it has produced positive net results from its activities. In 1963, the Bank was faced with such huge profits that the new president, George Woods, who only a short time before had been president of the First Boston Bank, proposed that the World Bank's managing committee should distribute dividends to its shareholders like any self-respecting bank.[1] The idea was abandoned as the managers felt that distributing dividends would give indebted developing countries a poor impression of the Bank. It was decided to transfer the profits to the Bank's reserves. In 2005, its total reserves came to $38.5 billion.

Since 1985, the revenues[2] of the Bank's main branch, the IBRD (International Bank for Reconstruction and Development), have exceeded a billion dollars every year. Exceptional results were registered for 1992 ($1,709 million of revenue), in 2000 ($1,991 million) and above all for 2003 ($3,021 million).

Figure 19.1 shows the growth of operations revenue from 1981 to 2005.

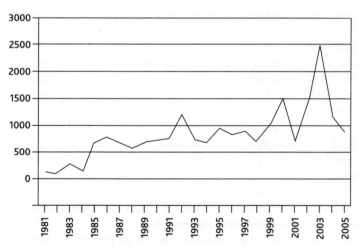

Figure 19.1   Growth of World Bank (IBRD) operations, 1981–2005 (US$ million)

Source: World Bank, *Global Development Finance*, 2005.

HOW DOES THE WORLD BANK MAKE ITS PROFITS?

The IBRD makes its profits through repayments received from indebted countries, mainly from a few big middle-income countries.[3] Indeed, the poorest countries cannot afford to borrow from the IBRD – they borrow instead from the IDA (International Development Agency).

The IBRD makes its profits on the difference between what the capital it borrows on the financial markets costs it, on the one hand, and what the developing countries repay it (amortization of borrowed capital + interest) on the other. Even then, the IBRD would have to ensure that the developing countries do actually repay it, and so it does: the IBRD manages to get repaid regularly. Of course there are a few exceptions and some countries are bad payers – as was the case of Mobutu's Zaire, for example.

Table 19.1 will give an idea of how seriously developing countries take their obligation to repay the IBRD. The developing countries can be seen to repay far more than the IBRD lends them. Developing countries' net transfer on debt has been negative since 1987. It is also apparent that despite the enormous amounts repaid, the total debt still owed to the IBRD has greatly increased.

Figure 19.2 shows the growth of stock and net transfer on debt for the same period.

The World Bank claims that the profits it makes from the IBRD are not enough to enable it to balance its accounts, because of a deficit in the IDA's accounts, which makes low-interest loans to the poorest countries. Figure 19.3 shows that if you add together IBRD and IDA loans, on the one hand, and subtract the total of the repayments made by all developing countries (including the poorest) to the IBRD and IDA, the Bank has been making a comfortable profit since 1990. So, from 1991 to 1996, net transfer has been systematically negative, as it has been since 2000.

From 1984, the World Bank decided to diversify where it placed its profits. Other than increasing its reserves, it used these in homoeopathic doses for certain UN programmes. Thus, in April 1984, the World Bank donated $2 million to the World Food Programme. This is referred to in the minutes of the Bank's managing committee meeting as 'a good and astute gesture'.[4]

Later, from 1985, the World Bank allocated part of its profits to special funds, usually trust funds, for limited purposes. These could be anything from the Bank's contribution to reducing poor countries'

Table 19.1 Growth in debt owed to the IBRD by all developing countries, 1970–2004 (US$ million)

Year	Stock total	Amounts lent	Amounts repaid	Net transfer
1970	4,377	672	491	181
1971	4,892	796	559	237
1972	5,517	928	630	298
1973	6,146	969	757	213
1974	7,136	1,338	883	456
1975	8,500	1,817	987	830
1976	9,984	1,937	1,151	786
1977	11,784	2,373	1,434	939
1978	13,812	2,661	1,780	881
1979	16,520	3,452	2,161	1,291
1980	20,432	4,224	2,666	1,558
1981	24,356	5,201	2,963	2,239
1982	28,570	5,828	3,611	2,217
1983	33,706	7,104	4,376	2,728
1984	33,426	7,917	5,217	2,700
1985	46,612	7,915	6,077	1,838
1986	63,411	9,768	8,881	887
1987	83,372	10,680	11,447	−767
1988	79,871	11,591	14,393	−2,801
1989	80,981	10,564	13,302	−2,738
1990	92,314	13,438	14,807	−1,369
1991	97,136	11,924	16,686	−4,762
1992	95,283	10,218	17,455	−7,237
1993	100,156	12,884	17,724	−4,840
1994	107,713	11,299	19,113	−7,814
1995	111,691	13,094	19,641	−6,548
1996	105,308	13,148	19,276	−6,128
1997	101,522	14,499	17,334	−2,835
1998	108,455	14,376	17,099	−2,723
1999	111,329	14,082	17,101	−3,019
2000	112,145	13,430	17,510	−4,079
2001	112,530	12,305	17,275	−4,970
2002	111,303	10,288	22,414	−12,126
2003	109,036	11,411	22,761	−11,350
2004	104,526	8,298	18,381	−10,084

Source: World Bank, *Global Development Finance*, 2005.

debt to aid for certain countries affected by the tsunami in December 2004, or donations to the Multilateral Investment Guarantee Agency, the fifth branch of the World Bank.[5] Generally, this use of the funds is criticized by the middle-income countries since it is through them that the Bank makes its profits. These countries denounce the fact

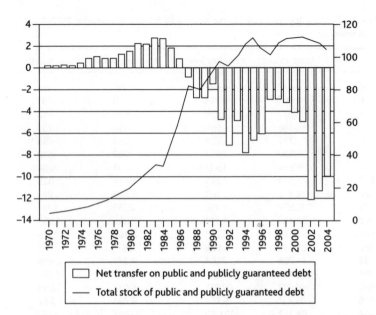

Net transfer on public and publicly guaranteed debt

Total stock of public and publicly guaranteed debt

Left-hand scale: Net transfer on debt owed to the IBRD by all the developing countries (US$ billion)
Right-hand scale: Growth in total debt owed to the IBRD by all developing countries between 1970 and 2004 (US$ billion)

Figure 19.2   Comparison between debt stock owed to IBRD and net transfers, 1970–2004

Source: World Bank, *Global Development Finance*, 2005.

that the rich countries use part of the profits made on their backs for noble gestures towards the poorest countries. They would prefer the Bank to charge them lower interest rates.

Note that the Bank is very active on the derivatives market, which feeds international speculation. In 2004, the Bank registered a shortfall of $4 billion from operations on derivatives in currency exchange. Although its usual activities had generated profits comparable to those made in previous years, this made a temporary impact on its net revenue.[6] However, all this is leading us to another of the World Bank's activities, which, however questionable, is beyond the scope of this chapter.

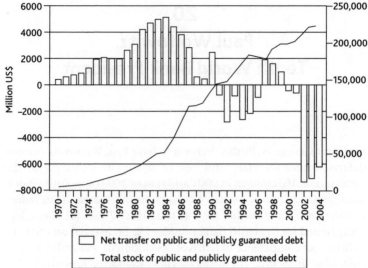

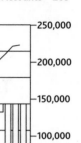

Left-hand scale: Net transfer on debt owed to the WB (IBRD + IDA) by all the developing countries (US$ million)
Right-hand scale: Growth in total debt owed to the WB (IBRD + IDA) by all the developing countries between 1970 and 2004 ($US million)

Figure 19.3   Comparison between debt stock owed to the World Bank (IBRD and IDA) and net transfers

Source: World Bank, *Global Development Finance*, 2005.

20
Paul Wolfowitz,
Tenth World Bank President

President George W. Bush's decision to have Paul Wolfowitz (former defense under-secretary and one of the main architects of the invasions of Afghanistan in 2001 and Iraq in 2003) appointed World Bank president was a source of controversy in March 2005. Before this decision some media, such as the British *Financial Times*, had campaigned for the tenth Bank president to be selected on the basis of his or her competence in terms of development, preferably among citizens of the South. The *Financial Times* supported Ernesto Zedillo, who had been President of Mexico at the end of the 1990s. George W. Bush's decisive choice in favour of Paul Wolfowitz clearly indicates who actually runs the World Bank. All 24 governors subscribed to this decision.

But who is Paul Wolfowitz? A pure product of the US state apparatus. He combines a short university career with a long-standing experience of power. A graduate in mathematics, he worked at the Bureau of the Budget (1966–67) when he was only 23. In 1969, he worked for a Congress committee that aimed at convincing the Senate that it was imperative to endow the US with an anti-missile umbrella against the USSR. He succeeded. From that point onwards Wolfowitz was fully involved in issues of military strategy. A leading thread can be detected in his strategic approach: adversaries (the USSR, China, Iraq, etc.) have to be exposed as more dangerous than they would appear, so as to justify an additional defence effort (a bigger budget, manufacture of new weapons, wider deployment of troops), including the launch of preventive strikes or wars intended to prevent potential threats rather than respond to actual attacks.

Wolfowitz taught at Yale for two years and received a doctorate in political science at the University of Chicago in 1972, i.e., in one of the intellectual centres of reactionary conservatism.[1] Afterwards he worked for four years with the Arms Control and Disarmament Agency (1973–77) in direct relation with George Bush Sr, who at the time was head of the CIA. Then he went straight into the Pentagon in 1977 and stayed there under Democrat President Jimmy Carter until 1980. He produced a file to show that the Soviet Union was developing new nuclear weapons. It later turned out that these allegedly new weapons in the Soviet hands were largely imaginary. Although he had worked for a Democratic President, after one year in limbo as a professor at the Johns Hopkins University, Wolfowitz managed to join the Reagan administration in 1981. He became Director of Policy Planning for the Department of State. From 1983 to 1986 he was Assistant Secretary of State for East Asian and Pacific Affairs. From 1986 to 1989 he was the US ambassador to Indonesia. From 1989 to 1993 he advised the Secretary of State for Defense, Dick Cheney, in the Bush Sr administration (first Gulf War) and after Clinton's two terms of office he became under-secretary of state for defense, running the wars against Afghanistan and Iraq along with Donald Rumsfeld. While Bill Clinton was President, i.e., from 1993 to 2001, he resumed his university career as dean of the Paul Nitze School of Advanced International Studies (750 students), which is part of the Johns Hopkins University. He worked miracles in collecting up to $75 million to finance the Paul Nitze School and did consulting work for one of the world's leading military corporations, Northrop Grumman. In 1997, Wolfowitz founded a neocon pressure group called PNAC (Project for a New American Century). Other members are Donald Rumsfeld (Defense Secretary until November 2006), Dick Cheney (then CEO of Halliburton and currently US vice-president), Jeb Bush (George W. Bush's brother), Richard Perle and Robert Kagan. From 1998 onwards, the PNAC campaigned for Clinton to launch a pre-emptive attack against Iraq and other potentially aggressive countries.

During the 1983–89 period when Wolfowitz was involved in US policy in East Asia, he actively supported dictatorships. Indeed, contrary to the image he likes to cultivate, he upheld the military dictatorships of Ferdinand Marcos in the Philippines, Chun Doo Hwan in South Korea and Suharto in Indonesia.

In the early 1980s he tried to save Marcos' position by persuading him to implement a number of democratic reforms. At that time, a powerful revolutionary guerrilla warfare was going on in the Philippines. The revolutionary movement was allied with a middle class that was strongly opposed to the dictatorship led by Aquino. It was close to bringing about another US defeat similar to the one in Nicaragua in 1979 when the Sandinistas had forged an alliance with the middle-class opposition led by Violetta Chamorro. It was not

Wolfowitz who chased Marcos from power in 1986 but the people's concerted action, with the US securing the dictator's flight to Hawaii (50th state of the United States of America).[2]

As to South Korea, Wolfowitz claims that he persuaded dictator Chun Doo Hwan (who had ordered massacres during the 1980 uprising) to withdraw in 1987. Actually the dictator's demise was the result of millions of students, workers and citizens demonstrating against him.

In Indonesia where actions against the dictatorship were less developed (with good reason too: when he seized power in 1965, Suharto had half a million civilians massacred), the USA supported the dictator as late as early 1998. Wolfowitz, who, as will be remembered, had been the US ambassador in Djakarta from 1986 to 1989, stated before a Congress meeting in May 1997 that 'any balanced judgment of the situation in Indonesia today, including the very important and sensitive issue of human rights, needs to take account of the significant progress that Indonesia has already made and needs to acknowledge that much of this progress has to be credited to the strong and remarkable leadership of President Suharto'.[3]

Wolfowitz's recent past is better known: he is one of the architects of the pre-emptive strategy developed in Afghanistan and Iraq from October 2001. He was one of the main originators of the lies disseminated through the media about the threat Saddam Hussein represented for the international community. He thought up the weapons of mass destruction theory and Saddam Hussein's alleged support to Al-Qaida and international terrorism. In the early days of the Iraq war he had claimed that US soldiers would always be seen as the liberators of Iraq and therefore cherished by the Iraqi people. Wolfowitz also asserted that Iraq would pay for its liberation itself thanks to its oil. Donald Rumsfeld, Paul Wolfowitz, George W. Bush and Dick Cheney have used the occupation and so-called 'reconstruction' of Iraq for the greater profit of US-based transnational corporations. There is thus a very real danger of seeing Wolfowitz do the same with 'linked' aid from the World Bank.

WASHINGTON'S OFFENSIVE AGAINST MULTILATERAL ORGANIZATIONS

The appointment of Paul Wolfowitz needs to be seen against the US offensive on several multilateral institutions.

Act One: On 18 January 2005, Kofi Annan, Secretary General of the United Nations Organization, decided to appoint Ann Veneman,

Secretary of Agriculture in the Bush administration, as executive director of UNICEF. It happens that the USA and Somalia are the only two countries that did not ratify the UN Convention on the Rights of the Child (ratified by 189 countries). We can easily imagine the kind of pressure Kofi Annan was under to make such a decision.

Act Two: On 7 March 2005, George W. Bush chose John Bolton as US ambassador to the UN. This ultraconservative figure feels a deep-seated hatred towards the UN, as testified by his oft-quoted statement that if the 38-storey UN building 'lost 10 storeys today, it wouldn't make a bit of difference'. He tried to organize the dismissal of Mohamed El Baradei (in charge of the UN mission that was to keep track of Iraq's disarmament programme shortly before the 2003 war). He also managed to see that the US did not ratify the International Criminal Court and withdrew from the UN conference on racism convened in Durban in August 2001. In his opinion the UN should never stand in the way of US foreign policy. He has even stated that the UN can only function if it is managed by the United States.

Act Three: On 10 March 2005, George W. Bush announced that Paul Wolfowitz was his candidate as president of the World Bank. On 31 March, the WB board of governors unanimously voted for Wolfowitz. Bush thus showed the international community and his supporters that he would and could increase US direct leadership on multilateral institutions.

The appointment of Paul Wolfowitz is in a way similar to that of Robert McNamara in 1968. McNamara had been Defense Secretary and was withdrawn from this post when the Vietnam War turned into a disaster. Wolfowitz had to leave his post when it appeared that the war in Iraq was a failure. Like McNamara, Wolfowitz knows how to manage a large administration: the Pentagon. Like McNamara, he was an adviser to the US President on foreign policy issues. In all likelihood Paul Wolfowitz, like Robert McNamara and in the wake of James Wolfensohn, will maintain the alibi of the fight against poverty. Like Robert McNamara, Paul Wolfowitz will know how to use both the stick and the carrot.

21
Structural Adjustment and the Washington Consensus: Are They Things of the Past?

During the 1980s, the International Monetary Fund (IMF) and the World Bank earned themselves the highly justified but less than enviable reputation of being responsible for very unpopular measures forced upon governments of developing countries – in short, of being the bane of the poor. It must be said that the governments themselves, often in cahoots with the ruling classes, found it convenient to place the blame on these distant institutions located on 19th Avenue in Washington. This dangerous reputation spread like wildfire and newspapers in the South began to give it ample coverage.[1]

Accustomed to making blunt recommendations for cuts in social expenditure or the privatization of public companies, these two institutions came to realize that plain speaking did not serve their interests. Very quickly, people recognized their leading role in unfolding economic and human disasters. Very quickly, the riots that followed price increases in essential goods were coined 'anti-IMF riots'. Very quickly, public opinion put pressure on governments to resist the decrees of the IMF or the World Bank. In short, it was becoming more and more difficult to get people to swallow such a bitter pill.

A major communication plan was therefore launched in the 1990s to deal with the serious and rightly deserved legitimacy crisis that the IMF and the World Bank were then facing (and still are). The argument focused on debt reduction and the fight against poverty. We have learned and we have changed, was the message. But the notorious ultra-liberal conditionalities that marked the structural adjustment programmes of the 1980s are still being practised. A series of recent examples on every continent testifies to the contradictions of these two institutions and the resistance movements that have ensued.

In **Sri Lanka**, the government refused a $389 million loan that was conditional on political reforms such as the restructuring of pension schemes and the privatization of water resources.[2]

In **Ecuador**, a popular uprising was responsible for the fall of President Lucio Guttierrez in April 2005. The government of the new president, Alfredo Palacio, has proved to be more touchy on the subject of economic sovereignty, much to the displeasure of the IMF and World Bank. It must be noted that in 2000, Ecuador ditched its domestic currency and switched to the US dollar, thus becoming totally dependent on Washington's monetary policy. In July 2005, the government decided to reform the use of oil resources. Instead of being entirely earmarked for paying back the debt, part of those resources would now fund social programmes, notably for the often under-privileged Indian communities. To show its displeasure, the World Bank withheld a $100 million loan to Ecuador. Rafael Correa, the popular finance minister who had initiated the reform, stated: 'It is an offence against Ecuador,' noting that 'no one has the right to punish a country for changing its own laws'.[3] In response, Ecuador looked for funding elsewhere: in Venezuela (where President Hugo Chávez, willing to support such measures, granted a $300 million loan)[4] and in China (whose flourishing economy requires increasing amounts of raw materials). This only highlighted the pressure exerted by Washington, ending in Correa's resignation. He was replaced by Magadalena Barreiro, who accepted the position on the condition that Correa give her his public support.

In **Haiti**, during 2003, the IMF put an end to government-controlled fuel prices, thereby making them 'flexible'. Within a few weeks, fuel prices rose by 130 per cent. The consequences were dramatic: problems with boiling water for drinking and cooking, and an increase in transportation costs, which small producers passed on to the market, thus increasing the price of numerous basic commodities. But as inflation is one of the IMF's bugbears, it promptly imposed a salary freeze. The daily minimum wage plummeted from $3 in 1994 to $1.50, which, according to the IMF, would attract foreign investors. It also served geopolitical interests, weakening President Jean-Bertrand Aristide and leading to his departure from office on 24 February 2004 – something the big powers had been pushing for.[5]

Even in oil-producing countries such as **Iraq** or **Nigeria**, the IMF imposed the same system of flexible pricing. Tariffs increased, leading to organized protests by the people affected, for example in Bassorah in December 2005.

In **Ghana**, former President Jerry Rawlings refused to adopt the Heavily Indebted Poor Countries (HIPC) initiative, but since John Agyekum Kufuor took power in January 2001, Ghana has been complying with conditions imposed by the IMF. One of these conditions – a significant one – concerned the water sector, for which the IMF demanded total cost recovery. In other words, households must bear the total cost of access to water, without the benefit of state subsidies. The price of a cubic metre of water had to be sufficient to recover total operating and management costs. Electricity was next in line and the same principle was applied. The goal was clear: to get the public company on an even keel before privatization. In May 2001 the price of water rose by 95 per cent, and it didn't stop there. The populations seriously affected by this measure formed the National Coalition against the Privatization of Water. With one out of three Ghanaians having no access to drinking water, the World Bank made another fateful move: in 2004, it granted Ghana a $103 million loan in exchange for the privatization of water supply to its main cities – awarding this prize to a multinational corporation. The privatization process is under way, but the people's struggle continues, backed by numerous international activist organizations.

In **Mali**, the cotton industry is in the line of fire. For decades, the entire cotton sector was controlled by the Compagnie malienne de développement des textiles (CMDT), jointly owned by the Malian government (60 per cent) and the French company Dagris (40 per cent). The CMDT, the real backbone of the Malian economy, was the biggest currency earner for the Malian state through profits and taxes. Its role extended beyond the mere production of cotton. It provided public services, from maintaining rural roads or eliminating illiteracy among rural communities, to the purchase of agricultural tools or the construction of vital infrastructures. Until 1999, production was constantly on the increase: 200,000 tonnes in 1988, 450,000 tonnes in 1997, 520,000 tonnes in 1998 and 522,000 tonnes in 1999. But CMDT's dubious management and very low prices triggered unrest among peasants, who refused to harvest in 1999/2000. Production that year fell by almost 50 per cent. The cotton sector's forum, the Etats généraux de la filière cotonnière, was held in April 2001. It was decided to introduce a series of drastic reforms, including a 23 per cent reduction in total expenditure on wages, partial or total debt cancellation for smallholders, layoffs (500 to 800 people out of 2,400), the freezing of a planned 7 per cent increase in salary, an increase in the guaranteed price paid to farmers from 170 FCFA/kg of cotton to 200 FCFA/kg, the opening up of capital, the reorganization of activities and the progressive withdrawal of the Malian state from the CMDT. In spite of the failed privatizations in the neighbouring countries (in Benin or Ivory Coast), the World Bank advocates outright privatization, causing great concern among the affected villagers. The first reorganizations, notably in the transport and management of fertilizers and pesticides, have already led to massive disruptions, seriously penalizing Malian producers and putting harvests at risk in 2003 and 2004.[6]

In order to accelerate the process even more, and dissatisfied with the CMDT's guaranteed price of 210 FCFA/kg, which it found too high, the World Bank put pressure on the government by freezing a $25 million aid payment. By so doing, it disregarded the two factors responsible for the success of the Malian cotton sector: a guaranteed minimum price and vertical integration. A World Bank study[7] published in May 2005 is explicit: 'In order to implement this strategy the plan of action was to create 3 or 4 different cotton processing companies by selling the state-owned share of the CMDT to private investors.' But the Malian government asked for a reprieve until 2008, 'so as not to be accused of dumping national industries in favour of foreign investors'. Pressure from the World Bank then increased: 'the privatization agenda is not set, the schedule is not clear and some decisions are made out of the blue, which is no guarantee of economic rationality or transparency'. The Bank then called for 'open talks on reforming the sector, adopting a firm schedule and a reasonable scenario towards privatization, as well as a plan to limit the impact of the company's deficit on the budget'.

Here too, the people continue their struggle in order to prevent the CMDT from paying the price of dubious management and the blindness of international organizations – the IMF and the World Bank being at the top of the list.

Will the cotton industry go the same way as water and electricity? Maybe, and the example is interesting because Mali has just regained its majority share in EdM (Energie du Mali), which was privatized to the benefit of La Saur, a Bouygues subsidiary, five years before. But the privatized EdM never fulfilled its contractual obligations (developing water and electricity networks by investing at least 600 million euros; reducing prices).[8] Advocated by the IMF and the World Bank, this privatization turned out to be a failure, even though it was presented as a showcase to neighbouring countries. Could renationalization be the way out?

In **Niger**, there was no period of grace following the re-election of President Mamadou Tandja in December 2004. In January 2005, on IMF instructions, a law amending finances was enacted increasing

VAT to 19 per cent on basic goods and services (wheat, sugar, milk, water and electricity). There was massive social mobilization. In March, the people, already impoverished by years of bad harvests (caused by droughts and invasions of desert locusts) and structural adjustment programmes (privatizations, cuts in social expenditure, layoffs and salary freezes in the civil service, etc.) took to the streets to express their dissatisfaction. The social movement, organized around three consumer groups, succeeded in creating a large unified front for a 'coalition against the high cost of living', bringing together 29 organizations and the four trade union federations. After several days of 'dead town' demonstration and arbitrary arrests, the mobilization forced the government to back down. The 19 per cent VAT no longer applies to milk and flour, and water and electricity are only concerned in the highest consumption brackets. Only sugar is still affected, but at the price of fierce social struggles to counter the wishes of the IMF, dutifully passed on by Niger's leaders.

In the **Democratic Republic of the Congo** (DRC), a parliamentary report published in February 2006 denounced the action of the World Bank with respect to the mining industry. Trouble broke out over the operation of a copper and silver mine in Dikulushi controlled by the Australian/Canadian company, Anvil Mining. In October 2004, Mai-Mai militants occupied the neighbouring town of Kilwa, from where extracted minerals are sent to Zambia. The Congolese army then launched an operation to repress this uprising, causing the death of several dozens of individuals suspected of supporting the rebels (at least a hundred people, according to the UN). Summary executions and plunder marked this strong-arm operation. Anvil Mining provided vehicles and equipment to the Congolese army, with a view to ensuring unhampered continuation of exports.

This did not prevent the Multilateral Investment Guarantee Agency (MIGA, an affiliate of the World Bank) from approving an insurance contract in April 2005 offering a guarantee of $13.3 million to cover political risks related to the expansion of this mining operation. We see here that the World Bank did not hesitate to support Anvil Mining's dubious activities. A report by the Congolese National Assembly Special Commission, entrusted with examining the validity of economic and financial agreements, written by 17 Congolese MPs from different parties and led by Christophe Lutundula, severely criticized 'the policy of splitting up the mining portfolio of the State' in which Anvil Mining was implicated, essentially 'to satisfy the immediate financial needs of governments'. According to this report, the collusion between the Congolese authorities and Anvil Mining was flagrant: 'tax, customs and para-fiscal exemptions were granted in an exaggerated fashion and for long periods, some 15 to 30 years. [...] The Congolese State has therefore been deprived of significant revenue resources indispensable to its development.' In spite of everything, control of Anvil Mining's operations was destined to fail: 'The public servants affected by the mining concessions were flagrantly being taken care of by the private operators whom they were supposed to audit. [...] These public servants also lacked full autonomy, independence and effectiveness.'

To cap it all, until March 2005 a significant shareholder of Anvil Mining was First Quantum, a Canadian company (17.5 per cent of shares), exposed in a 2002 UN report on the DRC for not respecting OECD guidelines governing multinationals. How can the World Bank, via MIGA, continue to offer guarantees to a company that has demonstrated how little it respects the fundamental rights of the people of the Kilwa region? To offer a guarantee in such circumstances is to make oneself a direct accomplice of the reprehensible actions of Anvil Mining.

In **Chad**, since the start of the project, numerous ecological, human rights and international solidarity organizations have been concerned by World Bank support for the construction of a 1,070-km pipeline linking the oil-producing region of Doba (Chad) to the maritime port of Kribi (Cameroon). From the outset, the ecological, human and financial risks were so great that interested investors Shell and Elf preferred to pull out. However, the final consortium consisting of Exxon Mobil, ChevronTexaco (USA) and Petronas (Malaysia) have carried through the $3.7 billion project, thanks to powerful strategic and financial support from the World Bank.

To justify its support, the World Bank committed to a pilot programme designed to allow Chadians to benefit from the profits made. In making this investment – the largest in Sub-Saharan Africa – it imposed its conditions: the Chadian President, Idriss Déby, must devote 90 per cent of the revenues earned from oil sales to social projects selected with WB approval and to investments in the Doba region. The remaining 10 per cent must be reserved for future generations: they were deposited in a blocked account at Citibank London, under WB control.

This arrangement failed since Déby appropriated the sums allocated for future generations: it is estimated that he helped himself to at least $27 million. Moreover, he changed the rules of the game by including security expenses in the definition of priority sectors to be financed by oil revenues. Weakened by high social tensions, attempts to overthrow him and army desertions, Déby sought to reinforce his military and repressive machine. In December 2005 the Bank reacted by blocking existing loans to Chad, pretending to discover the authoritative and corrupt nature of the regime, whereas this project, supported by the Bank for a decade already, has allowed Déby to strengthen his power base and bolster his personal fortune.

While the big winner in Chad-based oil operations is the consortium, Chad earns 12.5 per cent in royalties on direct oil sales, as well as various taxes and bonuses paid directly into the Treasury. Out of the first bonus, deposited in advance, $7.4 million was misappropriated. A further $4.5 million was diverted by the President's son for the purchase of helicopters. The Bank, aware of the situation but heavily involved in the project, turned a blind eye.

All the bombast by World Bank experts on good governance, corruption and reducing poverty is a dismal farce. It was clear from the beginning that this project would end up allowing a notorious dictator to get even wealthier, with total impunity. Each side did just what was expected of it. The Bank enabled the construction of a pipeline that allows oil multinationals to help themselves to a natural resource and their shareholders to reap juicy profits. Meanwhile, Chad's President helps himself to the wealth that belongs to the people.

Corruption and dictatorship in Chad must be denounced and fought, but that will not be enough. The World Bank is the determining element in a project that places a heavy burden of debt on Chad, increases corruption and poverty, damages the environment and allows a natural resource to be abusively exploited. In short, in Chad as elsewhere, the Bank knowingly supports a predatory model and a corrupt dictatorship.

HIPC: The announcement in June 2005 by the G8 Finance Ministers[9] regarding the cancellation of a $40 billion debt owed by 18 poor countries to the World Bank, the African Development Bank (ADB) and the IMF, was also a consequence of this logic. Erasing the debt of a small number of countries (representing only 5 per cent of the people in the 165 developing countries) is no gift: it is merely a compensation for the neoliberal straitjacket that has been imposed on them for years through the HIPC initiative. For at least four years, these 18 countries have had to implement neoliberal economic reforms strictly in line with structural adjustment policy: increased schooling costs, higher health care costs, increased VAT and the removal of subsidies for basic goods – four measures that particularly affect the poor; privatization, liberalization of the economy and the creation of unfair competition between local producers and transnationals. In other words, it's the carrot of debt cancellation after the stick of structural adjustment, which still takes a heavy toll.

22
The World Bank and Respect for Human Rights[1]

When I came to the Bank, we were not allowed to mention the word 'corruption'. It was called the 'c' word. Well, maybe we need to mention the 'r' word, which is 'rights'.

James Wolfensohn, 1 March 2004

The question of 'human rights' has never been a priority concern for the World Bank. Among the conditionalities fixed by the Bank, one right supersedes all others: the individual right to private property, which *in practice* works to the advantage of big property-holders, whether they be wealthy individuals or national and transnational corporations. In the conditionalities supported by the World Bank, there is no reference to the collective rights of peoples and individuals. If there is any consideration of human rights within the World Bank, it is not in the progressive sense expressed in the seminal documents of the United Nations. Evidently, ideologies like to interpret the concept of rights in their own specific way. As Jean-Philippe Peemans so accurately points out:

In any case, from the currently predominant western perspective, human rights are seen first and foremost as concerning individual freedom of action, non-interference in private business, the right to dispose freely of property, and above all, the obligation of the State to refrain from any act that violates the individual freedom to invest time, capital and resources in production and exchange... For neoliberals, social and cultural demands can be seen as legitimate aspirations, but never as rights... the neoliberal view rejects any collective approach to the question of rights. The individual is the only entity capable of demanding rights, and even those who violate rights are necessarily individuals who must take full responsibility for their actions. The violation of rights cannot be attributed to organizations or to structures.[2]

The World Bank, like the IMF, takes refuge in this postulate to divest itself of all responsibility in terms of respect for economic, social and cultural rights. Yet these rights are inseparable from civil and political rights: it is impossible to respect individual rights if collective rights are not taken into account. As multilateral institutions, the World Bank and the IMF are bound by the application of international treaties and the rights, both individual and collective, that are declared therein.

Transparency and good governance are standards that apply to all. The international financial institutions demand them from the governments of indebted countries, but feel free to ignore them when it comes to their own affairs. The obligation to evaluate and report on actions taken should not be limited to states but also extend to the private sector, and even more importantly, to the sphere of international organizations, since their activities, policies and programmes have a major impact on human rights.[3] Structural adjustment programmes have such negative consequences for economic, social and cultural rights (particularly among the most vulnerable), as well as for the environment, that these institutions should be obliged to account for their actions.

STRUCTURAL ADJUSTMENT IS NO RESPECTER OF HUMAN RIGHTS

In spite of the international texts that provide the legal framework for the protection of human rights, the IMF and the World Bank 'operate according to the logic of private financial enterprise and world capitalism, with little consideration for the social and political consequences of their actions'.[4]

The Common Report, presented to the United Nations Human Rights Commission by the Special Reporter and an independent expert, states:

For almost 20 years, the international financial institutions and the governments of creditor countries have played an ambiguous and destructive game which consists of remote-controlling the economies of the Third World and imposing unpopular economic policies on powerless countries, on the pretext that the bitter pill of macro-economic adjustment will in the end allow these countries to achieve prosperity and freedom from debt. After two decades, many countries are worse off than when they brought in the structural adjustment programmes enforced by the IMF and the World Bank. These drastically austere programmes have exacted a high social and ecological price and in many countries the human development index has taken a dramatic plunge.[5]

The report firmly recalls that

the exercise of the basic rights of the people of debtor countries to food, lodging, clothing, employment, education, health services and a healthy environment cannot be subordinated to the application of structural adjustment policies and economic reforms related to the debt...[6]

Yet the policies enforced by the IFI subordinate the respect for human rights and the legitimacy of governments to the dogmatic application of their programmes.[7] In practice, these structural adjustment programmes go beyond

the simple enforcement of a set of macro-economic measures at the domestic level. They [are] the expression of a political project, a deliberate strategy of social transformation on a global scale, whose aim is to make the whole planet a playing field in which transnational corporations will be able to operate with total impunity. In other words, the structural adjustment programmes (SAPs) act as a 'transmission belt' to facilitate a globalization process that is based on liberalization, deregulation and diminishment of the State's role in national development.[8]

The United Nations Human Rights Commission also pointed out that structural adjustment policies have serious repercussions on the ability of developing countries to implement national development policies whose prime objective is to respect human rights, and particularly economic, social and cultural rights, through improved living standards for local populations.[9]

According to the report of Bernard Muhdo, an independent expert, structural adjustment programmes – the result of a policy knowingly devised and applied by the directors of the IMF and the World Bank – have extremely negative consequences on economic, social and cultural rights,[10] especially in matters of health, education, access to drinking water, food safety, etc.[11] The expert also notes that the policies pursued by the IFI have been disputed by citizens through protest movements that have been brutally repressed by governments and public authorities to ensure the success of programmes imposed by these institutions (privatization of water and power, public transport and hospitals; unrestricted prices for medicines, bread and other basic necessities; protection of the interests of transnational corporations in the matter of investments and appropriation of common natural resources, etc.). Consequently there is a close link between these programmes and the massive violation of economic, social and cultural rights as well as of civil and political rights.

Having seen that the public authorities of the states concerned were committing violations, the IMF and the World Bank should have reminded them of their international obligations regarding the protection of civil and political rights and human rights in general. Instead of blocking or suspending the measures undertaken, these institutions continued to apply even more energetically. Such indifference and cynicism is bluntly revealed in a statement made at the meeting of the independent expert with the IMF directors: '... for the IMF, to block a programme for reasons of human rights violations was unwise'.[12]

A priori, this is a very serious state of affairs: these institutions behave as if they are bound by no international obligations whatsoever, unless they be linked to trade or investment agreements. But of course the underlying objective is clear. In 1999, the independent expert designated by the Human Rights Commission accurately identified the globalization process and the role of the financial institutions as being part of the 'neoliberal counter-revolution'.[13]

In international law, whether *contractual* or *customary*,[14] there are basic or fundamental legal principles and rules governing the international protection of human rights and whose scope extends to all subjects of international law.

STATES, INTERNATIONAL FINANCIAL INSTITUTIONS AND PRIVATE INTERESTS

The World Bank and the IMF are not abstractions. The decisions emanating from these institutions are taken by flesh-and-blood men, and sometimes women, who act on behalf of their states or groups of states. The states are themselves indisputably bound by the United Nations documents. The member states of the World Bank and the IMF are therefore, like all others, bound by the legal respect for human rights in the decisions they take.

One can pursue this even further. In the globalization process, thanks to the actions of transnational corporations, the G8 and the international financial institutions,[15] the national and local public authorities have been deliberately deprived of their powers in economic and social matters. The states intervene more and more frequently to ensure that private interests are served instead of ensuring the full enjoyment of human rights. For the World Bank, the whole problem of underdevelopment and poverty boils down to the fact that the public authorities interfere too much in social and economic affairs, often hindering the actions and business of the private sector. This is confirmed in a document entitled 'Private Sector Development', in which the president of the World Bank states that 'growth driven by the private sector is essential to sustainable development and the reduction of poverty'.[16]

The IFIs blame the states, yet in the report submitted to the United National General Assembly, the UN Secretary General affirms:

There is a general tendency today to ask Governments to carry too many responsibilities, without acknowledging that the old-fashioned view of the State's role in development is no longer valid; because of globalization, national Governments no longer have the same tools or resources at their disposal as they once had. Yet, while no mention is made of international responsibilities, or the role played by the current political system and the system of governance in the modern world, responsibilities which these systems do have, Governments are blamed for issues, difficulties and problems that are primarily created in the international arena. This kind of approach is neither objective nor fair, especially to *developing countries, which have very little say in the fundamental decisions taken on the international stage and yet are blamed for hampering the development process*, while underlying international inequities go unmentioned...[17] [author's emphasis].

It is therefore a fundamental error to consider the states as being *solely* responsible for human rights violations during the application of multilateral trade rules or following the application of measures enforced by the IMF and the World Bank.[18]

Yet this thesis is widely disseminated within the IMF and the World Bank: the real villains in the human rights story are the member states – taken individually – because it is they who finally decide on the policies these institutions must apply.

This denial of responsibility is unacceptable in international law.

The IMF, the World Bank and the WTO are above all *international organizations*[19] in the strict sense of the term. As such, they possess an international legal personality,[20] have their own bodies,[21] and are *given jurisdiction* by the treaty or basic agreement (absolute jurisdiction).[22] Most important, as international organizations they have rights and duties.

It goes without saying that no serious body, no international organization that claims to act as a subject of international law and intends to have jurisdiction and an international legal personality can reasonably argue that it is excused from international obligations, especially those governing the protection of human rights.[23] As a subject of international law, any and all international organizations are bound by this same international law, including the rules governing the protection of human rights.[24]

THE UNIVERSAL DECLARATION OF HUMAN RIGHTS

Incorporated in the body of customary law, the Universal Declaration of Human Rights is, as its name implies, universal; it binds the states and the other subjects of international law in the exercise of their specific actions and their responsibilities. No international organization can hide behind its rules of procedure to avoid having to respect the international agreements ratified by its members.[25]

International institutions therefore have a duty to create conditions favourable to the full enjoyment of all human rights, as well as to the respect, protection and promotion of these rights. However, structural adjustment programmes, as shown above, deviate in practice from this theory. Today renamed 'anti-poverty strategies', they stipulate that economic growth will in itself bring about development, a tenet that is contradicted by, among others, the annual reports of the United Nations Development Programme (UNDP). This so-called economic growth, as proposed by the international financial institutions, benefits mainly the most privileged classes and increases the Third World countries' state of dependency even further.[26] In addition, economic growth as it is actually practised is fundamentally incompatible with the preservation of the environment.

THE DECLARATION ON THE RIGHT TO DEVELOPMENT

This view of development, relentlessly maintained by the World Bank in spite of its patent failures, is incompatible with a text as laudable and eminently social as the Declaration on the Right to Development adopted by the United Nations in 1986:[27]

Article 1:1. The right to development is an unalienable human right...
Article 1:2. The human right to development implies the full realization of the right of peoples to self-determination, which includes [...] the exercise of their inalienable right to full sovereignty over all their natural wealth and resources.
Article 3:2. The realization of the right to development requires full respect for the principles of international law...

Article 8:1. States should undertake, at the national level, all necessary measures for the realization of the right to development... Appropriate economic and social reforms should be carried out with a view to eradicating all social injustices.

It was in March 1981 that the UN Human Rights Commission proposed to the Economic and Social Council the setting up of the first working group on the right to development. This group met a dozen or more times during the 1980s,[28] with the result that Resolution 41/128 of the UN General Assembly was adopted on 4 December 1986, subsequently to be known as the Declaration on the Right to Development.

Only one country dared vote against it: the United States, on the pretext that this Declaration was confused and imprecise, and rejecting the link between development and disarmament as well as the very idea of a transfer of resources from the developed North to the under-developed South. Eight countries abstained: Denmark, Finland, Federal Germany, Iceland, Israel, Japan, Sweden and Great Britain, insisting on the precedence of individual rights over the rights of peoples and refusing to consider development aid as an obligation under international law.[29]

THE CHARTER OF THE UNITED NATIONS AND SPECIALIZED AGENCIES

Although it is a resolution of the United Nations General Assembly, in practice the Declaration on the Right to Development does not have the binding force of international treaties. But other texts can play this role: the Charter of the United Nations (Preamble, paragraph 3 of Article 1 and Articles 55 and 56) is not only the constituent document of the UN, but also an international treaty that codifies the fundamental principles of international relations. The two covenants on civil and political rights and economic, social and cultural rights are also normative texts related to the right to development: all the rights stated in these covenants form part of the content of the right to development.[30]

The principal texts of the United Nations concern both individual rights and collective rights, the right to development and the right of the states to political and economic sovereignty. In practice, however, not only the World Bank but also the IMF, the WTO and transnational corporations have consistently refused to comply with their terms.

Until now, these institutions have been able to enjoy impunity on an alarming scale, because despite some interesting advances the present law is far from perfect. Of course, there are instruments and jurisdictions to deal with individual human rights and crimes against humanity, but other crimes that claim numerous victims throughout the world – economic crimes – are not at present subject to any international jurisdiction, agreement or definition.

THE WORLD BANK, A SPECIALIZED AGENCY OF THE UNITED NATIONS

Yet, in fact, the World Bank corresponds to the United Nations definition of one of the

specialized agencies established by intergovernmental agreement and having wide international responsibilities, as defined in their basic instruments, in economic, social, cultural, educational, health, and related fields....

Thus defined, the World Bank is linked to the UN system through the Economic and Social Council (known by the abbreviation ECOSOC, which acts under the authority of the General Assembly), as per Article 57, paragraph 1 of the Charter of the United Nations.

The UN system is based on international cooperation, and especially on international economic and social cooperation.

Under Article 55, with a view to the creation of conditions of stability and well-being that are necessary for peaceful and friendly relations between nations based on respect for the principle of equal rights and self-determination of peoples, the United Nations shall promote:

1. Higher standards of living, full employment, and conditions of economic and social progress and development;
2. Solutions of international economic, social, health, and related problems; and international and cultural cooperation;
3. Universal respect for, and observance of, human rights and fundamental freedoms for all, without distinction as to race, sex, language or religion.

The entire United Nations system is based on the two following principles: first, sovereign equality for all its members, and, second, members must in good faith fulfil the obligations they have undertaken by the terms of the Charter. Consequently, from a historic viewpoint and contrary to their pronouncements, the IMF and the World Bank are specialized agencies of the United Nations. As such, they are bound by the United Nations Charter.

Given this fact, it is impossible to evade the question: are the World Bank and the IMF legally bound to respect the obligations laid down in the United Nations Charter, including the obligation to respect human rights?

The International Court of Justice (ICJ) clearly ruled on this in the cases of Barcelone Traction and East Timor:[31] the articles of the World Bank are permeated with the obligations implied by customary law, in particular *erga omnes* obligations and *jus cogens* laws. These obligations, also called *imperative law*, mean that the rules of international law, whatever their nature, are always legally binding, and that their violation has specific legal consequences with regard to their corresponding obligations and rights. Among these, for example, are the principle of the sovereign equality of states, the prohibition of the use of force, of torture, of the forced disappearance of persons, all of which are imperative obligations. The *jus cogens* laws are an integral part of international public order from which no subject is exempt, whether or not that subject has ratified international treaties or agreements. The *erga omnes* obligations, very close to *jus cogens*, concern, as the International Court of Justice has noted, the legal obligation (or more specifically the obligation of prevention and repression) applicable to all subjects of international law, given the importance of the rights at stake, to protect these rights, and in particular the obligation to respect and ensure the respect of human rights at all times and in all circumstances.

While it is true that the World Bank and the IMF are independent of the UN at the operational level, it is nevertheless their duty to respect human rights and customary law in general.

The international financial institutions must incorporate this obligation in the implementation of their policies: no subject of international law can escape these obligations by invoking the absence of an explicit mandate or on the pretext of 'non-politicization', or even less by a restrictive interpretation of economic, social and cultural rights as being less binding than civil and political rights.

This last aspect has been effectively stressed by Eric David who states, as regards the laws applying to the IFI, that:

the rights more specifically affected by a situation of economic and social deterioration are economic, social and cultural rights. Such a situation in fact threatens the enjoyment of these rights by categories of the population in varying, but usually large proportions. It is not an exaggeration to say that situations of extreme poverty lead to a violation of practically all economic, social and cultural rights...[32]

He continues:

... if the rights affected by the SAPs are principally economic and social rights, the case also arises where, by a knock-on effect, the violation of these rights also leads to violation of the civil and political rights of the people concerned.[33]

CONCLUSION

Neither the World Bank nor the IMF should be able to invoke their 'constitutional right' in order to shirk their obligations to protect human rights, using the pretext that their decisions must be guided by economic considerations only.

It cannot be stated too emphatically: the policies pursued by the Bretton Woods institutions, whose field of action is planetary, have direct repercussions on the lives and fundamental rights of all peoples.[34]

APPENDIX

Declaration on the Right to Development
Adopted by General Assembly resolution 41/128 of 4 December 1986

The General Assembly,

Bearing in mind the purposes and principles of the Charter of the United Nations relating to the achievement of international co-operation in solving international problems of an economic, social, cultural or humanitarian nature, and in promoting and encouraging respect for human rights and fundamental freedoms for all without distinction as to race, sex, language or religion,

Recognizing that development is a comprehensive economic, social, cultural and political process, which aims at the constant improvement of the well-being of the entire population and of all individuals on the basis of their active, free and meaningful participation in development and in the fair distribution of benefits resulting therefrom,

Considering that under the provisions of the Universal Declaration of Human Rights everyone is entitled to a social and international order in which the rights and freedoms set forth in that Declaration can be fully realized,

Recalling the provisions of the International Covenant on Economic, Social and Cultural Rights and of the International Covenant on Civil and Political Rights,

Recalling further the relevant agreements, conventions, resolutions, recommendations and other instruments of the United Nations and its specialized agencies concerning the integral development of the human being, economic and social progress and development of all peoples, including those instruments concerning decolonization, the prevention of discrimination, respect for and observance of human rights and fundamental freedoms, the maintenance of international peace and security and the further promotion of friendly relations and co-operation among States in accordance with the Charter,

Recalling the right of peoples to self-determination, by virtue of which they have the right freely to determine their political status and to pursue their economic, social and cultural development,

Recalling also the right of peoples to exercise, subject to the relevant provisions of both International Covenants on Human Rights, full and complete sovereignty over all their natural wealth and resources,

Mindful of the obligation of States under the Charter to promote universal respect for and observance of human rights and fundamental freedoms for all without distinction of any kind such as race, colour, sex, language, religion, political or other opinion, national or social origin, property, birth or other status,

Considering that the elimination of the massive and flagrant violations of the human rights of the peoples and individuals affected by situations such as those resulting from colonialism, neocolonialism, apartheid, all forms of racism and racial discrimination, foreign domination and occupation, aggression and threats against national sovereignty, national unity and territorial integrity and threats of war would contribute to the establishment of circumstances propitious to the development of a great part of mankind,

Concerned at the existence of serious obstacles to development, as well as to the complete fulfilment of human beings and of peoples, constituted, inter alia, by the denial of civil, political, economic, social and cultural rights, and considering that all human rights and fundamental freedoms are indivisible and interdependent and that, in order to promote development, equal attention and urgent consideration should be given to the implementation, promotion and protection of civil, political, economic, social and cultural rights and that, accordingly, the promotion of, respect for and enjoyment of certain human rights and fundamental freedoms cannot justify the denial of other human rights and fundamental freedoms,

Considering that international peace and security are essential elements for the realization of the right to development,

Reaffirming that there is a close relationship between disarmament and development and that progress in the field of disarmament would considerably promote progress in the field of development and that resources released through disarmament measures should be devoted to the economic and social development and well-being of all peoples and, in particular, those of the developing countries,

Recognizing that the human person is the central subject of the development process and that development policy should therefore make the human being the main participant and beneficiary of development,

Recognizing that the creation of conditions favourable to the development of peoples and individuals is the primary responsibility of their States,

Aware that efforts at the international level to promote and protect human rights should be accompanied by efforts to establish a new international economic order,

Confirming that the right to development is an inalienable human right and that equality of opportunity for development is a prerogative both of nations and of individuals who make up nations,

Proclaims the following Declaration on the Right to Development:

Article 1

1. The right to development is an inalienable human right by virtue of which every human person and all peoples are entitled to participate in, contribute to, and enjoy economic, social, cultural and political development, in which all human rights and fundamental freedoms can be fully realized.

2. The human right to development also implies the full realization of the right of peoples to self-determination, which includes, subject to the relevant provisions of both International Covenants on Human Rights, the exercise of their inalienable right to full sovereignty over all their natural wealth and resources.

Article 2

1. The human person is the central subject of development and should be the active participant and beneficiary of the right to development.
2. All human beings have a responsibility for development, individually and collectively, taking into account the need for full respect for their human rights and fundamental freedoms as well as their duties to the community, which alone can ensure the free and complete fulfilment of the human being, and they should therefore promote and protect an appropriate political, social and economic order for development.
3. States have the right and the duty to formulate appropriate national development policies that aim at the constant improvement of the well-being of the entire population and of all individuals, on the basis of their active, free and meaningful participation in development and in the fair distribution of the benefits resulting therefrom.

Article 3

1. States have the primary responsibility for the creation of national and international conditions favourable to the realization of the right to development.
2. The realization of the right to development requires full respect for the principles of international law concerning friendly relations and co-operation among States in accordance with the Charter of the United Nations.
3. States have the duty to co-operate with each other in ensuring development and eliminating obstacles to development. States should realize their rights and fulfil their duties in such a manner as to promote a new international economic order based on sovereign equality, interdependence, mutual interest and co-operation among all States, as well as to encourage the observance and realization of human rights.

Article 4

1. States have the duty to take steps, individually and collectively, to formulate international development policies with a view to facilitating the full realization of the right to development.
2. Sustained action is required to promote more rapid development of developing countries. As a complement to the efforts of developing countries, effective international co-operation is essential in providing these countries with appropriate means and facilities to foster their comprehensive development.

Article 5

States shall take resolute steps to eliminate the massive and flagrant violations of the human rights of peoples and human beings affected by situations such as those resulting from apartheid, all forms of racism and racial discrimination, colonialism, foreign domination and occupation, aggression, foreign interference and threats against national sovereignty, national unity and territorial integrity, threats of war and refusal to recognize the fundamental right of peoples to self-determination.

Article 6

1. All States should co-operate with a view to promoting, encouraging and strengthening universal respect for and observance of all human rights and fundamental freedoms for all without any distinction as to race, sex, language or religion.
2. All human rights and fundamental freedoms are indivisible and interdependent; equal attention and urgent consideration should be given to the implementation, promotion and protection of civil, political, economic, social and cultural rights.
3. States should take steps to eliminate obstacles to development resulting from failure to observe civil and political rights, as well as economic social and cultural rights.

Article 7

All States should promote the establishment, maintenance and strengthening of international peace and security and, to that end, should do their utmost to achieve general and complete disarmament under effective international control, as well as to ensure that the resources released by effective disarmament measures are used for comprehensive development, in particular that of the developing countries.

Article 8

1. States should undertake, at the national level, all necessary measures for the realization of the right to development and shall ensure, inter alia, equality of opportunity for all in their access to basic resources, education, health services, food, housing, employment and the fair distribution of income. Effective measures should be undertaken to ensure that women have an active role in the development process. Appropriate economic and social reforms should be carried out with a view to eradicating all social injustices.
2. States should encourage popular participation in all spheres as an important factor in development and in the full realization of all human rights.

Article 9

1. All the aspects of the right to development set forth in the present Declaration are indivisible and interdependent and each of them should be considered in the context of the whole.

2. Nothing in the present Declaration shall be construed as being contrary to the purposes and principles of the United Nations, or as implying that any State, group or person has a right to engage in any activity or to perform any act aimed at the violation of the rights set forth in the Universal Declaration of Human Rights and in the International Covenants on Human Rights.

Article 10

Steps should be taken to ensure the full exercise and progressive enhancement of the right to development, including the formulation, adoption and implementation of policy, legislative and other measures at the national and international levels.

23
Time to Put an End to World Bank Impunity

IS IT POSSIBLE TO SUE THE WORLD BANK?

Contrary to popular notion, the World Bank is not entitled to immunity either as an institution or as a legal entity. Section 3 of Article 7 of the Charter (articles of agreement) explicitly states that the Bank may be taken to court under certain conditions. For example, it may be tried by a national court of justice in countries where it is represented and/or has issued bonds.[1]

The possibility of bringing an action against the Bank has existed since its foundation in 1944 and has never been modified until now for the simple reason that the Bank finances the loans it grants to member countries by borrowing (by issuing bonds) on the financial markets. Originally, these bonds were bought by the big, mainly North American, private banks. Now, other institutions, including pension funds and trade unions, buy them too.

The World Bank's founder countries estimated that they would not be able to sell the Bank's bonds unless they guaranteed buyers the right to sue the Bank in case of default. This is why there is a fundamental difference between the immunity status of the WB and the IMF. The IMF can have immunity since it finances its loans itself using the money paid in by its members in the form of *pro rata* shares. If the Bank does not enjoy immunity, it is not for humanitarian reasons but to provide creditors with the requisite guarantees.

It is therefore perfectly possible to sue the World Bank in the numerous countries where it has offices. It is possible in Djakarta or in Dili, the capital of East Timor, in Kinshasa, Brussels, Moscow or Washington, since the WB is represented in all those countries.

WHY SUE?

Since the World Bank has been making loans,[2] a good portion of them have been used to carry out policies that had a detrimental effect on the welfare of hundreds of millions of citizens. What do we mean by that? The WB has systematically given priority to loans for big infrastructures such as huge dams,[3] investment in industries that extract raw materials (for example, open-cast mines, numerous pipelines – of which the most recent are the Chad–Cameroon and the Baku–Tbilisi–Ceyhan[4] pipelines), agricultural policies in favour of 'all-export' at the expense of food security and food sovereignty, and power stations that devour tropical forests.

Moreover, the WB has frequently come to the aid of dictatorships known to be guilty of crimes against humanity. There were the dictatorships of the Southern Cone of Latin America from the 1960s to the 1980s, numerous African dictatorships (Mobutu from 1965 until his fall in 1997, the Apartheid regime of South Africa), regimes of the former Soviet bloc such as the Ceaucescu dictatorship in Romania, those of South-East Asia and the Far East, such as that of Marcos from 1972 to 1986 in the Philippines, Suharto from 1965 to 1998 in Indonesia, South Korea (1961–87) and Thailand (1966–88), up to and including today's dictatorship in China.

At the same time the WB, along with other actors, has contributed to the systematic destabilization of progressive and democratic governments by withdrawing all aid. This was the case for the Sukarno government in Indonesia until he was overthrown in 1965, the governments of Juscelino Kubitschek (1956–60) followed by Joao Goulart (1961–64) in Brazil, finally overthrown by a military *coup d'état*; Salvador Allende's government in Chile (1970–73), and so on.

Next, there are all the loans made by the WB to the colonial powers (Belgium, Great Britain, France, Italy, the Netherlands...) to enable them to exploit the natural resources of the countries they ruled until the 1960s. All those loans were later included in the external debt of the states when they became independent. For example, the independent state of Congo had to finish paying off the debt incurred by Belgium in its name. The same thing happened for Kenya, Uganda, Nigeria, Gabon, Mauritania, Algeria and Somalia for the debts contracted in their names by the colonial governments.

Then there are the structural adjustment loans that the World Bank has granted since the 1970s. These loans are not designed for any particular economic project, but are intended to help implement global policies with the ultimate aim of completely opening up the economies of the 'beneficiary' countries to investments and imports, mainly from the principal shareholders of the WB. This means that the Bank supports policies denationalizing the assisted countries to the advantage of a few of its members. Thus a handful of industrial powers impose their wishes on the majority of the inhabitants and the countries of the planet. The fact that all their remedies – whether long-term structural remedies or the 'short sharp shock' type – do more harm than good has been demonstrated repeatedly in the string of crises that began with the Tequila crisis that hit Mexico in 1994. The Bank's new priorities, such as the privatization of water and land, along with its recent refusal to apply the recommendations of the independent Commission on Extractive Industries, clearly indicate that the Bank has no intention of changing its course and that new social catastrophes are in preparation – powerful tsunamis caused by the cataclysmic interventions of the World Bank!

WHO MIGHT BRING A LEGAL ACTION?

Associations representing the interests of people adversely affected by WB loans and/or by its support for dictatorships could bring an independent action and sue the Bank for damages in national courts. Holders of World Bank bonds – there are not only bankers, but also trade unions – could sue the Bank over the use it makes of the money it borrows from them. There is no guarantee that such lawsuits would be successful, but it is hard to see why citizens' movements should not use their right to hold the WB accountable for its acts. It is inconceivable that the nefarious practices of an institution like the WB should not one day be sanctioned by a decision of justice.

WHY HAVE NO SUCH PROCEDURES EVER BEEN INITIATED?

The clause of the World Bank Charter (Article 7, Section 8) that grants immunity to the decision makers and officials in exercising their duties has tended to obscure the possibility of suing the WB as a legal entity (Article 7, Section 3: see endnote 1). Yet it is more important to be able to demand that the Bank answer for its actions as an institution than to simply hold its executives to account. Indeed, the same clause of its Charter (Article 7, Section 8) provides for the WB to decide to remove the immunity protecting its directors and officials. Actions could also be envisaged against high-ranking officials after they have left office.

Another reason why so far there have been no actions brought against the Bank is that it has taken a long time for the truth to emerge, and for people to realize just how systematic and generalized its reprehensible practices are. In the eyes of the citizens, it is often their national governments that are seen to be responsible for the policies demanded by the WB, so its true role passes unnoticed.

DOES THE UN CONVENTION OF 1947 NOT GIVE FULL IMMUNITY TO THE SPECIALIZED AGENCIES OF THE UNITED NATIONS TO WHICH THE WORLD BANK BELONGS?

A United Nations Convention on the Privileges and Immunities of the Specialized Agencies was approved by the General Assembly on 21 November 1947.[5] Article X, Section 37 of the convention, concerning the annexes and the application of the convention to every specialized institution, states that the convention

becomes applicable to each specialized agency when it has transmitted to the Secretary-General of the United Nations the final text of the relevant annex and has informed him that it accepts the standard clauses, as modified by this annex...

The Bank sent its copy back.

Annexe VI concerns the International Bank for Reconstruction and Development, and thus the World Bank. And what does it contain? This is where the Bank has actually inserted statutes that specify the circumstances under which it loses its immunity!

Within the United Nations, the World Bank thus prefers to conform to its status as a bank rather than take advantage of the immunity given to the UN's agencies. Here is the relevant paragraph:

The convention (including the current annexe) will apply to the International Bank for Reconstruction and Development (hereafter mentioned under the name of 'the Bank') with reservation of the following provisions: 1. The following text will replace the one of section 4: 'The Bank can only be sued in a court that has its jurisdiction in a member state where the Bank has a branch, where it has appointed an agent in order to accept demands or notice of demands or where it has issued or guaranteed transferable securities'.

It is therefore possible to sue the World Bank under the terms of the 1947 United Nations Convention and its annexes.

24
An Indictment of the World Bank

(1)   During its sixty years of existence, the World Bank has actively
        supported all the dictatorships and all the corrupt regimes of
        the US-allied camp.

(2)   Despite having detected massive misappropriations of funds,
        the Bank has maintained, and even increased, the amounts
        loaned (see the classic case of Congo-Zaire under Marshall
        Mobutu after the Blumenthal Report in 1982).

(3)   Through its financial support it helped prop up the dictatorial
        regime of Juvénal Habyarimana in Rwanda until 1992, thus
        allowing the army to increase its strength five-fold. The
        economic reforms it imposed in 1990 destabilized the country
        and aggravated the latent contradictions. The genocide that
        the Habyarimana regime had been preparing since the end
        of the 1980s was effectively perpetrated from 6 April 1994,
        leading to almost one million deaths among the Tutsis (and
        moderate Hutus). Subsequently, the World Bank demanded
        repayment of the debt contracted by the regime responsible
        for this genocide.[1]

(4)   The Bank supported a number of dictatorial regimes in the other
        camp (Romania from 1973 to 1982, China from 1980) in order
        to weaken the USSR before its collapse in 1991.

(5)   It has supported the worst dictatorships until they were
        overthrown. For example, its classic support for Suharto in
        Indonesia from 1965 to 1998, for Marcos in the Philippines
        from 1972 to 1986.

(6)   It has actively sabotaged progressive experiments in democracy
        (from Jacobo Arbenz in the first half of the 1950s in Guatemala,
        to the Sandinistas in Nicaragua in the 1980s, and of course
        Salvador Allende in Chile from 1970 to 1973).

(7)   The Bank finances tyrants and then demands that their victims
        repay the odious debts contracted by their oppressors.

(8)   In the same way, the Bank has forced countries gaining
        independence at the end of the 1950s and early 1960s to

repay odious debts contracted by former colonial powers for the purpose of colonizing these countries.

(9) The Bank has given financial support to countries (South Africa and Portugal) that were under a UN-decreed international financial boycott.

(10) The Bank has supported a country that annexed another by force (the annexation of East Timor by Indonesia in 1975).

(11) On the environmental front, the Bank continues to pursue a productivist policy that is disastrous for populations and detrimental to nature.[2]

(12) Among the projects least respectful of human rights and directly supported by the Bank is the 'transmigration' project in Indonesia, many components of which may well be classified as crimes against humanity (destruction of the natural environment of native populations, enforced displacement of populations).

(13) The World Bank (like the IMF) aided the emergence of factors that caused the outbreak of the debt crisis of 1982. To sum up: (a) the World Bank encouraged countries to contract debts in conditions that led to their overindebtedness; (b) it drove, and even forced, countries to remove capital movement and exchange controls, thereby increasing the volatility of capital and significantly facilitating its flight. This also gave considerable leverage to speculators (failing a return to strict control of capital movements); (c) it drove countries to abandon industrialization by import substitution and replace it with a model based on export promotion. The growth in exports from developing countries on the world market – where demand was stagnating – caused a fall in prices and a deterioration of terms of trade.

(14) The Bank concealed risks even after actually detecting them (overindebtedness, payment crises, negative net transfers, etc.).

(15) As soon as a crisis broke out, the World Bank systematically favoured the creditors and weakened the debtors.

(16) Together with the IMF, it has recommended, and even enforced, policies by which the burden of debt was borne by the people, while favouring the most powerful.

(17) Together with the IMF, it has continued the 'generalization' of an economic model that systematically increases the inequalities between countries, and within countries.

(18) The Bank has strengthened the large private corporations and weakened both the authorities of countries and the small producers. It has heightened the exploitation of workers and increased their precariousness. It has had the same detrimental effect on small producers.

(19) Its self-proclaimed fight against poverty fails to conceal a policy that in practice reproduces and aggravates the very causes of poverty.

(20) The liberalization of capital flows, which it has systematically encouraged, has increased the incidence of tax evasion, flight of funds and corruption.

(21) The liberalization of trade has strengthened the strong and further weakened the weak. The majority of small and medium producers in developing countries are unable to withstand competition from large corporations, whether in the North or the South.

(22) The World Bank operates in close cooperation with the IMF and the WTO to enforce an agenda that is radically opposed to the satisfaction of basic human rights.

(23) The Bank declares that it keeps up a permanent dialogue with civil society and with the poor, but this has not resulted in any positive changes in its policy. One observes repeated semblances of dialogue, in which the macroeconomic framework is the dominant, unchallengeable one promoted by the Bank.

(24) The Bank uses the groups made most vulnerable and deprived by its policies in order to give these policies a human and democratic face and to present them as being the conscious choice of these groups (women, the deserving poor, etc.).

(25) When independent commissions appointed by the Bank make recommendations that challenge the interests of its main stakeholders, the Bank refuses to follow them (see the report on extractive industries and on dams).

(26) It systematically piles up profits during the most severe economic crises. The Bank gets richer at the expense of indebted countries.

(27) It keeps these countries marginalized even though they represent the majority of its members, thus favouring a handful of governments in wealthy countries.

(28) The Bank has shown its complete inability to reform itself. The appointment of Paul Wolfowitz, one of the main strategists of

the criminal invasion of Iraq, as president of the World Bank, only emphasizes its destructive orientation.

(29) To sum up, the World Bank is a despotic instrument in the hands of an international oligarchy (a handful of major powers and their transnational corporations) who bolster an international capitalist system that is detrimental to mankind and the environment.

(30) A new international, democratic institution must urgently be found to promote a redistribution of wealth and to support the people's efforts towards development that is socially just and respectful of nature.

(31) It is necessary to make a radical break with the capitalist system of which the Bank is one of its mainstays.

Appendix
The World Bank Group Fact Sheet
International Bank for Reconstruction and Development (IBRD), World Bank Group

The International Bank for Reconstruction and Development was founded on the same day as the IMF. No such institution had existed before; and its basic structure, as laid down in the Articles of Agreement, has never changed. At present it employs about 12,300 people, of whom about 9,300 are based in Washington. These include about 800 economists.

The Bank's main purposes were: 'to assist in the reconstruction and development of territories of members by facilitating the investment of capital for productive purposes' and 'to promote the long-range balanced growth of international trade'. Article 1 also provides for improving 'productivity, the standard of living and conditions of labour' in the territories of member countries (Art. 1).

THE BANK'S MODE OF ADMINISTRATION

In principle, the Bank's highest instance is the Board of Governors, with each country being represented by a governor. The governors of the Bank are usually ministers of finance or the president of the respective nation's Central Bank.

The Bank's president is supposed to be chosen by the governors, but in practice, the president has always been a US citizen chosen by the US government, and usually by the Treasury Department.

The IBRD's board of directors consists of eight permanent representatives or Executive Directors (the United States, Japan, Germany, France, the United Kingdom, Saudi Arabia, China, Russia) and 16 executive directors who represent groups of countries (often led by a developed country).

In 2006, the ten richest industrialized countries controlled more than 58 per cent of the votes. On the other hand, 45 African countries had only 5.4 per cent of the votes between them, and two executive directors out of 24.

Table 25.1 Distribution of voting rights between administrators (or executive directors) of the World Bank in March 2006

Country	%	Group presided by	%	Group presided by	%
United States	16.39	Belgium	4.80	Indonesia	2.54
Japan	7.87	Netherlands	4.46	Kuwait	2.91
Germany	4.49	Spain	4.50	Switzerland	3.04
France	4.30	Italy	3.50	Brazil	3.59
United Kingdom	4.30	Canada	3.85	India	3.40
Saudi Arabia	2.78	Iceland	3.34	Algeria	3.19
China	2.78	South Korea	3.45	Peru	2.32
Russia	2.78	Burundi	3.41	Guinea-Bissau	1.99

Source: World Bank [Somalia did not take part in the election.]

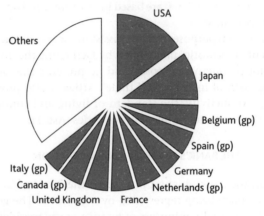

(gp) means the executive director represents a group of countries.

Figure 25.1 Voting rights of some of the executive directors of the IBRD in March 2006

Source: World Bank.

The executive directors reside in Washington, meet frequently (at least once a week) and must approve every loan and most of the Bank's policies. Everyday decisions require a simple majority of the votes but any action to change the articles of the constitutive charter or to modify the distribution of voting rights requires the approval of at least three-fifths of the membership and 85 per cent of total votes. With 16.39 per cent of the votes, the United States can veto any change in the statutes or the distribution of voting rights, that is to say, it can exercise its veto over any reform of the Bretton Woods institutions.[1]

PRESENTATION OF THE FIVE COMPONENTS OF THE WORLD BANK GROUP

The World Bank is a conglomerate of international institutions and organizations. The five component organizations are: the International Bank for Reconstruction and Development (IBRD), the International Development Association (IDA), the International Finance Corporation (IFC), the International Centre for Settlement of Investment Disputes (ICSID) and the Multilateral Investment Guarantee Agency (MIGA). The conglomerate is known as the World Bank Group and has local branches in 109 countries.

The International Bank for Reconstruction and Development (IBRD)

At first, its actions were directed towards both the industrialized and the developing countries. Today, the Bank finances sector-based projects, public or private, for Third World countries and the former Soviet bloc (which together constitute all the developing countries). The Bank has capital assets provided by the member countries, and mostly borrowed on the international money markets.

The International Bank for Reconstruction and Development (42 members, when it started out in 1947; 184 members in 2006) grants loans for the major activity sectors (agriculture and energy), mainly to middle-income countries.

Types of loan granted by the IBRD:

1. Project-loans, that is, standard loans for power stations, the petroleum sector, the forestry industry, agricultural projects, dams, roads, water distribution and purification, etc.
2. Sector-based adjustment loans for an entire sector of the national economy: energy, agriculture, industry, etc.
3. Loans to institutions that influence the policies of certain bodies in favour of foreign trade and foreign investments in the country. They also finance the privatization of companies and public services.
4. Structural adjustment loans.
5. Poverty reduction loans.
6. Others.

The Bank finances the loans it makes by issuing bonds, which may be considered as particularly safe investments, since they are guaranteed by the founding states, to the limit of 100 per cent of their respective shares.

The International Development Association (IDA)

The International Development Association, numbering 163 members in 2006, was founded in 1960, and specializes in very long-term loans (35 to 40 years, starting with ten years' grace) with nil or very low interest rates, to low-income countries.

The IBRD practises market rates, which are too costly for the poorest countries. So in order to succeed in its mission of financing development, the World Bank Group has equipped itself with an instrument of concessionary funding reserved for the poorest countries that do not have access to the capital markets.

The IDA is financed by public funds in the form of voluntary donations. However, budgetary restrictions and the developed countries' refusal to contribute to the IDA fund considerably limit the amount of credit destined for the poorest countries. The resources provided by the developed countries and a few emerging countries represent 90 per cent of total IDA funds. Moreover, the IBRD can raise money from its own income to subsidize the IDA. Whereas the IBRD regularly makes juicy profits (over a billion dollars a year, pushing its own capital up to $38 billion in 2006), the IDA shows a recurrent deficit. This forces the IDA to make regular appeals to the member states to replenish its funds.

The International Finance Corporation (IFC)

The International Finance Corporation is the subsidiary of the Bank in charge of financing private Third World businesses or institutions. The official statutes of the IFC were drawn up by the IBRD in 1955; and it came into being in the summer of 1956. When the IBRD was founded, several officials had pleaded in favour of creating another entity to complement the Bank's role. They wanted a companion institution for the Bank that would be entrusted with promoting private investment in poor countries. Towards the end of the 1940s, the president of the World Bank, Eugene R. Black, and the vice-president, former banker and director of General Foods Corporation, Robert L. Garner, set themselves to tackle this task. Garner, who was convinced that private enterprise had an important role to play, with his assistant Richard Demuth, came up with the idea of creating an institution affiliated to the World Bank, so that the Bank itself would not have to draw on its own resources for private-sector lending. The idea made its first official appearance in a report published in March 1951 by a consultative board on US development policy, presided by Nelson Rockefeller.

The IFC strives to promote private-sector investment, particularly by financing private-sector projects in the developing countries; by helping private companies in the developing countries to mobilize funds on the international money markets; and by providing advice and technical assistance to companies and governments.

The International Centre for Settlement of Investment Disputes (ICSID)

The ICSID was founded in 1966, with the purpose of providing a means of conciliation and arbitration to settle investment disputes between contracting states and nationals of other contracting states. To put it simply, it is an international arbitration tribunal that deals with disputes arising between a private investor from a contracting party state and the state where the investment is based. The ICSID's jurisdiction (Article 25) extends to disputes of a legal nature, relating directly to an investment, between a contracting state (or a government organization or body dependent on that state and designated by it to the ICSID) and a national from another contracting state.

The ICSID is usually designated as competent to deal with disputes arising within the context of bilateral investment agreements. Thus, almost 900 bilateral treaties on the promotion and protection of investments explicitly name the ICSID as the instance for settling disputes between the private investor of a contracting party, on the one hand, and the state where the investment concerned is based, on the other. The ICSID's arbitral sentence is mandatory and cannot be appealed against (Article 53). The ICSID is a member of the World Bank Group, but from an institutional point of view, it is an autonomous international organization that completes the Bank's range of intervention.

There is no obligation to have recourse to the ICSID for conciliation or arbitration. However, once the parties are engaged, neither may withdraw unilaterally from the ICSID's arbitration. Once the ICSID has made a decision, all the countries that have ratified the convention, even if they are not involved in the dispute, must acknowledge and apply the decision. Since 1978, the ICSID's area of jurisdiction has increased. A whole new set of rules allows it to intervene in cases that do not fall within the domain of the convention. Thus, it can now intervene in arbitration procedures even when one of the parties to the dispute is a state or the national of a state that has not ratified the convention. It can also be called on to witness the facts of a case.

Until the mid-1980s, the disputes dealt with by the ICSID arose from agreements made under investment contracts. Since then, it has dealt increasingly with disputes arising from agreements made under bilateral treaties. Because of this, cases submitted to the ICSID more often concern events like civil wars and problems of expropriation than investment contracts.

The Multilateral Investment Guarantee Agency (MIGA)

Founded in 1988 as a member of the World Bank Group, the mission of the MIGA is to promote foreign direct investment by offering the guarantees of an international institution to private investors and private creditors. It also encourages the developing countries to carry out reforms aimed at attracting private investments, while at the same time enhancing economic development.

CONCLUSION

The World Bank's subsidiaries – the International Finance Corporation (IFC); the Multilateral Investment Guarantee Agency (MIGA); the International Centre for Settlement of Investment Disputes (ICSID) – have been designed to weave a web of ever tighter mesh.

Let us take a theoretical example to illustrate the effects of their policies. The World Bank grants a loan to the government of a country on condition that it privatize its water distribution and purification system. The public company is thus sold to a private consortium including the IFC, a World Bank subsidiary.

Then the population affected by the privatization protests against the sudden sharp increase in rates and the fall in the quality of the service provided, and the government turns against the predatory transnational company, the dispute is dealt with by the ICSID, which thus finds itself on both sides of the judge's bench.

A situation has been reached where the World Bank Group is present at every level: it imposes and finances privatization via the IBRD and IDA; it invests in the privatized company through the IFC; it provides the company with guarantees covering it against political risk, through the good offices of the MIGA; and it judges any disputes that may arise through the ICSID.

This is exactly what happened in El Alto, in Bolivia, between 1997 and 2005 (see accompanying box).

The example of El Alto in Bolivia

On 13 January 2005, after three days of mobilization by the inhabitants of El Alto, the Bolivian president promised the population that he would terminate the 30-year concession granted to the transnational company, Suez.

What caused the popular uprising of January 2005 in El Alto?
On 24 July 1997, under pressure from the World Bank and the IMF, the Bolivian government granted a 30-year concession to the company Aguas del Illimani–Suez, for the distribution of drinking water and the treatment of sewage in the town of El Alto and the capital, La Paz. Aguas del Illimani is controlled by the Suez company, a world leader in the commercialization of water, along with Vivendi of France and Thames Water of Great Britain. The concession was attributed fraudulently, as the normal rules of calling for public tender were not respected. The call for tender was launched after a study carried out by the French bank, BNP Paribas. Only one company responded: Aguas del Illimani–Lyonnaise des Eaux (Suez). Instead of proceeding to make a second call for tender, to get several offers, the contract was signed in double quick time. This concession made to a transnational corporation was the result of the privatization of the public municipal company, Samapa, imposed by the World Bank, the IMF and the Inter-American Development Bank (IDB) when the Bolivian debt was rescheduled in 1996.

The World Bank was furthermore a direct receiver of the privatization since it holds 8 per cent of Aguas del Illimani shares through its private investment instrument, the International Finance Corporation. As for the Lyonnaise des Eaux–Suez, it holds 55 per cent of the shares.

In El Alto, Suez deprived 200,000 inhabitants of drinking water
Although Aguas del Illimani claimed that the whole population of El Alto had access to clean drinking water, the reality was quite a different story, with 70,000 people living in houses that were not connected to the water mains, as the cost of connection was exorbitant. It came to the astronomical sum of $445, i.e., approximately eight months of the minimum wage. Moreover, 130,000 people living on the territory of the Aguas del Illimani concession were outside the area covered by the transnational corporation.

Insufficient investment in the maintenance and improvement of the installations
According to the contract signed in 1997, Aguas del Illimani was under obligation to guarantee the maintenance and improvement of the water pipes and the sewers. In fact, its investments fell far short of meeting these requirements. Between 1997 and 2004, Aguas del Illimani only invested $55 million, mainly raised by loans from the Bank and the IDB or donations from foreign governments as part of their Official

▶

Development Assistance. This was the case for donations from Switzerland destined to guarantee access to clean drinking water for the poor. Insufficient investments resulted in pockets of contamination in certain areas owing to the distribution of insalubrious water.

Increased water rates
At the beginning of the contract, in 1997, water rates increased by 19 per cent. As for the cost of connection to the mains, that rose by 33 per cent. Despite the fact that Bolivian law prohibited the dollarization of prices (Law 2066 of 11 April 2000, Art. 8), Aguas del Illimani indexed its rates against the dollar.

Stealing from both the poor and the government
With its exorbitant rates, Suez redeemed its low investments and made a profit of 13 per cent. As if that were not enough, it used Article 26 of the contract to obtain the guarantee that in case of non-renewal of the concession in 2027, the government would have to reimburse the company for all the investments it had made. Furthermore, while Suez had agreed to pay Samapa $8 million a year, that company claims that it has only received $3.5 million a year.

World Bank: the judge and the judged
For these reasons, the entire population of El Alto took to the streets for three days running, demanding that Aguas del Illimani–Suez should leave and the distribution of water be returned to the public sector. After the Bolivian president's decree, Suez announced that it would lodge a complaint with the ICSID (the International Centre for Settlement of Investment Disputes), one of the five branches of the World Bank Group. Should the ICSID agree to deal with the complaint, any judgment it might pass should be declared null and void, since the World Bank would be both the judge and the judged. For as previously mentioned, the World Bank is a shareholder of Aguas del Illimani via the IFC.

Afterword
The World Bank: Hands Up,
This is a Hold-Up!

An Interview with Eric Toussaint
by Miguel Riera
(*El Viejo Topo*, Barcelona, No. 232, May 2007)

Having been accused of nepotism, Paul Wolfowitz had to resign as president of the World Bank. He is being replaced by Robert Zoelick, who has imposed bilateral free trade agreements on several countries of the South. The World Bank thus proves that it is incapable of becoming democratic and adopting policies that respect people's right to social justice and ecologically sustainable development. Fortunately, several South American governments have taken a strong stand: Ecuador has expelled the World Bank representative, Bolivia has withdrawn from the ICSID, Venezuela has announced its withdrawal from the WB and the IMF, and discussions are ongoing for the Bank of the South.

The first Spanish edition of the book *Banque Mondiale: le Coup d'état permanent* (The World Bank: A never-ending coup d'état), by Éric Toussaint, president of CADTM-Belgium (Committee for the Abolition of the Third World Debt), was published by *El Viejo Topo* in January 2007. This book, which meticulously analyzes the practices and objectives of the World Bank, situates the policies of the Bank in their political and geo-strategic contexts, bringing to light the hidden agenda of one of the most important international institutions.

The subtitle to the Spanish edition of your book, 'a never-ending coup d'état', is very provocative. Why did you choose this subtitle?

I wanted to emphasize the fact that, throughout its history, the World Bank (WB) has supported numerous despotic regimes that were allied to the United States or the imperial powers, which together with the US, control the WB, the IMF... I am thinking of England, France, Germany, Japan and other less important imperial powers. I wanted to highlight how the WB has supported despotic regimes or participated in the destabilization of democratic regimes. For example, I explain the contribution of the WB in destabilizing the Joao Goulart regime in Brazil in the early 1960s; it suspended loans to the government of Salvador Allende in Chile in the 1970s; it suspended financial aid to the Sandinistas in the 1980s. Contrary to popular belief that the WB is an effective instrument contributing to development, I show how in reality it serves the foreign policy aims of the US and directly intervenes in the political life of its member countries. I am talking about the political life of countries of the so-called Third-World, since of course the WB does not intervene in the economic and political life of the US, Belgium or Spain, etc. This is where the notion of 'coup d'état' comes from. It must also be added that using the external debt as leverage, the World Bank intervenes in the everyday governmental decisions of the debtor countries. For example, when in 2005, Rafael Correa, the current president of Ecuador, but the then finance minister, decided to allocate a larger percentage of his country's oil revenues to social programmes, the WB insisted that this policy be abandoned. The minister refused, but under pressure from Washington through local politicians, he had to resign. This is an external intervention of the World Bank, and in this case, with the support of the International Monetary Fund and which ended with the resignation of a minister.

Do you think that the World Bank's disregard for human rights and democracy is still topical today?

Yes, this disregard does still exist. However, there has been a change in discourse. The WB now integrates the question of human rights within its discourse, its public relations campaigns and its policies in a very clever way, in order to placate and co-opt organizations from the so-called civil society (NGOs, etc.) even though in fact the WB spends only a tiny fraction of its budget to finance NGO projects geared towards women, health or education. It pretends to promote human rights, but globally it persists with macroeconomic policies that undermine human rights as they are defined in the Universal Declaration of Human Rights 1948 and in various international conventions and treaties, such as the International Covenant on Economic, Social and Cultural Rights of 1966. The macroeconomic policies of the World Bank seek to increase privatization in developing countries, whereas privatization means, on the one hand, that key companies in the debtor countries are bought by Northern multi-nationals and on the other hand, that health, education and other vital services such as postal services, telecommunications and water distribution are privatized. It has been shown that such policies are completely incompatible with the application of human rights on the global level.

In relation to democracy, do you think that the World Bank continues to support despotic regimes or that it would do so in the future?

It's clear that the WB supports dictatorships. For example, Pakistan, a 'major client' according to WB terminology, is a military dictatorship, and manifestly, a strategic ally of the US in the region. We can also take the case of Turkey, which is not a dictatorship, but where there is a clear disregard for human and political rights, for example, towards the Kurds. Turkey has always been a 'client' of the WB. In Africa, the WB is present in Chad, a country ruled through the dictatorship of Idriss Déby, because of the presence of oil and because of important interests of North American corporations in the region. It signs agreements with Cameroon and Congo-Brazzaville, both dictatorships. The future actions of the WB will depend on the strategy of the US. Some analysts believe that US strategy, at least in parts of Asia, has once again turned towards direct support for dictatorships.

The second subtitle of your book, 'The hidden agenda of the Washington Consensus', seems to imply that right from the start of the World Bank and the International Monetary Fund, there was a hidden agenda, that the intention was to create a structure of domination.

When I talk about the Washington Consensus, I am referring to the general policies that have been applied since the 1980s and 1990s, when this concept came into being. With this subtitle, I want to highlight that the hidden aim of these policies, which affect the whole world, is to reconquer all the economies and to integrate them into the capitalist system, and that with this aim in mind, the types of measures that have been imposed become coherent. For example, I explain in my book that the type of policies imposed, in the context of structural adjustment, by the WB and the IMF already existed in the 1960s. However, with the Washington Consensus, the primary aspect of the reforms became privatization, and from the 1990s to 2000, there has been a major wave of takeovers, with big multinational companies acquiring the control of natural resources of so-called 'developing' countries and other strategic sectors of industry and services. This tactic is relatively new and it is part of this coherent strategy of planetary conquest that I mentioned.

Beyond the theme of privatization and the will to acquire the resources of developing countries, can you explain what are the key aspects of the Structural Adjustment Programmes?

Of course. There are two levels in structural adjustment. First comes 'shock therapy', which generally consists of brutal devaluation of a developing country's currency while brutally raising the internal interest rate. For example, the currency of 13 francophone African countries – these countries share a common currency, the CFA – was devalued by 50 per cent in 1994. Brazil's currency, the Real, was devalued by 44 per cent in 1999. Theoretically, these brutal devaluations serve to increase competitiveness of indebted countries on the global market, to increase export revenues and thus guarantee payment of external debts. The increase of internal rates supposedly serves to attract foreign investment, but in reality it gives rise to a general recession, as consumption decreases due to devaluation, which in turn occasions an internal price hike as many items have to be imported, and since the rise in interest rates denies the population access to credit, small and medium entrepreneurs, and sometimes even the big national producers, cannot increase their investments because the internal interest rates are too high. All this provokes chain bankruptcies, as we saw in South-East Asia in 1997–98; bankruptcies of banks, industries and services. This is generally what arises from shock therapy, causing a disaster: recession and increase in unemployment. For example, to return to the case of South-East Asia, in the space of six months of following IMF and WB policies, between 1997 and early 1998, 23 million people were left unemployed.

And after shock therapy?

The structural adjustment measures have as principal aim to open the economies of developing countries. This involves the abolition or the decrease of customs tariffs to allow importation without taxation, which increases competition between local and global producers. Generally, this leads to the bankruptcy of many local producers. Barriers to the movement of capital are also abolished. Free movement of capital, whether national or foreign, is supposed to increase foreign investment, but in fact it leaves the country at the mercy of international capital, which can enter and leave freely, sometimes even while attacking the host country through currency speculation (as was the case against Mexico in 1994–95; against the Asian countries I just mentioned, against Brazil, Argentina, Turkey, and Thailand recently). Furthermore, this allows the capitalists within the Southern countries to legalize capital flight. These days we cannot talk about capital flight, as it has become completely legal, and they can freely place their capital in the financial markets of the North. As I have already mentioned, an especially negative aspect is the privatization of key strategic companies, whether in the sector of natural resources or in services. There is massive pressure to privatize water distribution, the production and distribution of electricity, postal services, telecommunications... All these services must be privatized... This, in effect, is the policy of the World Bank and the IMF. This implies forcing the poor to pay for basic services, such as education and health. In Africa, 20 years ago, healthcare and the basic drugs were mostly free. The new policy consists in making these health services fee-paying. Families also have to pay the teacher of the small village primary school. This fundamental element of the structural adjustment is called 'policy of cost recovery'.

What about fiscal policy?

At the level of taxation, the measures insist on the progressive abolition of income tax and raising indirect taxation, such as VAT. In West Africa, there is a unique VAT rate of 19 per cent, even on water and electricity services. These policies increase in a structural way the subordination of the economies of the South to Northern capital, but are less advantageous to the capitalist classes of the South, which then have to find ways to increase their revenues. Consequently this deepens inequalities in the countries of the South and an increasing section of the population finds itself excluded from basic services.

Does this mean that the policies of the WB and the IMF, instead of reducing poverty, in reality increase it?

Indeed, we can assert that poverty is increasing in the countries of the South, even though the Bank claims the opposite.

What is the impact of the World Bank (and of course the IMF, an institution which we cannot ignore) on the capacities of countries of the South for food self-sufficiency?

This is a very important question. Since its creation in the mid-1940s, and despite its claims to promote the development of the countries of the South, the politics of the World Bank aim to increase exports of raw materials as well as agricultural products. What does this imply for Africa, for example? Up until the early 1960s, Africa was self-sufficient in the production of cereals to feed its population, but now Africa is a net importer of cereals. Under recommendations from the World Bank and other international organizations, which claimed that cereal production is better in the mild climates of the North and that the countries of the South could advantageously exchange their tropical products against the products of the North, especially cereals, Africa has increased its capacity to produce exportable agricultural products: coffee, tea, cotton, etc. and has decreased its production of cereals. Consequently, entire regions in the South have lost food sovereignty, that is they are no longer able to feed their population and have become dependent on imported cereals while exporting tropical produce.

In these conditions, are there any alternatives?

Of course. The need to propose alternatives imposed itself through the emergence of mass demonstrations. Already in the 1980s there were uprisings against the plans that the WB was defending: in April 1984 in the Dominican Republic; on 27 February 1989 in an uprising in Caracas against the IMF, etc. There have been numerous popular protests against the policies imposed by the WB and the IMF. As such, these governments created policies independent of the WB and the IMF, and politicians who went beyond the capitalist logic have been democratically elected, especially in Latin America. I am thinking of the election of Chávez in 1998 and his recent re-election, the election of Lula, of Tabaré Vásquez in Uruguay, Evo Morales in Bolivia, Rafael Correa in Ecuador, Nestor Kirchner in Argentina, and we can also include Daniel Ortega in Nicaragua... At present, an overwhelming majority of Latin American governments reject, on the rhetorical level, the policies of the World Bank.

In terms of action, I would say that the countries that really apply radically different programmes to those favoured by the IMF and the World Bank are Venezuela, Bolivia and possibly Ecuador, though it is still too early really to judge. Brazil, Uruguay, Chile and Argentina, on the other hand, have only slightly blocked the policies of the IMF and the WB, and in reality we cannot talk about a radical break in their case. This is certainly crystal clear in the case of Lula and Tabaré Vásquez. In Brazil, Lula maintains high interest rates, there is no control over the movement of capital, the Central Bank is still independent of the control of the government and the legislature, and an aid package has been negotiated with the WB that will guarantee the continuity if its policy framework. However, in the case of Venezuela and Bolivia, the renationalization and deprivatization schemes have been central to the radical departure from the policies of the WB and the IMF: renationalization of natural resources by Bolivia, renationalization in Venezuela of CANTV at the level of telecommunications and the announcement of the renationalization of the electricity sector, which can be added to PDVSA (Venezuela's oil company), which came under public control in 2002–03. This is the departure point for a radical break from WB policies. It remains to be seen what happens in relation to debts, as Venezuela is paying up its external debts and is transferring an important quantity of resources to its creditors. We will see, in this respect, if Venezuela, Bolivia and Ecuador will take more coherent measures that are in line with their political orientation.

Hugo Chávez, Evo Morales, Nestor Kirchner and Rafael Correa, are all in favour of a Bank of the South, and the creation of such a bank has been officially announced after a meeting between Kirchner and Chávez. What will be the role of this bank?

The conditions are present for the countries of the South to pull out of the World Bank and the IMF, and to form a multilateral Bank of the South that will back projects within the framework of twenty-first-century socialism, that is, projects that have nothing to do with capitalist development of their economies. There is a need for a Bank that backs the development of the public sector, cooperatives and the indigenous communities... That's the first possibility. The second is to have a public Bank of the South that reinforces the national capitalist development of the South, which will not constitute a true alternative. There needs to be a Bank that marks a radical break, and which creates a true alternative. The current political and economic climate favours that type of initiative. In Latin America, the conditions are much more favourable than during the lost decade of the debt crisis during the 1980s. The economic possibilities and the political will of the majority of the people of Latin America point towards an opportunity for a radical break with the capitalist system. The central problem is the political will. Clearly, Lula and Tabaré Vásquez do not have this political will, while Chávez, Morales and possibly Correa, lean more towards a radical break.

Whatever happens, and taking into account the high deficit in the US and its repercussions on the dollar, which will continue to fall, a united front of the countries of the South is needed that can place their reserves in a bank that serves their interests, and not invest them in US treasury bonds. An ALBA (Bolivarian Alternative for the Americas bank), which will be able to finance common projects covering infrastructures industrialization and the transformation of exports, while supporting the development of the internal market. Such a Bank will be a key element in the project for the development of twenty-first-century socialism.

Last question. Your book does not deal exclusively with economic policies tied to the political ideology of the World Bank: what about questions of a political nature?

Of course, it is written from a political point of view. The economic part has always been an important part of my work, but I have always taken into account the political and geostrategic factors. In the case of the book on the World Bank, it is mainly about politics and geostrategy. The World Bank is not an organization whose main preoccupation is economic; it is an instrument of the foreign policy of the great powers, led by the United States. This book is based on research from voluminous documentation from the WB itself. I have read more than 15,000 pages of documents, and the reader can find arguments and facts that are little known but whose sources are in the archives of the WB... By critically studying these documents, I have managed to reveal some facts that were never put forward before, for example, the fact that in the early 1960s, the WB forced the newly independent African countries to take possession of the debts accrued by Great Britain, France and Belgium in the exploitation of natural resources of colonized countries, odious debts that should never have been paid. I also show the importance of the impact of the Cuban revolution in 1959–60 on the policy of the US and the WB in Latin America, in the wake of the victorious revolution. There are documents that reveal how, within the WB, revolutionary contagion in Latin America was taken very seriously. Furthermore, this book shows that during its first 17 years of existence, the WB never granted a single loan for the construction of schools, for water projects and none for sewage treatment. Through a comparative study of official WB statements and the internal memos, I reveal the double discourse of the World Bank. Effectively, I don't think it is exaggerated to say that this book offers numerous new analyses that the reader can discover themself.

Translation: Diren Valayden, Coorditrad

Glossary

Author's note

In this book the following terms are used interchangeably: Third World, the countries of the South, the South, the Periphery, the Developing Countries or DCs. These terms are generally used in contrast to the Triad, the highly industrialized countries, the countries of the North, the Centre, the imperialist countries – also considered as synonymous. The countries of the former Soviet bloc are considered as part of the Periphery.

Balance of payments: A country's balance of current payments is the result of its commercial transactions (i.e. imported and exported goods and services) and of its financial exchanges with foreign countries. The balance of payments is a measure of the financial position of a country as regards the rest of the world. A country with a surplus in its current payments is a lending country for the rest of the world. On the other hand, if a country's balance is in the red, that country will have to turn to the international lenders to borrow what funding it needs.

BIS (The Bank for International Settlements): Founded at Basel as a public company in 1930 to handle German reparations after the First World War, the BIS manages part of the foreign currency reserves of the central banks of the highly industrialized countries and some others. The BIS plays an important role in gathering data on international banking transactions, published in a quarterly report since the early 1980s. It is responsible for handling financial risks associated with the liberalization of money markets. It also carries out banking transactions, receiving gold and currency deposits mainly from the central banks, selling the currency on the markets and granting loans to certain central banks.
Website: <www.bis.org>.

Central Bank: A country's central bank runs its monetary policy and holds the monopoly on issuing the national currency. Commercial banks must get their currency from it, at a supply price fixed according to the main rates of the central bank.

Conditionality: Covers a range of neoliberal measures imposed by the IMF and the World Bank on countries that sign an agreement, particularly to get their debt repayments rescheduled. The idea is that the measures will make the country more 'attractive' to international investors while penalizing the populations cruelly. By extension, the term is used for any condition imposed before granting aid or a loan.

Convertibility: This term designates the legal possibility of changing from one currency to another or from currency to the standard (traditionally gold) by which it is officially backed. In the present system of liberalized exchange rates, where it is supply and demand of currencies that determine their respective exchange rates – floating rates – currencies float with respect to the dollar (dollar-standard).

Currency market or money market: Market where currencies are exchanged and valued.

Debt

- **Debt rescheduling:** Modification of the terms of a debt, for example, by modifying the due dates or by postponing repayment of the capital sum and/or the interest. The aim is generally to give a bit of breathing space to a country in difficulty by extending the period of repayments so that the amounts can be reduced, or by granting a reprieve period when payments are not made.
- **Debt servicing:** Repayment of interest plus amortization of the capital sum.
- **Multilateral debt:** Debts due to the World Bank, the IMF, the regional development banks such as the ADB (African Development Bank), and other multilateral institutions such as the European Development Fund.
- **Net transfer on debt:** This refers to the subtraction of debt servicing (yearly payments – interest plus capital sum – to the industrialized countries) from the year's gross payments (loans) made by the creditors. The net transfer on debt is said to be positive when the country or continent concerned receives more (in loans) than it pays out. It is negative if the sums repaid are greater than the sums lent to the country or continent concerned.
- **Odious debt:** A legal concept according to which, if an illegitimate regime or a dictatorship should contract a debt contrary to the interests of the population, this debt shall be considered 'odious'. An ensuing democratic regime may denounce it. In this case, it will be deemed null and void, and need not be repaid.
- **Private debt:** Loans contracted by private borrowers, regardless of the lender.
- **Public debt:** All loans contracted by public borrowers.

Devaluation: A lowering of the exchange rate of one currency relative to others.

Direct Foreign Investment (DFI): Foreign investment can take the form of direct investment or portfolio investments. Even though it is sometimes difficult to distinguish between the two, for reasons of accountancy, jurisdiction or statistics, a foreign investment is considered to be a direct investment if the foreign investor holds 10 per cent or more of ordinary shares or voting rights in a company.

Eurodollars: The eurodollar market originated in the amount of American capital outflow in the second half of the 1960s. In 1963, the US authorities introduced a tax on non-resident borrowing, to slow down capital outflow. The result was a shift in the demand for financial backing in dollars from the US market to the European markets, where American bank subsidiaries could operate more freely.

Export Credit Agency: When private businesses of the North obtain a market in a developing country (DC), there is a risk that economic or political problems may prevent payment of bills. To protect themselves, they can take out insurance with an Export Credit Agency such as Eximbank in the US, COFACE in France, Ducroire in Belgium. If there is a problem, the agency pays instead of the insolvent client and the Northern business is sure of getting what is owed.

One of the main criticisms lodged against the agencies is that they are not very fussy about the nature of the contracts insured (arms, infrastructure and huge energy projects such as the gigantic Three-Gorges Dam project in China) nor about their social or environmental consequences. They often give their support to repressive and corrupt regimes.

Food crops: Crops destined to feed local populations (millet, manioc, etc.), as opposed to cash crops, destined for export (coffee, cocoa, tea, groundnuts, sugar, etc.)

G7: Germany, USA, France, UK, Japan, Italy and Canada. The seven heads of state generally meet annually in late June/early July. The first G7 summit was held in 1975 on the initiative of the French president, Valéry Giscard d'Estaing.

G8: Composed of the G7 plus the Russian Federation, which joined unofficially in 1995 and has been a full member since June 2002.

G77: The G77 arose from the group of Developing Countries that met to prepare the *first* UN Conference on Trade and Development (UNCTAD) in Geneva in 1964. The group provides a forum for the Developing Countries to discuss international economic and monetary issues.

GATT: The General Agreement on Tariffs and Trade, which was a permanent negotiating forum where States only had the status of 'contractual parties'. It was replaced by the WTO on 1 January 1995.

Gross domestic product (GDP): The GDP represents the total wealth produced in a given territory, calculated as the sum of added values.

Gross national product (GNP): The GNP represents the wealth produced by a nation, as opposed to a given territory. It includes the revenues of citizens of the nation abroad.

Heavily Indebted Poor Countries (HIPCs): The HIPC initiative, launched in 1996 and consolidated in September 1999, is supposed to reduce the debts of poor, heavily indebted countries, with the modest aim of making the debts sustainable.

It involves four demanding and complex stages that take an inordinately long time.

First of all, countries hoping to qualify must first submissively carry out an economic policy approved by the IMF and the World Bank, in the form of adjustment programmes. They continue to receive aid money from all the creditors concerned. Meanwhile, they must adopt a Poverty Reduction Strategy Paper (PRSP), sometimes just in the interim.

At the end of the three-year period comes the decision point: the IMF analyzes whether the candidate country's indebtedness is sustainable or not. If the net value of the ratio between external debt stock and export revenue exceeds 150 per cent, after traditional debt-reduction mechanisms have been applied, the country may be declared eligible. However, countries with high export levels (exports/GDP ratio of over 30 per cent) are penalized by this criterion, and their budgetary receipts are looked at rather than their exports. So if their indebtedness is clearly high despite good tax recovery (budgetary receipts of more than 15 per cent of the GDP, to avoid any laxity in this area), the objective retained is a ratio of net value of debt stock/budgetary receipts of more than 250 per cent.

If the country is declared eligible, it then benefits from some preliminary reductions on the part of creditor states and private banks and must pursue its implementation of policies approved by the IMF and the World Bank. The time this stage takes is determined by the satisfactory setting up of the key reforms agreed at the decision point, with a view to maintaining macroeconomic stability.

Lastly comes the completion point. The rest of the debt reduction is then applied, so that the country can get back to a situation of sustainable overall debt (in the terms described above) that is judged satisfactory.

The cost of the initiative is estimated at about $54 billion, i.e., about 2.6 per cent of the Third World's total external debt.

Altogether, there are only 42 HIPCs, of which 34 are in Sub-Saharan Africa, to which should be added Honduras, Nicaragua, Bolivia, Guyana, Laos, Vietnam, Yemen and Myanmar. By 31 March 2006, 29 countries had reached the decision point, and only 18 had reached completion point. The initiative, which was supposed to solve the problem of indebtedness for the 42 countries for once and for all, is a fiasco. Their debt has gone from $218 billion to $205 billion, a fall of only 6 per cent between 1996 and 2003. Confronted with these facts, the G8 Summit of 2005 decided an extra reduction concerning the multilateral part of the debt of the countries that have reached the decision point, i.e., the countries that have bowed to the will of the creditors.

Human Development Index (HDI): This instrument is used by the UN to estimate a country's degree of development, based on per capita income, the level of education and the average life expectancy of the population.

The International Monetary Fund (IMF): The IMF is the World Bank's sister institution, founded in Bretton Woods in July 1944. Its original purpose was to guarantee the stability of the international financial system based on fixed rates of exchange. After the end of the free convertibility of currencies to gold decided by the US government in August 1971, the financial markets came into play and interest rates became variable. In the wake of the debt crisis of 1982, the IMF was given the particular responsibility of intervening to help

developing countries with problems repaying their debt to achieve short-term economic stabilization, in order to reduce the country's budget deficit and limit the total amount of money in circulation. However, the IMF has also taken upon itself to impose structural economic reforms in the neoliberal sense. Its decision-making process is the same as the World Bank's and is based on distribution of voting rights according to the economic might of the member states; 85 per cent of the vote is required to modify the IMF Charter, so the USA has the power to block measures since it has over 17 per cent of the votes. The rich countries hold the majority of votes.
Website: <www.imf.org>.

IMF: distribution of administrators' votes in March 2006

USA	17.08%
Japan	6.13%
Germany	5.99%
Belgium	5.13%
United Kingdom	4.95%
France	4.95%
Netherlands	4.84%
Italy	4.18%
Canada	3.71%
Total (nine industrialized countries)	56.96%

Industrialization by import-substitution: This strategy mainly concerns a historic experiment in Latin America in the 1930s and 1940s, and the school of thought known as CEPAL (the UN Economic Commission for Latin America), and especially work published by the Argentine Raul Prebisch (who was to become the first Secretary General of UNCTAD in 1964). The starting point is the observation that when faced with a drastic reduction in foreign exchange, the main countries of Latin America had managed to respond to domestic demand by replacing imported products through the development of local production. The CEPAL theory holds that this process can be fruitfully extended to all sectors of industry, one after the other, and thus enable the country to 'disconnect' from the centre. A good dose of protectionism and coordinated state intervention are expected to promote the expansion of budding industries. South Korea applied the policy successfully but in special circumstances.

Inflation: The cumulative rise of prices as a whole (e.g. a rise in the price of petroleum, eventually leading to a rise in salaries, then to the rise of other prices, etc.). Inflation implies a fall in the value of money since, as time goes by, larger sums are required to purchase particular items. This is the reason why corporate-driven policies seek to keep inflation down.

Interest rates: When A lends money to B, B repays the amount lent by A (the capital) as well as a supplementary sum known as interest, so that A has an interest in agreeing to this financial operation. The interest is determined by the interest rate, which may be high or low. To take a very simple example: if A borrows $100 million for ten years at a fixed interest rate of 5 per cent, in the first year he will repay a tenth of the capital initially borrowed ($10 million) plus 5 per cent of the capital owed, i.e., $5 million, giving a total of $15 million. In the second year, he will again repay 10 per cent of the capital borrowed, but the 5 per cent now only applies to the remaining $90 million still due, i.e., $4.5 million, or a total of $14.5 million. And so on, until the tenth year when he will repay the last $10 million, plus 5 per cent of that remaining $10 million, i.e., $0.5 million, giving a total of $10.5 million. Over ten years, the total amount repaid will come to $127.5 million. The repayment of the capital is not usually made in equal instalments. In the initial years, the repayment concerns mainly the interest, and the proportion of capital repaid increases over the years. In this case, if repayments are stopped, the capital still due is higher.

The nominal interest rate is the rate at which the loan is contracted. The real interest rate is the nominal rate reduced by the rate of inflation.

The Least Developed Countries (LDCs): A notion defined by the UN on the following criteria: low per capita income, poor human resources and little diversification in the economy. The list includes 49 countries at present, the most recent addition being Senegal in July 2000; in the mid-1970s there were only 25 LDCs.

The London Club: The members are the private banks that lend to Third World states.

The Marshall Plan: A programme of economic reconstruction proposed in 1947 by the US State Secretary, George C. Marshall. With a budget of $12.5 billion (about $90 billion in 2003 terms) composed of donations and long-term loans, the Marshall Plan enabled 16 countries (especially France, the UK, Italy and the Scandinavian countries) to finance their reconstruction after the Second World War.

It would take $90 billion at 2006 rates to equate with the Marshall Plan. In the five years from 2000 to 2004 inclusive, the governments of all the DCs taken together gave their creditors the equivalent of three Marshall Plans via the negative net transfer on their external public debt.

Moratorium: A situation where a debt is frozen by the creditor, who forgoes payment until an agreed time. However, during the period of the moratorium, interest continues to accumulate. A moratorium can also be decided by the borrower, as was the case of Russia in 1998 and Ecuador in 1999.

New Deal: This term refers to the measures taken by President Franklin D. Roosevelt to end the deep economic crisis that the USA had been going through since 1929. From 1932 on, this interventionist policy was aimed at fighting instability of the financial markets by enabling the government to rationalize the economy, get the banking system back on its feet, help the unemployed and inject public funds to encourage consumption.

Non-Aligned Movement (NAM): A group of countries advocating neutrality, starting from the 1950s during the Cold War, towards the two blocs under the superpowers of the USA and the USSR. In April 1955, a conference of

Asian and African countries took place at Bandung, in Indonesia, in support of Third World unity and independence, decolonization and an end to racial segregation. It was initiated by Sukarno of Indonesia, Tito of Yugoslavia, Nasser of Egypt and Nehru of India. The Non-Aligned Movement really came into being in Belgrade in 1961. Other conferences followed in Cairo (1964), Lusaka (1970), Algiers (1973) and Colombo (1976). But unity turned out to be very difficult to attain between those who practised real neutrality (Yugoslavia), those who were drawn to the USSR because of anticolonialism (Egypt, India and Algeria) and those closely involved with the Soviet bloc (Cuba, China and Ethiopia) or the Western bloc (Saudi Arabia). Now made up of 114 countries, the Non-Aligned Movement has its headquarters in Lusaka (Zambia) but its field of action is very limited.
Website: <www.nam.gov.za>.

Official Development Assistance (ODA): Official Development Assistance is the name given to loans granted in financially favourable conditions by the public bodies of the industrialized countries. A loan has only to be agreed at a lower rate of interest than going market rates (a concessionary loan) to be considered as aid, even if it is then repaid to the last cent by the borrowing country. Tied bilateral loans (which oblige the borrowing country to buy products or services from the lending country) and debt cancellation are also counted as part of ODA.

Organization for Economic Cooperation and Development (OECD): Founded in 1960 and housed in the Château de la Muette in Paris, in 2002 the OECD included the 15 members of the European Union plus Switzerland, Norway and Iceland; in North America: the USA and Canada; and in Asia and the Pacific: Japan, Australia and New Zealand. The only Third World country to have been a member from the start for geostrategic reasons is Turkey. Between 1994 and 1996, two other Third World countries entered the OECD: Mexico, also part of NAFTA with its two North American neighbours, and South Korea. Since 1995, three countries of the former Eastern bloc have joined: the Czech Republic, Poland and Hungary. In 2000, Slovakia became the thirtieth member.
Website: <www.oecd.org>.

Organization of Petroleum-Exporting Countries (OPEC): OPEC is a group of eleven developing countries that produce petroleum: Algeria, Indonesia, Iran, Iraq, Kuwait, Libya, Nigeria, Qatar, Saudi Arabia, United Arab Emirates and Venezuela. These eleven countries represent 41 per cent of oil production in the world and own more than 75 per cent of known reserves. Founded in September 1960 and based in Vienna (Austria), OPEC is in charge of coordinating and unifying the petroleum-related policies of its members, with the aim of guaranteeing them all stable revenues. To this end, production is organized on a quota system. Each country, represented by its minister of energy and petroleum, takes a turn in running the organization.
Website: <www.opec.org>.

The Paris Club: This group of 19 lender states was founded in 1956 and specializes in dealing with non-payment by developing countries. From its beginnings, there has traditionally been a French president: in 2006, the Director of the French Treasury, Xavier Musca, was the incumbent. The member-states of the Paris Club have rescheduled the debts of some 80 DCs. The club members own nearly 30 per cent of Third World debt stock.

Links between the Paris Club and the IMF are extremely close, as witnessed by the observer status enjoyed by the IMF in the Paris Club's otherwise confidential meetings. The IMF plays a key role in the Paris Club's debt strategy, and the Club relies on IMF expertise and macroeconomic judgements in instigating one of its basic principles: conditionality. In return, the IMF's status as privileged creditor, and the implementation of its adjustment strategies in the developing countries, are bolstered by the Paris Club's actions.
Website: <www.clubdeparis.org>.

Poverty Reduction and Growth Facility: IMF credit facility endorsed in 1999, made available from the end of 2005 to 78 low-income countries (with GDP of less than $895 per capita in 2003). It carries the idea of fighting poverty, but within a global economic strategy always based on growth. Governments must then draw up a vast document – a Poverty Reduction Strategy Paper – which is a sort of structural adjustment programme with a slightly social feel, under agreement with the multilateral institutions. If deemed eligible, a country can borrow money within the framework of a three-year agreement. The amount is variable, depending on the country's balance of payments difficulties and past record with the IMF: usually no more than 140 per cent of its IMF quota. The annual rate is 0.5 per cent for a ten-year period, with five and a half years' grace.

Poverty Reduction Strategy Papers (PRSP): Set up by the World Bank and the IMF in 1999, the PRSP was officially designed to fight poverty. In fact, it turns out to be an even more virulent version of the structural adjustment policies in disguise, to try and win the approval and legitimization of the social participants.

Private loans: Loans granted by commercial banks, whoever the borrower.

Public loans: Loans granted by public lending institutions, whoever the borrower.

Recession: Negative growth of economic activity in a country or an area for at least two successive quarters.

Risk premium: When loans are granted, the creditors take account of the economic situation of the debtor country in fixing the interest rate. If there seems to be a risk that the debtor country may not be able to honour its repayments then that will lead to an increase in the rates it will be charged. Thus the creditors receive more interest, which is supposed to compensate for the risk taken in granting the loan.

Speculation: Activity destined to make a profit in the form of surplus value by betting on the future value of goods and financial or monetary assets. Speculation generates a divorce between the financial and the productive spheres. Currency markets are where most speculation takes place.

The Stock Exchange: The place where bonds and shares are issued and traded. A bond is loan paper while a share gives part ownership in a company. New securities are issued for the first time on the primary market. Bonds and shares can then be bought and sold freely on the secondary market.

Structural Adjustment Programmes (SAPs): As a reaction to the debt crisis, the rich countries entrusted the IMF and the World Bank with the task of imposing strict financial discipline on the over-indebted countries. The primary aim of Structural Adjustment Programmes, in the terms of the official discourse, is to restore financial equilibrium. To this end, the IMF and the World Bank make countries open up their economies to attract capital. Countries of the South that apply SAPs are supposed to export more and spend less, using two kinds of measures. The short-term measures are a kind of shock treatment with immediate effect. They involve eliminating subsidies on basic goods and services, reduction of social spending and the salaried workforce in the public sector, currency devaluation and raised interest rates. Structural reforms involve longer-term economic measures, such as specializing in certain export products (at the expense of food crops), economic liberalization through dropping control of capital flow and exchange control, opening up markets by lifting customs tariffs, privatizing public companies, generalizing VAT and taxation while preserving capital income. All this has dramatic consequences for the populations, and countries that apply the programmes to the letter find themselves faced with both disappointing economic results and galloping poverty.

Trade balance: The trade balance of a country is the difference between merchandise sold (exports) and merchandise bought (imports). The resulting trade balance either shows a deficit or is in credit.

Treasury bonds: Bonds issued by public Treasuries to fund government borrowing. They may be issued for periods from a few months to thirty years.

United Nations Conference on Trade and Development (UNCTAD): This was established in 1964, after pressure from the developing countries, to offset the effects of GATT.
See website: <www.unctad.org>.

United Nations Development Programme (UNDP): The UNDP, founded in 1965 and based in New York, is the UN's main agency of technical assistance. It helps the DCs, without any political restrictions, to set up basic administrative and technical services, trains managerial staff, tries to respond to some of the essential needs of populations, takes the initiative in regional cooperation programmes and coordinates, theoretically at least, the local activities of all the UN operations. The UNDP generally relies on Western

expertise and techniques, but a third of its contingent of experts come from the Third World. The UNDP publishes an annual *Human Development Report*, which, among other things, classifies countries by their Human Development Index (HDI).
See website: <www.undp.org>.

The World Bank: See fact sheet on the World Bank Group and also see website: <www.worldbank.org>.

World Trade Organization (WTO) (taken from M. Khor, 1997): The WTO, founded on 1 January 1995, replaced the General Agreement on Tariffs and Trade (GATT). Its role is to ensure that none of its members indulge in any kind of protectionism, and thus to accelerate the global liberalization of trade exchanges and facilitate the strategies of multinational corporations. It has an international court of law, the Dispute Settlement Body, which can try any apparent violations of its founding text drawn up at Marrakesh.

The WTO functions in 'one country, one vote' mode but the delegates from the countries of the South are overwhelmed by the tons of documents to study, the army of staff, lawyers, etc. of the countries of the North. Decisions are made by the powerful in the *green rooms*.
See website: <www.wto.org>.

Notes to the Text

ABOUT THIS BOOK

1. See Eric Toussaint, *Your Money [or] Your Life* (Chicago: Haymarket Books, 2004), chapter 16: 'Case study: Brazil', pp. 292–313.
2. They are chapters 3, 5 and 6 of Eric Toussaint, 'Enjeux politiques de l'action de la Banque internationale pour la Reconstruction et le Développement et du Fonds monétaire international envers le tiers-monde', doctoral thesis in political science (Universités de Liège et de Paris VIII, 2004).

TERMINOLOGY

1. Alfred Sauvy: 'We readily speak of two opposing worlds [the capitalist world and the socialist world: author's note], of their possible war, of their coexistence, etc., all too often forgetting that there exists a third one, the most important, and in fact the first one in chronological terms. This is the body of those that we call, in United Nations fashion, the underdeveloped countries. [...] The underdeveloped countries, the third world, have entered into a new phase [...]. Because at last this ignored, exploited Third World, looked down on as the Third State, also wants to be something else' (*L'Observateur*, No. 118 (14 August 1952), p. 14).

INTRODUCTION

1. The World Bank granted loans to Portugal until 1967.
2. The words used to define the countries that have received the WB's development loans have changed over the years. They were first called *backward areas*, then *underdeveloped countries*, and currently called *developing countries*, some of which are *emergent countries*.
3. World Bank, *Global Development Finance 2003* (Washington DC, 2003), p. 13. In the 2005 issue of the same publication, we read: 'Developing countries are now capital exporters to the rest of the world.' World Bank, *Global Development Finance 2005* (Washington DC, 2005), p. 56.
4. Source: World Bank, *Global Development Finance 2006* (Washington DC, 2006).

1 THE CREATION OF THE BRETTON WOODS INSTITUTIONS

1. This section is largely based on: (1) Robert W. Oliver, *International Economic Co-operation and the World Bank* (London: Macmillan, 1975); (2) Edward S. Mason and Robert E. Asher, *The World Bank since Bretton Woods* (Washington DC: Brookings Institution, 1973), chapter 1, pp. 11–35; (3) Devesh Kapur, John P. Lewis and Richard Webb, *The World Bank, Its First*

Half Century, Volume 1: History (Washington DC: Brookings Institution Press, 1997), specifically chapter 2, pp. 57–84; (4) Susan George and Fabrizio Sabelli, *Crédits sans Frontières: La Réligion Séculaire de la Banque Mondiale* (Paris: Eds La Découverte, 1994), chapter 1, pp. 28–45; (5) Bruce Rich, *Mortgaging the Earth* (London: Earthscan, 1994), chapter 3, pp. 49–80; (6) Michel Aguetta and Sandra Moatti, *Le FMI. De l'ordre monétaire aux désordres financiers* (Paris: Ed. Economica, 2000), chapter 1, pp. 8–31; (7) Catherine Gwin, 'US relations with the World Bank, 1945–1992', in Kapur, Lewis and Webb, *The World Bank, Its First Half Century, Volume 2: Perspectives* (Washington DC: Brookings Institution Press, 1997), pp. 195–200.

2. Eric Toussaint, *Your Money [or] Your Life: The Tyranny of Global Finance* (Chicago: Haymarket Books, 2005), chapter 7, pp. 131–6.

3. Oliver, *International Economic Co-operation and the World Bank*, pp. 72–5, 109.

4. John Maynard Keynes, *Collected Writings*, Vol. XXI (30 vols, London: Macmillan, 1971–80), quoted by Cheryl Payer, *Lent and Lost. Foreign Credit and Third World Development* (London: Zed Books, 1991), p. 20.

5. The US Department of State is the department responsible for administering the country's foreign policy.

6. The Chilean representative of the Inter-American Bank, Carlos Davila, wrote on 8 January 1940: 'In 1938, Germany absorbed 2 percent of the cacao exported by our countries; 25 percent of the cattle hides; 16 percent of the coffee; 19 percent of the corn; 29 percent of the cotton; 6 percent of the wheat; and 23 percent of the wool. [...] A new and closer form of association will be necessary in order to develop and exploit the mineral and agricultural resources of Latin America with a view to supplying and increasing the products saleable in the United States without domestic competition. A financial, technical and commercial collaboration which can be extended to the industrial field also, and which would permit creating or augmenting the production in Latin America of that large variety of manufactured articles which the United States now cannot or does not wish to import from other continents.

'It is advisable from every point of view that the necessary capital to carry out this program come from the United States and Latin America investors. Only thus would a page be turned over the history of the difficulties which United States investments by themselves have encountered.' Quoted by Oliver, *International Economic Co-operation and the World Bank*, p. 95.

7. Quoted by Oliver, *ibid.*, pp. 96–7.

8. Toussaint, *Your Money [or] Your Life*, chapter 7.

9. Quoted by Oliver, *International Economic Co-operation and the World Bank*, pp. 111–12.

10. For a full list of the proposals put forward by Harry White that were abandoned or seriously amended, see Oliver, *ibid.*, pp. 157–9.

11. Winston Churchill was uneasy about the United States' intentions. He told President Roosevelt: 'I believe you want to abolish the British Empire. [...] Everything you say is confirmation of this fact. Yet we know that you are our only hope. And you know we know it. Without America, the

British Empire will perish.' Quoted by George and Sabelli, *Crédits sans Frontières*, p. 31.

12. Bretton Woods is located in the mountains of New Hampshire.
13. Mason and Asher, *The World Bank since Bretton Woods*, p. 29.
14. On 30 August 1947: Australia (2.41 per cent), Belgium (2.67 per cent), Canada (3.74 per cent), Denmark (0.99 per cent), France (5.88 per cent), Greece (0.53 per cent), Luxembourg (0.37 per cent), Netherlands (3.21 per cent), Norway (0.80 per cent), United Kingdom (14.17 per cent), United States (34.23 per cent).
15. Damien Millet, *L'Afrique sans dette* (Paris: Edn CADTM/Syllepse, 2005), chapter 1.

2 THE FIRST YEARS OF THE WORLD BANK (1946–62)

1. Henry Morgenthau, a close collaborator of Franklin Roosevelt, clashed with his successor, President Truman, before the Potsdam Conference of July 1945 and handed in his resignation.
2. According to Oliver, Harry White was a progressive in political terms, sympathizing with workers' causes throughout the world and fraternizing with Communists. See R.W. Oliver, *International Economic Co-operation and the World Bank* (London: Macmillan, 1975), pp. 81–5.
3. During this hearing, he had the first warning signs of cardiac arrest.
4. Dwight D. Eisenhower, a general and a Republican politician, succeeded Harry Truman as US President in January 1953. He was re-elected in 1957 and ended his second term of office in 1961.
5. Executive Order 10422 of 9 January 1953, Part II.2c.
6. Letter, John D. Hickerson, Assistant Secretary of State, to President Eugene Black, 21 February 1953, in Devesh Kapur, John P. Lewis and Richard Webb, *The World Bank, Its First Half Century, Volume 1: History* (Washington DC: Brookings Institution Press, 1997), p. 1173.
7. From 1953, the World Bank not only borrowed from within the United States: it also issued bonds in Europe, then in Japan. In the 1970s, when oil prices surged, the Bank also borrowed from Venezuela and from oil-producing Arab countries.
8. Kapur, Lewis and Webb, *The World Bank, Its First Half Century, Volume 1: History*, p. 917.
9. Excerpts from Point IV and the conclusion of the inaugural address presented by G. Rist, *Le développement. Histoire d'une croyance occidentale* (Paris: Presses de Sciences Politiques, 1996), pp. 116–21. The other points concerned support for the United Nations system, the creation of NATO and the introduction of the Marshall Plan.
10. IBRD (World Bank), *Fourth Annual Report 1948–1949* (Washington DC, 1949), p. 58.
11. Almost 60 years later, the World Bank is still concerned with the eradication of malaria, the fatal disease of the poor. See Julie Castro and Damien Millet, 'Malaria and Structural Adjustment: Proof by Contradiction', in Christophe Boete, *Genetically Modified Mosquitoes for Malaria Control* (Georgetown: Eurekah-Landes Bioscience, 2006).

12. On the other hand, the concessional loans department of the World Bank, called the IDA (see next chapter), devoted exclusively to the poorest countries, lends them money from rich countries and from countries that have contracted debts with the IBRD at a rate lower than that of the market (around 0.75 per cent) over long periods (usually between 35 and 40 years, with an initial grace period of ten years).

13. The colonies concerned by World Bank loans were, for Belgium, the Belgian Congo, Rwanda and Burundi; for Great Britain, East Africa (including Kenya, Uganda and the future Tanzania), Rhodesia (Zimbabwe and Zambia), Nigeria, and British Guiana in South America; for France, Algeria, Gabon and French West Africa (Mauritania, Senegal, French Sudan [which became Mali], Guinée, Côte d'Ivoire, Niger, Haute-Volta [which became Burkina Faso] and Dahomey [which became Bénin]).

14. Kapur, Lewis and Webb, *The World Bank, Its First Half Century, Volume 1: History*, p. 687.

15. The fact that Belgium was the beneficiary of loans to the Belgian Congo can be deduced from a chart published in the fifteenth report of the World Bank for the year 1959–60. IBRD (World Bank), *Fifteenth Annual Report 1959–1960* (Washington DC, 1960), p. 12.

16. *Ibid.*, p. 52; IBRD (World Bank), *Annual Report 1965–1966* (Washington DC, 1966), p. 79.

17. Quoted by Alexander Nahum Sack, *Les Effets des Transformations des Etats sur leurs Dettes Publiques et Autres Obligations financières* (Paris: Recueil Sirey, 1927), p. 159.

18. *Ibid.*, p. 158.

19. Reparations should be demanded from the former colonial powers via the International Court of Justice in The Hague. It should be noted that as long as the UN agencies, of which the World Bank is one, continue to enjoy immunity, and as long as the Bank's statutes are not modified, the member states of the World Bank will have difficulty taking legal proceedings against it. On the other hand, citizens' associations representing the victims can take the Bank to court either in their own country or in a country where the Bank has an agency or where it has issued loans. This point will be developed later in the book.

20. Jacques Polack participated in the Bretton Woods conference of 1944. He was director of the research department of the IMF from 1958 to 1980, and IMF executive director for the Netherlands from 1981 to 1986.

21. Devesh Kapur, John P. Lewis and Richard Webb, *The World Bank, Its First Half Century, Volume 2: Perspectives* (Washington DC: Brookings Institution Press, 1997), p. 477.

22. This situation lasted until 1980, the year China returned to the World Bank and the IMF. At the United Nations, the situation lasted until 1971.

23. See Damien Millet and Eric Toussaint, 'India, 60 years after the long struggle for independence when will India's new liberation come?', in *Tsunami Aid or Debt Cancellation! The Political Economy of Post Tsunami Reconstruction* (Mumbai: VAK, 2005), chapter 4.

24. Poland withdrew from the World Bank in March 1950 and Czechoslovakia in December 1954, the Bank having refused to grant them a single loan.

25. Havana is some 200 km from the coast of the United States, which had been effectively controlling Cuba since 1898.
26. Kapur, Lewis and Webb, *The World Bank, Its First Half Century, Volume 1: History*, p. 163.
27. D. Eisenhower, *White House Years: Waging Peace, 1956–1961* (London: Heinemann, 1966), pp. 530–7.
28. John F. Kennedy, quoted in Richard Goodwin, *Remembering America* (Boston: Little Brown, 1988), p. 147.
29. *Ibid.*, p. 153. In his speech, Kennedy drew certain analogies with the Marshall Plan.
30. Kapur, Lewis and Webb, *The World Bank, Its First Half Century, Volume 2: Perspectives*, pp. 163–4.
31. The expedition took place on 17 April 1961. More than 1,500 anti-Castro mercenaries disembarked in the Bay of Pigs. The expedition was a monumental fiasco.
32. This text is taken from Kapur, Lewis and Webb, *The World Bank, Its First Half Century, Volume 1: History*, p. 165
33. This text was taken from *ibid.*, p. 166.

3   DIFFICULT BEGINNINGS BETWEEN THE UN AND THE WORLD BANK

1. The Economic and Social Council of the United Nations makes recommendations with a view to coordinating the programmes and activities of the specialized institutions of the UN (Article 58 of the United Nations Charter). To this end, ECOSOC enjoys powers that are granted to it by virtue of the terms of Chapter X of the Charter. Article 62, paragraph 1 thus states: 'The Economic and Social Council may make or initiate studies and reports with respect to international economic, social, cultural, educational, health, and related matters and may make recommendations with respect to any such matters to the General Assembly, to the Members of the United Nations, and to the specialized agencies concerned.'
2. Devesh Kapur, John P. Lewis and Richard Webb, *The World Bank, Its First Half Century, Volume 2: Perspectives* (Washington DC: Brookings Institution Press, 1997), p. 55.
3. *Ibid.*, p. 56.
4. *Ibid.*, p. 59.
5. This section is largely based on Aart van de Laar, *The World Bank and the Poor* (Boston/The Hague/London: Martinus Nijhoff Publishing, 1980), pp. 56–9; Edward S. Mason and Robert E. Asher, *The World Bank since Bretton Woods* (Washington DC: Brookings Institution, 1973), pp. 380–419; Catherine Gwin, 'US relations with the World Bank, 1945–1992', in Kapur, Lewis and Webb, *The World Bank, Its First Half Century, Volume 2: Perspectives*, pp. 205–9; Bruce Rich, *Mortgaging the Earth* (London: Earthscan, 1994), p. 77.
6. Mason and Asher, *The World Bank since Bretton Woods*, pp. 384–5; Gwin, 'US relations with the World Bank', p. 206; Van de Laar, *The World Bank and the Poor*, p. 57.

7. Kapur, Lewis and Webb, *The World Bank, Its First Half Century, Volume 2: Perspectives*, p. 1127.
8. Van de Laar, *The World Bank and the Poor*, p. 57; Gwin, 'US relations with the World Bank', pp. 386–7.
9. Kapur, Lewis and Webb, *The World Bank, Its First Half Century, Volume 1: History* (Washington DC: Brookings Institution Press, 1997), p. 1128.
10. Mason and Asher, *The World Bank since Bretton Woods*, p. 386.
11. *Ibid.*, pp. 380–1.
12. Kapur, Lewis and Webb, *The World Bank, Its First Half Century, Volume 1: History*, p. 1149.
13. UN Doc. A/AC.109/124 and Corr. 1 (10 June 1965).
14. Article 4, section 10 stipulates: 'The Bank and its officers shall not interfere in the political affairs of any member; nor shall they be influenced in their decisions by the political character of the member or members concerned. Only economic considerations shall be relevant to their decisions, and these considerations shall be weighed impartially in order to achieve the purposes (set by the Bank) stated in Article I.' See chapter 6 below.
15. Kapur, Lewis and Webb, *The World Bank, Its First Half Century, Volume 1: History*, p. 692.

4 THE POST-1945 CONTEXT –
THE MARSHALL PLAN AND US BILATERAL AID

1. John Maynard Keynes, who worked for the British Treasury, had participated in the negotiations leading to the Treaty of Versailles (1919), the peace settlement that was signed after the First World War ended. As he was against demanding such large amounts from Germany, he resigned from the British delegation and subsequently published a book called *The Economic Consequences of the Peace* (1919).
2. This is indeed what happened: the US trade balance, which used to be in the red, remained in the black until 1971. In other words, the US exported more than it imported.
3. 'Repayment in the form of imports has been traditionally opposed in this country on the ground that it causes competition for domestic producers and contributes to unemployment.' Randolph E. Paul, *Taxation for Prosperity* (Indianapolis: Bobbs-Merrill, 1947), quoted by Cheryl Payer, *Lent and Lost, Foreign Credit and Third World Development* (London: Zed Books, 1991), p. 20.
4. Information and table taken from the French page of Wikipedia: <http://fr.wikipedia.org/wiki/Plan_Marshall>.
5. 'Deutsche Auslandsschulden' (1951), pp. 7ff, in Philip Hersel, *El acuerdo de Londres de 1953* (III) <www.lainsigna.org/2003/enero/econ_005.htm>.
6. $US1 was worth DM4.2 at the time. West Germany's debt after reduction (i.e., DM14.5 billion) was thus equal to $3.45 billion,
7. Creditors systematically refuse to include this kind of clause in agreements with developing countries.
8. In allowing Germany to replace imports by home-manufactured goods, creditors accepted the reduction in their own exports to this country.

As it happened, for the years 1950–51, 41 per cent of German imports came from Britain, France and the United States. If we add the part of imports from other creditor countries that participated in the conference (Belgium, Netherlands, Sweden and Switzerland), the total amount reached 66 per cent.

9. 'The payment capacity of Germany's private and public debtors does not signify only the capacity to regularly meet payment deadlines in DM without triggering an inflation process, but also that the country's economy could cover its debts without upsetting its current balance of payments. To determine Germany's payment capacity we have to face a number of issues, namely, 1. Germany's future productive capacity with special consideration for the production of export commodities and of import substitution; 2. the possibility for Germany to sell German goods abroad; 3. probable future trade conditions; 4. economic and tax measures that might be required to insure a surplus in exports' ('Deutsche Auslandsschulden' (1951), pp. 7ff., in Hersel, *El acuerdo de Londres de 1953* (IV) <www.lainsigna.org/2003/enero/econ_010.htm>).

10. Author's computation. Sources: (1) World Bank Annual Reports 1954–61; (2) US Overseas Loans and Grants (Greenbook) <http://qesdb.cdie.org/gbk/index.html>.

5 A BANK UNDER THE INFLUENCE

1. 'But the only fully consistent hypothesis to reconcile the discordant elements of the Bank's actions, performance, and stated goals was that of a bureaucracy that had become an end in itself, driven by an institutional culture of expansion and a will to power for its own sake', in Bruce Rich, *Mortgaging the Earth* (London: Earthscan, 1994), p. 103.

2. This is a unique position. No other parliament had played as active a role as the United States in the World Bank Group (and the IMF). Besides the part of this chapter devoted to this question, chapter 18 on the Meltzer Commission will address the subject again.

3. See Catherine Gwin, 'US relations with the World Bank, 1945–1992', in Devesh Kapur, John P. Lewis and Richard Webb, *The World Bank, Its First Half Century, Volume 2: Perspectives* (Washington DC: Brookings Institution Press, 1997), p. 195.

4. Kapur, Lewis and Webb, *The World Bank, Its First Half Century*, Volumes 1 and 2, pp. 1275 and 766.

5. Gwin, 'US relations with the World Bank', p. 248.

6. *Ibid.*, p. 195.

7. *Ibid.*, p. 195.

8. *Ibid.*, p. 196.

9. *Ibid.*, p. 196.

10. *Ibid.*, p. 196.

11. *Ibid.*, p. 197.

12. Rich, *Mortgaging the Earth*, p. 64; Edward S. Mason and Robert E. Asher, *The World Bank since Bretton Woods* (Washington DC: Brookings Institution, 1973), p. 30.

13. This was the first and the biggest loan in its 50 years of existence (see Kapur, Lewis and Webb, *The World Bank, Its First Half Century, Volume 1: History*, p. 1218).

14. See Gwin, 'US relations with the World Bank', pp. 253–4. Note that Poland withdrew from the WB on 14 March 1950 and Czechoslovakia on 31 December 1954. The Soviet Union, which was present at the beginning of the Bretton Woods conference, did not participate in the system's implementation.

15. None of the sources I have consulted mentions the existence of an internal debate in the Board of Governors during which a different candidate from that of the government was proposed.

16. The US upheld this tradition so strongly that when it wished to propose a candidate who was not a US national – as happened in 1995 in the case of James Wolfensohn, an Australian – it quickly granted him citizenship to ensure it could offer him the position of president of the World Bank.

17. The second country in terms of percentage of voting rights was Great Britain with 14.52 per cent.

18. Japan had joined the Bank in 1952 at the same time as the Federal Republic of Germany.

19. Gwin, 'US relations with the World Bank', p. 244.

20. Mason and Asher, *The World Bank since Bretton Woods*, p. 915; Kapur, Lewis and Webb, *The World Bank, Its First Half Century*, Volumes 1 and 2, pp. 1275 and 766.

21. The Somoza family ruled Nicaragua from 1935, the year it was put in power by a US military intervention, to 1979 when a popular insurrection brought about the fall of dictator Anastasio Somoza and his flight to Paraguay, also ruled by a dictator, Alfredo Stroessner.

22. Kapur, Lewis and Webb, *The World Bank, Its First Half Century, Volume 1: History*, p. 103.

23. International Court of Justice, case concerning the military and paramilitary activities in and against Nicaragua, Judgment of 27 June 1986. Following this conviction, the US officially announced that it would not further acknowledge the competence of the ICJ.

24. Gwin, 'US relations with the World Bank', p. 258.

25. We will see much later that, on several occasions, the executive uses its direct influence on the Bank to bypass possible opposition from Congress or, in any case, avoid a debate that does not appear to it expedient.

26. George Kennan represented the State Department (NDA).

27. Kapur, Lewis and Webb, *The World Bank, Its First Half Century, Volume 1: History*, p. 103.

28. Gwin, 'US relations with the World Bank', pp. 256–7.

29. International Bank for Reconstruction and Development, Summary Proceedings of the 1972 Annual Meetings of the Boards of Governors (Washington, 1972), p. 55.

30. Gwin, 'US relations with the World Bank', p. 258.

31. *Ibid.*, p. 258.

32. The different examples concerning sectoral loans are from Gwin, *ibid.*, pp. 223–4 and 259–63.

33. According to Mason and Asher, it is unlikely that Prime Minister Nasser actively desired the support of the Soviets for the financing of the dam before the withdrawal of American and British offers. After this withdrawal, 17 months passed before he signed an agreement with the Soviets to finance the first phase of the construction of the dam (Mason and Asher, *The World Bank since Bretton Woods*, p. 642).

34. *Ibid.*, p. 636.

35. *Ibid.*, p. 641.

36. See Eric Toussaint, *Your Money [or] Your Life* (Chicago: Haymarket Books, 2004), chapter 16, pp. 327–38.

37. Horst Kölher resigned from his post on 4 March 2004 in order to be able to accept the position of President of Germany as proposed to him by the German Social-Christian opposition. Once released from his responsibilities at the IMF, Kölher made declarations in which he criticized the American occupation of Iraq. Rodrigo Rato, who was appointed on 4 May 2004 by the Board of Governors to succeed him, was until March 2004 minister of finance and economy in the José Maria Aznar government, a faithful ally of the US and the host of the conference of donors in October 2003.

38. More precisely: (1) an immediate cancellation of a part of the late payment interests representing 30 per cent of the debt stock on 1 January 2005. The non-cancelled debt stock was postponed until the approval date of a standard programme with the IMF. This reduction resulted in a cancellation of $11.6 billion; (2) with the approval of a programme with the IMF a reduction of 30 per cent of the debt stock would be implemented. The remaining debt stock would be rephased over a period of 23 years, including a grace period of six years. This step would reduce the debt stock of $11.6 billion, bringing the total cancellation rate to 60 per cent; (3) an additional debt reduction representing 20 per cent of the initial stock when the last review of the standard three-year programme of the IMF would be approved by the Board of Directors of the IMF. This reduction would involve $7.8 billion.

39. The agreement was confirmed and signed one year later, on 27 October 2005.

40. These facts are related by Catherine Gwin in 'US relations with the World Bank', p. 213.

41. David A. Stockman, *The Triumph of Politics: How the Reagan Revolution Failed* (New York: Harper & Row, 1986), pp. 116–19 (quoted by Gwin, 'US relations with the World Bank', p. 229).

42. Department of the Treasury, *Assessment of US Participation in Multilateral Development Banks in the 1980s* (Washington DC, 1982), chapter 3 (quoted by Walden Bello, *Deglobalization. Ideas for a New World Economy* (London/New York: Zed Books, 2002), pp. 59–60).

43 Bello, *Deglobalization. Ideas for a New World Economy*, p. 60.

44. Department of the Treasury, *United States Participation in Multilateral Development Banks*, p. 59 (quoted by Gwin, 'US relations with the World Bank', p. 270).

45. Department of the Treasury, *United States Participation in Multilateral Development Banks*, pp. 48, 52 (quoted by Gwin, 'US relations with the World Bank', p. 271).
46. Letter from President Ronald Reagan to Representative Robert Michel, 10 June 1988, p. 1 (quoted by Gwin, 'US relations with the World Bank', p. 271).
47. Gwin, 'US relations with the World Bank', pp. 271–2.

6   WORLD BANK AND IMF SUPPORT OF DICTATORSHIPS

1. Indonesian President Sukarno called the Bandung Conference in 1955, launching the non-aligned movement. Sukarno, Tito and Nehru were leaders who gave a voice to Third World hopes to overcome the old colonial system of rule. Here is an excerpt from Sukarno's speech at the conference opening: 'We are often told "Colonialism is dead". Let us not be deceived or even soothed by that. I say to you, colonialism is not yet dead. How can we say it is dead, so long as vast areas of Asia and Africa are unfree. [...] Colonialism has also its modern dress, in the form of economic control, intellectual control, actual physical control by a small but alien community within a nation. It is a skilful and determined enemy, and it appears in many guises. It does not give up its loot easily. Wherever, whenever and however it appears, colonialism is an evil thing, and one which must be eradicated from the earth' (Source: *Africa–Asia Speaks from Bandung* (Djakarta: Indonesian ministry of Foreign Affairs, 1955), pp. 19–29).
2. Bruce Rich quotes as examples of agencies founded through the World Bank: in Thailand, Industrial Finance Corporation of Thailand (IFCT), Thai Board of Investment (BOI), the National Economic and Social Development Board (NESDB) and the Electrical Generating Authority of Thailand (EGAT); in India, National Thermal Power Corporation (NPTC) and Northern Coal Limited (NCL) (see Bruce Rich, *Mortgaging the Earth* (London: Earthscan, 1994), pp. 13, 41).
3. Rich, *Mortgaging the Earth*, p. 76. Also see: Nicholas Stern and Francisco Ferreira, 'The World Bank as "Intellectual actor"', in Devesh Kapur, John P. Lewis and Richard Webb, *The World Bank, Its First Half Century, Volume 2: Perspectives* (Washington DC: Brookings Institution Press, 1997), pp. 583–5.
4. The period coinciding with the Cold War.
5. UNDP, *Human Development Report*, 1994, p. 76.
6. Mahbub ul Haq, 'The Bank's mistakes in Chile', 26 April 1976.
7. Kapur, Lewis and Webb, *The World Bank, Its First Half Century, Volume 1: History*, p. 301.
8. Memorandum, Mahbub ul Haq to Robert S. McNamara, 'Chile Country Program Paper – Majority Policy Issues', 12 July 1976.
9. An analysis of the facts summarized below is found in: Cheryl Payer, *The Debt Trap: the International Monetary Fund and the Third World* (New York/ London: Monthly Review Press, 1974), pp. 143–65.

10. In 1965 Brazil signed the Stand-By Agreement with the IMF, received new credits and had the United States, several European creditor nations and Japan restructure its debt. After the military coup, loans rose from zero to an average of US$73 million for the rest of the 1960s and reached almost half a billion dollars per annum in the mid-1970s.

11. Details in Kapur, Lewis and Webb, *The World Bank, Its First Half Century, Volume 1: History*, pp. 274–82.

12. World Bank, 'Notes on Brazil Country Program Review, December 2, 1971'. Details in Kapur, Lewis and Webb, *The World Bank, Its First Half Century, Volume 1: History*, p. 276.

13. *Ibid.*, p. 276.

14. Declaration of David Knox, vice-president of the World Bank for Latin America: 'One of my nightmares was what we would do were the Nicaraguans to start putting in place policies that we could support. I feared that political pressure, and not only from the United States, would be so great as to prevent us from helping the country', in Kapur, Lewis and Webb, *The World Bank, Its First Half Century, Volume 1: History*, p. 1058, note 95.

15. The historians of the Bank wrote that in 1982: '... lured by Mobutu's guile and promises of reform and by pressures from the United States, France and Belgium, the Bank embarked on an ambitious structural adjustment lending program to Zaire', in Kapur, Lewis and Webb, *The World Bank, Its First Half Century, Volume 1: History*, p. 702.

16. Aart van de Laar, *The World Bank and the Poor* (Boston/The Hague/London: Martinus Nijhoff Publishing, 1980), p. 40.

17. Kapur, Lewis and Webb, *The World Bank, Its First Half Century, Volume 1: History*, p. 1061.

7   THE WORLD BANK AND THE PHILIPPINES (1946–90)

1. Precisely, at the same time, Washington imposed a strict control on the outflow of capital and on the exchange rate. Do what I tell you to do, not what I do...

2. Devesh Kapur, John P. Lewis and Richard Webb, *The World Bank, Its First Half Century, Volume 1: History* (Washington DC: Brookings Institution Press, 1997), p. 558.

3. See Cheryl Payer, *Lent and Lost. Foreign Credit and Third World Development* (London: Zed Books, 1991), p. 82.

4. The World Bank historians made public one of the internal reports of a high-rank meeting between McNamara and his fellow workers: 'A rather surprising meeting! No more of the criticism of early years (politics, corruption, income inequality), but a rather general feeling that we should increase our lending program. And a flabbergasted Area Department trying to defend the cautious position taken in the Country Program Paper (CPP)! The order of the day is to work within the system. (Politics not necessarily worse than in Thailand but more publicized.)... We should aim to lend on average $120 million a year in FY74–78, 50 per cent more than proposed' (World Bank, *Notes on the Philippines*

Country Program Review, July 28, 1972, prepared by H. Schulmann on 15 August 1972; quoted by Kapur, Lewis and Webb, *The World Bank, Its First Half Century, Volume 1: History*, p. 303) 'A miracle has occurred in the Philippines. Philosophically, it is distressing, however, that the miracle occurred under the auspices of a military dictatorship. Mr. Cargill said he didn't believe the miracle would continue, "but while it does," interjected Mr McNamara, "and only as long as it does, let us continue to support it."' Memorandum, Alexis E. Lachman to John Adler, 27 December 1973, with attachment, *Philippines Country Program Review, December 19, 1973*, quoted by *ibid.*, p. 304).

5. In 1980, the World Bank lent $400 million.
6. Quoted by Kapur, Lewis and Webb, *The World Bank, Its First Half Century, Volume 1: History*, p. 304.
7. *Ibid.*, p. 563.
8. Paul Wolfowitz became president of the World Bank in 2005.
9. Ferdinand Marcos was transferred to Honolulu by the US Army and lived there until 1989.
10. Quoted by Kapur, Lewis and Webb, *The World Bank, Its First Half Century, Volume 1: History*, p. 565, note 102.
11. In 1987, a team of the World Bank led by Martin Karcher faced the possibility of a radical land reform, similar to the ones carried out in Japan, South Korea and Taiwan after the Second World War, as a consequence of the radicalization of the rural workers' struggle. The document delivered by this team in March 1987 recommended the limitation of land property to 7 hectares, which implied directly taking on the main growers of sugarcane (namely Corazon Aquino). This study by the World Bank suggested that the landless workers should obtain the lands in exchange for a one-off payment of 600 pesos (around $30 at the time). Needless to say, the study was never followed by concrete measures.

8 THE WORLD BANK'S SUPPORT OF THE DICTATORSHIP IN TURKEY

1. 'The Bank in the 1970s was at pains in Turkey not to overreach': Devesh Kapur, John P. Lewis and Richard Webb, *The World Bank, Its First Half Century, Volume 1: History* (Washington DC: Brookings Institution Press, 1997), p. 547.
2. Süleyman Demirel (1924–) served several times as Prime Minister (1965–71, 1975–78, 1979–80). He was head of government again in 1991 then President of the Republic from 1993 to 2000.
3. Turgut Özal (1927–93) was Prime Minister from 1983 to 1989, then President of the Republic from 1989 to his death in 1993. He worked at the Bank in Washington from 1971 to 1973.
4. Kapur, Lewis and Webb, *The World Bank, Its First Half Century, Volume 1: History*, p. 548, note 60.
5. *Ibid.*, p. 548.
6. In the mid-1980s Attila Karaosmanoglu became vice-president of the World Bank for East Asia and the Pacific. He had been responsible for

hiring Turgut Özal as head of planning in 1960 and was deputy prime minister immediately after the 1971 coup.

7. Munir Benjenk was vice-president of the World Bank for Europe, the Middle East and North Africa all through the 1970s. He was Robert McNamara's direct adviser for Turkey.

8. Later it would turn into quite a tradition with, for instance, Kemal Dervis, former vice-president of the World Bank, becoming Turkey's finance minister from March 2001 to August 2002. In 2005 he became director of the UNDP.

9. This continued in the 1990s and early 2000s.

10. Kapur, Lewis and Webb, *The World Bank, Its First Half Century, Volume 1: History*, p. 549, note 62.

11. At the time of the coup, tensions between the United States and Iran were very high since about a hundred American hostages were being detained in Teheran. The issue was at the core of the election campaign opposing Ronald Reagan and Jimmy Carter (running for a second term of office).

12. Kapur, Lewis and Webb, *The World Bank, Its First Half Century, Volume 1: History*, p. 547.

13. *Ibid.*, p. 550.

9   THE WORLD BANK IN INDONESIA – A TEXTBOOK CASE OF INTERVENTION

1. Bruce Rich, *Mortgaging the Earth* (London: Earthscan, 1994).

2. See Cheryl Payer, *The Debt Trap. The International Monetary Fund and the Third World* (London: Monthly Review Press, 1974).

3. See Devesh Kapur, John P. Lewis and Richard Webb, *The World Bank, Its First Half Century, Volume 1: History* (Washington DC: Brookings Institution Press, 1997).

4. 'Les mercredis de l'histoire', *Massacre en Indonésie*, Arte (2001), Australia, France, Thirteen WNET New York, Arte France,YLE TV2 Documentaries, Australian Film Finance Corporation, Hilton Cordell/Vagabond films production, BFC Productions.

5. Kapur, Lewis and Webb, *The World Bank, Its First Half Century, Volume 1: History*, pp. 467–71.

6. *Ibid.*, p. 469.

7. *Ibid.*, p. 470.

8. *Ibid.*, p. 493.

9. *Ibid.*, p. 469.

10. More than half of the Indonesian debt was contracted with the USSR, and when granting a moratorium on their debt, the Western creditors vouched for the repayment of the Soviet debt. In order to avoid any flow of capital towards the USSR, they granted this preferential treatment on condition that the Soviets did the same. The USSR accepted it for fear of not being fully repaid in the event of its refusal.

11. This new contract included the most favoured nation clause, which implied that the Soviet debt was to be repaid at a faster rate.

12. <www.infid.be/Statement-Debt-Swap-Germany.pdf>.
13. <www.asia-pacific-action.org/statements/infid_beyondmoratorium_110105.htm>.
14. 'A typically large resident staff': Kapur, Lewis and Webb, *The World Bank, Its First Half Century, Volume 1: History*, p. 495.
15. The World Bank, *Summary of RSI Staff Views Regarding the Problem of 'Leakage' from the World Bank Project Budget*, August 1997.
16. Kapur, Lewis and Webb, *The World Bank, Its First Half Century, Volume 1: History*, p. 491.
17. Extract from Memorandum, Jean Baneta: 'Meeting with President Suharto, 15 May 1979', 22 May 1979 ('The other country may have been Zaire', write the historians of the World Bank, *ibid.*, p. 492).
18. Kapur, Lewis and Webb, *The World Bank, Its First Half Century, Volume 1: History*, p. 538.
19. Daily newspaper *Libération*, 26 January 2006.
20. This section is largely inspired by the dissertation by Alice Minette, 'Anthropology of a misunderstanding. Analysis of the "Transmigration" development project in Indonesia and its consequences on the outer islands of the archipelago in general, and particularly on West New Guinea' (Université de Liège, unpublished). See also Damien Millet and Eric Toussaint, *Les tsunamis de la dette* (Paris: edn CADTM/Syllepse, 2005), chapter 3.
21. Kapur, Lewis and Webb, *The World Bank, Its First Half Century, Volume 1: History*, p. 489 (see note 60 for reference to the Board's decision on this matter in January 1979).
22. One of these camps is a small island off Java from which it was impossible to escape, and where the people known as 'undesirables' were inculcated in agricultural techniques and state ideology.
23. Millet and Toussaint, *Les tsunamis de la dette*, pp. 114–15.
24. Among the criticisms aimed at the Bank concerning the damage and non-observance of human rights caused by its support for the actions of the government in West New Guinea, the best known are: the letter addressed in 1984 to A.W. Clausen, the president of the Bank, by the Minority Rights Group (New York); the sentence declared by World Council of Indigenous People at its regional meeting in 1984; a petition addressed to the Inter-Governmental Group of Indonesia in 1984–85 by the Australian Council For Overseas Aid and by many associations for the defence of native rights. These complaints were taken into account neither by the Indonesian government, nor by the Bank, which maintained its support for the abuse of the rights of New Guinea's native populations.
25. The World Bank, *Indonesia Transmigration Sector Review*, quoted in Rich, *Mortgaging the Earth*.
26. This reinforcement, called 'Second Stage Development', consisted of the improvement of infrastructure and general living conditions in the transmigration villages, as well as the rehabilitation of sites with a high rate of desertion by transmigrants.
27. 'Indonesia Transmigration Program: a review of five Bank-supported projects', 1994; 'Impact Evaluation Report: Transmigration I, Transmigration II, Transmigration III', 1994.

28. IMF, *Annual Report 1997*, p. 90.
29. *Ibid.*, p. 91.
30. INFID, *Achieving Social Justice Through Poverty Eradication, Debt Cancellation and Civilian Supremacy in Post-Tsunami Indonesia*, Jakarta, 16–19 November 2005, p. 4.
31. See the decision of the Paris Club announced on 10 March 2005 on <www.clubdeparis.org>.
32. *Financial Times*, 1 March 2005.
33. Author's calculation, based on World Bank, *Global Development Finance*, 2005.

10 THE WORLD BANK'S THEORIES OF DEVELOPMENT

1. The terms used to designate the countries targeted for World Bank development loans have changed through the years. At first, they were known as 'backward regions', then 'underdeveloped countries' and, finally, 'developing countries'. Some of these have gone on to be called 'emerging countries'.
2. 'The period during which the Bank held firm views on the nature of the development process but did little to reach into it extended roughly up to the late 1950s, and coincided with a phase in Bank lending in which most lending was still made to developed countries (by 1957, 52.7 per cent of funding still went to such countries).' Nicholas Stern and Francisco Ferreira, 'The World Bank as "intellectual actor"', in Devesh Kapur, John P. Lewis and Richard Webb, *The World Bank, Its First Half Century, Volume 2: Perspectives* (Washington DC: Brookings Institution Press, 1997), p. 533.
3. 'The instruments of neoclassical analysis can be applied in a general way, quite unspecifically, to the questions posed by under-development. Under-development or blocked development is not subjected to systematic analysis in neoclassical theory.' Translated from Gerard Azoulay, *Les théories du développement* (Presses Universitaires de Rennes, 2002), p. 38.
4. Stern and Ferreira, 'The World Bank as "intellectual actor"', p. 533.
5. Edward S. Mason and Robert E. Asher, *The World Bank since Bretton Woods* (Washington DC: Brookings Institution, 1973), pp. 458–9.
6. World Bank (IBRD), *8th Annual Report 1952–1953* (Washington DC, 1953), p. 9.
7. Eugene Black, 'Tale of Two Continents', Ferdinand Phinizy Lectures, delivered at the University of Georgia, 12 April 1961, in Devesh Kapur, John P. Lewis and Richard Webb, *The World Bank, Its First Half Century, Volume 1: History* (Washington DC: Brookings Institution Press, 1997), p. 145. Eugene Black was president of the World Bank from 1949 to 1962.
8. World Bank, *Global Development Report 1987* (Washington DC, 1987), p. 4.
9. The predominance of exchanges between economies endowed with similar factors (exchanges of similar products between industrialized

economies) was established in the work of P. Krugman and E. Helpman in the 1980s.

10. Walt W. Rostow was an influential economist. He was also a high-ranking political adviser, becoming adviser to Robert McNamara during the Vietnam War. Some of the notes he addressed to McNamara can be consulted on the Net, dealing with the politico-military strategy to follow with regard to the North Vietnamese and their allies in 1964. One note entitled 'Military Dispositions and Political Signals', dated 16 November 1964, is particularly interesting, for it shows quite impressive mastery of the arts of war and negotiation (<www.mtholyoke.edu/acad/intrel/pentagon3/doc232.htm>). It is worth mentioning since it highlights once more the political stakes behind the operations of the IMF and the WB in countries of the Periphery. Thus economic policy has to be considered in the light of its political motivation and levers.

11. Walt W. Rostow, *The Stages of Economic Growth: a Non Communist Manifesto* (Cambridge: Cambridge University Press, 1960).

12. Note that Rostow claimed that Argentina had already reached the take-off stage before 1914.

13. Rostow also claimed that the USA had permanently reached the stage of mass consumerism just after the Second World War, followed by Western Europe and Japan in 1959. As for the USSR, it was technically ready to reach that stage but first needed to make some adjustments.

14. Paul Samuelson, *Economics*, 11th edn (New York: McGraw Hill, 1980), pp. 617–18.

15. Cheryl Payer, *Lent and Lost. Foreign Credit and Third World Development* (London: Zed Books, 1991), pp. 33–4.

16. Paul Rosenstein-Rodan, 'International Aid for Underdeveloped Countries', *Review of Economics and Statistics*, Vol. 43 (1961), p. 107.

17. Dragoslav Avramoviæ, *Economic Growth and External Debt* (Baltimore: Johns Hopkins Press for the IBRD), p. 193.

18. Max Millikan and Walt W. Rostow, *A Proposal: Keys to An Effective Foreign Policy* (New York: Harper, 1957), p. 158.

19. In 1970, Hollis Chenery became adviser to Robert McNamara, then president of the World Bank. Soon after, in 1972, the post of vice-president linked to that of chief economist was created for Chenery by McNamara. Since then, it has become part of the tradition. Chenery served as chief economist and vice-president of the World Bank from 1972 to 1982. Chenery remains the longest-serving occupant of the post of chief economist. Previous and later incumbents stayed between three and six years, according to each case. Source: Stern and Ferreira, 'The World Bank as "intellectual actor"', p. 538.

20. Hollis B. Chenery and Alan Strout, 'Foreign Assistance and Economic Development', *American Economic Review*, Vol. 56 (1966), pp. 680–733.

21. Charles Oman and Ganeshan Wignarja, *The Postwar Evolution of Development Thinking*, OCDE 1991, cited by Stephanie Treillet, *L'Economie du développement* (Paris: Nathan, 2002), p. 53.

22. Keith B. Griffin and Jean Luc Enos, 'Foreign Assistance: Objectives and Consequences', *Economic Development and Cultural Change*, No. 18 (1970), pp. 319–20.

23. Hollis B. Chenery, 'Objectives and Criteria of Foreign Assistance', in *The United States and the Developing Economies*, ed. G. Ranis (New York: W.W. Norton, 1964), p. 81.

24. Max Millikan, who was a member of the Office of Strategic Services (OSS) then of the Central Intelligence Agency (CIA) as it became, was the director of CENIS (Center for International Affairs at the Massachusetts Institute for Technology), with direct links to the State Department.

25. Max Millikan and Donald Blackmer, *The Emerging Nations: their Growth and United States Policy* (Boston: Little, Brown & Co., 1961), pp. x–xi.

26. *Ibid.*, pp. 118–19.

27. Chenery and Strout, 'Foreign Assistance and Economic Development', pp. 682, 697–700.

28. Bela Balassa, *Development Strategies in Some Developing Countries: a Comparative Study* (Baltimore: Johns Hopkins Press for the World Bank, 1971); Jagdish Bhagwati, *Anatomy and Consequences of Exchange Control Regime* (Cambridge, MA: Ballinger for the National Bureau of Economic Research, 1978); Anne Krueger, *Foreign Trade Regimes and Economic Development: Liberalization Attempts and Consequences* (New York: National Bureau of Economic Research, 1978).

29. Anne Krueger became chief economist and vice-president of the World Bank in 1982 (when President Reagan let Chenery go and brought in supporters of his neoliberal orientations) and kept the post until 1987.

30. Krueger, *Trade and Development: Export Promotion vs. Import Substitution* (New York: National Bureau of Economic Research, 1978), cited by Stephanie Treillet, *L'Economie du développement* (Paris: Nathan, 2002), p. 37.

31. Kapur, Lewis and Webb, *The World Bank, Its First Half Century, Volume 1: History*, pp. 215–33.

32. *Ibid.*, p. 218.

33. See especially James P. Grant, 'Development: the End of Trickle-down', *Foreign Policy*, Vol. 12 (Fall 1973), pp. 43–65.

34. For the period 1974–81, they wrote: 'Attention began to shift away from direct targeting of Bank investments on the poor to the enhancement of indirect benefits through increased urban employment. In effect, the strategy was falling back on the trickle down approach', in Kapur, Lewis and Webb, *The World Bank, Its First Half Century, Volume 1: History*, p. 264.

35. On the change of direction of 1981–82, they wrote: 'Poverty reduction would thus have to depend on growth and trickle-down', in Kapur, Lewis and Webb, *The World Bank, Its First Half Century, Volume 1: History*, p. 336.

36. Hollis B. Chenery, *Redistribution with Growth* (London: Oxford University Press for the World Bank and the Institute of Development Studies, 1974).

37. Simon Kuznets, 'Economic Growth and Income Inequality', *American Economic Review*, Vol. 49 (March 1955), pp. 1–28.

38. Cited by Kapur, Lewis and Webb, *The World Bank, Its First Half Century, Volume 1: History*, p. 171.

39. François Bourguignon, 'The Poverty–Growth–Inequality Triangle', paper presented at the Indian Council for Research on International Economic Relations (New Delhi, 4 February 2004).

40. World Bank, *Global Development Report 2006, Equity and Development* (Washington DC, 2005) <http://siteresources.worldbank.org/INTWDR2006/Resources/477383-1127230817535/WDR2006overview-fr.pdf>.

11   SOUTH KOREA: THE MIRACLE UNMASKED

1. Choy Bong-young, *A History of the Korea Reunification Movement: Its Issues and Prospects* (Peoria IL: Bradley University, 1984).

2. Roy E. Appleman, *South to the Naktong, North to the Yalu* (Washington DC: Center of Military History, US Army, 1961), p. 18.

3. The UN granted the US a mandate to intervene against North Korea. The expeditionary corps under Washington's leadership included 16 countries. How could the UN Security Council take such a decision when China and the USSR were permanent members with the power of veto? Since the People's Republic of China had been banned from the UN and the Security Council after the victory of the revolution in China, the latter was represented by the delegate for the anti-communist Taiwan government led by General Chiang Kai-shek from 1949 to 1971. He supported the US intervention in Korea. In the context of the Cold War the Soviet Union would not participate in the Security Council meetings and could therefore not exert its veto power.

4. The figure of 100,000 deaths is taken from the book by Gregory Henderson, a diplomat in Korea at the time, *The Politics of the Vortex* (Cambridge MA: Harvard University Press, 1968).

5. Until 1945 over 90 per cent of the money invested in Korean economy outside farming depended on Japan.

6. Mahn-Je Kim, 'The Republic of Korea's Successful Economic Development and the World Bank', in Devesh Kapur, John P. Lewis and Richard Webb, *The World Bank, Its First Half Century, Volume 2: Perspectives* (Washington DC: Brookings Institution Press, 1997), p. 25. See also US Overseas Loans and Grants (Greenbook) <http://qesdb.cdie.org/gbk/index.html>.

7. 'The reform similarly eliminated the last key issue on which the left wing could have hoped to develop substantial rural support in Korea': David C. Cole and N. Lyman Princeton, *Korean Development, The Interplay of Politics and Economics* (Cambridge MA: Harvard University Press, 1971), p. 21, quoted by Anne Krueger, *Studies in the Modernization of the Republic of Korea: 1945–1975. The Development Role of the Foreign Sector and Aid* (Cambridge MA and London: Council on East Asian Studies, Harvard University, 1979), p. 21.

8. Forty per cent of the farmland was owned by the Japanese.

9. The same kind of reform was implemented in Taiwan.

10. Krueger, *Studies in the Modernization of the Republic of Korea: 1945–1975*, p. 20. See also Sarah Sugarman, 'Land Rights and Establishing Desirable Production and Consumption Outcomes for Agricultural Households',

2 October 2002. <www.reed.edu/~sugarmas/LandRights&desirable. pdfwww.reed.edu/~sugarmas/LandRights&desirable.pdf>.

11. To increase their income peasants greatly increased their productivity and volume of production, particularly for products where prices remained free, such as fruit.

12. See Jean-Philippe Peemans, *Le développement des peuples face à la modernisation du monde* (Louvain-la-Neuve: Academia-Bruylant; Paris: L'Harmattan, 2002), p. 373.

13. *Ibid.*, p. 374.

14. Bank of Korea, National Accounts (1987), quoted by Mahn-Je Kim, 'The Republic of Korea's Successful Economic Development and the World Bank', p. 25.

15. According to Mahn-Je Kim, between 1953 and 1961, US military aid in the form of grants amounted to $1,561 million. According to US Overseas Loans and Grants (Greenbook) <http://qesdb.cdie.org/gbk/index.html>, the amount was $1,785 million.

16. An analysis of Park Chung Hee's regime can be found in Paik Nak-chung's speech when opening the international conference of Korean studies at the University of Wollongong, Australia, 10–13 November 2004 on 'The Park era: a new evaluation after 25 years'. The text of the speech is available in French, English and Korean (www.korea-is-one.org/article. php3?id_article=2291>). See also the Changbi publishing house website <www.changbi.com/english/html/intro.asp>. Paik Nak-chung, director of the Changbi publishing house, was a victim of the repression under Park's dictatorship. Changbi was closed under the dictatorship of General Chun Doo Hwan, 1980–87.

17. He also acted as a minister under president Kim Young Sam in the 1990s.

18. Mahn-Je Kim, 'The Republic of Korea's Successful Economic Development and the World Bank', p. 46.

19. In 1984 Pierre Rousset described the stunning development of the Daewoo group: 'While it started only 17 years ago as a small textile company it now has 70,000 employees. Thanks to Park Chung Hee's support, Kim Woochong has built an empire in trade, shipbuilding, construction, car manufacturing, textiles, finance, telecommunications, electronics, clothing. He owns the largest textile plant in the world and an ultramodern shipyard. He has launched substantial projects in the Middle East. Now he is investing in semiconductors.' Pierre Rousset, 'La Corée du Sud, second Japon?', *Croissance des jeunes nations*, No. 265 (October 1984).

20. Mahn-Je Kim, 'The Republic of Korea's Successful Economic Development and the World Bank', p. 33.

21. See chapter 10.

22. Mahn-Je Kim, 'The Republic of Korea's Successful Economic Development and the World Bank', p. 35.

23. See *Lutte de Classe*, No. 26 (March 1997), 'Corée du Sud – Du mythique «miracle économique» aux traditions de lutte de la classe ouvrière'.

24. Mahn-Je Kim, 'The Republic of Korea's Successful Economic Development and the World Bank', p. 35.

25. Jimmy Carter was US President from 1977 to 1980. During his term of office, several of Washington's allies collapsed or were destabilized: the Shah of Iran fled his country in February 1979, driven out by violent popular protest; the Nicaraguan dictator Anastasio Somoza was ousted in July 1979 by the Sandinista revolution; the Korean dictatorship was under threat from October 1979 to May 1980. Enough was enough – it was vital to keep this valuable strategic ally. Yet Jimmy Carter was known as a vocal advocate for human rights on the international political scene.

26. See Jun Yasaki, 'La crise du régime sud-coréen et le soulèvement de Kwangju', *Inprecor*, No. 80 (26 June 1980), p. 25.

27. Estimates as to how many demonstrators were killed vary widely. The lowest figure, put forward by the government, is 240. Other sources mention one to two thousand dead. The 28 May 1980 issue of the *New York Times* claims that 50 troops were killed in one single confrontation (see Kim Chang Soo, 'Le Soulèvement de Kwangju', *Inprecor*, No. 97 (16 March 1981), pp. 35–9).

28. Jun Yasaki, 'La crise du régime sud-Korean et le soulèvement de Kwangju', p. 25 and Kim Chang Soo, 'Le Soulèvement de Kwangju', pp. 35–9.

29. Kim Chang Soo, 'Le Soulèvement de Kwangju', p. 35.

30. Ronald Reagan was US President from 1981 to 1988.

31. 'South Korea also got special help from Japan under the formal guise of reparations. The fact that the postwar treaty had been a dead letter for many years did not worry either party. The Japanese government was aware that putting up $3 billion to help Korea service its large foreign debt was going to be in the long term interests of the many Japanese companies with investments and joint ventures in Korea. The result was that in a subsequent phase of the debt crisis, the Korean government never had to negotiate with foreign bankers or with the IMF.' In Susan Strange, *Rival States, Rival Firms, Competition for World Trade Shares* (CSRI, 1991), p. 46.

32. Krueger, *The Development Role of the Foreign Sector and Aid*, p. 256.

33. Figures given by Kang Min Chang, chief of national police. Quoted in *Korea Communiqué Bulletin*, special issue, July 1986.

34. For example, the storming of the Konkuk campus on 31 October 1986.

35. David Cameron, 'The Working Class takes up the Struggle', *Inprecor*, No. 248 (7 September 1987), pp. 4–5.

36. Figures from the Ministry of Labour, quoted in the *International Herald Tribune*, 26 August 1987.

37. 'From July to September 1987, the number of strikes reached 3,372': Hermann Dirkes, 'The New Trade Union Movement', *Inprecor*, No. 281 (6 February 1989).

38. In October 1995 there occurred the biggest scandal since the end of the Korean War, implicating three successive presidents. Following an accusation by an opposition member of parliament, the former President of the Republic, Roh Taewoo (1987–93) was arrested on the grounds of having received $369 million in bribes. His predecessor Chun Toowhan (1980–87) suffered the same fate. Kim Youngsam found himself in an embarrassing position, having won his election victory largely thanks to Roh Taewoo's support. He admitted to receiving money during his

electoral campaign. The industrial world also came under fire: many of the *chaebols* were implicated in some way or another in the scandal.

39. The Uruguay round is the name of the last round of negotiations of the GATT (General Agreement on Tariffs and Trade). It led among other developments to the establishment of the WTO, which replaced the GATT in 1995. The GATT was created in 1948 after the International Trade Organization (created on paper in 1946 at the Havana Conference) was wound up by the United States.

40. International Monetary Fund, *Annual Report 1997* (Washington DC, 1997), p. 60.

41. *Ibid.*, p. 61.

42. *Ibid.*, p. 61.

43. UNCTAD, 2000c, pp. 65–6, quoted by Eric Toussaint, *Your Money [or] Your Life* (Chicago: Haymarket Books, 2004), chapter 17, p. 357.

44. I made a detailed analysis of the Asian crisis of 1997–98 in my book *Your Money [or] Your Life*, chapter 17.

45. For information on the KCTU action and social movements in general, see: <www.kctu.org>.

12   THE DEBT TRAP

1. Among the countries for which the World Bank does not provide data are Cuba, Iraq, Libya, North Korea and South Korea.

2. However, the number of countries with arrears on their payments to the World Bank, and/or who manifested the need to renegotiate their multilateral debt went up from three to 18 between 1974 and 1978!

3. See Eric Toussaint, *Your Money [or] Your Life* (Chicago: Haymarket Books, 2004). Chapter 8 gives an analysis of the debt crisis that exploded in 1982. See also Damien Millet and Eric Toussaint, *Who Owes WHO? 50 Questions about World Debt* (London: Zed Books, 2004), question 8.

4. It was the Latin American countries that had mainly taken out variable rate loans from private banks who were especially affected by the rise in interest rates combined with the fall in export revenue.

5. For more about risk premiums, see Toussaint, *Your Money [or] Your Life*, pp. 156–8.

6. *Ibid.*, p. 320.

7. In order to obtain the amount of the external debt owed by the private sector of a DC, the public debt (column 4) has been subtracted from the total debt (column 2).

8. During this period, the public treasuries received $2,402 billion in loans and repaid $2,873 billion, i.e., a net negative transfer of $471 billion. Source: World Bank, *Global Development Finance*, 2005.

9. See chapter 10.

10. Thailand did that in 2003; Brazil and Argentina did the same thing in January 2006.

11. The countries given in brackets are not taken into account in the World Bank's statistics concerning indebted nations.

12. The country given in brackets, Afghanistan, is not taken into account in the World Bank's statistics concerning indebted nations.
13. The country given in brackets, Namibia, is not taken into account in the World Bank's statistics concerning indebted nations.
14. The countries given in brackets are not taken into account in the World Bank's statistics concerning indebted nations.
15. The countries given in brackets are not taken into account in the World Bank's statistics concerning indebted nations.
16. Since 2003, the World Bank has no longer considered South Korea as a developing country since the annual revenue per inhabitant has risen above the ceiling, fixed at present at $9,385 dollars. Henceforth, South Korea is considered as a developed country.

13 THE WORLD BANK SAW THE DEBT CRISIS LOOMING

1. Devesh Kapur, John P. Lewis and Richard Webb, *The World Bank, Its First Half Century, Volume 1: History* (Washington DC: Brookings Institution Press, 1997), p. 599.
2. The Yugoslav Dragoslav Avramoviæ was chief economist at the World Bank from 1963 to 1964. Thirty years later, he became the governor of the Central Bank of Yugoslavia (1994–96) during the government of Slobodan Milosevic.
3. Dragoslav Avramoviæ and Ravi Gulhati, *Debt Servicing Problems of Low-Income Countries 1956–58* (Baltimore: Johns Hopkins Press for the IBRD,1960), pp. 56, 59.
4. World Bank, *Annual Report 1963–4*, p. 8.
5. World Bank, *Annual Report 1965*, p. 54.
6. *Ibid.*, p. 55.
7. Note that at this time the World Bank was directing its loans towards export crops and activities exporting raw materials.
8. World Bank, *Annual Report 1965*, p. 61.
9. For a brief account of the creation of UNCTAD and its subsequent development, see Eric Toussaint, *Your Money [or] Your Life* (Chicago: Haymarket Books, 2004), pp. 99–104. See also CETIM, *ONU. Droits pour tous ou loi du plus fort?* (Geneve: Cetim, 2005), pp. 207–19 and Jean-Philippe Therien, *Une Voix du Sud: le discours de la Cnuced* (Paris: L'Harmattan, 1990).
10. World Bank, *Annual Report 1966*, p. 45.
11. World Bank, *Annual Report 1965*, p. 62.
12. Paradoxically, while the WB argues for freer movement of capital between the DCs and developed countries, Washington for its own part has set up severe restrictions on capital flow out of the USA since 1963. These restrictions have accelerated the development in Europe of the market for eurodollars, which are recycled as loans to the DCs. See Toussaint, *Your Money [or] Your Life*, p. 189 and Philippe Norel and Eric Saint-Alary, *L'endettement du Tiers-Monde* (Paris: Syros la Découverte, 1988), pp. 41ff.
13. World Bank, *Annual Report 1966*, p. 45.

14. Nelson Rockefeller, *Report on the Americas* (Chicago: Quadrangle Books, 1969), p. 87, cited by Cheryl Payer, *Lent and Lost. Foreign Credit and Third World Development* (London: Zed Books, 1991), p. 58.

15. *Banking*, November 1969, p. 45, cited by Payer, *Lent and Lost*, p. 69.

16. Task Force on International Development, *U.S. Foreign Assistance in the 1970s: a new approach*, Report to the President (Washington DC: Government Printing Office, 1970), p. 10.

17. Robert S. McNamara, *Cien países, Dos mil millones of seres* (Madrid: Tecnos, 1973), p. 94.

18. IMF, *Annual Report 1975*, p. 3.

19. It was in this context that the World Bank went to great lengths to persuade China to join its ranks (much to the chagrin of the government of Taiwan, who had occupied China's seat at the Bank from 1949 to 1979). In fact, the People's Republic of China returned to the World Bank at the end of Robert McNamara's presidency.

20. In 1976–78, the commercial banks made loans to Brazil at an average rate of 7.4 per cent while the World Bank was lending at 8.7 per cent (Kapur, Lewis and Webb, *The World Bank, Its First Half Century, Volume 1: History*, p. 281 and Table 15.5, p. 983).

21. Cited by Nicholas Stern and Francisco Ferreira, 'The World Bank as "intellectual actor"', in Devesh Kapur, John P. Lewis and Richard Webb, *The World Bank, Its First Half Century, Volume 2: Perspectives* (Washington DC: Brookings Institution Press, 1997), p. 558.

22. In the medium term, they were right. The vision expressed in McNamara's words was confirmed in the 1980s when debt payments were suspended for short periods and rescheduling was agreed between the big US banks and the governments of Latin America, with the support of the IMF and the WB. As Citibank claimed, interest rates and differentials were usually revised upwards when a loan was rescheduled. That was exactly what happened. As the next two chapters show, big banks made enormous profits out of the indebted countries.

23. *Global Financial Intermediation and Policy Analysis* (Citibank, 1980), quoted in 'Why the Major Players Allowed it to happen', *International Currency Review* (May 1984), p. 22, cited by Payer, *Lent and Lost*, p. 72.

24. Kapur, Lewis and Webb, *The World Bank, Its First Half Century, Volume 1: History*, p. 598.

25. *Ibid.*, p. 599.

26. This scenario, though closer to what actually happened, was still too optimistic.

27. Cited by Stern and Ferreira, 'The World Bank as "intellectual actor"', p. 559.

14 THE MEXICAN DEBT CRISIS AND THE WORLD BANK

1. Devesh Kapur, John P. Lewis and Richard Webb, *The World Bank, Its First Half Century, Volume 1: History* (Washington DC: Brookings Institution Press, 1997), p. 499.

2. *Ibid.*, p. 499.

3. Memorandum to files, 'Mexico: Present Economic Situation – Problems and Policies', 14 August 1981.
4. Carlos Salinas de Gortari became President of Mexico in 1988 as a result of a massive fraud to rob the Progressive candidate Cuauthémoc Cardenas of his victory. He left the presidency in 1994, shortly after ratifying the North American Free Trade Agreement (NAFTA). See next chapter.
5. Here is what historians of the World Bank write: 'The economist (at the time of writing still with the Bank) had taken a much more alarmed view of Mexico's macro prospects in 1981 and wrote up his dissenting economic analysis in the form of a memo to the files. His subsequent career at the Bank was jeopardized: after an embattled few years, he was reinstated after a legal battle.' Pieter Bottelier, interview with the authors, 19 January 1993, in Kapur, Lewis and Webb, *The World Bank, Its First Half Century, Volume 1: History*, p. 603.
6. José Lopez Portillo was President from 1977 to 1982.
7. Letter, A.W. Clausen to His Excellency José Lopez Portillo, President, United Mexican States, 19 March 1982, in Kapur, Lewis and Webb, *The World Bank, Its First Half Century, Volume 1: History*, p. 603.
8. Morgan Guaranty Trust Co. of New York, *World Financial Markets* (March 1986), p. 15.
9. The consequences of structural adjustment policies in Mexico are analyzed in the first edition of *Your Money [or] Your Life*, 'The Tyranny of Global Finance', chapter 15, case study 2.

15   THE WORLD BANK AND THE IMF: THE CREDITORS' BAILIFFS

1. Karin Lissakers, *Banks, Borrowers and the Establishment: a Revisionist Account of the International Debt Crisis* (New York: Basic Books, 1991), p. 194.
2. Devesh Kapur, John P. Lewis and Richard Webb, *The World Bank, Its First Half Century, Volume 1: History* (Washington DC: Brookings Institution Press, 1997), p. 636, note 132.
3. The Argentine companies with parent companies outside Argentina are: Renault Argentina, Mercedes-Benz Argentina, Ford Motor Argentina, World Bank Argentina, Citibank, First National Bank of Boston, Chase Manhattan Bank, Bank of America, Deutsche Bank. The Argentine state reimbursed the private creditors of the following companies, i.e., their parent companies: Renault France, Mercedes Benz, City Bank, Chase Manhattan Bank, Bank of America, First National Bank of Boston, Crédit Lyonnais, Deutsche Bank, Société Générale. In short, the Argentine taxpayer repaid the debt incurred by subsidiaries of transnational corporations towards their parent companies or international bankers. One may surmise that those transnationals had created a debt on behalf of their Argentine subsidiaries by sleight of hand. The Argentine government had no access to their accounts.
4. In Kapur, Lewis and Webb, *The World Bank, Its First Half Century, Volume 1: History*, Tables 1–5, p. 642.
5. UNDP (1992), p. 74.

6. IBRD, Operations Policy Staff, 'Debt and Adjustment in Selected Developing Countries', Sec. M84–698, 1984, in Kapur, Lewis and Webb, *The World Bank, Its First Half Century, Volume 1: History*, p. 615.

7. Fax message, Ernest Stern to Luis de Azcarate, director, CPDDR, 15 May 1984, in *ibid.*, p. 616.

8. Memorandum, Ernest Stern to members of the managing committee, 'Conference at the Federal Reserve Bank of New York', 11 May 1984, p. 1, in *ibid.*, p. 616.

9. Andres Bianchi, Robert Devlin and Joseph Ramos, 'The Adjustment Process in Latin America 1981–1986', paper prepared for the World Bank–IMF Symposium on Growth-Oriented Adjustment Programmes, Washington DC, 25–27 February 1987, Table 9 in *ibid.*, p. 627, note 105 ('By way of comparison, the war reparations imposed on Germany between 1925 and 1932 amounted to 2.5 percent of GDP').

10. Memorandum, Ernest Stern to Munir Benjenk, 'Draft Speech for Davos', 16 January 1984, p. 2, in *ibid.*, p. 616.

11. In drawing up Table 15.4, I took into account loans made by the IBRD branch of the World Bank, which grants loans to middle-income countries. I did not take into account loans made by the IDA to low-income countries.

12. Kapur, Lewis and Webb, *The World Bank, Its First Half Century, Volume 1: History*, p. 1194.

13. *Ibid.*, p. 1193, note 47.

14. *Ibid.*, p. 624.

15. *Ibid.*, p. 617.

16. World Bank, *World Development Report 1986*, p. 33, in *ibid.*, p. 617.

17. Letter, Ernest Stern to Carlos F. Diaz-Alejandro, 10 September 1984, pp. 3–4, in *ibid.*, p. 618.

18. Memorandum, Stanley Fisher to Ibrahim Shibata, May 26, 1990 in *ibid.*, p. 618.

19. *Ibid.*, p. 626.

20. *Ibid.*, p. 662. They based this on estimates from Miguel A. Rodriguez, 'Consequences of Capital Flight for Latin American Debtor Countries', in Donald Lessard and John Williamson, *Capital Flight and Third World Debt* (Washington DC: Institute for International Economics, 1987), Table 6.1, p. 130.

21. Kapur, Lewis and Webb, *The World Bank, Its First Half Century, Volume 1: History*, p. 678.

22. Memorandum, Stanley Fisher to Jacob A. Frenkel, 'Coordination of Forecasts', 27 June 1989, in *ibid.*, p. 611, note 45.

23. Memorandum, Jacob A. Frenkel to Stanley Fisher, 'Coordination of Forecasts', 14 July 1989, pp. 1–2, in *ibid.*, p. 611, note 45.

24. John Williamson, 'What Washington Means by Policy Reform', in *Latin American Adjustment: How much has happened?* (Washington DC: Institute of International Economics, 1990).

25. William B. Dale, 'Financing and Adjustment of Payment Imbalances', in John Williamson, ed., *IMF Conditionality* (Washington: Institute for International Economics, 1983), p. 7.

26. Nicholas Stern and Francisco Ferreira, 'The World Bank as "intellectual actor"', in Devesh Kapur, John P. Lewis and Richard Webb, *The World Bank, Its First Half Century, Volume 2: Perspectives* (Washington DC: Brookings Institution Press, 1997), p. 540.

27. *Ibid.*, p. 543.

28. In 1989 the two institutions agreed to share responsibilities, as a means of limiting the clashes between their recommendations (as occurred, for example, in Argentina in 1988, when the World Bank backed conditions that the IMF found unsatisfactory). The term 'concordat', used by the institutions themselves, was significant. It meant that the disagreements and tensions between them were considerable. It was agreed that the IMF would mainly examine the global aspects of macroeconomic policies, particularly concerning budget, prices, currency, credit, interest rates and exchange rates. The World Bank, on the other hand, would concentrate on development strategies, projects and sector-based aspects. Sharing the tasks in this way required various forms of collaboration but rivalry between the two institutions remains intense. On top of this institutional rivalry there are differences of corporate culture.

29. World Bank, *Accelerated Development in Africa South of the Sahara*, Programme indicatif d'Action (Washington DC, 1981), p. 151.

30. Kapur, Lewis and Webb, *The World Bank, Its First Half Century, Volume 1: History*, p. 1193.

31. *Ibid.*, p. 620.

32. *Ibid.*, p. 615, note 64.

33. *Ibid.*, p. 679.

34. Alfredo Eric Calagno and Alfredo Fernando Calagno, *El universo neoliberal: recuento de sus lugares comunes* (Buenos Aires: Alianza Editorial, 1995), p. 378.

35. This was the case for Brazil, which suspended external debt payments to banks from January 1987 to January 1988. See Eric Toussaint and Arnaud Zacharie, *Le Bateau ivre de la mondialisation, Escales au sein du village planétaire* (Bruxelles: CADTM; Paris: Syllepse, 2000), pp. 67–8.

36. See the complete text reproduced in Damien Millet, *L'Afrique sans dette* (Liège: CADTM; Paris: Syllepse, 2005), p. 205.

37. Jean-Philippe Peemans, *Le développement des peuples face à la modernisation du monde* (Louvain-la-Neuve: Academia-Bruylant; Paris: L'Harmattan, 2002), p. 367.

38. Argentina, Bolivia, Brazil, Chile, Colombia, Ivory Coast, Ecuador, Mexico, Morocco, Nigeria, Peru, the Philippines, Uruguay, Venezuela and Yugoslavia: in Kapur, Lewis and Webb, *The World Bank, Its First Half Century, Volume 1: History*, p. 626.

39. Concerning the issue of who makes the important decisions, it is significant that the US Treasury informed the World Bank of the existence of the 'Baker plan' only 48 hours before it was made public.

40. Kapur, Lewis and Webb, *The World Bank, Its First Half Century, Volume 1: History*, p. 648.

41. Letter, Stanley Fisher to Nicholas Stern, 19 May 1992, in *ibid.*, p. 1195.

42. <www.clubdeparis.org/fr/presentation/presentation.php?BATCH=B03WP01>.

43. This phenomenon has continued to grow.

16   PRESIDENTS BARBER CONABLE AND LEWIS PRESTON (1986–95)

1. Devesh Kapur, John P. Lewis and Richard Webb, *The World Bank, Its First Half Century, Volume 1: History* (Washington DC: Brookings Institution Press, 1997), pp. 1199–201.
2. Chico Mendès, one of the leaders of the Brazilian protest, was assassinated in December 1988 by hired thugs in the pay of big landowners who profit from World Bank subsidies.
3. Bruce Rich, *Mortgaging the Earth* (London: Earthscan, 1994), pp. 145–70.
4. *Ibid.*, p. 150.
5. The World Bank's policy on the environment will be analyzed in my next book on the World Bank, entitled *L'horreur productiviste*.
6. Rich, *Mortgaging the Earth*, p. 252.
7. Quoted by Carol Lancaster, 'Governance and Development: the views from Washington', *IDS Bulletin*, No. 24 (1993), p. 10.
8. See the complete report devoted to the BCCI in 1992 by Senators John Kerry and Hank Brown: <www.fas.org/irp/congress/1992_rpt/bcci/>. See also: <http://en.wikipedia.org/wiki/Bank_of_Credit_and_Commerce_International>.
9. Rich, *Mortgaging the Earth*, pp. 21–2.
10. Address by Lewis T. Preston to the Board of Governors of the World Bank Group, World Bank press release, 15 October 1991.
11. It should be added that at the time when Preston was making his address, the end of the USSR was being sealed. The final thrust in favour of the dissolution of the USSR came from Boris Yeltsin in August 1991 in Moscow. The USSR was dissolved in December 1991.
12. Rich, *Mortgaging the Earth*, p. 24.
13. Lawrence H. Summers, World Bank office memorandum, 12 December 1991, quoted by Rich, *ibid.*, p. 247.
14. The British daily paper *The Financial Times* devoted a long article to the subject, written by Michael Prowse, on 10 February 1992; its title was 'Save the Planet Earth from Economists'.
15. Lawrence H. Summers, World Bank office memorandum, 12 December 1991, quoted by Rich, *Mortgaging the Earth*, p. 247.
16. Boris Yelstin was President of Russia from 1992 to 1999. The situation that Joseph Stiglitz describes occurred in 1993.
17. Joseph E. Stiglitz, *Globalization and its Discontents* (London: Allen Lane, 2002), p. 136.
18. *Ibid.*, pp. 144–5.
19. *Ibid.*, p. 144.

17   JAMES WOLFENSOHN SWITCHES ON THE CHARM (1995–2005)

1. The Schroder Bank financed Hitler and the SS from the 1920s through to the fall of the third Reich. This bank was later a base for Allen Dulles, later the director of the CIA. The Schroder Bank was involved in the financing of several *coups d'état*: the overthrow of Iranian Prime Minister Mohammad Mossadegh in 1953, the military *putsch* against

Jacobo Arbenz in Guatemala in 1954, the Bay of Pigs invasion of Cuba in 1961, covert action in Chile between 1970 and 1973, then Pinochet's military Junta.

2. Patrick Bond, *Elite Transition, From Apartheid to Neoliberalism in South Africa* (London/Sterling VA: Pluto Press; Pietermaritzburg: University of Natal Press, 2000), p. 164.

3. The Bilderberg Conference is an annual conference that brings together, by invitation only, some 130 of the world's most influential bankers, economists and politicians, who call themselves 'Bilderbergers' or the 'Bilderberg group'. Their initial aim, in the context of the Cold War, was to reinforce cooperation between the United States and its European allies in opposition to communism. It was also the time to create a united front to combat the nationalist uprisings in the colonies. The aims of the Bilderberg group have moved on to promoting ultra-liberalism. It is of course resolutely transatlantist. The Bilderberg group's meetings never reach the media. At its beginnings, the group was financed by the Dutch firm Unilever and the CIA. James Wolfensohn participated in the May 2005 meeting in good company (Pascal Lamy, John Bolton, Robert Zoellick). See <http://en.wikipedia.org/wiki/Bilderberg_Group>. In 1973, the Trilateral Commission was founded by key members of the Bilderberg group and of the 'Council on Foreign Relations', such as David Rockefeller and Henry Kissinger. See: <http://en.wikipedia.org/wiki/Trilateral_Commission>.

4. <www.globalpolicy.org/socecon/bwi-wto/wolfsohn.htm>.

5. The WB/IMF/WTO triad will be analyzed in my next book, *L'horreur productiviste*.

6. Walden Bello and Shalmali Guttal, 'The Limits of Reform: the Wolfensohn Era at the World Bank', 26 April 2005, <www.focusweb.org/content/view/596/27/>.

7. *Ibid*.

8. *Ibid*.

9. Quoted in *ibid*.

10. In December 2005, the World Bank had to withdraw its support from the pipeline, which was already in use, in order to try to avoid a scandal; the President of Chad had pocketed the income from the oil that the World Bank had intended for future generations. Numerous organizations had warned Wolfensohn of the risk of taking on such a project with the dictator Idriss Déby Itno. In the end, however, the World Bank only suspended its support to the dictator for a short period. In April 2006, under pressure from the United States, the Bank began to provide loans once again, even accepting the terms fixed by Idriss Déby Itno.

11. See <www.50years.org>.

12. James Wolfensohn press conference, Washington, 12 April 2003.

18   DEBATES IN WASHINGTON AT THE START OF THE TWENTY-FIRST CENTURY

1. That is to say a commission comprised of Democrats and Republicans.

2. <www.house.gov/jec/imf/meltzer.htm or http://phantom-x.gsia.cmu. edu/IFIAC>.
3. Jerome Levinson was assistant director of USAID in Brazil from 1964 to 1966.
4. Anne Krueger, 'Whither the Bank and the IMF?', *Journal of Economic Literature*, Vol. XXXVI (December 1998), pp. 1987, 1999.
5. *Ibid.*, p. 2010.
6. *Ibid.*, p. 2006.
7. *Ibid.*, p. 2015.
8. Since 2001, given the Republican majorities in the Senate and Congress, these types of attacks on the executive from Congressional commissions have ceased. It remains to be seen whether this will change.

19   THE WORLD BANK'S ACCOUNTS

1. Devesh Kapur, John P. Lewis and Richard Webb, *The World Bank, Its First Half Century, Volume 1: History* (Washington DC: Brookings Institution Press, 1997), p. 177.
2. From here on in the text, the word 'revenue' will be used to avoid repeating 'net operations revenue' throughout.
3. Middle-income countries are those with a gross domestic income between $766 and $9,385 per inhabitant in 2003. They borrow from the Bank at rates close to market rates.
4. Minutes of managing committee meeting, 9 April 1984, cited by Kapur, Lewis and Webb, *The World Bank, Its First Half Century, Volume 1: History*, p. 341.
5. Complete list of these funds: Environment Trust Fund, Special Facility to Sub-Saharan Africa, Technical Assistance Trust Fund for the Soviet Union, Trust Fund for Gaza and West Bank, Trust Fund for East Timor, Emergency Assistance for Rwanda, Debt Reduction Facility for IDA-countries only, Trust Fund for Bosnia and Herzegovina, HIPC Debt Initiative Trust Fund, Capacity Building in Africa, Trust Fund for Kosovo, Trust Fund for Federal Republic of Yugoslavia, Multilateral Investment Guarantee Agency, Low-Income Countries Under Stress Implementation Trust Fund, Trust Fund for Liberia, Multi-Donor Trust Fund for Aceh and North Sumatra, and Trust Fund for Tsunami Disaster Recovery in India.
6. See World Bank, *Annual Report 2005* (Washington DC), vol. 2, pp. 3ff.

20   PAUL WOLFOWITZ, TENTH WORLD BANK PRESIDENT

1. Milton Friedman, one of the star professors at the University of Chicago, and the *Chicago boys* were to influence dictator Augusto Pinochet's economic policy after the coup of September 1973. See Eric Toussaint, *Your Money [or] Your Life* (Chicago: Haymarket Books, 2005), chapter 14: 'Neoliberal Ideology and Politics: Historical perspective', pp. 263, 264, 268.
2. See Walden Bello, *US Sponsored Low Intensity Conflict in the Philippines* (San Francisco: Institute for Food and Development Policy, 1987).
3. Tim Shorrock, 'Paul Wolfowitz, Reagan's Man in Indonesia, Is Back at the Pentagon', *Foreign Policy in Focus* (February 2001), p. 3.

21   STRUCTURAL ADJUSTMENT AND THE WASHINGTON CONSENSUS: ARE THEY THINGS OF THE PAST?

1. The source for this chapter is a document co-written by Damien Millet and the author at the beginning of 2006, as well as various CADTM press releases.
2. See the *Sunday Observer* (Sri Lanka), 6 November 2005, <www.sundayob-server.lk/2005/11/06/ne>.
3. Quoted by *Le Figaro*, 11 August 2005.
4. It should be said in passing that after the April 2002 *coup d'état* in Venezuela, which brought Carmona to power for less than two days, the IMF, through its spokesperson, Thomas Dawson, immediately offered assistance to this illegitimate government ('We would hope that these discussions could continue with the new administration, and we stand ready to assist the new administration in whatever manner they find suitable'): <www.imf.org/external/np/tr/2002//tr0>.
5. See <http://endehors.org/news/4518.shtml>.
6. See Damien Millet, *L'Afrique sans dette* (Bruxelles: CADTM; Paris: Syllepse, 2005).
7. D. Craig [World Bank director of operations for Mali], 'The Present Situation of Challenges and Issues of the Cotton Industry in Mali', <www.afribone.com/article.php3?id_ar>.
8. See <www.acme-eau.com>.
9. Canada, France, Germany, Great Britain, Italy, Japan, the US and Russia.

22   THE WORLD BANK AND RESPECT FOR HUMAN RIGHTS

1. The author wishes to thank Hugo Ruiz Diaz Balbuena, whose work has been one of the main sources of inspiration in the writing of this chapter. Of particular importance is the study entitled *Les politiques menées par les IFI et leur responsabilité pour les violations massives des droits humains suite à l'imposition des programmes d'ajustement structurel* [IFI policies and their responsibility for the massive violations of human rights following the enforcement of structural adjustment programmes], 3 October 2004.
2. Jean-Philippe Peemans, *Le développement des peuples face à la modernisation du monde* (Louvain-la-Neuve: Academia-Bruylant; Paris: L'Harmattan, 2002), p. 349.
3. Nicolas Angulo Sanchez, *El Derecho Humano al Desarollo frente a la mundialización del Mercado* (Madrid: Iepala, 2005), p. 145.
4. M. Benchikh, R. Charvin and F. Demichel, *Introduction critique au droit. international* (Lyon: Presses Universitaires de Lyon, 1986), p. 12.
5. UNHRC, 'Debt Relief and Local Investment: Coordination between the HIPC (Highly Indebted Poor Countries) Initiative', Common Report by Ronaldo Figueredo (Special Reporter) and Fantu Cheru (Independent Expert), 14 January 2000, E/CN.4/2000/51, paragraph 1.
6. *Ibid.*, paragraph 5.

7. Notably, the massive impoverishment of entire strata of populations in Third World countries. We should recall that poverty is considered '... *as being a state of denial, even of violation, of human rights'*. Cf, UNHRC, 'Implementation of the Right to Development in the Present Global Context: Examination of the Sixth Report of the Independent Expert on the Right to Development', E/CN.4/2004.18/4, 17 February 2004, paragraph 12.

8. UNHRC, 'Effects of Structural Adjustment Policies on the Full Enjoyment of Human Rights', Report by the Independent Expert Mr Fantu Cheru, E/CN.4/1999/50, paragraph 31.

9. *Consecuencias de las políticas de ajuste económico originadas por la deuda externa en el goce efectivo de los derechos humanos y, especialmente, en la aplicación de la Declaración sobre el derecho al desarrollo*, Resolución de la Comisión de Derechos Humanos 1999/22.

10. The massive and constant violation of economic, social and cultural rights is inseparable from the entire body of human rights because this violation usually goes hand in hand with serious violations of civil and political rights. Cf. Jacques Fierens, 'La violation des droits civils et politiques comme conséquence de la violation des droits économiques, sociaux et culturels', *Institutions financières, l'exception aux droits humains* (Centre de droit international de l'Université libre de Bruxelles, December 1998, Revue belge de droit international, 1991–1).

11. UNHRC, 'Effects of Structural Adjustment Policies and Foreign Debt on the Full Enjoyment of Human Rights, Especially Economic, Social and Cultural Rights', E/CN.4/2003/10, paragraph 42.

12. UNHRC, 'Fourth Report by the Independent Expert Mr Arjun Sengupta', E/CN.4/2002/WG.18/2/Add. 1, 5 March 2002, paragraph 21.

13. UNHRC, 'Effects of Structural Adjustment Policies on the Full Enjoyment of Human Rights', Report by the Independent Expert Mr Fantu Cheru, E/CN.4/1999/50, paragraphs 28–30.

14. Contractual law is written law, the rules of which are contained in international agreements, such as the International Covenant on Economic, Social and Cultural Rights. Customary law is unwritten law, which is binding, such as the prohibition of crimes against humanity, crimes of aggression, non-intervention, the rights of peoples to their natural resources, etc.

15. Alejandro Teitelbaum describes them as 'instruments and representatives of the major powers and big capital ...'. See A. Teitelbaum, *El Papel de las sociedades transnacionales en el mundo contemporáneo* (Buenos Aires: AAJ, Producciones Gráficas, 2003), p. 104.

16. Note by the president of the World Bank, 28 September 2004. Quoted by Hugo Ruiz Diaz Balbuena in *IFI Policies and Their Responsibility for the Massive Violations of Human Rights Following the Enforcement of Structural Adjustment Programmes*, 3 October 2004.

17. GA/UN, *Human Rights Questions: Human Rights Questions, Including Alternative Approaches for Improving the Effective Enjoyment of Human Rights and Fundamental Freedoms. Globalization and its Impact on the Full Enjoyment of Human Rights*, Report of the Secretary General, 7.08.2003, paragraphs 16–17.

18. Making only the states responsible is, in practice, 'to hold the executing entities responsible while the main institutions that are in charge of the adoption of these policies enjoy full impunity...'. Cf. UNHRC, 'Globalization and its Effects on the Full Enjoyment of Human Rights', E/CN.4/Su.2/2003/14, paragraph 37. Not emphasized in the document.
19. See J.A.P. Ridruejo, *Cours général de Droit international public*, Recueil des Cours de l'Académie de Droit international (RCADI) (1998), tome 274, pp. 193–8.
20. Cf. CIJ, *Réparation des dommages subis au service des Nations Unies (Affaire Bernadotte)* (Recueil, 1949), p. 174.
21. J. Verhoeven, *Droit international public*, Précis de la Faculté de Droit de l'UCL (Larcier, Bruxelles, 2000), p. 205.
22. J. Combacau and S. Sur, *Droit international public*, 2nd edn (Paris: Montchrestien, 1995), pp. 731–2.
23. E/CN.4/Su.2/2003/14, paragraph 37.
24. P.M. Dupuy, *Droit international public*, 3rd edn (Paris: Dalloz, 1995), p. 115.
25. Gustave Massiah in *ONU. Droits pour tous ou loi du plus fort?* (CETIM, 2005), pp. 404–5.
26. Sanchez, *El Derecho Humano al Desarollo frente a la mundialización del Mercado*, p. 16.
27. The full text of the Declaration can be found at: <www.ohchr.org/english/law/rtd.htm>.
28. The 1980s is a paradoxical decade. During this period we see the birth of a potentially marvellous legal instrument on the global level with the adoption of the Declaration on the Right to Development. It is also one of the most negative decades in terms of human rights and the right to development as a result of the explosion of the debt crisis, deteriorating trade terms, the widening equality gap between the countries of the Centre and the countries of the Periphery, and between people within each country.
29. Sanchez, *El Derecho Humano al Desarollo frente a la mundialización del Mercado*, pp. 36–7.
30. *Ibid.*, p. 288.
31. ICJ, *Yearbook 1970* and *Yearbook 1996*.
32. E. David, 'Conclusions de l'atelier juridique: les institutions financières internationales et le droit international', *Les institutions financières internationales et le droit international* (Bruxelles: ULB, Bruylant, 1999), p. 2.
33. *Ibid.*, p. 4.
34. Cf. UNHRC, 'The Effects of Structural Adjustment Policies and Foreign Debt on the Full Enjoyment of All Human Rights, in particular Economic, Social and Cultural Rights', E/CN.4/2003/10: Analysis of the Case of Bolivia.

23   TIME TO PUT AN END TO WORLD BANK IMPUNITY

1. Section 3 of Article 7: 'Actions may be brought against the Bank only in a court of competent jurisdiction in the territories of a member state in

which the Bank has an office, has appointed an agent for the purpose of accepting service or notice of process, or has issued or guaranteed securities.'

2. The first loan dates back to 1947.
3. According to the report of the Commission on Large Dams, 60 to 80 million people have been displaced as a result of the construction of large dams. In many a case, the rights of these people in terms of compensation and resettlement have not been respected.
4. According to the report of the Commission on Extractive Industries published in December 2003, a large portion of the projects financed by the WB have had negative effects on the populations of the countries concerned. See chapter 17.
5. In Article I of the Convention entitled 'Definition and Application', Section 1, the specialized institutions mentioned by name are the following: International Labour Organization (ILO), the United Nations Food and Agricultural Organization (FAO), the United Nations Educational, Scientific and Cultural Organization (UNESCO), the Organization of International Civil Aviation, the International Monetary Fund (IMF), the International Bank for Reconstruction and Development (IBRD), the World Health Organization (WHO), the International Postal Union and the International Telecommunications Union.

24   AN INDICTMENT OF THE WORLD BANK

1. Eric Toussaint, *Your Money [or] Your Life* (Chicago: Haymarket Books, 2005), chapter 16: 'Rwanda: the genocide's financiers'.
2. Point 11, and also points 19, 22 and 24, will be developed in my next book, *L'horreur productiviste*.

APPENDIX: THE WORLD BANK GROUP FACT SHEET

1. The definition of the requisite majority was modified in the 1980s in response to the growth in the number and the relative importance of new members, in order to guarantee the USA their veto however the institution might evolve. When the World Bank was founded, the required majority was 80 per cent, and the USA had 37.20 per cent of the votes. From 1989, when the US quota fell below 20 per cent, the required majority was brought up to 85 per cent.

Bibliography

Adams, Patricia. *Odious Debts* (Toronto: Probe International, 1991).

Aglietta, Michel and Moatti, Sandra. *Le FMI. De l'ordre monétaire aux désordres financiers* (Paris: Ed. Economica, 2000).

Angulo Sanchez, Nicolas. *El Derecho Humano al Desarollo frente a la mundialización del Mercado* (Madrid: Iepala, Colección Cooperación y Desarollo, 2005).

Arruda, Marcos. *External Debt. Brazil and the International Financial Crisis* (London: Pluto Press, 2000).

Attac. Harribey, Jean-Marie, sous la coordination de, *Le développement a-t-il un avenir? Pour une société solidaire et économe* (Paris: Fayard, collection Mille et une nuits, 2004).

Avramoviæ, Dragoslav and Gulhati, Ravi. *Debt Servicing Problems of Low-Income Countries 1956–58* (Baltimore: Johns Hopkins Press for the IBRD, 1960).

Azoulay, Gérard. *Les théories du développement, Du rattrapage des retards à l'explosion des inégalités* (Rennes: Presses Universitaires de Rennes, 2002).

Bank for International Settlements (BIS). 1995. *65th Annual Report*, Basel.

Bank for International Settlements (BIS). 2000. *70th Annual Report*, Basel.

Bank for International Settlements (BIS). 2001. *71st Annual Report*, Basel.

Bank for International Settlements (BIS). 2002. *72nd Annual Report*, Basel.

Bank for International Settlements (BIS). 2003. *73rd Annual Report*, Basel.

Bank for International Settlements (BIS). 2006. *76th Annual Report*, Basel.

Bello, Walden. 'The Prague Castle Debate: Hard Answers, Please, Gentlemen', in *Transfer of Wealth* (Bangkok: Focus on the Global South, 2000).

Bello, Walden. *Deglobalization. Ideas for a New World Economy* (London/New York: Zed Books, 2002).

Bond, Patrick. *Elite Transition, From Apartheid to Neoliberalism in South Africa* (London/Sterling VA: Pluto Press; Pietermaritzburg: University of Natal Press, 2000).

Bond, Patrick. *Against Global Apartheid, South Africa meets the World Bank, IMF and International Finance* (Lansdowne: University of Cape Town Press, 2001).

Boote, A. ,Thugge, K., Kilby, F. and van Trosenburg, A. *Debt relief for low-income countries. The HIPC debt initiative.* Pamphlet series 51 (World Bank/IMF, 1988).

Brooks, R. et al. *External debt histories of ten low-income developing countries: lessons from their experience*, Working Paper/98/72 (Washington DC: FMI, 1998).

Bulow, Jeremy I. 'First World Governments and Third World Debt', *Brookings Papers on Economic Activity*, No. 1 (2002).

Bulow, Jeremy I. and Rogoff, Kenneth. 'A Constant Recontracting Model of Sovereign Debt', *Journal of Political Economy*, Vol. 97, No. 1 (February 1989).

304

Bulow, Jeremy I. and Rogoff, Kenneth. 'Cleaning Up Third World Debt Without Getting Taken to the Cleaners', *Journal of Economic Perspectives*, Vol. 4, No. 1 (Winter 1990).

Calcagno, Alfredo Eric. *La perversa deuda* (Buenos Aires: Editorial Legasa, 1988).

Calcagno, Alfredo Eric and Calcagno, Alfredo Fernando. *El universo neoliberal: recuento de sus lugares comunes* (Buenos Aires: Alianza, 1995).

Castro, Fidel. *La Cancelación de la deuda externa y el nuevo orden económico internacional* (La Habana: Editora Política, 1985).

Centre Tricontinental. 'Les Organismes financiers internationaux, instruments de l'économie politique libérale', *Alternatives Sud*, Vol. VI, No. 2 (Louvain-la-Neuve/Paris/Montréal: L'Harmattan, 1999).

Centre Tricontinental. 'Raisons et déraisons de la dette. Le point de vue du Sud', *Alternatives Sud*, Vol. IX, No. 2/3 (Louvain-la-Neuve/Paris/Montréal: L'Harmattan, 2002).

Cetim. *ONU. Droits pour tous ou loi du plus fort?* (Geneva: CETIM, 2005).

Chang, Ha-Joon. *The Rebel Within: Joseph Stiglitz and the World Bank* (London: Anthem Press, 2001).

Charvin, Robert. *L'investissement international et le droit au développement* (Paris: L'Harmattan, 2002).

Chenery, Hollis B. and Strout, Alan. 'Foreign Assistance and Economic Development', *American Economic Review*, Vol. 56 (1966).

Christen, Ivan. *La Banque mondiale* (Paris: PUF, Que sais-je?, 1995).

Comanne, Denise. 'Quelle vision du développement pour les féministes?', *Les Autres Voix de la Planète*, No. 28 (2005).

Commission des Finances, de l'Economie générale et du Plan (rapporteur Yves Tavernier). *Rapport d'information sur les activités et le contrôle du Fonds Monétaire International et de la Banque mondiale*, Assemblée Nationale, Paris (13 December 2000).

Delgado, Gian Carlo, *Agua y Seguridad Nacional. El recurso natural frente a las guerras del futuro* (Mexico: Random House Montadori, 2005).

Edwards, Sebastian. *Crisis y Reforma en América Latina* (Buenos Aires: Editorial Emecé, 1997).

Fonds Monétaire International. *Rapport annuel 1997* (Washington DC, 1997).

George, Susan. *Jusqu'au cou* (Paris: La Découverte, 1989).

George, Susan. *L'effet Boomerang* (Paris: La Découverte, col. Essais, 1992).

George, Susan and Sabelli, Fabrizio. *Crédits sans Frontières* (Paris: La Découverte, col. Essais, 1994).

International Monetary Fund/The World Bank. *External Comments and Contributions on the Joint Bank/Fund Staff Review of the PRSP Approach* (Washington DC, February 2002).

Jadhav, Narendra. *Synopses of External Comments and Contributions on the Joint IMF/World Bank Staff Review of the PRSP Approach* (International Monetary Fund/World Bank, February 2002).

Kapur, Devesh, Lewis, John P. and Webb, Richard. *The World Bank, Its First Half Century, Volume 1: History* (Washington DC: Brookings Institution Press, 1997).

Kapur, Devesh, Lewis, John P. and Webb, Richard. *The World Bank, Its First Half Century, Volume 2: Perspectives* (Washington DC: Brookings Institution Press, 1997).

Krueger, Anne O. *Studies in the Modernization of the Republic of Korea: 1945–1975. The Development Role of the Foreign Sector and Aid* (Cambridge MA/London: Council on East Asian Studies, Harvard University, 1979).

Krueger, Anne. 'Whither the Bank and the IMF?', *Journal of Economic Literature*, Vol. XXXVI (December 1998).

Land Research and Action Network. *The Destructive Agrarian Reform Policies of the World Bank* (São Paulo, nd).

Lissakers, Karin. *Banks, Borrowers and the Establishment: A Revisionist Account of the International Debt Crisis* (New York: Basic Books, 1991).

McNamara, Robert S. *The Essence of Security: Reflections in Office* (London: Hodder & Stoughton, 1968).

McNamara, Robert S. *Cien países, Dos mil millones de seres* (Madrid: Tecnos, 1973).

McNamara, Robert S. *In Retrospect: The Tragedy and Lessons of Vietnam* (New York: Times Books, 1995).

Maddison, Angus. *Progreso y política económica en los países en vías de desarrollo* (Mexico: Fondo de Cultura Económica, 1988).

Mandel, Ernest. *Late Capitalism*, rev. edn, trans. Joris de Bres (London: Humanities Press, 1975).

Mandel, Ernest. *La Crise, 1974–1982* (Paris: Champs Flammarion, 1982).

Mandel, Ernest. *L'Annulation de la dette du tiers monde*, Dossier Rouge 29 (Paris, 1989).

Mason, Edward S. and Asher, Robert E. *The World Bank since Bretton Woods* (Washington DC: Brookings Institution, 1973).

Millet, Damien. *L'Afrique sans dette* (Liège: CASDTM; Paris: Syllepse, 2005).

Millet, Damien and Toussaint, Eric. *50 Questions/50 Réponses sur la dette, le FMI et la Banque mondiale* (Bruxelles: CADTM; Paris: Syllepse, 2002).

Millet, Damien and Toussaint, Eric. *The Debt Scam* (Mumbai: Vikas Adhyayan Kendra, 2003).

Millet, Damien and Toussaint, Eric. *Les Tsunamis de la dette* (Liège: CADTM; Paris: Syllepse, 2005).

Millet, Damien and Toussaint, Eric. 'Les faux semblants de l'aide au développement', *Le Monde diplomatique* (July 2005).

Millikan, Max and Blackmer, Donald. *The Emerging Nations: Their Growth and United States Policy* (Boston: Little Brown & Co., 1961).

Morrisson, Christian. 'La Faisabilité politique de l'ajustement', *Cahiers de politique économique*, No. 13 (Paris: Centre de développement de l'OCDE, 1996).

Narayan, Deepa et al. *Voices of the poor. Can Anyone Hear Us?* (New York: Oxford University Press for the World Bank, 2000).

Ndikumana, Leonce and Boyce, James. *Congo's Odious Debt: External Borrowing and Capital Flight* (Amherst: University of Massachussetts, Department of Economics, 1997).

Norel, Philippe and Saint-Alary, Eric. *L'Endettement du tiers-monde* (Paris/ Montréal: Syros et Alternatives-St Martin, 1992).

Ocde. *Statistiques de la dette extérieure. Principaux agrégats: 1998–1999* (Paris: OCDE, 2001).

Oliver, Robert W. *International Economic Co-operation and the World Bank* (London: Macmillan Press, 1975).

Payer, Cheryl. *The Debt Trap: The International Monetary Fund and the Third World* (New York/London: Monthly Review Press, 1974).

Payer, Cheryl. *The World Bank. A Critical Analysis* (New York/London: Monthly Review Press, 1982).

Payer, Cheryl. *Lent and Lost. Foreign Credit and Third World Development* (London: Zed Books, 1991).

Peemans, Jean-Philippe. *Le développement des peuples face à la modernisation du monde* (Louvain-la-Neuve: Academia-Bruylant; Paris: L'Harmattan, 2002).

Rich, Bruce. *Mortgaging the Earth* (London: Earthscan, 1994).

Rostow, Walt W. *The Stages of Economic Growth: A Non-Communist Manifesto* (Cambridge: Cambridge University Press, 1960).

Ruiz Diaz Balbuena, Hugo. *La Responsabilité internationale des institutions financières internationales* (December 2003).

Ruiz Diaz Balbuena, Hugo. *Le Traitement de la dette par l'ONU. L'Assemblée générale et la dette: entre le désir de solution durable de la dette et l'acceptation des relations économiques internationales inéquitables* (December 2003).

Sack, Alexander Nahum. *Les Effets des Transformations des Etats sur leurs Dettes Publiques et Autres Obligations Financières* (Paris: Recueil Sirey, 1927).

Sanchez Arnau, J.-C. *Dette et développement (mécanismes et conséquences de l'endettement du Tiers Monde)* (Paris: Editions Publisud, 1982).

Saxe-Fernandez, John and Delgado-Ramos, Gian Carlo. *Imperialismo y Banco Mundial* (Madrid: Editorial Popular, 2004).

Saxe-Fernandez, John and Delgado-Ramos, Gian Carlo. *Imperialismo en Mexico. Las operaciones del Banco Mundial en nuestro país* (Mexico: Random House Montadori, 2005).

Saxe-Fernandez, John and Nunez Rodriguez, Omar. 'Globalización e imperialismo: la transferencia de excedentes de America latina', in Saxe-Fernandez, John and Petras, James, *Globalización, imperialismo y clase social* (Buenos Aires/Mexico: Grupo Editorial Lumen, 2001).

Shapley, Deborah. *Promise and Power. The Life and Times of Robert McNamara* (Boston/Toronto/London: Little Brown and Co., 1993).

Shiva, Vandana. *The Violence of the Green Revolution* (Penang: Third World Network, 1993).

Shiva, Vandana. *La Nature sous licence ou le processus d'un pillage* (Geneva: CETIM, 1994).

Soros, George. *Soros on Soros* (New York: John Wiley & Sons, 1995).

Soros, George. *The Crisis of Global Capitalism* (New York: Public Affairs, 1998).

Stiglitz, Joseph E. *Globalization and its Discontents* (London: Penguin, 2002).

Teitelbaum, Alejandro. *El Papel de las sociedades transnacionales en el mundo contemporáneo* (Buenos Aires: Asociación Americana de Juristas, Producciones Gráficas, 2003).

Thérien, Jean-Philippe. *Une Voix du Sud: le discours de la Cnuced* (Paris: L'Harmattan, 1990).

Toussaint, Eric. *Your Money or Your Life. The Tyranny of Global Finance*, trans. by Raghu Krishnan and Vicki Briault-Manus (London: Pluto Press, 1999).

Toussaint, Eric. 'Enjeux politiques de l'action de la Banque internationale pour la Reconstruction et le Développement et du Fonds monétaire international envers le tiers-monde' (unpublished doctoral thesis, Universités de Liège et de Paris VIII, 2004).

Toussaint, Eric. *Globalisation: Reality, Resistance and Alternatives*, trans. by Vicki Briault-Manus (Mumbai: Vikas Adhyayan Kendra, 2004).

Toussaint, Eric. *Your Money [or] Your Life. The Tyranny of Global Finance*, trans. by Vicki Briault-Manus (Chicago: Haymarket Books, 2005).

Toussaint, Eric and Millet, Damien. *The Debt Scam*, trans. by Vicki Briault-Manus (Mumbai: Vikas Adhyayan Kendra, 2003).

Toussaint, Eric and Millet, Damien. *Who Owes Who?*, trans. by Vicki Briault-Manus (London: Zed Books, 2004).

Toussaint, Eric and Zacharie, Arnaud. *Le Bateau ivre de la mondialisation, Escales au sein du village planétaire* (Bruxelles: CADTM; Paris: Syllepse, 2000).

Toussaint, Eric and Zacharie, Arnaud. *Afrique: Abolir la dette pour libérer le développement* (Bruxelles: CADTM; Paris: Syllepse, 2001).

Toussaint, Eric and Zacharie, Arnaud. *Sortir de l'impasse. Dette et ajustement* (CADTM-Bruxelles/Syllepse-Paris, 2002).

Treillet, Stéphanie. *L'Économie du développement* (Paris: Nathan, 2002).

Unctad. *World Investment Report* (Geneva: UNCTAD, 2005).

Unctad/Undp. *Debt Sustainability, Social and Human Development, and the Experiences of the Heavily Indebted Poor Countries (HIPCs)* (Geneva: UNCTAD; New York: UNDP, 1997).

Undp. *Global Human Development Report* (annual 1990–2005, New York).

Van de Laar, Aart. *The World Bank and the Poor* (Boston/The Hague/London: Martinus Nijhoff Publishing, 1980).

Webb, Richard. *Peru*, Country Study 8 (United Nations University: WIDER, 1987).

Williamson, John. 'What Washington means by policy reform', in *Latin American Adjustment: How much has happened?* (Washington DC: Institute of International Economics, 1989).

World Bank. *Annual Reports* (1946–2006, Washington DC).

World Bank. *World Development Report* (1981, 1982, 1983, 1990, 1991, 1992, 1994, 1996, 1997, 1998, 2000, Washington DC). [Each report consists of 250 to 340 pages.]

World Bank. *Governance and Development* (Washington DC, 1992).

World Bank. *World Debt Tables 1992–1993*, Vol. 1 (Washington DC, 1992).

World Bank. *World Development Report, Investing in Health* (Washington DC, 1993).

World Bank. *The Asian Miracle* (Washington DC, 1993).

World Bank. *World Development. Labour in an Economy without Borders* (Washington DC, 1995).

World Bank. *Promoting Social Development. The World Bank's Contribution to the World Social Summit* (Washington DC, 1995).

World Bank. *Global Development Finance* (annual, 1997–2006, Washington DC).

World Bank. *World Development Indicators* (Washington DC, 2003).

World Bank/International Monetary Fund. 'The HIPC Debt Initiative: Elaboration of Key Features and Proposed Procedures' (unpublished confidential document, 1996).

World Bank/International Monetary Fund. *Estimated Potential Cost of the HIPC Debt Initiative Under Alternative Options* (1996)

Ziegler, Jean. *L'Empire de la Honte* (Paris: Fayard, 2004).

Index